# PeopleSoft

## ADMINISTRATOR'S GUIDE

# PeopleSoft®

## ADMINISTRATOR'S GUIDE

**Darrell Bilbrey**

SYBEX®

**San Francisco • Paris • Dusseldorf • Soest • London**

Associate Publisher: Richard Mills
Contracts and Licensing Manager: Kristine O'Callaghan
Acquisitions Editor: Krista Reid-McLaughlin
Developmental Editors: Krista Reid-McLaughlin, Brenda Frink
Editor: Sarah Lemaire
Project Editor: Raquel Baker
Technical Editor: Roger Rudenstein
Book Designer: Franz Baumhackl
Graphic Illustrator: Tony Jonick
Electronic Publishing Specialist: Franz Baumhackl
Production Coordinator: Julie Sakaue
Indexer: Ted Laux
Cover Designer: emdesign
Cover Photographer: emdesign

Library of Congress Card Number: 99-60011
ISBN: 0-7821-2396-1

Manufactured in the United States of America

10 9 8 7 6 5 4 3 2 1

Screen reproductions produced with Collage Complete. Collage Complete is a trademark of Inner Media Inc.

SYBEX is a registered trademark of SYBEX Inc.

PeopleSoft, PeopleTools, PeopleBooks, PeopleCode, and PS/nVision are registered trademarks of PeopleSoft, Inc. PeopleSoft is not the publisher of this book and is not responsible for it in any way. PeopleSoft owns the copyrights to all screen reproductions from PeopleSoft software products or documentation contained in this publication.

TRADEMARKS: SYBEX has attempted throughout this book to distinguish proprietary trademarks from descriptive terms by following the capitalization style used by the manufacturer.

The author and publisher have made their best efforts to prepare this book, and the content is based upon final release software whenever possible. Portions of the manuscript may be based upon pre-release versions supplied by software manufacturer(s). The author and the publisher make no representation or warranties of any kind with regard to the completeness or accuracy of the contents herein and accept no liability of any kind including but not limited to performance, merchantability, fitness for any particular purpose, or any losses or damages of any kind caused or alleged to be caused directly or indirectly from this book.

*This book is dedicated to my wife, Jodie,*

*and my daughter, Alexis.*

# ACKNOWLEDGMENTS

Writing this book has been a far more challenging project than I could ever have imagined. I am grateful for all the support and encouragement that I have received during this process.

First, I need to thank the team at Sybex for their dedication to this book. I would like to thank Krista Reid-McLaughlin, who initiated this project. Thanks to Richard Mills for keeping the project moving. Brenda Frink stepped in and offered the encouragement that got the first draft back on track and offered guidance on the early chapters.

Thanks to Roger Rudenstein, the technical editor, for pointing out technical issues that needed clarification. Thanks most of all to Raquel Baker of Sybex, the project editor, for shepherding the book through the editorial and production process, and to Sarah Lemaire, the editor, for improving the readability and organization of the chapters.

Thanks also to the individuals working behind the scenes to convert my rough sketches into production art and the desktop publishers for all their hard work in preparing the book for publication.

A special thanks to my wife, Jodie, and my daughter, Alexis, for their support and sacrifices during my nocturnal periods, when all Alexis wanted to do was use the "pewter."

I would also like to thank my boss, Rick, for his support and encouragement during this project. Thanks to Vicki for all the support and for getting me started with People-Soft in the first place. Thanks to Sam for reviewing several chapters, especially with regards to PeopleSoft Security. Thanks to Steve, Leslie, Brian, and Elizabeth for the encouragement along the way.

Thanks also to Bonnie for the advanced "marketing." Is there anyone in Emeryville who doesn't know about the book?

# CONTENTS AT A GLANCE

# TABLE OF CONTENTS

## PART IV     EXPANDING THE SYSTEM    439

### Chapter 18    Extending PeopleSoft to the Enterprise    441

### Chapter 19    Planning for the Future    453

# INTRODUCTION

This book is designed to be a comprehensive reference for the new (or almost new) PeopleSoft system administrator. This book should answer 75–80 percent of the basic questions that you will have. This book is not designed to be the complete guide to PeopleSoft. That would require volumes. I have attempted to give you the information necessary to answer many of your everyday questions, while pointing you to sources for more detailed information if needed. In this book, I have consolidated information on PeopleSoft administration from many different sources.

This book will help you get started with PeopleSoft, even if you do not already have the software installed at your company. You will learn what steps you need to take and which business processes need to be in place before you even begin the implementation of your PeopleSoft system.

Once you've implemented the PeopleSoft applications successfully, this book will help you manage the day-to-day operations of the applications. You'll learn about tools provided by PeopleSoft and other vendors that can help you:

▶ Configure and implement the PeopleSoft applications in a three-tier configuration with an application server and a database server.

▶ Develop new applications that work with the PeopleSoft applications.

▶ Automate certain business processes.

▶ Customize panels and menus.

▶ Design business processes made up of individual activities. Represent those business processes graphically.

▶ Improve system performance.

▶ Develop applications for the Web using Java applets provided by PeopleSoft.

▶ Implement PeopleSoft upgrades, including the periodic tax updates.

▶ Troubleshoot problems in your system.

▶ Recover from system crashes or other disasters.

▶ Maintain and customize your online and offline documentation.

# PeopleSoft Version

The screens and examples in this book come from PeopleSoft version 7.5. At the time this book is being published, PeopleSoft has indicated that version 8 will be released in the first half of the year 2000.

Version 7.5 is a significant improvement over versions 6 and 7. PeopleTools Version 7 included functionality for three-tier client-server configurations, Web applications, and OLAP. Version 7.5 includes some enhancements to PeopleTools but is primarily the application upgrade for the PeopleSoft applications. Enhancements to business processes have been made in all application modules. For those customers currently operating on version 5.x and earlier, the upgrade to version 7.5 requires that you upgrade your client operating system to 32-bit Windows 95 or to Windows NT.

Version 7.5 applications provide enhanced support for global companies. New Payroll versions were added, along with support for the European Monetary Unit (EMU).

# Who Should Read This Book

This book is for system administrators who are implementing and managing a PeopleSoft system. While most of the topics deal with the technical aspects of administrating a PeopleSoft installation, managers of the functional areas that use the PeopleSoft applications may find some useful information to help them better understand their PeopleSoft system.

This book assumes that you have:

► A working knowledge of SQL to help you understand many of the discussions and examples.

► A good understanding of networks and client-server systems.

► A working knowledge of what it takes to make production systems work.

# How This Book is Organized

This book is organized into five parts. However, it is not my intent that the book be read in that order. You may find that you need to jump from chapter to chapter to find specific information. You may refer to some chapters frequently to address issues that arise in your day-to-day operations.

Part One provides a basic introduction to the PeopleSoft applications. It describes what you need to do to plan for the implementation of your PeopleSoft system, how to customize the system to meet the unique needs of your company, and the importance of running your business processes in parallel with the PeopleSoft applications to ensure that the implementation is successful.

Part Two describes the tools that are delivered by PeopleSoft to help you administer your system, add new functionality, and empower your users through data access. Part Two also discusses the importance of securing your PeopleSoft system from external and internal threats, and describes the tools provided by PeopleSoft to help you manage and implement a security plan. The SQR reporting tool, developed by SQRIBE Technologies, is a powerful production tool that can be especially useful for doing batch reporting.

Part Three covers a number of situations that you will encounter in maintaining your PeopleSoft system over time:

- ▶ Preparations and precautions you should take when upgrading your system as new versions of the PeopleSoft applications are released.

- ▶ The tax updates provided by PeopleSoft on a regular basis.

- ▶ The importance of documenting changes to the applications.

- ▶ The need to monitor the performance of the applications.

- ▶ How to troubleshoot any problems that you may encounter.

- ▶ How to develop procedures for implementing a disaster recovery plan.

Part Four leaves you with some thoughts on methods to extend the PeopleSoft modules to your entire company. The final chapter of the book gives you insight on the long-term issues related to your PeopleSoft system and tells you how to monitor and influence the PeopleSoft strategy in order to make your installation a continued success.

Part Five contains the appendices. The appendices provide examples of programs and reports that are discussed throughout the book. Appendix A provides full code samples that were discussed in several of the chapters, plus an example of an include file for SQR programs. Appendix B contains sample output from the database audit reports discussed in Chapter 6, "Data Management Tools." Finally, a Microsoft Excel function that I created for use with PeopleSoft HRMS is provided for your use.

# Conventions Used in This Book

There are numerous figures and tables in each chapter that are designed to provide you with a visual reference for the material being covered. Many of the panels you will encounter while administering the PeopleSoft applications are included. There are also practical examples used to explain possible methods or use of the applications and tools. Most of these examples are being used successfully at my company.

This book uses various conventions to present information in as readable a manner as possible. The Notes, Tips, and Warnings throughout the book, shown here, highlight important information.

 **NOTE**   Notes emphasize the important points in each section.

 **TIP**   Tips explain how to accomplish a specific task.

 **WARNING**   Warnings alert you to issues that you should be on the lookout for.

This book takes advantage of several font styles. **Bold font** in the text indicates something that the user types. A `monospaced font` is used for PeopleCode, command names, URLs, and filenames.

# Sybex Technical Support

If you have questions or comments about this book (or other Sybex books) you can contact Sybex directly.

## For the Fastest Reply

E-mail us or visit the Sybex Web site! You can contact Sybex through the Web by visiting `http://www.sybex.com` and clicking Support. You may find the answer you're looking for on this site in the FAQ (Frequently Asked Questions) file.

When you reach the support page, click `support@sybex.com` to send Sybex an e-mail. You can also e-mail Sybex directly at `support@sybex.com`.

Make sure you include the following information in your e-mail:

**Name**    The complete title of the book in question. For this book, it is *PeopleSoft Administrator's Guide*.

**ISBN number**    The ISBN that appears on the bottom-right corner of the back cover of the book. This number looks like this:

0-7821-2396-1

**Printing**    The printing of the book. You can find this near the front of the book at the bottom of the copyright page. You should see a line of numbers as in the following:

10 9 8 7 6 5 4 3 2 1

Tell us what the lowest number is in the line of numbers. This is the printing number of the book. The example here indicates that the book is the first printing.

**NOTE**    The ISBN number and printing are very important for Technical Support because it indicates the edition and reprint that you have in your hands. Many changes occur between printings. Don't forget to include this information!

## For a Fast Reply

Call Sybex Technical Support and leave a message. Sybex guarantees that they will call you back within 24 hours, excluding weekends and holidays.

Technical Support can be reached at (510) 523-8233, ext. 563.

After you dial the extension, press 1 to leave a message. Sybex will call you back within 24 hours. Make sure you leave a phone number where you can be reached!

## Other Ways to Reach Sybex

The slowest way to contact Sybex is through the mail. If you prefer, you can write Sybex a small note and send it to the following address:

SYBEX Inc.
Attention: Technical Support
1151 Marina Village Parkway
Alameda, CA 94501

Again, it's important that you include all the following information to expedite a reply:

**Name**    The complete title of the book in question.

**ISBN number**    The ISBN that appears on the bottom-right corner of the back cover of the book and looks like this:

0-8721-2258-2

**Printing**    The printing of the book. You can find this near the front of the book at the bottom of the copyright page. You should see a line of numbers as in the following:

10 9 8 7 6 5 4 3 2 1

Tell us what the lowest number is in the line of numbers. This is the printing number of the book. The example here indicates that the book is the first printing.

**NOTE**    The ISBN number and printing are very important for Technical Support because it indicates the edition and reprint that you have in your hands. Many changes occur between printings. Don't forget to include this information!

**Page number**    Include the page number where you have a problem.

No matter how you contact Sybex, Technical Support will try to answer your question quickly and accurately.

# PART I

# GETTING STARTED WITH PEOPLESOFT

*You've decided to purchase a PeopleSoft system to address the ERP needs of your company. But how do you get started? Part I outlines the steps required to ensure a smooth transition from your existing system to the PeopleSoft ERP system.*

*Chapter 1, "The Fundamentals of PeopleSoft," describes the characteristics of ERP systems in general and specifically of the PeopleSoft applications. This chapter discusses the PeopleSoft business solutions and the hardware and software requirements for running PeopleSoft applications. Chapter 2, "Basic Implementation," outlines the procedures and steps to follow before implementing your PeopleSoft system, from the planning process through the completed PeopleSoft configuration. Chapter 3, "Customization," provides the guidelines you should be familiar with before customizing your PeopleSoft system during the implementation. Chapter 4, "Parallel Operations," describes what to consider when preparing your new PeopleSoft system for production. In particular, this chapter outlines the importance of running parallel operations before switching fully to the production system.*

# The Fundamentals of PeopleSoft

**FEATURING:**

▶ **WHAT IS ERP?**

▶ **AN OVERVIEW OF PEOPLESOFT APPLICATIONS**

▶ **THE PEOPLESOFT TECHNICAL ENVIRONMENT**

**W**hat is PeopleSoft? Is it a company or is it an application? These are questions that merit answers. PeopleSoft is a software company that produces application modules that are designed to help you run your company. The type of functionality that is delivered by these application modules is generally grouped around the concept of enterprise resource planning (ERP).

This chapter will introduce you to the concept of ERP and explain how PeopleSoft applications can be used in your company. This chapter provides you with the background you need to understand future chapters that will help you with the specifics of administering your PeopleSoft system.

## What Is ERP?

ERP is the concept of building applications that are fully integrated and can be used to automate many of the routine functions of running a company. The advantage of ERP is the ability to integrate the data across a company. Manufacturing companies have been early adopters of ERP systems like PeopleSoft. ERP systems allow these companies to adjust production and inventory automatically to meet fluctuating sales. ERP systems can be used for everything from demand planning to labor force planning.

ERP systems also provide global companies an opportunity to consolidate and integrate data from all over the world into a single corporate system. The benefits they derive may include lower warehousing costs, lower cost of materials due to consolidated purchasing, and better management of assets.

However, most companies do not implement ERP systems just to lower costs; they want better control of the data. As a matter of fact, many of the ERP systems are expensive on the front end of their implementation. However, installing an ERP system can result in savings over the long term, once the system has been in production for several years.

## An Overview of PeopleSoft Applications

PeopleSoft is a company that produces a wide range of applications designed to help large, multi-tiered organizations run efficiently and effectively. PeopleSoft has become a leader in the field of ERP by providing a wide range of business solutions that can be customized to meet the unique needs of your company. PeopleSoft offers approximately 40 application modules, including:

- ▶ Human Resources
- ▶ Payroll
- ▶ General Ledger
- ▶ Budgets
- ▶ Asset Management
- ▶ Enterprise Planning
- ▶ Production Planning
- ▶ Production Control
- ▶ Student Records
- ▶ Student Financials
- ▶ Project Management
- ▶ Performance Management
- ▶ Supply Chain Management
- ▶ Procurement

**N O T E**   The source of most of this information is the PeopleSoft Web site at `http://www.peoplesoft.com`.

# PeopleSoft Solutions

PeopleSoft has introduced a new enterprise solution methodology. They are now offering specific solutions built around your particular industry. In this model, PeopleSoft uses a pyramid to represent the general-to-specific characteristics of a PeopleSoft solution. Figure 1.1 illustrates this pyramid.

**Business Management**   The Business Management solutions are those designed to support processes that are common across all companies. Some examples of PeopleSoft's Business Management solutions are Human Resources, Accounting and Control, Project Management, Treasury Management, and Company Performance.

**Supply Chain Management**   The management of the supply chain is critical to any company, whether they produce goods or services. The PeopleSoft Supply Chain solution helps support the interaction between the customer and the company. PeopleSoft divides the solutions into two classes: Product Industries and Service Industries. The Product Industries solutions include Supply Chain Planning, Materials Management, and Sales and Logistics. The Service Industries solutions include Procurement and Service Revenue.

**Industry Operations**   PeopleSoft's Industry Operations solutions cover the functionality for a specific industry. Some examples include Student Administration, Merchandise Management, Product Development, and Management.

**Sub-Industry**   Sub-Industry solutions are targeted at specific categories of companies inside an industry. For example, there are opportunities to differentiate between banks and insurance companies in the Financial Services area. PeopleSoft's recent acquisition of the insurance software manufacturer TriMark Technologies is one of the first steps in this direction.

**Firm (Company-Specific Attributes)**   The specific attributes of each individual company represent a challenge for PeopleSoft. There are no current solutions at this level. This is where the PeopleSoft Alliance Partners and the PeopleSoft Professional Services Group can provide help in building a custom application solution for a company that is fully integrated into the PeopleSoft architecture.

**FIGURE 1.1**   Enterprise solution assembly

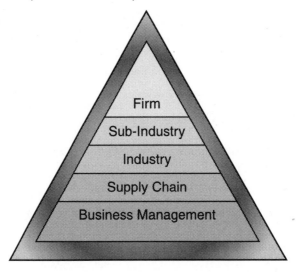

# Business Process Solutions

PeopleSoft has recently begun marketing its applications based on business solutions. These business processes, as they are called, group PeopleSoft applications together to provide a specific organizational function. Table 1.1 provides several examples of PeopleSoft's Business Process solutions.

**TABLE 1.1**   PeopleSoft Business Solutions

| Business Process | Applications That Comprise the Business Process |
|---|---|
| Treasury Management | Cash Management, Payables, Expenses, Receivables, Budgets, Deal Management, Risk Management |
| Project Management | Projects, Purchasing, Payables, Expenses, Asset Management, Inventory, Time and Labor, Payroll, Budgets |
| Procurement | Purchasing, Inventory, Payables, Expenses, Asset Management |

# Functional Areas

Let's look at the functional areas that are defined by PeopleSoft.

## Human Resource Management System (HRMS)

The HRMS application modules represent the oldest group of PeopleSoft products. PeopleSoft began as a software company producing Human Resources and Payroll systems. The Human Resources and Payroll products are the most widely installed and the most mature applications. The new applications in this product group have been added largely to meet the demands of existing customers or to appeal to a wider group of employers.

The HRMS application modules include:

- ► Human Resources

- ► Payroll

- ► Benefits Administration

- ► Pension Administration

- ► Flexible Spending Account (FSA) Administration

- ▶ Payroll Interface
- ▶ European Payroll
- ▶ Stock Administration
- ▶ Time and Labor

## Financials

PeopleSoft formerly grouped many of their applications under the Financials label. The current trend toward Business Process solutions has broken some of the traditional boundaries that were previously defined. However, the core products are still found in the PeopleSoft Accounting and Control solution.

These application modules include:

- ▶ General Ledger
- ▶ Payables
- ▶ Receivables
- ▶ Expenses
- ▶ Asset Management
- ▶ Purchasing
- ▶ Cost Management
- ▶ Cash Management

## Manufacturing

The manufacturing industry is being served by the new Business Process solutions that are being rolled out. Manufacturing solutions include the following application modules:

- ▶ Human Resource Management
- ▶ Accounting and Control
- ▶ Treasury Management
- ▶ Project Management

### Public Sector

PeopleSoft markets specific business solutions to the government agencies in the public sector. These business solutions include:

▶ Human Resources Management for Education and Government

▶ Financial Management for Education and Government

Let's look at the technical environment that must exist for the PeopleSoft applications to work successfully.

# The PeopleSoft Technical Environment

PeopleSoft software is built around the client-server model. The client-server model is a system where the vital data is centralized and stored on a database on a server. The application processing logic resides on and is executed from multiple clients accessing the database.

The panels and application logic are stored in the PeopleSoft database along with the data. One advantage this gives you over traditionally designed client-server systems is in the area of version control. If you modify a panel or other object that is stored in the database, the end user automatically gets the new object the next time they access it. The only time you have to visit the workstation is during an upgrade to a newer version. This saves you much time during troubleshooting since you don't have to worry if the user has the latest object.

PeopleSoft provides two types of desktop clients: a traditional client that runs on either Windows 95 or Windows NT and, beginning with Version 7.x, a Java-based client that runs in an Internet browser or applet. The traditional client runs either the Windows 95 or Windows NT operating system and can be connected in either a two-tier client-server configuration or a three-tier configuration that includes an application server. Figure 1.2 illustrates the differences between a two-tier and three-tier client-server configuration. Chapter 5 discusses this concept in more detail.

On a Java-based client, Web applets are provided that can be launched using an Internet browser. Microsoft Internet Explorer is the preferred browser with PeopleSoft 7; Internet Explorer is required with PeopleSoft 7.5. Plans for version 8 include adding support for other browsers.

You must also have a database server. PeopleSoft supports several major database platforms: Oracle, DB2, Sybase, Microsoft SQL Server, and Informix. The Process

Scheduler and the Tuxedo application server that are delivered with PeopleSoft require either UNIX (HP-UX, AIX, SUN, or DG-UX) or Windows NT.

Additionally, a file server must be available onto which you can load the PeopleSoft executable files and other files necessary to run the applications and utilities provided by PeopleSoft. Supported network operating systems include Novell NetWare, Windows NT, and UNIX.

**NOTE**   PeopleSoft maintains a database of supported hardware and software platforms on their Web site that is updated frequently.

**FIGURE 1.2**    **Two-tier and three-tier client-server architecture**

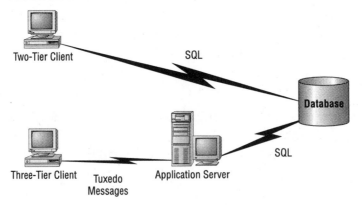

# Summary

This chapter introduced you to the concept of enterprise resource planning (ERP) and how it can help your company run more efficiently and effectively. PeopleSoft provides a comprehensive suite of ERP applications that can be customized to meet the unique needs of your company. You are now familiar with the major applications available in a PeopleSoft system.

This chapter also described the technical requirements, both hardware and software, that you need to consider before starting the implementation of your PeopleSoft system. Chapter 2, "Basic Implementation," will help you build and execute an implementation plan that will ensure that the PeopleSoft system is a success for your organization.

# *Basic Implementation*

**FEATURING:**

▶ **SELECTING THE TEAM**

▶ **PREPARING THE IMPLEMENTATION PLAN**

▶ **CONFIGURING THE SOFTWARE**

▶ **LINKING TO EXTERNAL APPLICATIONS**

Once you have purchased your PeopleSoft applications, you are faced with the task of implementation. Many factors can influence the scope of this task. The number of employees in your company can affect an HRMS implementation, while the total sales or the number of product lines can impact both the Financials and Manufacturing applications.

You need to develop an implementation plan that is both comprehensive and realistic for the selected applications. There are no firm guidelines that will cover all companies. The technical capabilities and PC experience of your functional users can greatly affect the length of time required for a successful implementation. The members of your implementation team must have experience with your current system and be familiar with all the areas to be implemented. For example, do not attempt to implement the General Ledger module without an implementation team member who is familiar with your current General Ledger system.

In addition, you must have all the financial and personnel resources required to accomplish the implementation. The project must have a corporate sponsor at the executive level. If the scope of your project affects multiple divisions of the company, then the level of executive from which you must gain support must be higher than a project that impacts just a single division. For example, a project for HRMS must have the support of the Vice President of Human Resources; a combined Financials and Manufacturing implementation should probably have the support of the Chief Operating Officer. Upper management support is critical for acquiring the technical resources for the implementation project.

**WARNING**  Do not attempt implementation without 100 percent support from upper management to provide necessary resources for the project.

This chapter will provide you with guidelines to assist with the implementation of your PeopleSoft system. The specific examples are based on PeopleSoft HRMS, but you can apply many of the ideas and procedures to other PeopleSoft modules.

Let's begin with a discussion designed to help you select the members of your implementation team.

## Selecting the Team

The success or failure of your project depends directly on the quality of the implementation team that you assemble. Make sure to select people from both the functional and technical communities for the implementation team. The functional experts can assess the PeopleSoft functionality for their area and determine how best to configure the required parameters. This information is used to configure the control tables for the specific PeopleSoft modules that are being implemented. Technical experts can make sure you are adhering to all the company guidelines. They can also handle all the technical questions and problems that arise during the implementation.

The project leader function should be filled by a manager from the functional area. You should also have a technical project leader who can focus on all the technical issues involved in the implementation (and there will be many). At my company, we find that separating these functions between two individuals provides a good balance. The project leader is free to keep track of the overall project while the technical project leader concentrates on the technical aspects of the implementation, including database setup, data migration, LAN and workstation setup, and interface implementation. The project leader and the technical project leader can work together to coordinate any requested modifications or customizations.

Another consideration when planning your implementation is whether to bring in an implementation partner or to perform the implementation yourself. Let's look at some of the factors to consider when choosing an implementation partner.

## Should You Choose an Implementation Partner?

When implementing PeopleSoft, the inevitable question that must be answered is whether to bring in an implementation partner or not. The alternative is to perform the implementation without outside help.

To answer this question, consider the answers to two other questions first. The first question is: Do you have the skills in house that are required to perform the implementation? The answer to this question must take into account both the technical and functional aspects of the implementation. A functional consultant understands the function being performed and how PeopleSoft performs that function. Technical consultants can supplement your own technical staff with an individual who is knowledgeable about the PeopleSoft technology.

One word of caution: Review the consultant's qualifications and interview any consultant before you use them. Check the references provided by the individual and the company. Treat this as seriously as if you were hiring the consultant to be an employee of your company.

A consultant can also manage the project, but I have found it better to use internal personnel for project management. Internal personnel are more familiar with your corporate culture, which should allow the project to be best positioned for success in your environment. However, if you have a shortage of personnel with project management skills, consider using a consultant as the project manager. Make sure to conduct interviews with prospective project managers to determine how well the consultant meshes with your company's management style and corporate culture in general.

If you answered yes to the first question, then the second question is: Are the in-house personnel available for your project during the desired implementation window? If not, you either have to delay the start of your implementation project or bring in outside expertise in the form of an implementation partner or consultants.

Let's take a look at the members of the internal implementation team.

## Internal Team Members

In addition to the project leader and the technical project leader, there are two basic categories of internal team members: technical and functional, as outlined in the previous section.

The technical team should include a database administrator (DBA). The DBA is responsible for building all the databases necessary for the implementation. The DBA is also responsible for running the installation scripts that load the base system. The DBA has on-going support responsibilities for data integrity, performance tuning, and upgrading.

The LAN administrator plays a critical role in the storage and backup of the application directories. The LAN administrator also installs and provides database connectivity for each workstation that will be running the PeopleSoft application.

The operating system (OS) administrator (e.g., UNIX, Windows NT, MVS) for the database platform should also be included on the implementation team. The OS administrator installs and configures the initial PeopleSoft environment on the database server. The OS administrator must also ensure that the server is configured with the appropriate version of the COBOL and C compilers.

The programmers who have been supporting your existing system and who will support your new system should be included on the implementation team as well. The programmers may be involved in the migration of current system data into your PeopleSoft system. They will also define and develop any necessary interfaces that must continue between the PeopleSoft system and other systems.

The functional team should include area experts for each module that you are attempting to install. For example, to perform a PeopleSoft HRMS implementation of the

Human Resources, Payroll, and Benefits Administration modules, you should include experts from the Employment, Training, Payroll, and Benefits departments on the project team.

Once you have identified your team members, assemble the team and begin building the implementation plan.

# Preparing the Implementation Plan

The implementation plan that you and your team develop is critical in determining the level of success you achieve. You must define clear, concise, and achievable goals for the project. Providing additional incentives to your implementation team should be a priority; define these incentives during the planning phase as well.

Begin your team planning meetings by outlining all the steps required to implement the chosen PeopleSoft applications. Developing these steps before establishing project goals helps you define more achievable goals. For example, by determining the target database platform, you can identify additional training that might be required in the goal-setting process.

The following steps are the initial implementation questions that have to be answered in order to begin the goal-setting process. Depending on your environment, you may need to answer additional questions:

▶ Which database platform (Oracle, Sybase, DB2/UNIX, Informix, Microsoft)?

▶ Which server operating system (HP, Sun, IBM, DEC, Windows NT)?

▶ Do we need additional database management tools?

▶ How large do the databases need to be?

▶ How large does the database server need to be (e.g., for memory, storage, fault tolerance)?

▶ Will additional internal support be required to support the current system during the implementation?

▶ Is extended system availability required (hours per day and days per week)?

▶ Do we need to hire or contract the needed personnel resources?

▶ What are the workstation requirements?

The answers to these questions should help you set better goals. You should be able to identify additional training, software, configuration, and personnel requirements.

In addition to building the implementation plan, you also need to develop a system administration plan. This plan defines the maintenance of the system after its implementation. You need to address many considerations. Some of them require you to gather information before the implementation begins to gauge the current system administration requirements. The following considerations should be included in the overall implementation planning process:

▶ Create a disaster recovery plan.

▶ Determine the current level of network utilization.

▶ Forecast utilization growth with the new system.

▶ Determine if any changes need to occur on the network.

▶ Define a plan for periodic review and initial actions when utilization problems occur.

▶ Establish security plans and procedures.

▶ Establish audit plans and procedures.

▶ Define standards for documentation and programming.

▶ Implement procedures for managing changes to the system (change control).

▶ Identify any external linkages.

Once you have answers to all or most of the above questions, the team can begin to set goals for the implementation project. Let's look at this goal-setting process.

## Establishing Goals

The goals that you establish for your project are critical to its success. The more realistic and detailed you are in setting the project goals, the more likely your project will be successful.

The first step of the goal-setting process is to consider the phased implementation approach. If your environment has many locations or if you are implementing several applications, a phased approach works better than implementing all locations or all applications at once. Early in the process, you should identify each phase and which applications should be implemented during that phase. For example, for PeopleSoft HRMS products, the first application you must configure is Human Resources. The other applications then connect to the basic personnel information defined in the

Human Resources tables. For the PeopleSoft Financial applications in a large multi-company environment, you may want to define the basic roll-up reporting structures at the corporate level and then implement the structures one company at a time.

Second, list the tasks in the order in which they are to be completed. Surprisingly, when my company began to plan for the PeopleSoft implementation, our list closely matched the PeopleSoft installation instructions:

1. Complete the configuration of the application control tables.

2. Load the test data.

3. Complete the configuration testing.

4. Customize the software.

5. Define the acceptance testing criteria for use during parallel operations.

6. Reload the database with updated conversion data.

7. Begin parallel operations (concurrent keying).

8. Complete the critical interfaces and prepare for testing.

9. Begin production.

Once you have defined your goals, assign target dates for each goal and build a delivery schedule for the project. Let's take a look at the process of scheduling.

## Setting the Schedule

At this point, begin establishing target dates for the completion of each phase. A good target date for a payroll implementation, for example, is the first payroll of the year. This way, you don't have to maintain and report tax information from two discrete systems. A target date for a General Ledger application might be the beginning of a new fiscal year. If it is not possible to start with the first payroll of the year, I recommend the beginning of a quarter. Decide what works best for your environment and is least stressful to the functional staff that will be coordinating the transition from the old system to the new.

The following list contains the first tasks that should be defined in the implementation plan. You should clearly identify the deadlines and ensure that the technical team understands and agrees with those deadlines. These items should not be allowed to delay other aspects of the project:

1. Hardware installation

2. Hardware configuration

3. Relational database management system (RDBMS) installation

4. RDBMS configuration

5. Additional database management tool installation if required

6. Software installation

At our company, we allowed one month between the installation of the software and the beginning of the configuration. This gave us ample time to test the technical parts of the installation. This also allowed us to evaluate and understand how the PeopleSoft table structures and indexes are designed. You can compress this to one or two weeks, but reserve some time for the DBA to become familiar with the People-Soft database environment.

After modifying the checklist from above with dates for each step, the implementation schedule that my company developed for PeopleSoft Human Resources and Payroll looked similar to Table 2.1.

**TABLE 2.1**   Implementation Schedule for the Human Resources and Payroll Phase

| Date | Task to Be Completed |
| --- | --- |
| 3/15 | Hardware installation. |
| 3/25 | Hardware configuration. |
| 4/1 | Relational database management system (RDBMS) installation. |
| 4/6 | RDBMS configuration. |
| 4/10 | Additional database management tool installation if required. |
| 4/15 | Software installation. |
| 8/31 | Complete the configuration company tables. |
| 8/31 | Load the test data. |
| 9/30 | Complete the configuration testing. |
| 10/20 | Complete the software customization. |
| 10/20 | Define the acceptance testing criteria for payroll for use during parallel operations. |
| 10/20 | Reload the database with updated employee data. |

**TABLE 2.1  (continued)**    Implementation Schedule for the Human Resources and Payroll Phase

| Date | Task to Be Completed |
|------|----------------------|
| 11/1 | Begin parallel operations (concurrent keying). |
| 12/1 | Critical interfaces to be completed and ready for testing. |
| 1/1 | Begin production. |

**TIP**   You must maintain both systems during the implementation. Consequently plan for additional manpower to handle the concurrent keying required during parallel operations.

Another aspect of the implementation that should not be overlooked is the incentives for the team members to meet their deadlines. Let's look at some ideas on how to create those incentives.

## Creating the Incentives

I cannot take credit for the next idea. My company has a tremendous corporate performance management program that provides incentives for superior work performance. Our project used the incentive procedures already in place to implement a performance management project for our PeopleSoft implementation project.

**NOTE**   For a more detailed explanation of performance management, I recommend the book *Performance Management, Improving Quality Productivity through Positive Reinforcement*, by Aubrey Daniels, Ph.D. My company continues to maintain a close alliance with his company, Aubrey Daniels and Associates, for advice and materials for our Performance Management program.

Using performance management techniques, assign small definable goals throughout the implementation and reward the project team as those goals are achieved. This system does not have to track goal accomplishment using traditional project management methods like Gant charts. You can be as creative as you want in your goal tracking.

Whatever method you use for providing incentives to the project team, be consistent. Remember to reward behaviors that you want to continue. This may prevent members of your implementation team from leaving the company after the implementation is complete.

**NOTE** To date, my company has maintained 100 percent retention of the technical implementation team!

Now that you have some guidelines for building your plan, let's learn how to configure the PeopleSoft software.

# Configuring the Software

The first step that the technical team should take in configuring the software is to load the software onto the file server. To do this, run the setup routine for People-Tools and all the applications to be implemented. Additionally, you need to perform the setup for PeopleBooks, Crystal Reports, and any of the other included third-party applications (Cognos PowerPlay, Arbor Essbase, or Actuate). These installations require significant resources on your file server. For example, HRMS version 7.5 requires over 500MB of space on the file server.

At the end of the file-loading process, the PeopleSoft setup routine prompts you to accept the default name for this installation group or give it the name of your choice. This group contains the programs that are required to get your system up and running. The most important programs are Data Mover, Database Setup, PeopleTools, and Workstation setup.

Use the Workstation setup program to configure any environment variables that are required for the users. The configuration can be exported to a file and then applied to each workstation. I prefer to create multiple profiles based on the programs that the user needs to access. For example, not all users need access to the SQRW program from the command line. None of the end users require access to the Data Mover program, so that program is loaded only in the profile for the technical users.

At this point, you have all the scripts extracted, so that the DBA can begin building the databases. Let's look at how to build a database.

## Building the Database

The first step the DBA needs to perform is to size and establish a database into which the empty PeopleSoft shell will be installed.

At my company, I took a conservative approach with my databases. I created several additional databases as the implementation proceeded. We used one, the development database, for the configuration and testing of all the application control tables. Concurrently, I created an empty PeopleSoft database that became the production database. The production database allowed us to make a clean conversion to production once we were ready to begin parallel operations. You can accomplish this by migrating the data contained in the application control tables from the development database into the target production database. I then loaded clean employee data into the production database. Synchronizing the new database with the current employees in the old system allowed parallel testing to begin.

Sizing the production database is affected by a number of factors, depending on which PeopleSoft application you are configuring, the volume of transactions that have been planned, and the history that will be available from day one of your new system. PeopleSoft now provides a configuration lab to help you with sizing your databases for the initial installation. Take advantage of it!

PeopleSoft provides an installation guide for each supported database platform. This document contains examples of how to create the database. You should build the script using information found in the installation guide for your database platform and combine it with sizing information that you have calculated or received from the People-Soft sizing center. A sample script for creating a 1.6GB database with a 400MB log for Sybase on a UNIX server is shown below:

```
use master
go
disk init
  name = "db_hrprod",
  physname = "/dev/vg01/rdb_hrprod",
  vdevno = 20,
  size = 819200
go
disk init
  name = "tr_hrprod",
  physname = "/dev/vg01/rtr_hrprod",
  vdevno = 21,
  size = 204800
go
create database HRPROD
 on db_hrprod = 1600
 log on tr_hrprod = 400
```

```
go
sp_dboption HRPROD,trunc,true
go
sp_dboption HRPROD,allow,true
go
sp_dboption HRPROD,bulkcopy,true
go
sp_dboption HRPROD,ddl,true
go
use HRPROD
go
checkpoint
go
```

**NOTE** I will often use examples that are specific to my environment. I provide them to give you an idea of what will occur. I do not attempt to provide examples for platforms for which I cannot test the script to ensure that it works.

This script first initializes the database device. Then the database and log are created using this device. Finally, the database options that control creation and loading of the database tables are executed.

Once you have created the database, run the script provided by PeopleSoft to add several data types to your database. This script is called addobj.sql. These data types are used by PeopleSoft to provide a consistent date and time data type for the supported database platforms.

Now that you have created the empty database to house your PeopleSoft data, it is time to load any code that will run on the database server.

## Loading the Software

The PeopleSoft system has a Process Scheduler program that is used to schedule and run programs for both yourself and the users. The Process Scheduler is a COBOL process that must be compiled for the platform on which it runs. First, load all source code to the target server. Then compile the COBOL source and link the COBOL to the database connectivity routines by executing psrun.mak, located in the PeopleSoft installation directory on your target server. PeopleSoft recommends that you run your Process Scheduler and any other batch programs, such as the Payroll process, on the same machine as your database.

**N O T E** Chapter 5, "Administration Tools," discusses the Process Scheduler and Application Server applications in greater detail.

PeopleSoft provides a program called Server Transfer, located in the PeopleSoft Installation program group, to build a script that can be used to transfer these files to your server using the ftp program. Carefully review the script that is generated to ensure that the files are being placed in the directories that you have designated on the server.

If you choose to run the Process Scheduler on a separate machine, you may have to create a custom transfer script. One way to do this is to copy the PeopleSoft-generated transfer script to a new file and delete the objects that you do not need.

Occasionally, I found it necessary to create my own scripts to move many files from the file server to other servers. I developed a method to create a script quickly that I would like to share with you. The most common situation where I used this method is when moving custom SQR programs that have been developed.

1. Place all the files in a single directory or directory structure.

2. Obtain a list of files and write it to a text file using the command `ls *.sqr >files.out` on UNIX or `dir /B *.sqr >files.out` in a DOS window on Windows 95 or Windows NT.

3. Open the file using MS Excel (or another spreadsheet program).

4. Copy the files to additional columns as shown in Figure 2.1.

5. Edit the first cell in both the first and third columns to reflect the source and target directories. Then copy the edited cells down the column as shown in Figure 2.2.

6. Save the file as a text file.

7. Open the file in a text editor.

8. Use search and replace to remove the spaces between the directories and the filenames.

9. Add target and login instructions to the top of the file and add exit information at the bottom.

10. Your script is now complete and ready to run.

11. From the Windows NT command line, type `ftp -s:filename.txt` to run the script. The script can also be executed from a DOS window on Windows 95/98.

**FIGURE 2.1**     Script creation–Step 4

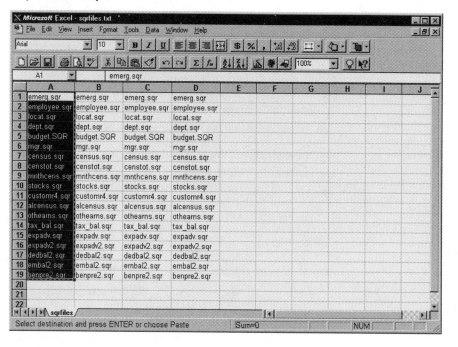

**FIGURE 2.2**     Script creation–Step 5

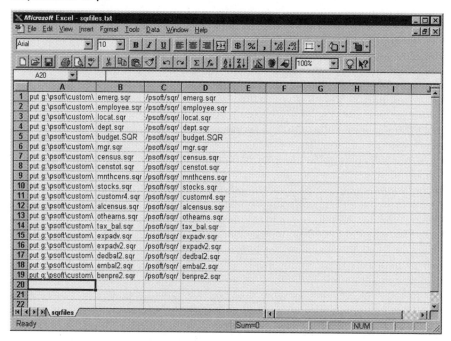

After completing these steps, a directory listing that looked like the following:

```
emerg.sqr
employee.sqr
locat.sqr
dept.sqr
budget.sqr
mgr.sqr
census.sqr
censtot.sqr
mnthcens.sqr
stocks.sqr
customr4.sqr
alcensus.sqr
othearns.sqr
tax_bal.sqr
expadv.sqr
expadv2.sqr
dedbal2.sqr
ernbal2.sqr
benpre2.sqr
```

looks like this:

```
open target-server
loginid
password
ascii
put g:\psoft\custom\emerg.sqr /psoft/sqr/emerg.sqr
put g:\psoft\custom\employee.sqr /psoft/sqr/employee.sqr
put g:\psoft\custom\locat.sqr /psoft/sqr/locat.sqr
put g:\psoft\custom\dept.sqr /psoft/sqr/dept.sqr
put g:\psoft\custom\budget.sqr /psoft/sqr/budget.sqr
put g:\psoft\custom\mgr.sqr /psoft/sqr/mgr.sqr
put g:\psoft\custom\census.sqr /psoft/sqr/census.sqr
put g:\psoft\custom\censtot.sqr /psoft/sqr/censtot.sqr
put g:\psoft\custom\mnthcens.sqr /psoft/sqr/mnthcens.sqr
put g:\psoft\custom\stocks.sqr /psoft/sqr/stocks.sqr
put g:\psoft\custom\customr4.sqr /psoft/sqr/customr4.sqr
put g:\psoft\custom\alcensus.sqr /psoft/sqr/alcensus.sqr
put g:\psoft\custom\othearns.sqr /psoft/sqr/othearns.sqr
put g:\psoft\custom\tax_bal.sqr /psoft/sqr/tax_bal.sqr
put g:\psoft\custom\expadv.sqr /psoft/sqr/expadv.sqr
```

```
put g:\psoft\custom\expadv2.sqr /psoft/sqr/expadv2.sqr
put g:\psoft\custom\dedbal2.sqr /psoft/sqr/dedbal2.sqr
put g:\psoft\custom\ernbal2.sqr /psoft/sqr/ernbal2.sqr
put g:\psoft\custom\benpre2.sqr /psoft/sqr/benpre2.sqr
bye
```

The advantage of this procedure is that I am able to create a script for 40 files or 800 files in almost the same amount of time. This script also allows me to easily copy files to both my test and production servers by just changing the target. This guarantees that both servers have the same files.

**NOTE**  I use this script building as one example, there are other methods for moving mass quantities of files, such as the UNIX mput command. There are also utilities that allow for point-and-click mass transfer of files. Your server administrator will be able to provide suggestions for which works best in your environment.

The next section describes the procedures for loading the PeopleSoft data into your databases.

## Loading the Tables

There are two basic databases that must be established for you to begin configuring the PeopleSoft application for your environment. First, create the Demo database using the Data Mover script that is created by running the database setup program. This program is installed on the workstation from which you install the software to your file server. Figure 2.3 illustrates the database setup options for PeopleSoft HRMS version 7.5.

The Demo database contains both the PeopleTools data and test data supplied by PeopleSoft. This database will be used often during the implementation phase as a reference for how PeopleSoft uses a particular object or function. You can also use it for training your end users, but my company found that it was better to use our own test data and all of our application control table information to build our own training database.

**NOTE**  My company sent a few individuals to PeopleSoft instructor-led training to prepare them to teach the rest of our user population.

**FIGURE 2.3**   Demo Database Setup

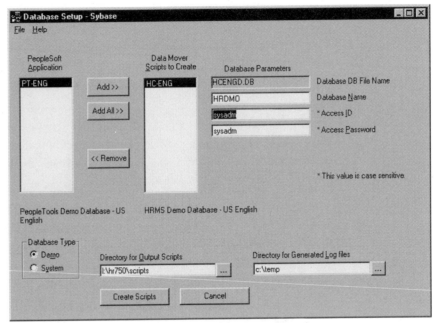

Using the Database Setup application, select the Demo database type using the radio button in the lower-left corner of the screen. You are then given a choice of configuring the HRMS Demo version or the PeopleTools Demo version. To complete configuration, follow these steps:

1. Select the HRMS demo.

2. Enter the target database name.

3. Enter your Access ID and Password. The PeopleSoft logon process uses the initial operator information to look up security settings for the user. The logon process then disconnects the user and reconnects using this Access ID that you created. The Access ID should generally be the database owner, who ensures that full rights to the database exist. This reconnection process is important because all your users appear to be connected using the same ID, and they are connected when using many of the standard database tools. PeopleSoft provides additional information about the connection that can be used to identify the user. The location and nature of this information varies from database to database.

4. Verify or enter the directory where the output script is to be placed.

**5.** Verify the output directory for the log file.

**6.** Click the Create Scripts button.

The script is generated and placed in the selected directory. The Demo database is used for future upgrades for comparison and is also quite helpful for use as a reference when trying to decide how to configure certain aspects of your application.

The second database you need to load is the empty System database, using another Data Mover script created with the same database setup program as above. Select the System database radio button in the lower-left corner of Figure 2.3. This second database will be a shell database that contains only PeopleTools data. This is the database into which you load your own information.

**NOTE**   The system table will also contain tax information for federal, state, and local tax localities for payroll customers.

There are two ways to load information. The first way is to create load scripts of your own. This method provides the best performance on large data loads. The disadvantage of creating load scripts is that you *must* add code to verify the integrity and validity of the data that you are loading. This added code should match the logic that is used by the PeopleSoft online system, or your data will be inaccessible or will cause the system to operate improperly.

**WARNING**   You *must* add validation code that matches the PeopleSoft validation code when creating import scripts instead of using Import Manager.

The second option is to use the PeopleSoft Import Manager. Import Manager allows you to define a file format and map it to the record definition for the table you want to load. The data is then validated using the appropriate PeopleCode. The disadvantage in using Import Manager is speed. Import Manager is not a good option for tables larger than about 3,000 records. Chapter 6, "Data Management Tools," provides a more detailed explanation of Import Manager.

While you are extracting the data from your old system to load into the PeopleSoft database, the functional users should be configuring all the tables that they need for their applications. For HRMS, the pay groups and salary ranges should be configured. PeopleSoft provides a detailed listing of the tables that must be configured for each application. In general, all prompt tables must be completed before a record can be loaded. You should also have all your translate table values configured. Chapter 7, "Development Tools," contains more detailed information about prompt tables using the Record Designer.

There is also a specific load order for the PeopleSoft tables that is provided by PeopleSoft in their documentation. For example, in HRMS, all employee-level database tables use the personal data table to validate that an employee ID exists before it accepts information for that employee.

Another key concept that you should be aware of as the administrator is the effective dating of information. PeopleSoft uses effective dates on many of the tables in the system. This allows history to be maintained online in the system. This will be a new concept to many of your users. You may be more familiar with a flat-file legacy database where history, if maintained at all, had to be accessed by a different panel of function keys. All that is required in PeopleSoft is to select Display All when opening an effective dated panel.

Another aspect of the implementation that you need to address is the links to other applications. You may have to bring in information from external systems for payments or bonuses. You also have to test the links to external systems, such as for sending direct deposits to the bank or financial information to your parent company. Let's look at how to create these links.

# Linking to External Applications

When you have other systems with which you must exchange information, you have two options: You can rewrite and convert the existing functions so that they directly access the needed information, or you can write programs that extract data and serve as an interface between the systems. The choice you make depends on your access to the external system. If it is internal to your company, then you may be able to create direct access routines for the data. Otherwise, you have to create files to pass between the two systems.

An example of a system that you may be able to rewrite is a timecard system. PeopleSoft has a Time and Labor application module but it currently does not support timecards. You may choose to write a timecard program to capture employees' time and update the Payroll system with hours-worked data.

Suppose, for example, that your General Ledger system is a non-PeopleSoft application, but you have PeopleSoft installed. These two applications will need to exchange data. You will need to write a routine that creates an extract file that can be loaded into the General Ledger system.

Let's look at the conversion of existing functions.

## Converting an Existing Function

Converting an existing function to access the PeopleSoft application and or tables directly is a good long-term solution if you have the capability and the manpower to modify the existing function. Simply write the new application to link directly to the PeopleSoft tables.

Another option is to rewrite the current application using the PeopleTools development environment to fully integrate the new application into the PeopleSoft architecture.

A third option is to rewrite the new application using another development tool and accessing the needed PeopleSoft application using the PeopleSoft Message Agent application programming interface (API). The Message Agent API is limited in its capabilities and cannot perform all the access functions to the PeopleSoft system.

A fourth option that is used by some companies is to create the routine using the SQR application, which provides the ability to directly access the database.

As the system administrator, you have to decide which option is best, then pass the development task on to the developers to create the necessary programs. Chapter 7, "Development Tools," provides an overview of the PeopleSoft development environment.

Let's look at the other option for building interfaces to the external systems.

## Interfaces to External Applications

The most common resolution to the problem of linking to external systems is to write procedures that export the data out of one system and create a file that can then be imported into the other. This is most often used when the data mappings between the two systems are dissimilar.

For example, consider an interface from the PeopleSoft system to an external system that can read a non-delimited text file. A non-delimited text file is a file with fixed-width fields containing no characters to represent the beginning or ending of the fields. To obtain the simplest output using delivered PeopleSoft tools, write an SQR report to create this file for you. A Structured Query Report (SQR) is a delivered reporting tool that also has the capability to perform database insertions, updates, and deletions using the SQR command structure. The SQR report syntax is covered in more detail in Chapter 10, "SQR."

To build an extract program using SQR, follow these steps:

1. Determine what information is required by the external application.

2. Determine which tables contain the needed information.

3. Write the SQR.

4. Test the SQR.

5. Send the test file to the external system.

The following script illustrates what an extract looks like. This program creates a flat-file listing of the location table.

```
! locat.sqr 06/04/97 Create extract file from database table.

begin-report
 do main
end-report

begin-procedure main
move 0 to #totrec
begin-select
A.LOCATION    (0,0,005)
A.DESCR    (0,0,030)
A.ADDRESS1    (0,0,035)
A.ADDRESS2    (0,0,035)
A.CITY    (0,0,030)
A.COUNTY    (0,0,015)
A.STATE    (0,0,002)
A.ZIP    (0,0,010)
 add 1 to #totrec
 new-page
from HRPROD..PS_LOCATION_TBL A
where A.EFF_STATUS = 'A'
 and A.EFFDT =
 (SELECT MAX(H.EFFDT)
   FROM HRPROD..PS_LOCATION_TBL H
  where H.LOCATION = A.LOCATION
    and H.EFFDT <= getdate())
order by A.LOCATION
end-select
end-procedure
```

```
begin-setup
 page-size 1 162
 no-formfeed
end-setup
```

**WARNING** Some of the functions in this example may not be available on your database platform. For example, the getdate() command is specific to Sybase.

**NOTE** This script was designed for use in automated scripts being executed with the cron functionality of UNIX. I use the database name with a double dot and the table name to ensure that the data is retrieved from the production table, even if a SQR command line parameter gets inadvertently changed.

In this script, the positioning data that is in parentheses immediately following each column in the select statement tells the program to list the contents of the field at that position. The SQR reads the setup information and determines that the page size is 1 row by 162 columns. This specifies that there will be one record per page (or per select statement in this case). The new-page command can also be used without the setup command to return the pointer back to column one. The output is a fixed-length file format that is easily ready by other systems.

You can also provide print statements for the output, which allow you to perform some processing action. The following code example illustrates this functionality. This example is designed to build a semi-colon–delimited file that can be easily ready by Microsoft Excel. This file is used to build an organizational chart for my company using the Organization Chart Wizard feature of Visio Professional. The only thing you have to do before running the Wizard is to open this file, delete the reports to column for your top level (the CEO), and save the file in Microsoft Excel format.

```
! mgr.sqr 10/16/97 Create extract file for Managers
!  target ----------- Excel
! Created by Darrell Bilbrey

begin-report
 do main
end-report

begin-procedure main
move 0 to #totrec
move 'A' to $pholder
```

```
move ';' to $delim
begin-select
A.EMPLID
A.NAME
A.SAL_ADMIN_PLAN
A.DEPTNAME
A.DEPTID
A.LOCATION
 move ' ' to $deptmgrid
 move 'Non-Manager' to $nonmgr
 move &A.EMPLID to $employeeid
 move &A.DEPTID to $empldeptid
 do Check_Mgr
 do Get_Manager_Info
 if $deptmgrid <> ' '
 print &A.NAME    (0,0,050)
 print $delim     (0,0,001)
 print $depname    (0,0,030)
 print $delim     (0,0,001)
 print &A.LOCATION  (0,0,002)
 print $delim     (0,0,001)
 print &A.DEPTID   (0,0,010)
 print $delim     (0,0,001)
 print $deptmgrname  (0,0,050)
 end-if
 add 1 to #totrec
from HRPROD..PS_EMPLOYEES A
where A.SAL_ADMIN_PLAN <> 'NEX'
end-select
end-procedure

begin-procedure Check_Mgr
begin-select
D.MANAGER_ID
D.DEPTID
D.DESCR
 move &D.DEPTID to $deptmgrid
 move &D.DESCR to $depname
from HRPROD..PS_DEPT_TBL D
where D.MANAGER_ID=$employeeid
and D.COMPANY = 'BC1'
and D.EFF_STATUS = 'A'
```

```
    and D.DEPTID = (select min(J.DEPTID) from HRPROD..PS_DEPT_TBL J
        where J.MANAGER_ID = D.MANAGER_ID)
    and D.EFFDT = (select max(K.EFFDT) from HRPROD..PS_DEPT_TBL K
        where K.DEPTID = D.DEPTID
          and K.EFFDT <= getdate())
end-select
end-procedure

begin-procedure Get_Manager_Info
begin-select
F.DEPTID
F.MANAGER_ID
 move &F.MANAGER_ID to $mgrid2
 do Get_Mgr_Name
from HRPROD..PS_DEPT_TBL F
where F.DEPTID = $empldeptid
 and F.EFFDT = (select max(L.EFFDT) from HRPROD..PS_DEPT_TBL L
     where L.DEPTID = F.DEPTID
       and L.EFFDT <= getdate())
end-select
end-procedure

begin-procedure Get_Mgr_Name
begin-select
G.NAME
 move &G.NAME to $deptmgrname
from HRPROD..PS_EMPLOYEES G
where G.EMPLID = $mgrid2
end-select
end-procedure

begin-setup
 page-size 1 146
 no-formfeed
end-setup
```

Another example of an interface is one that moves data from an external system into the PeopleSoft system. Let's look at a process for updating the pay sheets in the payroll process with updated time information from an external time system that provides the same non-delimited text file for your use.

PeopleSoft provides a SQR program called `payupdt.sqr` that you can use or modify to load pay information from the Payroll tables. You execute the payroll calculation program just as you would if the pay information had been created internally. My company modified payupdt.sqr to edit the information being entered and also to make it respond to other inputs from the online run control panel so that this one program could be used to load information from all of our external sources.

**N O T E**  The run control panels are used by PeopleSoft to initiate jobs via the Process Scheduler. This is where any needed runtime parameters are entered. The information is stored in a run control table and retrieved by the program when the Process Scheduler executes the program. The Process Scheduler is explained in more detail in Chapter 5, "Administration Tools."

# Summary

Careful preparation will ensure the success of your PeopleSoft system implementation. The first step is to select a team to do the implementation. This team should include the following members:

- ▶ Project leader
- ▶ Technical project leader
- ▶ Implementation consultants (if required)
- ▶ Technical experts (database administrator, LAN administrator, operating system administrator, programmers)
- ▶ Functional experts

The second step is to prepare an implementation plan which does the following:

- ▶ Outlines the implementation steps
- ▶ Describes a system administration plan
- ▶ Establishes goals
- ▶ Considers a phased implementation approach
- ▶ Lists all the tasks to be completed
- ▶ Sets the schedule
- ▶ Creates incentives for implementation team members

Once the plan is prepared, the implementation begins. Technical team members need to configure the software, including building both the Demo database and the System database. The technical team must also address issues related to other applications, both internal to the PeopleSoft applications and external applications developed by third-party vendors. If necessary, the programmers on the implementation team should develop or modify any code that acts as an interface to any other applications. We will discuss issues surrounding the customization of the PeopleSoft application in Chapter 3, "Customization."

Once the implementation is complete, you should run the new system in parallel with the current system for a period of time. Chapter 4, "Parallel Operations," describes this period of parallel operations.

# *Customization*

**FEATURING:**

▶ **DEFINING THE OBJECTIVES**

▶ **MINIMIZING CUSTOMIZATION**

▶ **MAKING THE CUSTOMIZATION**

▶ **DOCUMENTING THE CUSTOMIZATION**

During the implementation, you are faced with many decisions about whether to customize the PeopleSoft application or to adopt PeopleSoft's way of performing tasks. Chapter 2 briefly discussed customization. This chapter examines this topic in more detail. We will discuss an assessment methodology for you to use when considering a customization. We will then describe some of the tools used in performing an impact analysis. Finally, we will explore the customization steps in three examples that my company has performed.

**N O T E**   The issue of customization merits your consideration during the implementation phase, which is why I have included it in Part One. You may want to return to the examples in this chapter after you complete Part Two and have a better understanding of the tools used in these examples.

One of the primary considerations when evaluating a proposed customization is whether the customization can be easily maintained in the future as application upgrades are delivered by PeopleSoft. First, consider seriously modifying your business practices to accommodate the PeopleSoft methodology. PeopleSoft can accomplish most required business tasks. There will be cases where the functionality for a company-specific process does not exist. This is the ideal place to add a customization to extend the PeopleSoft system. This ability to customize the system to perform almost any task is one of the strengths of the PeopleSoft system. Additionally, the PeopleSoft system is easy to customize compared to mainframe systems. However, you do not want to modify the existing screens merely for cosmetic reasons like, for example, moving fields around on a panel to make it look like your old system.

You do not want to severely limit your ability to upgrade by performing unnecessary customization. If PeopleSoft does not perform the function you need, your only alternative may be customization. Customizations will not prevent upgrades; they make the process much slower, and they require more testing to ensure that your customizations are still working as designed after upgrades are completed.

**W A R N I N G**   Use caution when customizing the delivered PeopleSoft application. Making changes without conducting a full impact analysis can render other functions unusable.

**N O T E**  It is not my intent to scare you away from making customizations. Almost all companies make customizations to their PeopleSoft system. Just be aware of the system-wide impact a customization can have before you begin.

If you choose to proceed with a customization, first define the objectives that you are trying to achieve.

# Defining the Objectives

The first step in the assessment methodology is to define the objectives of the customization. This gives both the technical and functional users a clear understanding of the goals of the customization.

Next, the technical team must perform an impact analysis to determine if there will be any adverse effects on other modules of the PeopleSoft application. This is an important step because you do not want to make changes that could render other functions inoperable.

Let's use a proposed field change as an example. Your user gives you the name of the panel on which the field appears. You use this information to determine the record that contains the field by following these steps:

**1.** Open the panel in the Application Designer. Figure 3.1 contains an example of a panel. Open the panel by selecting File > Open and choose the panel type from the Object Type drop-down list, as shown in Figure 3.2.

**2.** Highlight the field you want to change. Right-click that field and select Panel Field Properties to get information about the object. The Record Name and Field Name boxes should provide you with the needed information, as illustrated in Figure 3.3.

**3.** To determine which other panels and records contain the field, open the record that contains the desired field. Highlight that field. Select Edit > Find Object References.

**4.** A list of other panels and records that contain this field appears in the output window at the bottom of the Application Designer window, as shown in Figure 3.4.

**FIGURE 3.1**    Application Designer panel

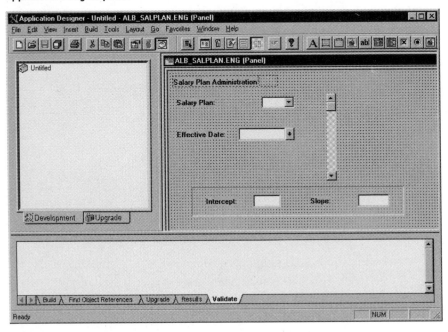

**FIGURE 3.2**    File open for panel

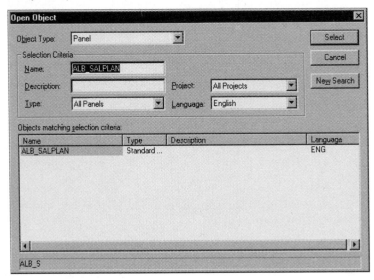

**FIGURE 3.3**    Panel Field Properties dialog box

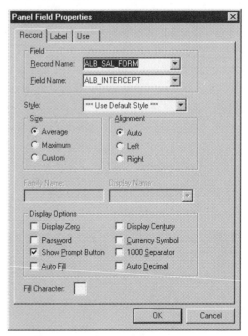

**FIGURE 3.4**    Find Object References tab

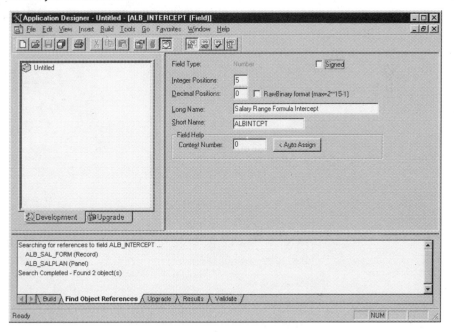

**5.** Review the list, researching any records that are listed to determine if they are used by other online panels or batch processes. You can use the Find function of Windows Explorer to search the stored statement Data Mover scripts for references to the record.

**6.** If any records for online panels are found, review the PeopleCode found in the record to determine if the proposed change will have any effect on this record. To access the PeopleCode for a record, open the record by selecting File **>** Open, and then selecting the Record type. Then select View **>** PeopleCode. Figure 3.5 contains an example of a record showing which fields have the associated People-Code. (This figure illustrates a different record since there was no PeopleCode associated with the record shown in Figure 3.3.)

**FIGURE 3.5**    Record showing PeopleCode

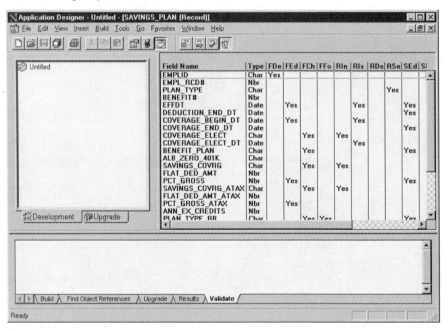

**7.** If any records used by batch processes are found, review the code for the batch process itself to determine if the change to the field will cause any problems with the batch processes. (The most common type of change that might affect batch processing is changing the numeric type on a field.)

**8.** Review any reports to determine if there is any special formatting for the field in the reports that might be affected. The best way to do this is to use the grep command and search for the field name in your SQR directories. You can use the Find function of Windows Explorer if you have only Windows 95 or Windows NT available.

**TIP**   If you have UNIX available, use the grep command because it is faster than the Explorer Find function.

# Minimizing Customizations

One thing to consider when preparing proposed customizations is that you will be forced to review and carry forward any customizations during future upgrades. There are several actions you can take to help minimize the number of customizations that you make:

1. Create a review process in which the functional area managers must review any proposed changes before the request is even considered. It is important that the managers know what their group is requesting.

2. Don't make any customizations merely for cosmetic reasons. The PeopleSoft documentation emphasizes this point. Take it seriously. You do not want to rearrange the order of fields on a panel merely for aesthetic reasons.

3. Check PeopleSoft Customer Connection for possible alternatives using PeopleSoft-delivered functionality to perform the task. Don't forget to review the discussion areas to see if other PeopleSoft customers are facing the same problem.

4. Use PeopleSoft Account Manager to help identify other customers who have encountered this situation. They may be able to find a reference that is not mentioned on Customer Connection.

5. Review any information concerning a future release. The functionality you need may be planned for the next release, which is due to ship in a short period of time. You can then approach the user who requested the change to determine the feasibility of delaying a decision until the new functionality is reviewed.

**WARNING**   Remember: Any change, even the movement of an existing field on a panel, is automatically stamped as a customization. You have now taken "ownership" of the panel in PeopleSoft's view.

If you have tried all the above steps and still need to customize, do not give up hope. You may be able to minimize the impact on future upgrades. If the functionality can be contained in its own custom record, panel, panel group, or menu item, then you can easily move the customization forward during an upgrade. Let's take a look at how to make a needed customization.

# Making the Customization

Once all the research and evaluation has been completed, you are ready to perform the approved customization.

The first step that the technical team should perform after the research and evaluation is complete is to plan how the customization will be implemented. This plan should include all the procedures necessary to make the change and to train the end user in the functionality. Once you have your plan, you are now ready to perform the change. Take the following steps:

1. Assign a name to the project for use in your test system. The development team should document this name for use when moving the program from the test environment into production.

2. The developer or developers should make the changes necessary to implement the customization. This may include new fields, records, panels, PeopleCode, SQRs, menu items, or even COBOL SQL programs. Modifying COBOL and COBOL SQL should be done infrequently, if at all. Changes to these applications are not easy to make and may potentially impact other processes. The PeopleSoft COBOL is not easy to modify, even for veteran COBOL programmers.

3. The next step after development is complete should be testing the change.

4. Once testing is complete and the end users are satisfied with the results, you are ready to migrate the change into production. The tools used to migrate changes are explained in Chapter 7, "Development Tools."

5. The person designated to maintain your customization log should update the log with any pertinent information, including the date the program was moved into production.

6. The end users should receive detailed instructions, which may include written procedures on how to use the new functionality.

**7.** You should also add the customization project to the Custom project that you must maintain beginning with PeopleSoft version 7.5. The Custom project identifies all of your customizations and is used during an upgrade to help prevent your customizations from being inadvertently overwritten.

# Adding One or Two Elements to a Panel

You will encounter situations where the users only want one or two elements added to a delivered panel. This situation calls for a different approach. If the field that they want exists in the field definitions, add it to the record definition for the panel being updated, then use it in the panel. However, I generally like to create a custom field using the approved custom naming standards. This has two advantages: First, this prevents a change that PeopleSoft makes to the record definition from affecting the field in use. Second, when looking at the field list on a panel, it is much easier to see that the field has been added as a customization. This can be a real timesaver during an upgrade when you must decide whether to keep customized panels or to re-create the customization on the new panel.

Chapter 12, "Upgrading Your PeopleSoft System," discusses upgrades in much more detail. However, in the situation just described, I recommend that you reapply your customization to the panel delivered by PeopleSoft in the new version if PeopleSoft has made significant changes to the panel.

The next section describes three examples of customizations made at my company.

# Customization Examples

This section describes three examples of a customization and lists all the steps that were required to take this change from proposal to production.

**N O T E**   The following examples are in this chapter to keep them near the discussion about the customization process. You should review the contents of Part Two to gain a better understanding of the tools and concepts being utilized in the examples.

### Example 1

My company wanted to incorporate our formula for calculating salary ranges into the PeopleSoft system. This would allow us to update the ranges based on the approved percentage increase. We wanted the flexibility to run this for a single salary administration plan at any time during the year. A salary administration plan is a group of employees with the same pay structures. For example, exempt and non-exempt employees are in different salary administration plans. The salary administration plans are established as part of the payroll setup. The following steps outline how we implemented this customization while making it easy to carry forward during an upgrade.

 **N O T E**   This example uses many procedures. I will explain why I used them as I mention them and refer you to the later chapters that explain them in more detail.

First, we created the plan for how to implement the customization using the requirements for the change gathered from the users. In reviewing the request for the salary range update, I determined that the best approach was to implement an SQR that used information retrieved from two custom records. One of the records would be updated using a custom panel to insert new salary formulas for selected salary administration plans.

Using the general steps that were defined earlier in this section, we implemented the customization by taking the following steps:

1. Create the record definitions.

2. Create the SQR.

3. Create the panel for parameter input.

4. Create the run control panel.

5. Create the menus for the panels.

6. Add the menus to security.

7. Test the customization.

8. Move the customization into production.

9. Train the end users.

10. Document the new process.

Let's discuss each step in more detail while explaining why we developed the customization in this order.

**Step 1: Create the record definitions**    During the analysis phase, we determined that our salary formula required that two variables be entered for a proposed change. We defined a record for entering the variables for a specific salary administration plan and effective date. Figure 3.6 contains the record definition we created.

**FIGURE 3.6**    ALB_SAL_FORM record definition

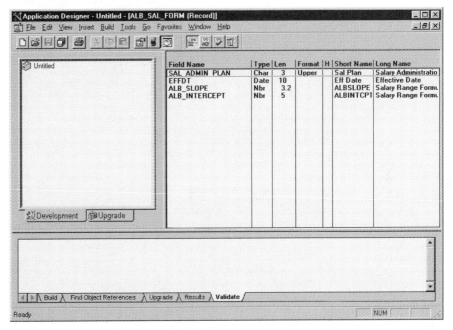

The ALB_GRADE_PTS table holds the Hay points number for each defined grade. This is the final piece of the salary formula. This rarely changes, but we wanted to make it table driven so that additions to the grade table would be automatically included in the formula. Figure 3.7 contains the record definition for this table.

**Step 2: Create the SQR**    An SQR program was created that selected the current salary range information from PS_SAL_GRADE_TBL. The selection was based on the salary administration plans that had new factors defined in the PS_ALB_SAL_FORM table for the new effective date.

**N O T E**    Chapter 10, "SQR," contains a more detailed explanation of the SQR product.

**FIGURE 3.7**    ALB_GRADE_PTS record definition

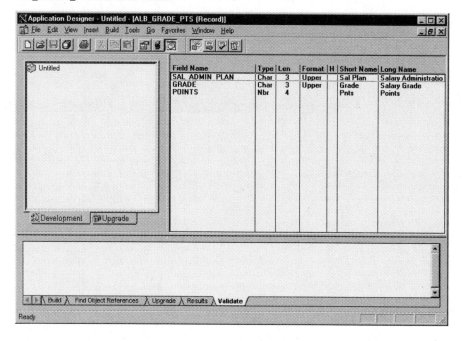

The following program excerpt shows the selection of the old ranges:

```
begin-select
A.SAL_ADMIN_PLAN
A.GRADE
A.EFFDT
A.EFF_STATUS
A.DESCR
A.DESCRSHORT
A.SALARY_MATRIX_CD
A.RATING_SCALE
A.MIN_RT_HOURLY
A.MID_RT_HOURLY
A.MAX_RT_HOURLY
A.MIN_RT_MONTHLY
A.MID_RT_MONTHLY
A.MAX_RT_MONTHLY
A.MIN_RT_ANNUAL
A.MID_RT_ANNUAL
A.MAX_RT_ANNUAL
A.STEP_INCREM_TYPE
```

```
A.STEP_INCREM_ACCUM
B.POINTS
. . .
from PS_SAL_GRADE_TBL A, PS_ALB_GRADE_PTS B
where A.EFFDT = $ThruDate
and B.SAL_ADMIN_PLAN = A.SAL_ADMIN_PLAN
and B.GRADE = A.GRADE
end-select
```

**NOTE**  Appendix A, "Sample Programs," contains a complete listing of ALB_SLGR. Only the pertinent information is included here.

The new slope and intercept were selected from the PS_ALB_SAL_FORM table defined in step 1 using the following code:

```
begin-procedure Get-Sal-Form
begin-select
F.SAL_ADMIN_PLAN
F.ALB_SLOPE
F.ALB_INTERCEPT
 . . . .
from PS_ALB_SAL_FORM F
where F.EFFDT = $FromDate
end-select
end-procedure
```

A calculation was performed using the slope and intercept values to calculate the new salary ranges. The calculation steps were as follows:

```
if $salplan = 'NEX'
let #tempmid = (#nexslope * #grpts) + #nexintrcpt
let #minannual = round(#tempmid * .8,0)
let #maxannual = round(#tempmid *1.2,0)
end-if
 . . . .
let #midannual = round((#minannual + #maxannual)/2,0)
let #minmonth = round((#minannual/12),2)
let #midmonth = round((#midannual/12),2)
let #maxmonth = round((#maxannual/12),2)
let #minhrly = round((#minannual/2080),3)
let #midhrly = round((#midannual/2080),3)
let #maxhrly = round((#maxannual/2080),3)
```

The new ranges were inserted into the PS_SAL_GRADE table using the following code:

```
Begin-SQL
Insert into PS_SAL_GRADE_TBL
(SAL_ADMIN_PLAN,
GRADE,
EFFDT,
EFF_STATUS,
DESCR,
DESCRSHORT,
SALARY_MATRIX_CD,
RATING_SCALE,
MIN_RT_HOURLY,
MID_RT_HOURLY,
MAX_RT_HOURLY,
MIN_RT_MONTHLY,
MID_RT_MONTHLY,
MAX_RT_MONTHLY,
MIN_RT_ANNUAL,
MID_RT_ANNUAL,
MAX_RT_ANNUAL,
STEP_INCREM_TYPE,
STEP_INCREM_ACCUM)
Values
(&A.SAL_ADMIN_PLAN,
&A.GRADE,
$FromDate,
&A.EFF_STATUS,
&A.DESCR,
&A.DESCRSHORT,
&A.SALARY_MATRIX_CD,
&A.RATING_SCALE,
round(#minhrly,4),
round(#midhrly,4),
round(#maxhrly,4),
round(#minmonth,2),
round(#midmonth,2),
round(#maxmonth,2),
round(#minannual,0),
round(#midannual,0),
```

```
round(#maxannual,0),
&A.STEP_INCREM_TYPE,
&A.STEP_INCREM_ACCUM)
end-SQL
```

**Step 3: Create the panel for parameter input**    The next step was to create the panel that the end user could use to enter the effective date of the new salary ranges and the salary administration plan that the change would affect, as shown in Figure 3.8. This panel is also used to enter the slope and intercept criteria for the plan. This information is used by the range calculation equation to create the new range. For additional information about working with panels, see Chapter 7, "Development Tools."

**FIGURE 3.8**    Salary Administration panel

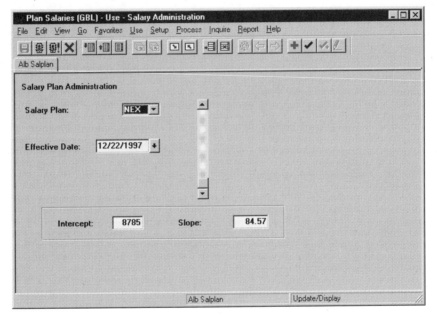

**Step 4: Create a run control panel**    There was also a requirement for a run control panel. Run control panels are used to start programs from inside the People-Soft application. When you choose the server as the run location, the Process Scheduler process that is running on your server starts the application. Figure 3.9 illustrates a run control panel. The user must enter the effective dates of the old ranges and the new

ranges. The SQR then loads the new ranges for any salary administration plan that has a new slope and intercept that matches the new effective date you have defined.

**FIGURE 3.9**   **Salary Grade run control panel**

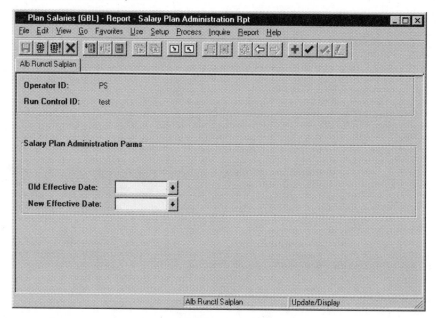

**Step 5: Add the new panels to a menu**   We had to add the new panels to a menu. To do this, we opened the existing menu that we wanted to add the panels to. First, we added the panels to a panel group. In this example, we created a new panel group called ALB_SALPLAN and inserted the panel ALB_SALPLAN into that group, as shown in Figure 3.10. We also had to add the run control panel to a panel group (not shown).

For this example, we added the two panels to the Plan Salaries menu. As illustrated in Figure 3.11, we added the Salary Form panel shown in Figure 3.8 to the Use menu item and called it Salary Administration. To add the panel to the menu, click the blank space at the bottom of the menu to get the Menu Item Properties panel shown in Figure 3.12. Enter the Menu Items Name and Label fields. Select the PeopleCode type, press the Panel Group Select button, and select the Panel Group you have created. Select OK and then save the menu.

**FIGURE 3.10**    Panel group: ALB_SALPLAN

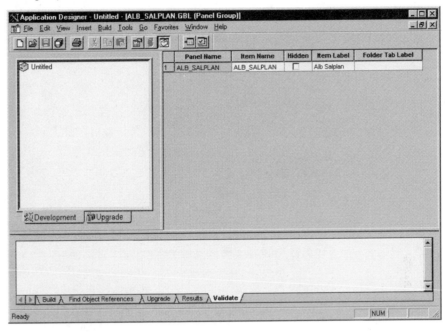

**FIGURE 3.11**    Salary grade menu items

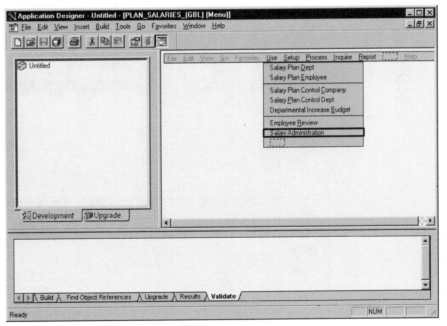

**FIGURE 3.12** Menu Item Properties dialog box

**Step 6: Add the menu to security** The next step was to assign security to the new menu items to allow the users to access them. To do this, select Go > PeopleTools > Security Administrator. Select File > Open and select the group or operator that needs access to the new menu items. Then click the Menu Items icon to view all the menu names that are available. Figure 3.13 shows the PLAN_ SALARIES menu selected.

**FIGURE 3.13** Menu security: menu name selection

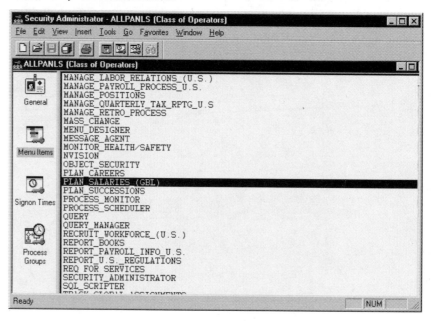

PART

I

Getting Started with
PeopleSoft

Double-click the PLAN_SALARIES item to open the Menu Item list. Scroll down the
list of menu items to locate the new menu item that was added. Highlight the access
that the user needs. Figure 3.14 shows the Select Menu Items panel with the REVIEW_
RATING_TABLE menu item selected. To grant the user access, highlight the menu
item and action. In this example, we gave the user all rights to the ALB_SALPLAN
menu item. Note that the REVIEW_RATING_TABLE menu item shows that the user
does not have authority for the actions Add or Correction.

**FIGURE 3.14**    Menu security: adding a menu item

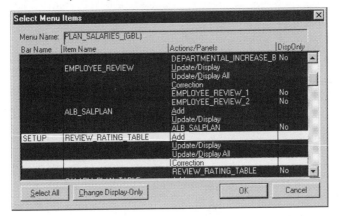

### Step 7: Test the customization
Once we completed steps 1–6, we were
ready to test the new application. First, we entered sample data to create new salary
range information for the salary administration plans. Then we opened the run control panel and started the update program just as the users might. The final step of
the testing was to validate that the salary grade table had been updated correctly.

**TIP**  Use the report generated by the SQR to let the end users verify that the changes
have been made correctly.

### Step 8: Move the customization into production
Once the end users
were satisfied that the test results were correct, we moved the new records, menus,
and panels into the production environment. The Application Designer upgrade
Copy function copied the project from the test database into the production database. Then we were ready to train the end users.

**Step 9: Train the end users**   Training the end users is a critical step. We provided the end users with adequate documentation and/or instruction on how to use the new process. For this change, we actually used the testing phase to train the end user that would be responsible for running the program. This helped the user better understand the program in an environment where mistakes were not critical. This also helped us determine the level of documentation about the new process that we would need to generate.

**Step 10: Document the customization**   The final step is, in my opinion, the most important: *Document the changes.* The documentation should be comprehensive and it should explain what was done and why it was done. This will make the upgrade process run more smoothly and it will prevent you from relying on the development team remembering the changes that have been made.

Now that we have walked through the process of implementing a customization, let's look at another example that affects your online processing.

## Example 2

The second example is a customization to an online panel that my company implemented. The Benefits and Payroll users both needed an additional field to track information about participants in the 401K program. We decided to add a field to an existing PeopleSoft record and panel. In addition, we had an interface program that imported information from our voice response unit (VRU) that had to be modified to accommodate the adjustment.

This change was designed to keep track of those personnel who had been contributing to their 401K, but wished to stop contributing temporarily. We wanted to distinguish them from those employees who had never contributed. We created a check box that represented a zero deferral rate. This allowed the Benefits users to gain the functionality they needed for reporting.

**Step 1: Create the new field definition**   To create this customization, we created a new custom field called ALB_ZERO_401K, as shown in Figure 3.15.

**Step 2: Update the record definition**   We added the new field to the existing record definition. The SAVINGS_PLAN record was edited and the new field was inserted, as shown in Figure 3.16. To insert a new field, select Insert **>** Field and select the new field.

**Step 3: Update the panel**   Figure 3.17 shows the original SAVINGS_PLAN1 panel.

Figure 3.18 shows the modified SAVINGS_PLAN1 panel. We inserted the check box Zero Defer onto the line beneath the Participation Election line as highlighted by the arrow.

**FIGURE 3.15** ALB_ZERO_401K field definition

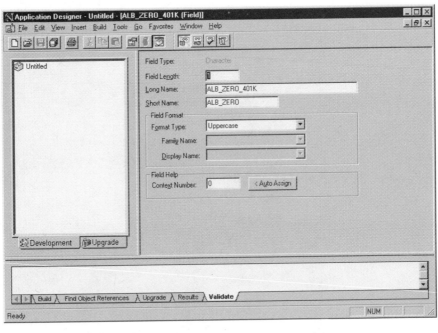

**FIGURE 3.16** SAVINGS_PLAN record definition

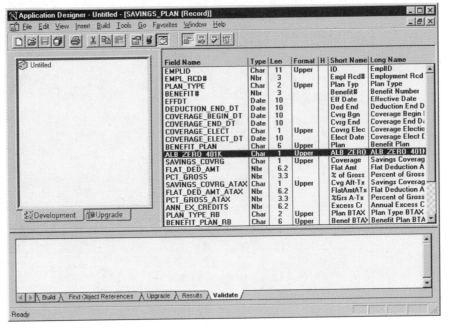

**FIGURE 3.17**    SAVINGS_PLAN1 panel definition (before)

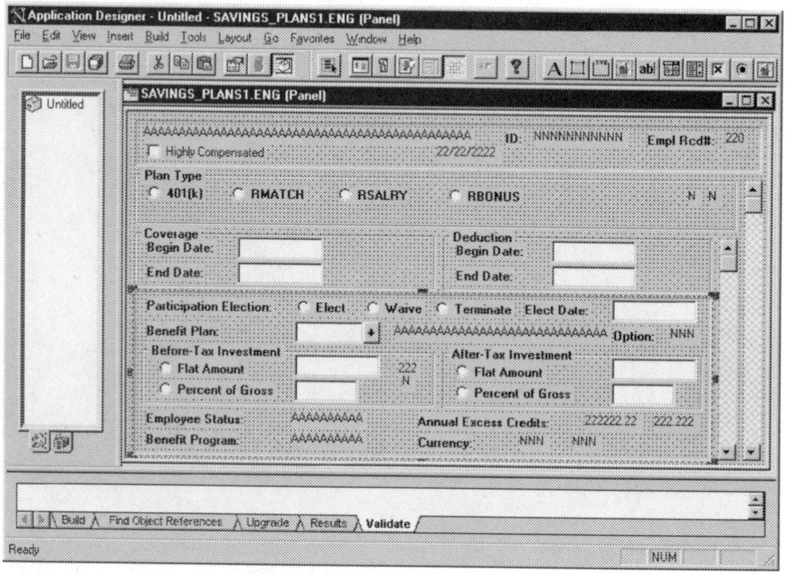

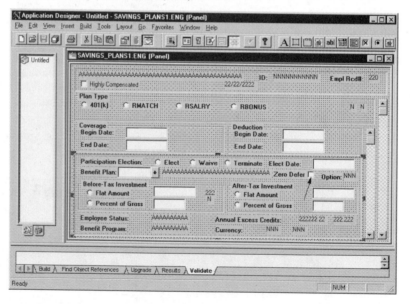

**FIGURE 3.18**    SAVINGS_PLAN1 panel definition (after)

**Step 4: Add PeopleCode**    Next, we added the PeopleCode that allows the user to check the Zero Defer check box only when the Participation Election option is changed to Waive. Figure 3.19 shows the PeopleCode that was inserted into the FieldChange PeopleCode object. We added the RowInit PeopleCode as shown in Figure 3.20 so that the field is initialized correctly when the panel is opened for each employee.

**NOTE**    PeopleCode is discussed in more detail in Chapter 7, "Development Tools."

**FIGURE 3.19**    Record PeopleCode FieldChange

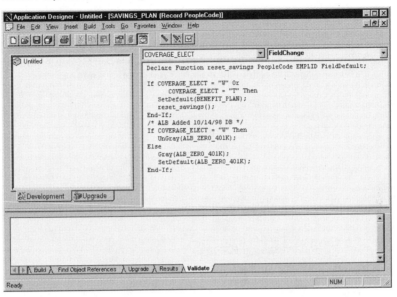

**FIGURE 3.20**    Record PeopleCode RowInit

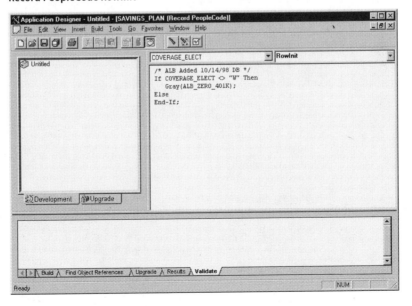

**Step 5: Update the SQR**     The interface SQR that loads information from our voice response unit (VRU) had to be updated to handle the insertion of new records after the new field was added. The insert step would have failed if we had not added the new field. The field was added simply by adding the field name to the field list and the variable name for the value into the values list of the `insert` statement. The `insert` statement is shown in the following code. The new code we added is shown in **boldface**.

**N O T E**     The entire code for this program is *not* shown in Appendix A due to proprietary company code in the module that contains this routine.

```
begin-sql
insert into PS_SAVINGS_PLAN
( EMPLID,
  EFFDT,
  DEDUCTION_END_DT,
  COVERAGE_BEGIN_DT,
  COVERAGE_END_DT,
  COVERAGE_ELECT,
  COVERAGE_ELECT_DT,
  BENEFIT_PLAN,
  ALB_ZERO_401K,      !new code 004
  FLAT_DED_AMT,
  SAVINGS_COVRG_ATAX,
  FLAT_DED_AMT_ATAX,
  PCT_GROSS_ATAX,
  PLAN_TYPE_RB,
  BENEFIT_PLAN_RB,
  DEDCD_RB,
  DED_CLASS_RB,
  EMPL_RCD#,
  PLAN_TYPE,
  BENEFIT#,
  SAVINGS_COVRG,
  PCT_GROSS,
  ANN_EX_CREDITS,
  PLAN_TYPE_RA,
  BENEFIT_PLAN_RA,
  DEDCD_RA,
  DED_CLASS_RA)
VALUES
( $s_emplid,
  $mkdate,
```

```
        $ded_end_dt,
        $coverage_dt,
        $ded_end_dt,
        $cov_elect,     !new code 001
        $mkdate,
        $planhold,
        $zerodefer,     !new code 004
        0,
        $sav_covrg_atax,
        0,
        ROUND(#s_pct_gross_atax,2),
        ' ',
        ' ',
        ' ',
        ' ',
        0,
        $s_plan_type,
        ROUND(#s_benefit,2),
        $sav_covrg,
        ROUND(#s_pct_gross_btax,2),
        0,
        ' ',
        ' ',
        ' ',
        ' ')
    end-sql
```

**Step 6: Test the customization**    Again, we tested the customization to ensure that it was functioning as required. Figure 3.21 contains the final updated Savings Plan panel.

**Step 7: Move the customization into production**    The customization was moved into our production database when the testing was complete.

**Step 8: Train the end users**    We demonstrated the new functionality to the end users. In our environment, we involved them in the test phase so that their training was complete when we moved into production.

**Step 9: Document the customization**    Always document any customization as described in Example 1. We added the change to our customization log and documented the SQR programs that were affected by the change to the Savings Plan record definition. If you are using PeopleSoft version 7 or higher, do not forget to add each change to your Custom project that is used during upgrades.

**FIGURE 3.21** Savings Plans panel (final)

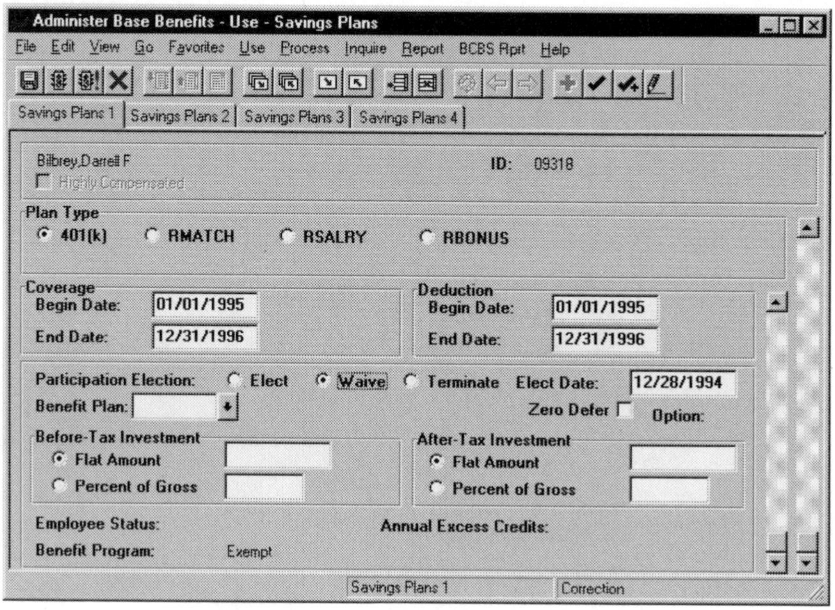

## Example 3

The final customization example is a custom view that my company created. The functional users in our Benefits area needed an easy way to run queries that used information about employees that were married to other employees. PeopleSoft does not readily provide this functionality.

One option we tried was showing the users how to execute this query with the People-Soft Query tool. But using the PeopleSoft Query tool, the data could not be joined in the way we needed it. We decided to explore the creation of a custom view that could be used more easily by the PeopleSoft Query tool. Creating the custom view involved fewer steps than in the previous two examples.

**Step 1: Create the record definition**   We created a new record definition containing the required fields. Figure 3.22 contains that record definition.

First, we created the SQL to be used by the view. I wrote the SQL using the SQL tools for my RDBMS. This allowed us to test the SQL to ensure that it was returning the required data. Next, I copied the SQL code and pasted it into the View windows, as shown in Figure 3.23. To reach this view, select File > Object Properties, and select the Type tab. Set the record type to SQL View and then paste the SQL into the window. Close the Record Properties window and save the record definition.

**FIGURE 3.22**    ALB_SPOUSE_VW record definition

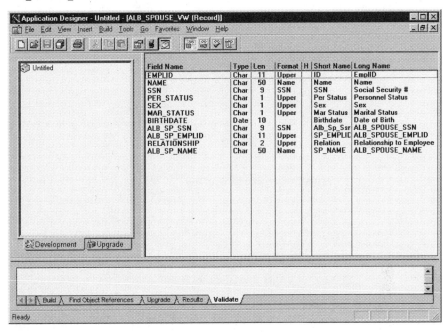

**FIGURE 3.23**    Record Properties dialog box: SQL View

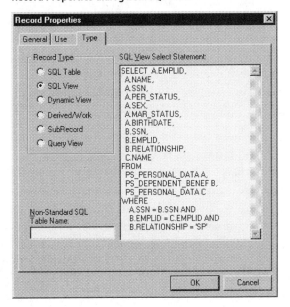

**N O T E**   This view uses the Social Security Number to join the tables. If you do not have the Social Security Number for all the spouses of your employees, then you will have to add code to prevent those spouses without Social Security Numbers from being included in the view.

**N O T E**   Our company is in the process of modifying this view to support new table structures introduced in PeopleSoft version 7.5.

**Step 2: Create the view**   Once the definition was defined and saved, we executed the build process to generate a SQL script file. To do this, select Build **>** Current Object. (Chapter 6, "Data Management Tools," describes this process in more detail.) The script must be executed using the SQL tool to create the view in the RDBMS.

You can create the database objects, using Data Designer, for a specific database. However, I recommend using the script since your DBA will want to review any generated SQL, especially for views, to ensure that the code is correct and will work efficiently on your particular database platform.

**Step 3: Add the record to query security**   Since the primary purpose of the Spouse View was to make the users self-sufficient using the PeopleSoft Query tool, the next step was to grant their security group query access to this object. This was accomplished by selecting Go > Tree Manager, then opening the Default group and the tree under which access is required. In the example shown in Figure 3.24, I inserted the ALB_SPOUSE_VW under the EE BENEFIT INFO tree branch. To insert the record into the tree, right-click the tree branch and select Add Child. Then select Record and enter the record name.

**Step 4: Test the customization**   Testing the Spouse View was very straightforward. The view was tested using PeopleSoft query to ensure that it worked properly. We verified the list against another report that had been generated from our old system. The testing for this view was much easier than in the previous examples, since there was no panel for updates involved. This was created merely as a convenience for use with the PeopleSoft Query tool.

**Step 5: Move the customization into production**   After the users were satisfied with our test results, we migrated the record definition to our production database using Application Upgrade. We then updated the SQL script for our production database and executed it to create the view.

**FIGURE 3.24** Query Security

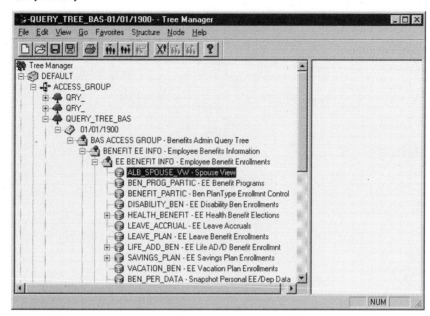

**Step 6: Train the end users**   For this customization, we demonstrated the use of the view using the PeopleSoft Query tool. We described the available fields. All of the Benefits users had already had basic query training, so they were using the view on their own within minutes.

**Step 7: Document the customization**   The final step in the process was to add the change to our customization log. We also added it to our security log, showing that the Benefits group had been granted query access to this object.

# Documenting the Customization

Document thoroughly all customizations that you have made to the delivered People-Soft functionality. Chapter 14, "Documentation," covers the topic of documentation in much more detail. However, this is such an important issue that I would like to emphasize two points that are valid during the implementation phase.

Create a customization log to store information about the changes that have been made. During the implementation, you may want to maintain a separate list of all proposed customizations and your decisions. This will be useful during your first one to two years of production in case your users request the customization again.

By maintaining a customization log, much of the research is complete and you just have to update the log when any changes in the situation occur.

Consider assigning someone the responsibility of maintaining the customization log. The best person for this role is the person that you assign to migrate all the changes into production. This person is in the best position to monitor and verify when changes are made to your production system.

# Summary

Before customizing your PeopleSoft system, there are a number of issues you need to consider:

▶ Evaluate the maintainability issues. Will the customization cause problems with future upgrades of the system?

▶ Prepare an impact analysis.

▶ Create a review process.

▶ Don't make changes that are purely cosmetic.

▶ Consult other PeopleSoft users to see if they've developed a work-around that might solve your problem.

▶ See if your problem will be resolved by a future PeopleSoft release.

Once you've decided to implement the customization, the technical team takes over. They develop the code for the change, test the change, migrate the change to the existing system, document the change in a customization log, and train the end users. The examples in this chapter showed how these steps were applied to three distinct customizations.

Now that we have reviewed the customization process, let's move on to Chapter 4, which discusses parallel operations.

# Parallel Operations

**FEATURING**

▶ DEFINING THE SCOPE OF PARALLEL OPERATIONS

▶ DEVELOPING A PARALLEL TEST PLAN

▶ PERFORMING THE TESTS

▶ MOVING TO PRODUCTION

Once you have completed your implementation, the next task is to conduct parallel operations with your existing system; run the PeopleSoft system concurrently with your existing operating procedures. Running parallel operations ensures that your PeopleSoft system is configured and operating as expected. To make sure of this, compare the output data from the PeopleSoft system with the output from your existing system.

**N O T E** PeopleSoft calls the process of parallel operations the "parallel system approach." I prefer the term "parallel operations," because you must run many processes in parallel, including data entry. This gives you a chance to validate all your input processes as well as any calculations or reports.

In addition to ensuring that the new system is running properly, a parallel operations period offers another advantage. During parallel operations, users have the opportunity to verify and validate the new system firsthand. Any glitches can be worked out without negatively affecting normal business operations.

PeopleSoft offers two alternatives to the parallel approach in their Production Readiness white paper. The first they call the "Big Bang" approach in which you begin using the new system without any synchronization. You simply load all your data into the PeopleSoft system and begin operations.

The second approach requires that you maintain two production systems and is recommended only for HRMS implementations. In this approach, an employee is migrated to the new system and all information about that employee is now on the new system. Over time, you will migrate your employee data from the old to new system. This method requires a lot of synchronization and dual reporting from two systems.

I recommend the parallel operations approach because it provides better data integrity during the conversion process. However, it does require more manpower, since both systems must be updated during the parallel period. The amount of effort required for duplicate data entry depends on the duration of parallel operations and the amount of data that is entered daily or weekly.

The duration and scope of your parallel operations is a decision that both the implementation team and upper management of your company will have to make jointly using some of the following factors:

► How comfortable your company is when implementing change. Conservative companies tend to require longer parallel operations periods.

- ▶ The level of confidence that management has in the implementation team.

- ▶ The scope of your project. A large project moving a multinational company from one financial system to another will probably require a much longer parallel cycle, or the project will need to be broken up into smaller pieces.

The scope of the project will greatly influence the approach you take. Let's see how to define the scope of your parallel operations.

# Defining the Scope of the Parallel Operations

The scope of the parallel operations should closely follow the scope of the entire project as defined in your implementation plan. The scope of the parallel operations is different from the implementation plan in that the parallel operations focuses on the big picture of what functions should be included in the parallel operations. The implementation plan takes those boundaries and describes each step in more detail.

The first step in defining the scope is to compile a list of what functions need to be tested. Create a checklist that describes in detail all the PeopleSoft processes that you need to compare with your existing system. PeopleSoft provides a checklist of items to check during an implementation. Use this checklist as a starting point and add your own tests to the checklist to prevent you from forgetting to validate an important area.

A good checklist should include all the major business processes that are targeted for production during your initial implementation phase. During this phase, make sure to list any major interfaces that must be in place and working properly so that you can include them in your test plan.

The second step in defining the scope is to identify how long the parallel operations will last. Most financial implementations will probably involve at least one full month of parallel operations to ensure that all monthly processes are working correctly and that the results are consistent with those from the current system. Payroll systems may use one full payroll cycle, including biweekly and monthly payrolls. However, I recommend at least a full month of parallel operations for HRMS as well.

 **N O T E** My company performed two full months of parallel operations before implementation. Upper management also mandated that the old system be kept available and current in case any unforeseen problems occurred during the first few payroll cycles after moving to the new system.

PART
I

Getting Started with
PeopleSoft

The following lists contains some of the checklist items that my company created using the PeopleSoft list and our implementation plan:

### FUNCTIONAL TEAM MEMBERS

**Verify Employee Information**    Verify that all the employee information that has been converted is correct.

**Verify Tax Calculations**    Verify that all federal, state, and local tax calculations are being calculated correctly.

**Verify Benefit Deductions**    Verify that all benefit deductions are being calculated correctly. Check to verify that the special accumulators are working correctly.

**Verify Autonumbering**    Verify that the autonumbering for the employee ID field is working properly.

**Test Hire Process**    Use the PeopleSoft Hire Workforce application to ensure that all items are functioning properly.

**N O T E**    Verify that your conversion scripts are working correctly. My company did a 100 percent validation of our test population, which included approximately 50 employees. We executed all the conversion scripts that had been created and then validated all the information. We then performed random sampling of employee information from the final conversion data. There were a few employees that were specifically checked due to known issues in the past.

### TECHNICAL TEAM MEMBERS

**Audit Database Structure**    The database administrator (DBA) should run the DDDAUDIT.SQR report to ensure that all tables, views, and indexes have been created and are working properly.

**Verify Extract Interfaces**    Run the extract interfaces and send the test samples to external systems to verify that the file is readable and in the proper format.

**Validate Security Profiles**    A designated security manager should verify that all the profiles have the proper security set for the parallel testing.

**T I P**    I recommend that you create a file to contain this checklist as soon as possible after your decision to implement a PeopleSoft application. Make the checklist a "living" document that is continually adjusted during the implementation. Add items to your checklist as new ideas occur.

When developing your parallel operations plans, don't forget to allow for the duplicate data entry that may be necessary to conduct the tests. Allow yourself ample time to conduct the tests.

Allow time for testing important interfaces to other systems. For example, allow time for the bank to validate your extract file that contains any direct deposit transactions. The PeopleSoft application may provide the information in a different format, so let the bank know what to expect. You may have to customize the program that generates the file to make sure the output format matches the bank's requirements.

Now let's turn the scope of the parallel operations into a detailed test plan for your system.

# Developing a Parallel Test Plan

The development of your parallel test plan should be the result of a joint effort by the functional and technical teams. Each team has specific tests that they need to perform to validate that the system is working properly. The parallel test plan is also known as the acceptance test plan. You should attach criteria for acceptance of a test as part of the parallel test plan.

**N O T E**   Keep the wording of the test plan understandable while avoiding a lot of technical (or functional) jargon. The testers should be able to follow the test scripts without having to constantly ask for assistance in interpreting the meaning of a test.

Use the documents you created when you defined the scope as the outline when writing the detailed parallel test plan. Create your test plans around specific functions. Each functional team member should define the tasks that they will be performing and then create a checklist of the functions to be tested. For detailed processes, the user may want to specify some critical individual steps for the process in the plan. They should also create a plan to mirror the test on both your new system and old system in order to validate the results.

**N O T E**   All checklists should include space for the person conducting the test to sign and enter the date that the test was completed. The checklist should also allow space to explain any abnormal conditions or problems that were encountered (even if they have already been corrected).

Another item to include in the parallel test plan is a set of procedures that will reconcile any differences between the new and old systems. Defining the procedures in the test plan will minimize delays when differences occur during the parallel testing.

The following list shows some of the items on the parallel test plan that the implementation team at my company developed:

► Update personal data on both systems to ensure that all functions are working and to keep the two systems synchronized.

► Process new employees through the Hire Workforce process, including their benefit deductions and W-4 tax withholding.

► Create pay sheets and calculate checks for all pay groups. Ensure that the calculated gross pay for individuals is correct. Total gross pay should balance between both systems.

► Verify that local tax withholding is working correctly, especially if you have personnel who are in exempt status.

**NOTE**   Pay particular attention to local taxes. You may find differences between People-Soft and your old system. You should identify which is correct. If PeopleSoft is not calculating the tax correctly, verify that you have the latest tax updates installed before calling for support. Chapter 13, "Tax Updates," provides more information on the tax update process.

**TIP**   The quality of your parallel test is only as good as the test plan you create. Plan! Plan! Plan!

# Performing the Tests

Once you have established your test plan and acceptance test criteria, you are ready to begin testing. Each functional user begins performing the tasks that have been assigned on the test plan. The technical staff tests some of the technical components, including PeopleSoft Query, to verify that everything is working correctly. The technical team should also be available to assist in resolving any problems that are uncovered during the test.

# Functional Tests

The functional users should be conducting tests for all functional areas that have been configured. The functional users understand the processes and should be able to quickly identify any problems as they occur.

For example, let's define the functional tests that are required to validate the tax calculations mentioned in the previous section.

**N O T E** This scenario assumes that the setup tables for payroll and base benefits have been configured.

- ▶ Create the pay sheets.

- ▶ Run the pay calculation.

- ▶ View the tax deduction information from PeopleSoft.

- ▶ Compare the taxes being deducted to the same information in the current system.

- ▶ Reconcile any differences to determine if there is a problem or if the tax deductions match and are correct.

For large payroll operations, you may want to create an automated procedure to compare each deduction line by line and report any differences. You can use SQR (Structured Query Report) for this or other programming languages with which you are familiar.

While pay sheets are being created and the checks are being calculated, you can also verify the deduction calculations using the same calculation process as before. To validate the deduction calculations, you would additionally:

- ▶ View the general deduction information from PeopleSoft.

- ▶ Compare the deductions to the current system.

- ▶ Reconcile any differences between the two systems.

Validate all deductions in this manner. PeopleSoft uses two types of deductions: general and benefit. General deductions are all deductions not associated with a benefit plan, such as United Way contributions or wage garnishments. Benefit deductions are any deductions that are taken due to a benefit plan.

**TIP** You may find test results that do not agree between the two systems. First, check the new system, but don't forget to verify that your current system is performing the function correctly. You may have an error in your current system that was never discovered. My company found just such an instance!

## Technical Tests

The technical team should conduct tests of the interfaces between PeopleSoft and any external systems. Make sure that you provide samples of your output to any recipients. For example, in an HRMS project, have the Payroll personnel calculate the paychecks. Then print some sample checks to send to the bank to ensure that the check-printing routines are correct. The bank will verify that the check is in the correct format and the bank routing codes are in the correct font and position on the check. A financial project would probably also want to send to the bank *all* information that they exchange with that bank to verify that the format is correct.

An important test that the technical team can perform concurrently with parallel testing is to run the database audit report and system audit report and take any necessary actions to correct problems. The number of problems should be minimal if you are implementing the same version that you originally purchased, you have few customizations, and your implementation has moved quickly.

**NOTE** The database audit (DDDAUDIT.SQR) and system audit (SYSAUDIT.SQR) reports are explained in more detail in Chapter 6, "Data Management Tools."

The technical team should also use the parallel operations period to test and refine any change control processes that have been implemented. Document and log any changes that you are making to your system. During the parallel test, make your users submit formal requests for changes.

## Benchmarking

The parallel operations period also offers you a great opportunity to develop some baseline performance statistics. You can create run statistics from all your processes as they are being tested. You can also acquire information from both network and database monitoring tools to determine if they are configured correctly.

The LAN administrator should use your company's network analysis tools to provide you with information regarding bandwidth utilization. I recommend that you obtain this information before you begin testing. During the testing, the benchmark data provides statistics from which you can interpolate what your total usage will be when the system is completely online. It is better to discover that you need to reconfigure your network before your scheduled production date instead of waiting until everything is at a standstill during your first weeks of production operations.

The DBA should also take this opportunity to begin tuning the database to provide a good balance between the batch and online environment that you have configured. This is a good opportunity for the DBA to begin the process of tuning the application to your specific RDBMS.

Keep both the network statistics and database statistics that you obtain during this time. You can use them as baseline data as you begin to accumulate production data in your database. By comparing the production data to the baseline data, you can determine if and how quickly you are experiencing performance degradation. Revisit the benchmark numbers at least once per quarter and compare your current performance to these original benchmarks.

**N O T E**    Performance tuning is covered in detail in Chapter 11, "Performance Tuning."

# Moving to Production

Now that you have completed the acceptance tests during parallel operations and you have verified that your configuration is correct, you are ready to move your system into production. There are several methods you can use. These methods involve the use of tools provided by PeopleSoft, database tools provided by your RDBMS vendor, or a combination of the two.

When conducting parallel operations prior to moving your system into production, you are duplicating all the system data to allow for complete comparisons. For the HRMS system implementation, the move to production should be simple to outline. The following list includes some of the tasks that you need to perform to clear out any calculations created during the parallel testing from your database tables:

▶ Remove all check and direct deposit advice information.

▶ Delete all balance information.

▶ Remove special accumulator balances.

▶ Remove all pay sheet records.

▶ Remove all pay earnings records.

▶ Remove pay calendar information.

▶ Remove or update savings bond information if you are using this functionality.

Once all these tasks are complete, you should have a clean system on which to begin production operations. Performing these cleanup tasks prevents you from retaining any information that may not exactly match the information from the old system. These tasks also help prevent any duplication of data when merging historical information from your old system.

Make sure to update several system parameters that are used throughout your People-Soft application. Figure 4.1 shows the Installation Table 1 panel that is used to set up several system default settings and to specify the modules that you are running from this database. To display this panel, select Go **>** Define Business Rules **>** Define General Options. Select Setup **>** Installation Table from the menu.

**FIGURE 4.1**    Installation Table 1 panel

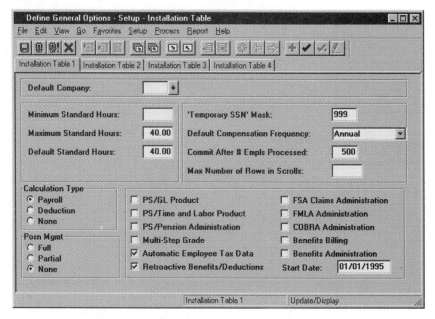

 **NOTE**    Most of the parameters in the installation table should have been configured during the configuration process. You should verify all the information at this point to ensure that everything is in order.

The Commit After # Empls Processed field is an important parameter that can affect the performance of your system, especially batch processes. This parameter determines how many records are processed before a database commit occurs. I recommend a value of 300 or higher.

For HRMS users, set the last employee ID number assigned if you plan to use the autonumbering functionality as shown in Figure 4.2. The remaining entries on this panel are used by autonumbering functions throughout the PeopleSoft applications.

**FIGURE 4.2**  Installation Table 2 panel

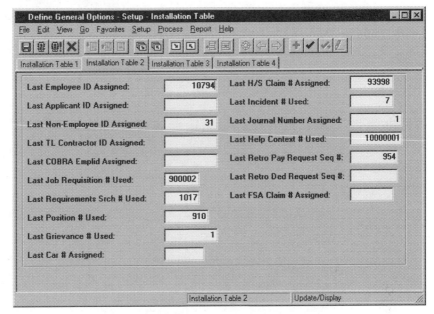

Figure 4.3 illustrates the Installation Table 3 panel, which contains the International and Canadian Parameters information. You must specify the default country in the Country field. HRMS users must specify the countries for which they want to enable Global HR Functionality.

Figure 4.4 contains the Installation Table 4 panel that is used for the integration of third-party tools. For HRMS customers using the Organization Charting interface, you can specify your charting tool. Visio is the only software that is directly supported currently.

**FIGURE 4.3**  Installation Table 3 panel

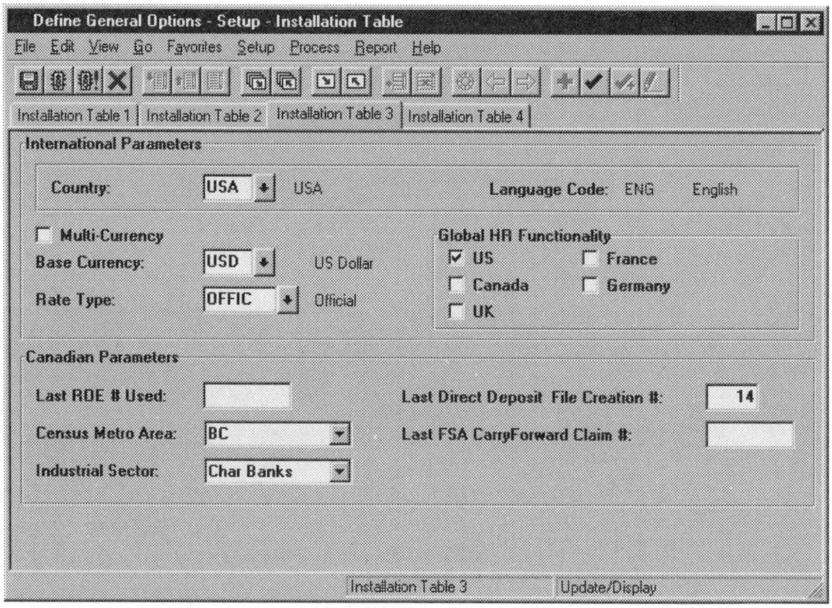

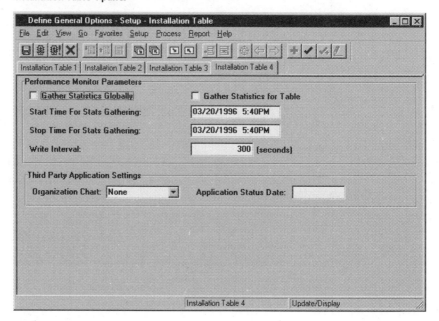

**FIGURE 4.4**  Installation Table 4 panel

If you are implementing a payroll system, don't forget to update the installation table to set the last check number used by your old system. To do this, select Go > Define Business Rules > Define Payroll Process from any menu. Then select Setup > Form Table and select the form ID for the check value that you need to set. Figure 4.5 contains this panel. You can also set the number for your direct deposit advice form using this panel.

**FIGURE 4.5**    Define Payroll Process panel

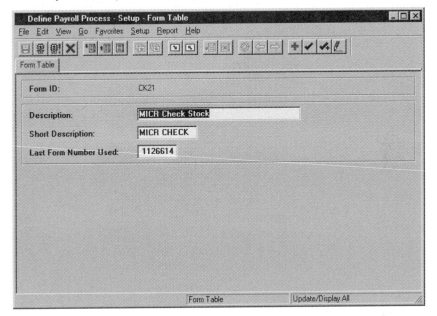

## Summary

Parallel operations are an important step you must take before moving your People-Soft system to production. Parallel operations help ensure data integrity, give the users a chance to work out the kinks in the new system, make sure the new system is configured and installed properly, and provide benchmark data for system performance.

To ensure a successful parallel operations period, take the following steps:

▶ Define the scope of the parallel operations.

▷ Make a checklist of functions to be tested.

▷ Identify the length of the parallel operations period.

▶ Develop a test plan that's easy for the testers to use.

▶ Perform the tests.

  ▷ Functional

  ▷ Technical

  ▷ Benchmark

▶ Move the new system to production.

Now that we have covered the implementation and rollout of your PeopleSoft application, the next part of the book discusses the tools that make up your PeopleSoft environment.

# PEOPLETOOLS

*Part II explores the PeopleSoft tools that are available to you and describes the functionality of the tools available to your end users.*

*Chapter 5, "Administration Tools," describes the tools to manage and automate your PeopleSoft system. Chapter 6, "Data Management Tools," provides an overview of the tools that manage and manipulate your table structures. Chapter 7, "Development Tools," describes the tools that help you develop new functionality for your PeopleSoft environment and the tools used during a system upgrade. Chapter 8, "End-User Tools," discusses the functions that the end users can use to make their jobs easier. Chapter 9, "Security," provides an overview of the security tools that help establish and maintain the security of your PeopleSoft system. Chapter 10, "SQR," reviews the command structure and usage of the SQR program.*

# Administration Tools

## FEATURING

▶ CONFIGURATION MANAGER

▶ APPLICATION SERVER

▶ PROCESS SCHEDULER

▶ PEOPLETOOLS UTILITIES

Thisn chapter provides you with an overview of the administration tools delivered by PeopleSoft. These tools are designed for use by the system administrator to help you manage and automate your system. This chapter discusses the functionality of these tools and give you some practical tips on when these tools can help you. Examples are provided to show you how these tools can be used in your company.

# Configuration Manager

The Configuration Manager application makes the administration of your workstations easier. You can specify installation-specific settings that allow you to quickly configure the paths to directories or identify which default options the users have. The Configuration Manager automatically sets or adjusts the Windows 95 or Windows NT Registry setting, making it unnecessary for you to adjust them manually.

Configuration Manager is located in the PeopleSoft Installation folder and also in the PeopleSoft folder on the desktop. There are 14 folders to select from, each controlling a different set of parameters that are used to configure the workstation. Let's look at some of the configuration options in these folders and see how these options can make your job easier.

## Startup Folder

The first configuration panel that is displayed after starting the Configuration Manager is the Startup folder. Figure 5.1 illustrates the Startup folder. The initial window allows you to specify the PeopleSoft menu item that is initially displayed on startup. For example, the technical team usually starts with the Application Designer window; Payroll users may start with the Compensate Workforce window.

**N O T E**   None of the parameters on this screen are mandatory but the user can be forced to enter all of these manually. I recommend that you use the Startup folder to make it easier for your users to get logged in to the system by designating several parameters for them.

Let's examine how you specify login defaults for your users. The following information is specified on the Startup folder. This information is database dependent.

**Database Type**   The Database Type is the database type, such as Oracle, DB2, or Sybase (as shown in the figure). This parameter can be restricted.

**FIGURE 5.1**   Configuration Manager–Startup folder

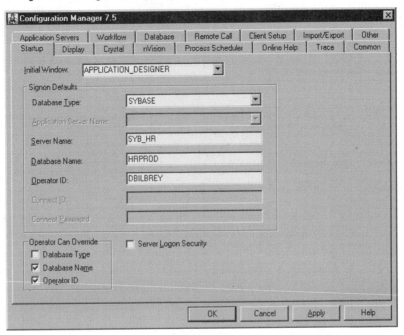

**Application Server Name**   The Application Server Name is the name of the application server to which the user will attach. This box is dimmed unless the database type APPSRV is selected.

**Server Name**   The Server Name is the name of the server to which the user will attach (SYB_HR in Figure 5.1). This parameter is only available if your database type is Sybase, DB2, Informix, or Microsoft SQL Server.

**Database Name**   The Database Name is the name of the database to which the user will attach. This parameter can be restricted. This parameter is not changeable when connecting to the application server.

**Operator ID**   The Operator ID is the default ID for the workstation. If you have a small number of users, entering a value here can reduce the number of keystrokes they have to perform to get into the system.

**Connect ID**   The Connect ID is specific to DB2 and Informix. This represents the user's account on the host system for those databases. The Connect ID is used in place of the PeopleSoft ID used by the other RDBMS platforms.

**Connect Password**   The Connect Password is used to specify a default when using the Connect ID field. This is *not* recommended, since saving a default password into a configuration file is viewed as a security violation; anyone can gain access when using a machine that is configured with this default password.

**NOTE** The login defaults are defaults that can be modified at the time of login unless they are restricted by the Operator Can Override settings.

The final settings that you specify in Configuration Manager are located at the bottom of the Startup folder. The options under Operator Can Override control what database type and/or database name the user can access. When any of these three boxes (Database Type, Database Name, and Operator ID) is checked, the user is allowed to modify that parameter.

Unless your PeopleSoft system operates in a multi-database environment, the Database Type box under Operator Can Override should not be checked. Leaving this box unchecked prevents the user from inadvertently selecting another database type and then not being able to sign on correctly. The Database Name box should be checked if users need to access multiple databases. If you have users who only need access to a single database, I recommend removing the check from this box, again to prevent the user from attempting to sign on to another database. This can reduce the number of support calls you and your staff receive.

The Server Logon Security checkbox specifies that the user will be authenticated by the server and will not use the PeopleSoft security profile. This is most commonly used when your database platform is DB2/MVS, where you use the security on the mainframe for controlling access.

## Display Folder

The Display folder is used to select the resolution to be used as the default for the panels when they open. Figure 5.2 contains the Display folder. The PeopleSoft default is 640 × 480. When using a higher resolution, the panels open as windows that are not full screen. If your users always want the panel to open in full-screen mode, select the video resolution that matches the default resolution setting for the PC, or set the panel to scale by selecting Scale from the Panel Sizing drop-down list. If you select Clip, the panel uses the amount of the screen required to support the selected resolution. For example, if your screen resolution is set to 800 × 600 and you selected Clip, your Display Size value is 640 × 480 and the PeopleSoft panels open in a 640 × 480 window on the desktop.

**FIGURE 5.2**    Configuration Manager–Display folder

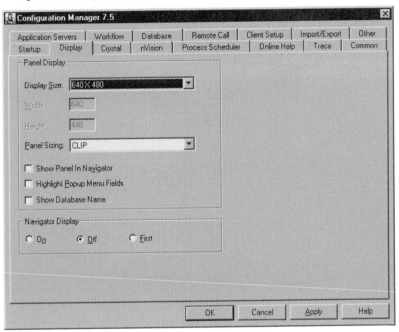

Additional information that can be supplied on the Display folder includes:

▶ The panel name displayed in the status bar.

▶ The database name displayed in the status bar and the minimized taskbar icon on Windows 95 or Windows NT workstations.

▶ Pop-up menu fields may be highlighted with a black rectangle to visually alert the user that a pop-up menu exists for that field.

## Crystal Folder

The Crystal folder, illustrated in Figure 5.3, is used to specify the location of the Crystal Reports executable files as well as the search paths to be used when searching for Crystal Reports report (`*.rpt`) files.

Two additional options can be set on the Crystal folder:

▶ To disable the automatic inclusion of columns in a new Crystal Report, uncheck Report Columns.

▶ To turn the trace option on to log execution to a specified log file, check Use Trace During Execution and specify the trace file name.

**FIGURE 5.3**    Configuration Manager–Crystal folder

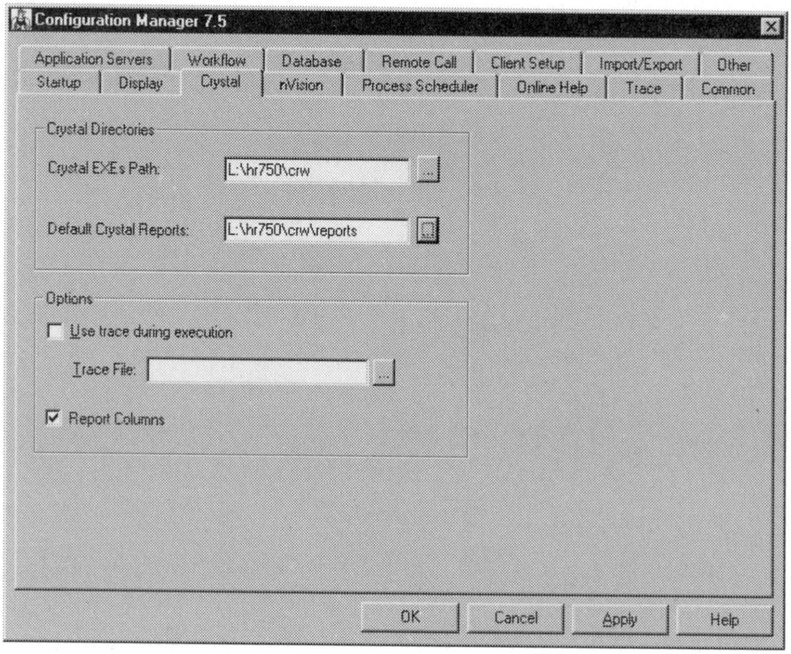

# nVision Folder

Use the nVision folder (see Figure 5.4) to specify the parameters that are used by nVision to locate executable programs, layouts, instances, and templates.

The SpreadSheet field specifies the spreadsheet application that you are using for nVision. At this time, PeopleSoft only supports Microsoft Excel so the only valid option is Excel. The drop-down list box allows PeopleSoft to add additional support as needed.

The second item on the nVision folder is the Space Between Query Columns option. This option affects the layout of the report. Set the Space Between Query Columns to 0 so that an empty column is not inserted between your data columns in queries. I recommend this choice because, in my experience, most users get annoyed when blank columns are inserted between each column in the data that is returned from a query.

The Directory Paths section of the nVision folder allows you to specify the directory paths where various files can be found. The Microsoft Excel directory should point to the user's copy of the Microsoft Excel executable file. This will be either the local drive or the network drive if you run the applications from your network. By default, all the other directories point to either the Excel or nVision subdirectories located under your PeopleSoft home directory on your file server. The PeopleSoft home directory shown in Figure 5.4 is 1:\hr750\.

**FIGURE 5.4**    Configuration Manager–nVision folder

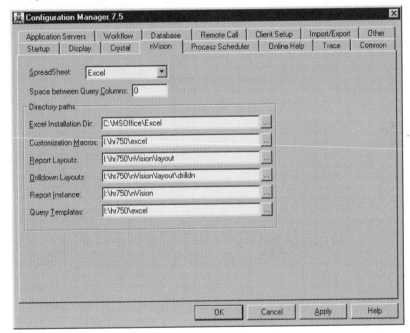

PART

II

PeopleTools

## Process Scheduler Folder

The Process Scheduler folder allows you to specify directory information for processes as well as specific command line options, or flags, as PeopleSoft calls them. Figure 5.5 contains the Process Scheduler folder. Table 5.1 explains each of the parameters on the Process Scheduler folder in detail.

**FIGURE 5.5**   Configuration Manager–Process Scheduler folder

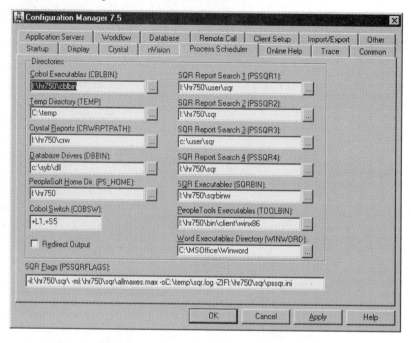

**TABLE 5.1**   Process Scheduler Parameters

| Parameter | Description |
|---|---|
| CBLBIN | The location of the compiled COBOL code. |
| TEMP | The designated temporary directory. |
| CRWRPTPATH | The location of the Crystal Reports executable file. |
| DBBIN | The location of your database drivers. |
| PS_HOME | Your PeopleSoft home directory. The location of all files required by clients. |
| COBSW | COBOL switches that control COBOL program behavior. Beginning with version 7.5, this is a dynamic parameter that can be set in Configuration Manager and does not require a machine reboot to change. These switches are:<br>+L = suppresses Application Completed message box<br>+S5 = redirects display statements to log<br>-L = displays Application Completed message box |

**TABLE 5.1 (continued)** Process Scheduler Parameters

| Parameter | Description |
|-----------|-------------|
| PSSQR1 | The search order for SQR programs. You can also have three other search parameters: PSSQR2, PSSQR3, and PSSQR4. |
| SQRBIN | The location of the SQR executable program. |
| TOOLBIN | The location of PeopleTools executable files. |
| WINWORD | The location on the client for your Microsoft Word executable file. |
| SQR Flags | Command-line switches that control SQR reports. Table 5.2 lists the most commonly used command-line SQR switches. The flags entered in this box in Configuration Manager are also used by the SQRW program when it is launched by Process Scheduler. |

**TABLE 5.2** SQR Command-Line Switches

| SQR Switch | Description |
|------------|-------------|
| -I | Location of *.SQC or other include program files |
| -m | SQR configuration file used to modify default SQR properties |
| -o | Filename for the log file |
| -DEBUG | Used in conjunction with the #debug command to display additional information when troubleshooting SQR programs |

## Online Help Folder

The Online Help folder, illustrated in Figure 5.6, allows you to specify the directory where your help files are stored. In addition, you can specify the order in which your PeopleBooks are searched on global searches and you can specify the function keys that are associated with starting help files. In Figure 5.6, the F1 key is assigned to PeopleSoft Help.

PART

II

PeopleTools

**FIGURE 5.6**   Configuration Manager–Online Help folder

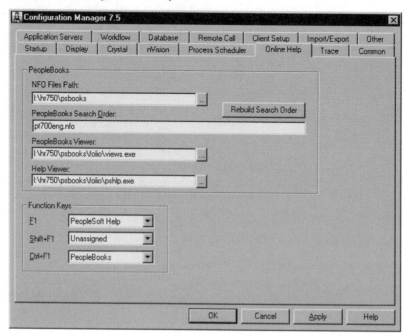

## Trace Panel Folder

The Trace Panel folder allows you to specify the trace functions that you want for SQL, PeopleCode, or Message Agent. Figure 5.7 contains the Trace Panel folder. At the bottom of the Trace Panel folder, you must specify the path and filename where you want to store the trace information. The trace functions are most often used in the problem isolation stages of troubleshooting. Chapter 17, "Troubleshooting," discusses trace functions in more detail.

## Common Settings Folder

The Common Settings folder (see Figure 5.8) allows you to specify the language in which the workstation will be operating. The default language is English. In this folder, you also specify the location of the cache files for the machine and the default Data Mover settings for the location of the input, output, and log files.

**FIGURE 5.7** Configuration Manager–Trace folder

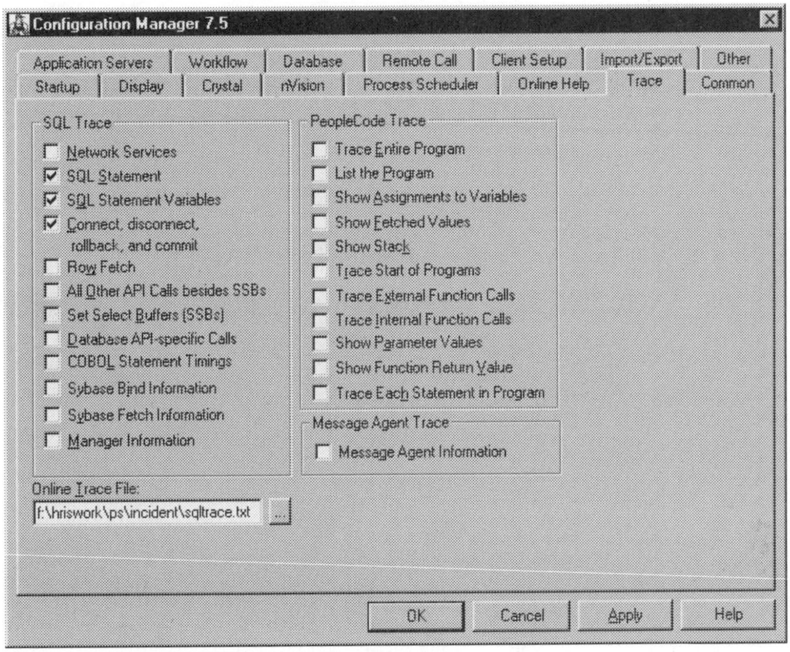


**FIGURE 5.8** Configuration Manager–Common Settings folder

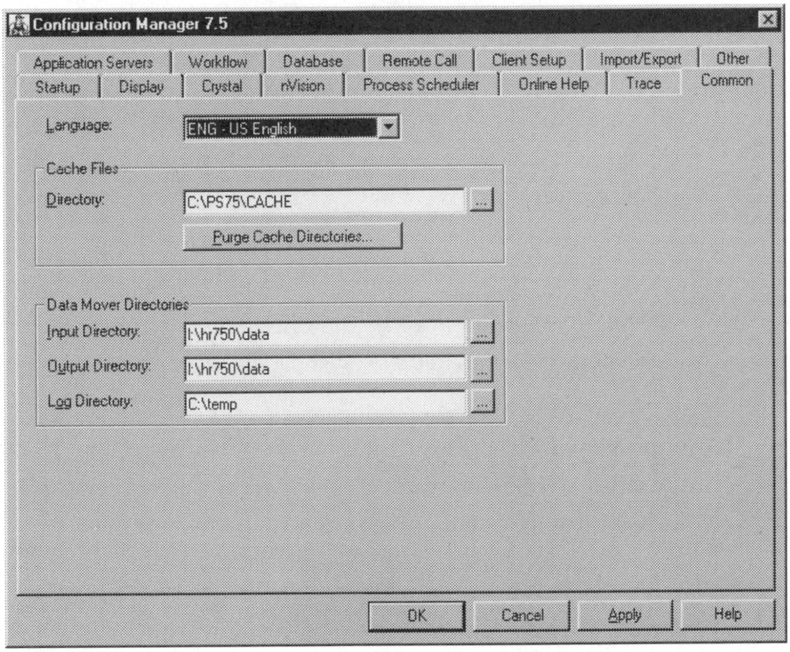


PART II

PeopleTools

# Application Servers Folder

The Application Servers folder, illustrated in Figure 5.9, allows you to specify the application servers (if any) that your users are able to attach to. You must specify the application server name that you want the user to use. You also specify both the IP (Internet Protocol) address and port number for the workstation listener on the application server that is configured to handle the workstation requests.

**FIGURE 5.9**    Configuration Manager–Application Servers folder

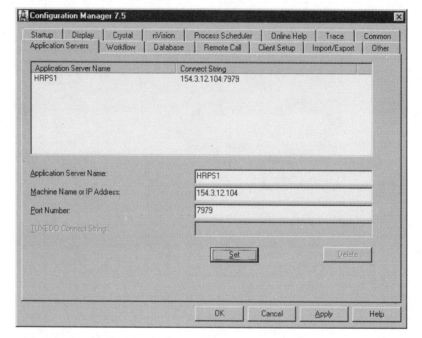

Figure 5.9 contains an example application server named HRPS1, with a connect string of 154.3.12.104:7979. You specify this configuration in the Application Server Name, Machine Name or IP Address, and Port Number fields at the bottom of the Application Servers folder by clicking the Set button.

The TUXEDO Connect String field is used in a multi-application server environment to provide for load balancing and failover capability. If you specify a value here, the workstation automatically attempts to connect using this configuration if the selected application server is not responding to your request.

## Workflow Folder

The Workflow folder (see Figure 5.10) allows you to define the message agent server and the forms server that are used by the workflow processes defined in your system. The Mail Protocol and Mail DLL Path options on the Workflow folder should be set to the type of e-mail protocol that you have and for the path to the *.dll file for your e-mail system respectively.

**FIGURE 5.10**    Configuration Manager–Workflow folder

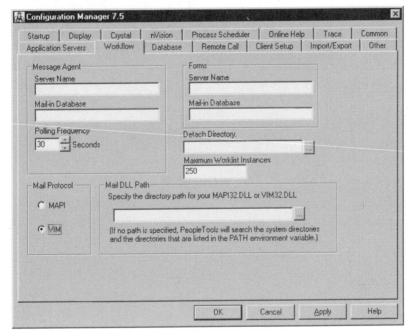

**NOTE**    PeopleSoft supports both the VIM and MAPI e-mail protocol. The VIM32.DLL or MAPI32.DLL are called by the PeopleSoft application to route e-mail messages created as part of a workflow process to designated addresses.

## Database Folder

The Database folder, illustrated in Figure 5.11, allows you to specify specific database settings on some RDBMS platforms. For example, you can set the DB2 Message Size option, but only if you are accessing DB2 through the Centura SQLNetwork product.

PART

II

PeopleTools

You can also set the Sybase Packet Size option. This allows you to match your packet sizes to the best size for your network topology. If you are uncertain about the best value for your network, consult your LAN administrator before changing this value from the default setting.

**FIGURE 5.11**    Configuration Manager–Database folder

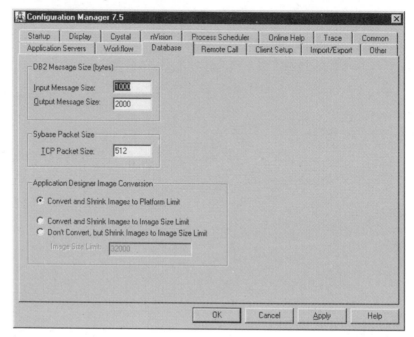

## Remote Call Folder

The Remote Call folder in Figure 5.12 allows you to use the remote call capabilities of the Tuxedo application server, which will be described later in this chapter. The remote call functionality is a holdover from PeopleSoft version 6 before the full three-tier capabilities were introduced. Remote call is still useful for short transactions, such as online manual checks, where the user spends more time waiting for the Process Scheduler to poll, find work, and execute the process. Remote call execution is instantaneous. You can set the timeout value that the client will wait for a response from the server; the default value is 50. PeopleSoft recommends limiting the use of the remote call functionality to transactions that take 15 seconds or less so the default value should be adequate. You can also set the debugging options to redirect the output using this folder or to support COBOL animation.

The Show Window State option allows you to control the appearance of the remote call execution on the desktop. You can hide the execution, show it on the taskbar only, or allow a DOS window to open. I suggest either hiding the execution or showing it on the taskbar only, unless you need it in the development environment for debugging purposes.

**FIGURE 5.12**    Configuration Manager–Remote Call folder

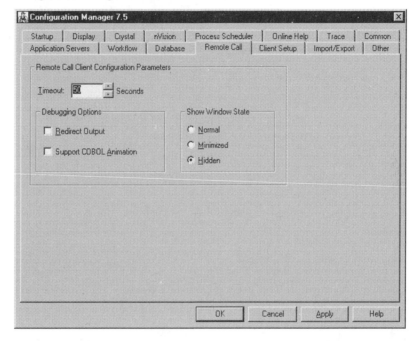

PART

II

PeopleTools

# Client Setup Folder

The Client Setup folder, illustrated in Figure 5.13, allows you to specify the program group name to be created on the client desktop. The first section of the Client Setup folder allows you to specify which applications have a shortcut link. For example, you will probably not give your normal users the Data Mover, PeopleTools RPT Converter, or SQA Robot Setup shortcut links.

You can also specify the installation of the PeopleSoft ODBC driver on the Client Setup folder. Crystal Reports use this driver to attach directly to your database. The connection passes through all PeopleSoft security to execute queries defined by the PeopleSoft Query tool. PeopleSoft says that a future release will allow the execution of any SQL, which would allow you to completely define the query using Crystal Reports or another third-party application.

Beginning with version 7.5, the Three-Tier Minimal Install option is available. This option allows you to load a smaller amount of code on client machines that are only going to have three-tier access to your PeopleSoft application.

When all the Configuration Manager folders have been completed, you are ready to check the Install Workstation box on the Client Setup folder. The client machine then updates the client machine's registry and installs any selected shortcuts to the desktop.

**FIGURE 5.13**    Configuration Manager–Client Setup folder

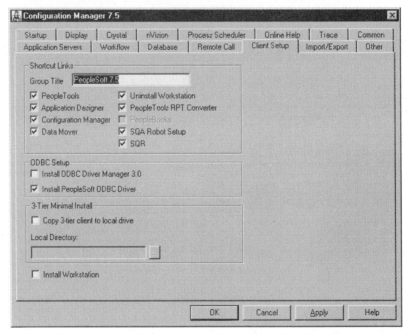

 **N O T E**   You do not have to reinstall your PeopleSoft system to update the settings on a workstation. Simply change the setting and click the Apply button.

## Import/Export Folder

The Import/Export folder (see Figure 5.14) allows you to export the Configuration Manager settings to a file. This folder also allows you to import the configuration file you created. You can open the Configuration Manager on another workstation and import the file; the settings will be identical on the two machines.

**FIGURE 5.14**    Configuration Manager–Import/Export folder

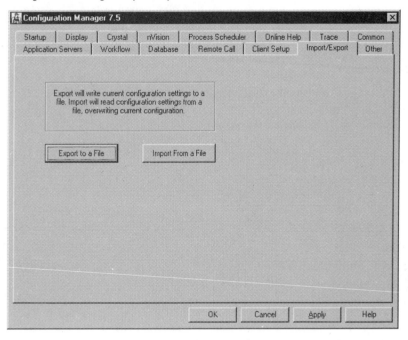

The Import/Export feature is a time-saving tool for the system administrator. For example, suppose you have established configuration files for the Payroll, Accounting, and Purchasing departments. You can then import the Purchasing profile to all machines in the Purchasing department to give each user an identical configuration.

## Other Folder

The Other folder, illustrated in Figure 5.15, allows you to update settings that are used by the PeopleSoft Manufacturing applications' Quality Server. You must specify the directory that contains the data files you want to analyze and the directory where the SQR programs should store the analysis files created by the Quality Server processes.

Configuration Manager can also be used ad hoc to change the settings on a workstation at any time. You don't need to click the Install Workstation button except during the initial setup when you want to create the program group icons. At other times, you just need to click the Apply button to initiate your changes.

PART

II

PeopleTools

**FIGURE 5.15**    Configuration Manager–Other folder

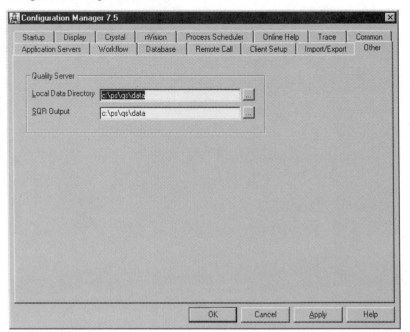

# Application Server

An application server is designed to remove intensive application or database access processing from the client and locate it on a machine that has a higher bandwidth connection to the server. This provides two benefits. One, remote clients can achieve performance close to that of central site clients, since all the database access is performed at the central site and the results are sent to the remote client. Two, you can extend the life of older clients at the central site by running them in three-tier mode. For example, my company extended several 486 computers for months by using a three-tier configuration. The performance of these computers was equal to or better than higher speed Pentium clients. Adding an application server and creating a three-tier environment does this.

A three-tier client-server system has a workstation, a database server, and an application server, each performing separate tasks. The application server may run on a separate computer from the database server in a physical three-tier arrangement. Another option is to have the application server and database server coexist on the same computer, creating what is called a logical three-tier system.

PeopleSoft has historically been a two-tier client-server system with the client communicating directly with the database. Beginning with PeopleTools version 7, PeopleSoft began to support the use of three-tier client-server processing. Figure 5.16 illustrates the differences between the two-tier and three-tier system architecture. In a three-tier system, the application server runs the PeopleSoft application and exchanges SQL messages with the database server, requesting information and sending database changes. The client does not directly access the database; instead, the application server uses Tuxedo messages to service requests to and from the client. PeopleSoft licenses the BEA Tuxedo application server for use in PeopleSoft installations. Tuxedo can run on both Unix and Windows NT servers.

**FIGURE 5.16**    Two-tier and three-tier client-server architecture

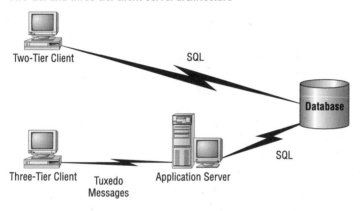

PeopleSoft recommends the use of a logical three-tier system if your database and operating system support it. This provides better performance since the intensive database access functions do not have to travel across your network. However, PeopleSoft does not support the application server on all platforms; on some platforms, a physical three-tier setup is the only option. The specific installation instructions that accompany your PeopleSoft application describe the recommended configuration for your environment.

**N O T E**    PeopleSoft began providing Remote Call Support with PeopleTools version 6.

There are two types of clients: Windows and Web. The Windows client is the standard workstation configuration. The Web client is a Java-based client that can run on any platform that supports the Java Virtual Machine (JVM). Beginning with PeopleTools 7.5, the supported Web browser is Microsoft Internet Explorer 4.x or higher with the Microsoft JVM. PeopleSoft has stated that support for Netscape will be available with version 8.

With a generic application server, you can write your own programs to carry out many types of transactions. You can also modify the configuration of the application server itself to better handle your specific applications. The version of Tuxedo that ships with PeopleSoft is a runtime version. This means that Tuxedo has already been adjusted to work with the PeopleSoft applications. This is all it can be used for because of the licensing provided by PeopleSoft and since you cannot completely control the application server operation. Now let's look at the components that make up the PeopleSoft Application Server.

## Components

The PeopleSoft Application Server application contains the following components:

**Tuxedo**   Tuxedo is a transaction monitor that listens for work and then schedules processes to handle the requests. Tuxedo consists of workstation listeners and workstation handlers that provide the communication interfaces for the Windows clients.

**Jolt**   Jolt is a product designed to communicate with Web clients for Tuxedo. Jolt takes the place of the workstation listeners and handlers for Web clients.

**Jolt Internet Relay and Jolt Relay Adapter**   The Jolt Internet Relay and Jolt Relay Adapter are products that are required to transfer Web client requests from your Web server to the Jolt listeners on your application server if they are located on separate machines.

## PSADMIN

The PSADMIN utility is designed to assist you in configuring and administering your server. PSADMIN allows you to establish an application server domain. Each domain is configured to support one database connection. The domain includes all processes required to support your mix of clients. You generate one PSTUXCFG configuration file for each domain you establish.

As you create the domain, PSADMIN guides you through the choices required to configure the new domain. You will be prompted to provide the names and port numbers for listeners and the minimum and maximum number of connections that you want for the domain.

When the configuration is complete, you are ready to start your application server. There is a menu item to boot the application server. The first process to start is the Bulletin Board Liaison (BBL) process, which is the primary Tuxedo process. The next module to start is the Workstation Listener (WSL). This process monitors the assigned IP port number for connection requests from Windows workstations.

When the WSL process detects a request, it assigns the request to a Workstation Handler (WSH) process. The WSH process handles all subsequent client communications and the WSL process continues listening for new connection requests.

The Jolt Station Listener (JSL) and Jolt Station Handler (JSH) perform the same functions for the Web client.

The PeopleSoft extensions to Tuxedo are the processes that begin with the prefix "PS." The PeopleSoft Tuxedo Authentication (PSAUTH) process is used to link requests to the security table PSOPRDEFN for user authentication and login.

The main process that PeopleSoft uses to handle requests is the PeopleSoft Application Server Manager (PSAPPSRV). PSAPPSRV processes all client requests and sends the results back to the client.

**TIP**  I recommend that you download the "Three-Tier Answerbook" white paper from Customer Connection for help in planning, implementing, and administering your application server. It contains more detailed information about the Application Server application than any other PeopleSoft sources that I have read. The PeopleBooks for Application Server and the Tuxedo installation guide can also provide you with valuable information.

# Process Scheduler

The PeopleSoft Process Scheduler is an application that handles requests from users to execute batch programs and reports that have been defined using the Process Scheduler definitions. The Process Scheduler is a COBOL SQL application that must be compiled for the server platform on which you are running it. PeopleSoft recommends that the Process Scheduler for the Unix environment be compiled and run on the same physical server as the RDBMS if possible. The other supported environment for the Process Scheduler is Windows NT. The Process Scheduler for the DB2/MVS environment must be run on either a Unix or Windows NT server; it cannot run on the mainframe.

There are three distinct areas of the Process Scheduler application:

1. The server agent runs on the server and executes the processes that have been submitted. The server agent does this by polling the PSPRCSRQST table, looking for work.

2. The Process Monitor window is used by the user submitting the job to receive an update on the status of that job.

3. The Process Scheduler PeopleTool is used to create and configure processes so that the server agent can execute them. This tool is discussed later in this chapter.

**N O T E**    Process Monitor is discussed in more detail in Chapter 8, "End-User Tools."

Beginning with version 7.5, PeopleSoft has included the configuration and management of the Process Scheduler server in the PSADMIN program. The only supported platforms for Process Scheduler are UNIX and Windows NT, since PSADMIN is not supported on other platforms. The following steps outline the processes required to get the Process Scheduler server running. The examples are for the UNIX Process Scheduler, which has a character-based menu system.

1. Load all PeopleTools COBOL and PeopleSoft database connectivity programs onto the Process Scheduler platform.

2. Load PeopleTools-stored statements into the PS_SQLSTMT_TBL table using the Data Mover program.

3. Compile the COBOL code and link the database connectivity programs to create the PSRUN file.

4. Start the PSADMIN program. You will see the following menu:

```
--------------------------------
PeopleSoft Server Administration
--------------------------------

  1) Application Server
  2) Process Scheduler
  3) Web Components
  q) Quit

Command to execute (1-3, q):
```

**5.** Select option 2, Process Scheduler, from the previous menu, and then select option 4, Create a Process Scheduler Server Configuration, from the following menu:

```
-------------------------------------------
PeopleSoft Process Scheduler Administration
-------------------------------------------

  1) Start a Process Scheduler Server
  2) Stop a Process Scheduler Server
  3) Configure a Process Scheduler Server
  4) Create a Process Scheduler Server Configuration
  5) Delete a Process Scheduler Server Configuration
  6) Edit a Process Scheduler Configuration File
  7) Show Status of a Process Scheduler Server
  8) Kill a Process Scheduler Server

  q) Quit

Command to execute (1-8, q) :
```

**6.** Enter the name of the database and select UNIX from the menu. You will return to the previous menu. Select option 3, Configure a Process Scheduler Server. Complete the sections per the installation manual for your RDBMS. The following dialog shows the configuration steps for my test server, which uses Sybase:

```
Values for config section - Startup
  DBName=HRTEST
  DBType=SYBASE
  OprId=PS
  OprPswd=XXXXXX
  ConnectId=
  ConnectPswd=
  ServerName=SYB_HR

Do you want to change any values (y/n)? [n]:

Values for config section - Database Options
  SybasePacketSize=512
  UseLocalOracleDB=0

Do you want to change any values (y/n)? [n]:n

Values for config section - Trace
  TraceSQL=0
```

PART

II

PeopleTools

```
Do you want to change any values (y/n)? [n]:

Values for config section - Process Scheduler
 LogFence=5
 ProgramName=PSRUN PTPUPRCS
 PrcsServerName=PSUNX
 PSSQR1=%PS_HOME%/sqr
 PSSQR2=
 PSSQR3=
 PSSQR4=
 PSSQRFLAGS=-i%PSSQR1%/,%PSSQR2%/,%PSSQR3%/,%PSSQR4%/[break here]-
 m%PSSQR1%/allmaxes.max -ZIF%PSSQR1%/pssqr.unx
 Log Directory=%PS_SERVDIR%/logs
 OutputDirectory=%PS_SERVDIR%/output/

Do you want to change any values (y/n)? [n]:n
```

**7.** Once you have completed the configuration, you are ready to select option 1, Start a Process Scheduler Server. Select your server from the list and PSADMIN will attempt to start it. If you have errors, check your configuration and try again. You should receive output similar to the following output if your configuration is successful.

```
**************************************************
** Logfiles will be found in /sybase/psupg/appserv/prcs/HRRCVR/logs
**
** Stdout and stderr sent to PSPT_PSUNX.stdout
**************************************************
 UID PID PPID C STIME TTY TIME COMMAND
 psupg 1272 1271 7 16:30:27 ttyp1 0:01 PSRUN PTPUPRCS
PeopleSoft Process Scheduler Started Normally
```

**NOTE** This has been a general overview of the procedures required to get the Process Scheduler running in your environment. Consult the installation manual for your specific RDBMS for more detailed information.

## Creating a Process Scheduler Process

To configure a process to be executed by the Process Scheduler, you must first create a Process Definition. To do this, open the Process Definition panel by selecting Go > PeopleTools > Process Scheduler. Then select Use > Process Definition > Add from the Process Scheduler menu. Figure 5.17 illustrates the Process Definition panel.

**FIGURE 5.17**    Process Scheduler–Process Definition panel

Process Scheduler - Use - Process Definitions

File  Edit  View  Go  Favorites  Use  Process  Help

Process Definitions | Process Definition Options | Panel Transfers |

Process Type:   SQR Report
Process Name:   ALB_BOND

Description:      Savings Bond Balancing Rpt

Process Class:  SQR Report                                          ☑ Log client request
                                                                    ☐ SQR Runtime
Server Name:    PSUNX    ⬦    UNIX Server Agent                      ☑ API Aware

Priority:       High

Run Location:   Server          Recurrence Name:

Long            Savings Bond Balancing Rpt
Description:

Panel Groups                        Process Security Groups
RUN_ALB_BOND                        HRALL

                    Process Definitions          Update/Display

When adding a new definition, you need to enter a process type and process name.
These are displayed in read-only mode on the Process Definition panel. In Figure 5.17,
the process type is SQR Report and the process name is ALB_BOND. To finish creating the definition, you must enter the following:

▶ A description of the process

▶ The process class, which is selected from the drop-down list based on the process type

▶ The priority of the process

▶ The run location—whether you want the process to run on the client, the
server, or on either

▶ The panel groups associated with the process

▶ The process security groups that have access to the process

To complete the definition, select the Process Definition Options tab to get the panel
illustrated in Figure 5.18. The parameters on this panel are optional and are only used
to override the default environment settings that are established for your entire system.
My company found that there were very few instances when we needed to override our
defaults for a specific process.

PART

II

PeopleTools

**FIGURE 5.18** Process Scheduler–Process Definition Options panel

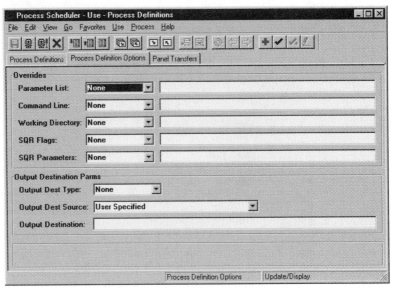

The final panel to configure a new process is the Panel Transfers panel. Figure 5.19 illustrates this panel. The settings on this panel control what events should occur after the execution of the process you are creating. You can specify that another panel be started and the user be pointed to a particular menu item on that panel. My company has never added panel transfer information for any processes that we have defined.

**FIGURE 5.19** Process Scheduler–Panel Transfers panel

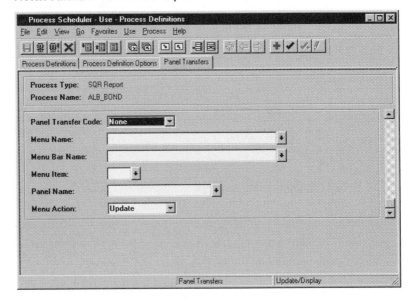

# PeopleTools Utilities

PeopleSoft provides a set of PeopleTools utilities designed to simplify the administration of various aspects of your PeopleSoft applications. To access the Utilities menu, select Go > PeopleTools > Utilities from any panel. PeopleSoft organizes the utilities into eight categories:

**Performance Monitoring**    Performance Monitoring includes the Trace People-Code and Trace SQL utilities. These utilities are available using the Configuration Manager. However, if you turn them on for a given application, that application must be restarted. You can turn on Trace PeopleCode and Trace SQL from the Utilities menu dynamically. This is useful when you want to limit the amount of data that is logged and you have isolated the problem to an area that can be analyzed using these functions.

**Text Control**    The Text Control utilities include the Message Catalog and the Strings Table capabilities. The Message Catalog is where system error messages are stored and is discussed in more detail later in this chapter. The Strings Table allows you to enter custom field descriptions for use as headers in SQR reports.

**Control Tables**    Control Tables allow you to share common functions throughout your company using the TableSet ID, Record Group, and TableSet Control functions.

**System Control**    The System Control utility allows you to define system settings to control the performance of applications. The primary System Control areas are PeopleTools Options, DDL Definitions, and Query Security. The PeopleTools Options allow you to specify the language. DDL Definitions are discussed later in this chapter. Query Security is discussed in detail in Chapter 9, "Security."

**Record Cross-Reference**    The Record Cross-Reference utility is used to find out where records are used in your system. This utility is discussed later in this chapter.

**International Settings**    International Settings are used to temporarily adjust the users' language preference when multiple languages are installed. You can also expand the amount fields in your applications by selecting the International Field Size. This is used if the currency you are tracking has very large numbers.

**Web Client Security**    Web Client Security is used to provide security information for your Web clients. You can configure alias types and values using the panels in Web Client Security.

**Utility Processes**    There are two utility processes: the System Audit utility, which is discussed in detail in Chapter 6, "Data Management Tools," and the Change Base

Language utility. The Change Base Language utility is used to convert your system to a new base language in a multi-language installation.

Let's take a look at a few of these utilities in detail and see how you can use these functions to help you perform your job better.

## Message Catalog

You can edit delivered messages or add messages for your custom applications by selecting Use > Message Catalog from the Utilities menu. PeopleSoft reserves the message numbers up to 20,000. Use a number larger than 20,000 to guarantee that your messages are not overwritten during an upgrade. The Message Catalog panel is shown in Figure 5.20.

**FIGURE 5.20**    Message Catalog utility

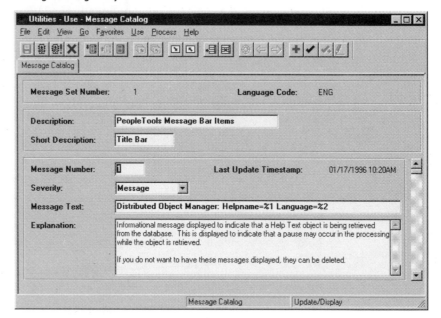

## DDL Definitions

Dynamic Definition Language (DDL) is the set of commands that your RDBMS needs to perform tasks. PeopleSoft provides definitions for all the supported database platforms so that the Data Mover and Application Designer Build applications work properly.

Figure 5.21 shows the DDL Model Defaults for Sybase. The statement type is displayed with the corresponding Model SQL in an edit box immediately below it. The

SQL contains variable replacement information that is used by the Data Mover and the Build applications to create dynamic SQL for online database modification. The variable replacement information can also be used to generate SQL scripts that your database administrator (DBA) can execute to create the object in your RDBMS.

The DDL Parm field matches the **CLUSTER** code shown in the Model SQL field in Figure 5.21. The DDL Parameter Value of CLUSTERED is used in its place at execution.

During the upgrade process, you are usually asked to review the DDL definitions in a Data Mover script. This allows your DBA to review these settings before they are updated on your system. If you update without reviewing them and later find you are having problems, then the DDL Definitions utility is where you go to fix the problem.

**FIGURE 5.21**   Utilities–DDL Model Defaults

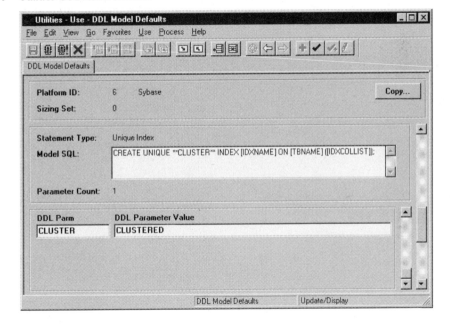

## Record Cross-Reference

As stated earlier, the Record Cross-Reference utility allows you to locate where a record is used in the system. There are two basic functions of Record Cross-Reference. The first function displays where a record is used. Some examples are:

**Panels**   The panels on which a record is used

**Search records**   The panels that define the specified record as a search record

**Views**   The views that use the record

**Projects**   The projects in the Application Designer that contain the specified record

The second function in Record Cross-Reference displays how a record is used. Some examples are:

**PeopleCode**   The PeopleCode programs that reference the record

**Prompts**   The records that use the specified records as a prompt table

**Group boxes**   The group boxes for which the record is the default table

**N O T E**   Prompt tables are used in data validation to help ensure the integrity of the database. For example in HRMS, many fields on panels prompt against the PS_PERSONAL_ DATA table to determine if an employee exists in this table before allowing information to be inserted into another table.

The Record Cross-Reference utility is useful in many ways. It can help you identify where record objects are used when you are performing an impact analysis before a customization is made. Record Cross-Reference is also useful in troubleshooting. It can help you identify the record or field that is causing the error message to appear by checking to see if the record is being used as a prompt table where you did not expect it.

# Summary

This chapter described several administration tools provided by PeopleSoft to simplify the administration of your PeopleSoft system.

The Configuration Manager provides the capability to specify workstation-specific characteristics about the database, the display, online help, the format and location of report files, and the processes.

The Application Server application allows you to configure and maintain an application server in a three-tier client-server system.

The Process Scheduler application handles requests from users to execute batch programs and reports that have been defined using Process Scheduler definitions. Using

Process Scheduler, you create a process and specify its priority, class, run location, security, and other characteristics.

PeopleSoft also provides you with several PeopleTools utilities. This chapter described:

▶ Message Catalog, which allows you to edit delivered messages or add your own messages for use by your custom applications

▶ DDL Definitions, which helps you manage the definitions for your database platform

▶ Record Cross-Reference, which allows you to determine where and how a record is used

The next chapter, Chapter 6, "Data Management Tools," discusses the tools provided by PeopleSoft to maintain your database.

PART

II

PeopleTools

# Data Management Tools

FEATURING

- ▶ DATA INTEGRITY TOOLS

- ▶ DATA MOVER

- ▶ IMPORT MANAGER

- ▶ MASS CHANGE

- ▶ TRANSACTION SET EDITOR

- ▶ CUBE MANAGER

T
he tools that are used to monitor and manage your database are extremely important to your PeopleSoft system. The database contains the definitions for all your menus and panels. In addition, most of the business rules that you have developed are stored in the database tables. As the system administrator, you need to ensure the integrity of the data stored in the database. You also have to move data in and out of the database for synchronization with external software. You may have to provide data for further analysis to other areas of your company.

The PeopleSoft database consists of two distinct groups of tables. The first group is the PeopleTools tables, which serve as the foundation for all other objects and applications in the database. This book refers to these tables as the system tables. The second group is the application-specific tables. These tables contain all the data that is specific to your company, for example, your employees or your financial records. This differentiation between system tables and application-specific tables is why upgrades are divided into two distinct parts. Chapter 12, "Upgrading," discusses this issue in more detail.

PeopleSoft provides several tools to help you maintain your database. These tools range from those designed to maintain the integrity of your database to those that allow you to perform batch conversions and transformations of your data. This chapter discusses both types of tools. This chapter also describes the programming interface that allows you to expand PeopleSoft edits to non-PeopleSoft tables.

# Data Integrity Tools

PeopleSoft delivers three tools that help you verify the integrity of your data. However, there is really one tool and two reports. The tool is SQL Alter. The reports are DDDAUDIT.SQR and SYSAUDIT.SQR. Let's take a look at SQL Alter.

## SQL Alter

SQL Alter is a small component of the Application Designer application. The other components of the Application Designer are discussed in more detail in Chapter 7, "Development Tools."

SQL Alter is used to verify that the underlying database tables are synchronized with the definitions defined in the Record Designer. SQL Alter only validates that the tables, which PeopleSoft calls records, and fields, are correctly defined.

SQL Alter has several modes of operation. The first is the online mode. Database tables can be updated online as the verification occurs. Online mode is limited to certain RDBMS platforms and is generally not recommended.

SQL Alter can also be run in audit-only mode. A list of discrepancies is generated when running in audit-only mode. You must decide how to fix the discrepancies that are found. PeopleSoft recommends that you rerun SQL Alter in script creation mode to fix the discrepancies.

Script creation mode is the mode that I recommend for all SQL Alter operations. This mode generates a script that is specific to your RDBMS because SQL Alter performs the comparison. The script that is generated in script creation mode contains the SQL that is necessary to perform updates to the database tables. Figure 6.1 shows the first panel you see when preparing to run SQL Alter. (This process has been moved into the Build function in the newer releases of PeopleSoft.) To access the Build panel, select Build **>** Project from the Application Designer window. Select only the current or selected objects to build. Make sure to keep an updated project that contains all the tables in your system. When you want to audit the system, open this project and build the script to alter the tables based on any differences that are found.

**FIGURE 6.1**    **SQL Alter–Build panel**

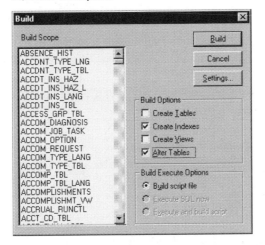

Figure 6.1 shows the Build Scope down the left side of the window. The Build Scope lists all the tables that will be checked by the audit process. You must also select the type of build that you want to perform. For audit-only mode, choose the Alter Tables check box. The Create Indexes check box will automatically be checked. One of the radio buttons must be selected in the Build Execute Options group. I recommend that you always build to a script file so that you have a chance to review the changes before they are actually executed against your database. Before you click the Build button, select the Settings button. Figure 6.2 contains the Build Settings panel.

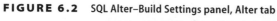

FIGURE 6.2    SQL Alter–Build Settings panel, Alter tab

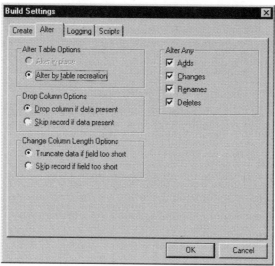

In Figure 6.2, the Alter tab of the Build Settings panel shows the options you have in controlling what actions will be detected and scripted. You can decide if you want to drop columns that contain data or truncate data if the new field definition is shorter than the existing definition and data. You can also limit the build with respect to additions (adds), changes, renamings, or deletions. When building a script, select the Scripts tab, shown in Figure 6.3.

FIGURE 6.3    SQL Alter–Build Settings panel, Scripts tab

Figure 6.3 shows the options that affect the script being generated. You can specify that comments be written to the script. You can also specify whether to create a single script or separate files. You must also designate the filename and location where you want the generated script file to be stored.

The following excerpt is from a script for Sybase that was created using SQL Alter. This script shows all the steps that are required to modify one table.

```
/* Do not perform deletes at this time */

/* Alters for record PS_SAL_PLAN_CONTRL */
/* ANNIVERSARY_SW - add */
/* NEW_HIRE_ELIG_DT - change */

/* Initialize SQL */
USE HRTEST
GO

/* Start the Transaction */
BEGIN TRANSACTION
GO

/* Drop the TMP table, just in case it exists */
DROP TABLE PS_1
GO
DROP VIEW PS_1
GO

/* Create Tmp Table */
CREATE TABLE PS_1 (COMPANY CHAR(3) NULL,
  BUDGET_START_DT PSDATE NULL,
  BUDGET_END_DT PSDATE NULL,
  SAL_PLAN_START_DT PSDATE NULL,
  ANNIVERSARY_SW CHAR(1) NULL,
  Z_TMP_ALTER_1 PSDATE NULL,
  SAL_PLAN_EFFDT PSDATE NULL,
  CURRENCY_CD CHAR(3) NULL,
  NEW_HIRE_ELIG_DT PSDATE NULL)
GO

/* Copy to Tmp Table */
INSERT INTO PS_1 (
  COMPANY,
  BUDGET_START_DT,
  BUDGET_END_DT,
  SAL_PLAN_START_DT,
```

PART

II

PeopleTools

```
                    SAL_PLAN_EFFDT,
                    CURRENCY_CD,
                    NEW_HIRE_ELIG_DT)
                    SELECT
                    COMPANY,
                    BUDGET_START_DT,
                    BUDGET_END_DT,
                    SAL_PLAN_START_DT,
                    SAL_PLAN_EFFDT,
                    CURRENCY_CD,
                    NEW_HIRE_ELIG_DT
                     FROM PS_SAL_PLAN_CONTRL
                    GO

                    /* Convert Data */
                    UPDATE PS_1 SET Z_TMP_ALTER_1 = NEW_HIRE_ELIG_DT
                    GO

                    /* Set Default Values */
                    UPDATE PS_1 SET ANNIVERSARY_SW = 'N'
                    GO

                    /* TMP Table is now complete */
                    /* CAUTION : Drop Original Table */
                    DROP TABLE PS_SAL_PLAN_CONTRL
                    GO
                    DROP VIEW PS_SAL_PLAN_CONTRL
                    GO

                    /* Create New Table */
                    CREATE TABLE PS_SAL_PLAN_CONTRL (COMPANY CHAR(3) NOT NULL,
                     BUDGET_START_DT PSDATE NOT NULL,
                     BUDGET_END_DT PSDATE NOT NULL,
                     SAL_PLAN_START_DT PSDATE NOT NULL,
                     ANNIVERSARY_SW CHAR(1) NOT NULL,
                     NEW_HIRE_ELIG_DT PSDATE NULL,
                     SAL_PLAN_EFFDT PSDATE NULL,
                     CURRENCY_CD CHAR(3) NOT NULL)
                    GO

                    /* Copy from Tmp Table */
                    INSERT INTO PS_SAL_PLAN_CONTRL (
                     COMPANY,
                     BUDGET_START_DT,
```

```
        BUDGET_END_DT,
        SAL_PLAN_START_DT,
        ANNIVERSARY_SW,
        SAL_PLAN_EFFDT,
        CURRENCY_CD,
        NEW_HIRE_ELIG_DT)
        SELECT
        COMPANY,
        BUDGET_START_DT,
        BUDGET_END_DT,
        SAL_PLAN_START_DT,
        ANNIVERSARY_SW,
        SAL_PLAN_EFFDT,
        CURRENCY_CD,
        Z_TMP_ALTER_1
        FROM PS_1
GO

/* Drop Tmp Table */
DROP TABLE PS_1
GO
COMMIT
GO

/* Recreate indexes */
CREATE UNIQUE INDEX PS_SAL_PLAN_CONTRL ON PS_SAL_PLAN_CONTRL (COMPANY)
GO
COMMIT
GO

/* Done */
/* Job Summary: */
/*   Data base: HRTEST */
/*   Operator: PS */
/*   Start: 8:43:30 AM 7/28/98 */
/*   End: 8:43:53 AM 7/28/98 */
/*   Errors: 0 Warnings: 0 Informational: 1 */
/*   >>Script completed successfully<< */
```

Note that several lines in the previous excerpt are highlighted in **bold**. These are references to data elements that are changing the data in your table. Note also that the job summary for this script is included at the bottom of the code listing. The job summary contains any errors or warnings that occurred as the script was generated.

PART

II

PeopleTools

Prior to version 7.5, PeopleSoft generated scripts for altering the database that created a temporary table, copied the existing data to the temporary table, dropped the original table, created a new table with the new structure, and then copied the data into the new table from the temporary table. This was not very efficient. Beginning with version 7.5, PeopleSoft creates a temporary table with the new format, copies the data from the original table into the temporary table, drops the original table, and renames the temporary table to the original name. This is more efficient. Work with your database administrator (DBA) to determine the best methodology for altering your tables. You will want to use the most efficient method possible for your RDBMS, especially on larger tables.

There are other methods for auditing the record definition. Let's first look at the data designer audit report—DDDAUDIT.SQR.

## DDDAUDIT.SQR

DDDAUDIT.SQR is an SQR report that is used to validate the record definitions for tables, views, and indexes in your RDBMS. The report consists of nine queries, of which three queries check indexes, two queries check views, and four queries check the tables.

To run this report, select SQR for Windows from the Windows Start button. It should be located in your PeopleSoft group. We recommend putting a shortcut to this program on the desktop for members of the technical group.

**TIP** I have found that having a shortcut on the Windows Desktop to the PeopleSoft program group is also useful, especially when I am using multiple versions of PeopleSoft during the upgrade process.

Figure 6.4 shows the SQRW dialog box that is used to start the DDDAUDIT.SQR report. You must specify the full path to the audit report. Select the file from a standard Windows file dialog box by clicking the Files button. Enter a valid user and password. All users who need to run a DDDAUDIT.SQR report must have the authority to select from both the PeopleSoft system tables and RDBMS system tables without going through PeopleSoft security. The report arguments are populated when the program is started. You may, however, have to add some arguments for your specific environment. Once you have entered the information to control the run, press OK and wait for the report to complete.

**FIGURE 6.4**    SQRW dialog box–DDDAUDIT.SQR

```
SQRW: Structured Query Report Writer V3.0.18.1.1

Report name    I:\hr700\sqr\dddaudit.sqr        OK

Username       user                             Cancel

Password       xxx                              Files

Report arguments:                               Help
-il:\hr700\sqr\
-ml:\hr700\sqr\allmaxes.max                     About
-FC:\temp\ -xp -cb -USYB_HR
-DBHRPROD
```

DDDAUDIT.SQR generates a report for you to use in validating and updating your
system. A sample excerpt from this report follows. A more detailed report is shown
in Appendix B, "Sample Reports."

```
(TABLE-3) SQL Table defined in the Database
and not found in the Data Designer:

SQL Table Name
------------------
PS_CLOSE_EARN_TMP
PS_CLOSE_LEDG_LOG
PS_CLOSE_LEDG_TMP

(VIEWS-1) Views defined in the Data Designer
and not found in the Database:

Record Name
------------------
ALB_PE_SCR_VW
IMAGE_VW1
IMAGE_VW2
IMAGE_VW3

(VIEWS-2) Views defined in the Database and
not found in the Data Designer:

View Name
------------------
PS_SKILLS
PS_SRCH_PTS_LICENS
PS_SRCH_PTS_SKILL
PS_SRCH_PTS_TEST
```

The Table-3 query in this report shows tables that are still defined in your RDBMS
but are not defined in the PeopleSoft record definitions. This condition is usually

created during an upgrade when PeopleSoft tables are deleted. You must manually delete these tables from your database.

The Views-1 query lists all the views that are defined in the record definitions but are not defined in the database. If these views should be in the database, you need to generate a script to create these views in the database.

Let's look at the SYSAUDIT.SQR report, which is used to validate the integrity of other PeopleSoft objects.

# SYSAUDIT.SQR

SYSAUDIT.SQR is used to search for "orphaned" PeopleSoft objects. PeopleSoft defines orphaned objects as those objects or code that refer to objects that no longer exist. Figure 6.5 shows the System Audit panel. The System Audit dialog box is used to specify which objects SYSAUDIT.SQR should check when executed.

**FIGURE 6.5**    System Audit panel

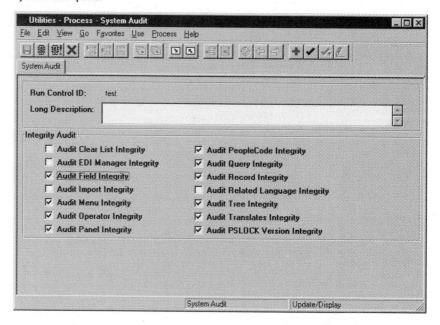

This panel is used to set the audit parameters before running the SYSAUDIT.SQR program. To reach this panel, select Go **>** PeopleTools **>** Utilities and then selecting **>** Process **>** System Audit from the Utilities menu. You can choose to audit any of the parameters shown. Figure 6.5 shows the normal configuration we use at my company when using the System Audit feature.

SYSAUDIT.SQR generates a report that details any problems discovered with People-Soft objects. A sample excerpt from this report follows. The report showing more object types is shown in Appendix B, "Sample Reports."

```
Report ID: SYSAUDIT PS SYSTEM TABLE AUDIT REPORT

(AUTHS-1) Authorized Signon Operator does
not exist in Operator Definition table: No rows found.

(PNLDF-1) Panel Definition Field count does
not match the record count in Panel Field
table:

Lang Field Record
Panel Name Code Count Count
---------------------------------------------
BAS_PARTIC_ENT2 ENG 46 48

(PNLGR-3) Panel Group Definition contains
Search Panel Name that does not exist in
Panel Definition table:

Panel Group Name Search Panel Name
---------------------------------------------
RUN_PER003M RUNCTL_PER003M

(PCMPR-1) PeopleCode Program table contains
Program name not currently in use:

PeopleCode Name
Program Name Count
---------------------------------------------
PCM55050 18

(PCMNM-2) PeopleCode Name table contains
Record/Field name that does not exist in
ProgName table:

PeopleCode
Prog Name Record Name Field Name
---------------------------------------------
PCM55050 RC_PAYINIT COMPANY

(QRYFD-2) Query Definition Field name does
not exist in the Field Definition table:

Oper ID Query Name Record Name Field Name
---------------------------------------------
BJones earn EARNINGS_BAL MONTHCD
```

PART

II

PeopleTools

The AUTHS-1 query lists any authorized signon operators that are not defined in the Operator Definition table. This report example found none.

The PNLDF-1 query reports any discrepancies between the Panel Field and the Panel Definition Field tables. The field counts should be equal to the record counts. In this example, they are not equal.

The PNLGR-3 query in this report lists all panel groups whose definition contains search panels that no longer exist in the panel definition table. This can be attributed to upgrades where new search panels were created without deleting previous search panel definitions.

The PCMPR-1 query is useful in finding PeopleCode programs that are not currently in use. This helps you locate and delete the orphaned code.

The PCMNM-2 query helps identify orphaned PeopleCode that is usually left after an upgrade. In this example, the PeopleCode Program Name does not have a match in the Program Name table.

The QRYFD-2 query helps you identify queries that contain field names that no longer exist in the system. These queries can then be modified or deleted.

Another critical issue with maintaining your data is the movement of data into and out of your production database. Data Mover is one tool that can help make this process less cumbersome. Let's take a look at Data Mover in more detail.

# Data Mover

Data Mover is a utility that updates tables in your PeopleSoft system. The most common use of Data Mover is to load new data into your PeopleSoft system tables. (System tables are sometimes called tools tables.) Other scripts that utilize Data Mover include tax table updates and stored statement updates. Data Mover is also used to export data from one database into another to facilitate moving data from development to production or from one RDBMS to another.

The two most common processes that require the use of Data Mover for running scripts are when conducting an upgrade and when applying tax updates. Both of these topics are covered in detail in Chapter 12, "Upgrading Your PeopleSoft System," and Chapter 13, "Tax Updates." This section gives you an overview of the Data Mover functionality.

Figure 6.6 shows the Data Mover panel. Data Mover is started using the icon placed in the PeopleSoft Release folder or the PeopleSoft Installation folder. The dialog box is split horizontally into two areas. The input area is on top and shows any loaded scripts. The output area is on the bottom and shows the results of each step of the process defined in the input area. Error messages are displayed in the output window and logged to the log file that you designate.

**FIGURE 6.6**    Data Mover dialog box

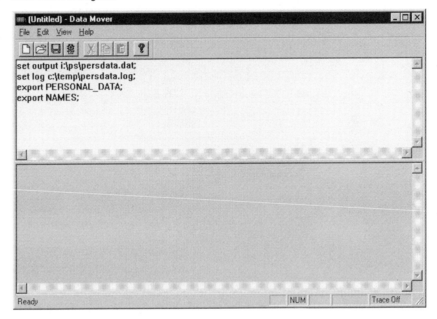

Data Mover has several rules that your scripts must adhere to for them to complete successfully:

▶ All command lines must end in a delimiter. A semicolon is the delimiter that must be used.

▶ Commands may be longer than one line in length.

▶ Comment lines require no delimiter but must begin with either REM, REMARK, or --. Comment lines cannot be more than one line in length.

▶ Command statements are *not* case sensitive.

▶ Strings constants *are* case sensitive.

There are several commands that can be used with Data Mover:

▶ The SET command, when used with valid parameters, controls how Data Mover functions when running scripts.

▶ The IMPORT and EXPORT functions are used to move data in and out of database tables. You can apply conditions on the EXPORT only to select certain records. This is done using standard SQL syntax. The IMPORT function inserts all data into a table. If the table does not exist, the table and any indexes are created by Data Mover before inserting any records.

The Data Mover commands are outlined in Table 6.1 for your reference.

**TABLE 6.1**   Data Mover Commands

| Command | Function |
| --- | --- |
| IMPORT | Used to insert data into records from a file that was generated by the EXPORT command. IMPORT creates a tablespace, the table, and indexes when a table does not exist in the target database. In the installation procedure, the IMPORT command creates the demo and system databases. |
| EXPORT | The EXPORT command selects records from a table and places them into a file that can be read by the IMPORT command or other programs that are written to understand it. You can combine SQL commands to select subsets of information from the source table. The EXPORT command is useful in making a backup of a table before performing a mass change. |
| REPLACE_ALL | Similar to IMPORT, the REPLACE_ALL command drops the table and indexes and recreates the table using the structure and data contained in a file created by the EXPORT command. |
| REPLACE_DATA | The REPLACE_DATA command deletes all data in the table (it truncates the table) and then inserts the data contained in a file created by the EXPORT command. |
| REPLACE_VIEW | The REPLACE_VIEW command recreates views in the database for the specified tables. |
| SET | The SET command is used to specify parameters that Data Mover uses when executing scripts. Typical parameters are for input file location and names and log file location and name. |
| RUN | The RUN command executes other Data Mover scripts. This command cannot be nested. The most common usage is for the stored statement Data Mover scripts. PeopleSoft provides a single Data Mover script for PeopleTools that calls all stored statement scripts. Each installed application likewise has a single script to execute. |
| ENCRYPT_PASSWORD | The ENCRYPT_PASSWORD command encrypts the passwords in the PSOPRDEFN table for the specified operator. |

**TABLE 6.1** **(continued)** Data Mover Commands

| Command | Function |
|---------|----------|
| GRANT_USER | The GRANT_USER command gives specified users the ability to log in. |
| RENAME | The RENAME command can be used to rename a record, a field in a single record, or a field in all records. |
| REM | The REM command is used for comment lines. |

The Data Mover commands support the wildcard * to signify that the command should apply to all parameters. For example, the command GRANT_USER *; gives access to all users defined in the PSOPRDEFN table.

**WARNING** All Data Mover command lines must end in a semi-colon ( ; ).

Data Mover is quite useful when testing new SQL that is designed to insert or update data into production tables. At my company, we simply create an export script and move all the current data in a production table into a file. Then, if errors are encountered with the update program, we use the REPLACE_ALL command in Data Mover to move the original data back into place. The scripts used to perform these procedures follow.

To export data from the database, use the following script as an example:

```
set output i:\ps\persdata.dat;
set log c:\temp\persdata.log;
export PERSONAL_DATA;
export NAMES;
```

To import the exported data back into the database, execute the following script:

```
set input i:\ps\persdata.dat;
set log c:\temp\persin.log;
replace_all PERSONAL_DATA;
replace_all NAMES;
```

Let's look at Import Manager, a tool that allows you to move data into your system from external sources.

PART

II

PeopleTools

# Import Manager

Import Manager is the tool that PeopleSoft provides to help you with the conversion of your data during implementation. It can also be used periodically when you want to validate incoming data against the existing data or rules already defined in your system. Consider the following example: You want to verify that the employee IDs are valid on data that you are importing from external systems. The Import Manager validates your data one row at a time. Import Manager is limited to the insertion of data; updates cannot be performed.

Figure 6.7 shows an Import Manager definition called BOND_SPDAT. To start Import Manager, select Go >PeopleTools > Import Manager.

**FIGURE 6.7**    Import Manager–BOND_SPDAT definition

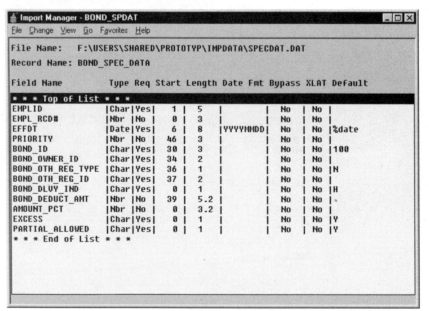

This figure contains the import definition that our company used for loading one of the savings bond tables. There are two parts to an import definition: the header and the field load definitions. When creating a new import definition, you must designate the record name that you want to load in the header. Once the record is selected, it populates your import definition with a list of all the fields for that record. Figure 6.8 contains the Import Header Information panel. You must also designate the full path name for the data file from which you want to import data. You can enter it at this time or you can save the definition and edit this later if you do not know the name.

**FIGURE 6.8**   Import Manager–Import Header Information panel

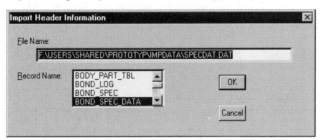

The next step is to define the start position for each field for which you have data. Note that several of the fields have a starting value of 0. This signifies that there is no data to import. You can then load the default value or a space. You must specify the length of the field in the data file. If you are importing a date field, you must specify the date format from the data file. The default parameter allows you to specify the value to load if you are importing no data for a field or if some of your records may contain no information for a field.

In the example in Figure 6.7, the BOND_ID field is required and data from the file SPECDAT.DAT will be loaded. The data will start in position 30 and be three characters long. A default value of 100 is specified. This loads a value of 100 for records that contain no information. We chose this value after scrubbing our data and determining that due to past practices, if a user had no value, a $100 bond was mandated.

**TIP**   If you are loading large amounts of data or have a short window for loading the data, you should write your own scripts. Import Manager is very slow compared to other utilities for loading data. The PeopleSoft validation slows it down.

The next section describes the Mass Change utility that can be used to update large amounts of data using SQL statements that have been predefined by a developer.

# Mass Change

When you have large amounts of data that needs to be updated, Mass Change is a good tool to consider. This is especially true if the type of update you need to perform will be required on a regular basis. Mass Change is similar to the PeopleSoft Query utility, except that Mass Change does updates.

Mass Change has three components: types, templates, and definitions. This section describes these three components. Each component should be defined in the order that they are discussed here.

## Types

Mass Change types control the structure of the SQL that is generated. You must be very familiar with SQL and the design of the PeopleSoft database design in order to create effective types. There are four Mass Change Type panels.

Figure 6.9 contains the Description panel. This panel is used to specify the owner and identify whether this is a public use Mass Change. There is a text area into which you can enter a detailed description of the purpose and usage of the Mass Change program.

**FIGURE 6.9**    Mass Change Type–Description panel

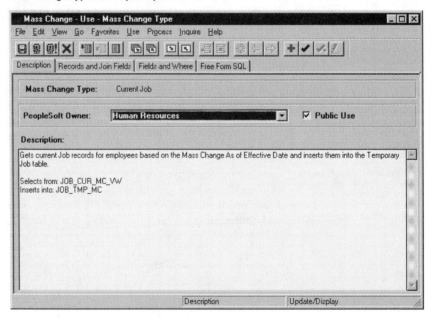

Figure 6.10 shows the Records and Join Fields panel. This panel is where the records and join fields are defined. You must specify the execution sequence and the type of SQL action to be performed. You can also specify if this program is used for file upload or download and whether any free-form SQL is used with this program. If free-form SQL is used, it is entered in the Free Form SQL panel shown in Figure 6.11.

**FIGURE 6.10**    Mass Change Type–Records and Join Fields panel

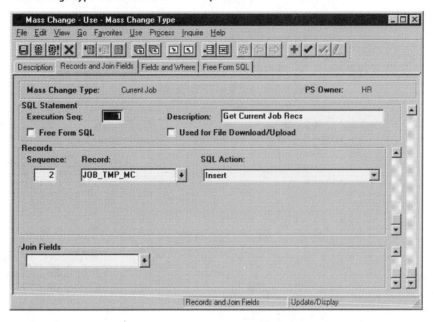

**FIGURE 6.11**    Mass Change Type–Free Form SQL panel

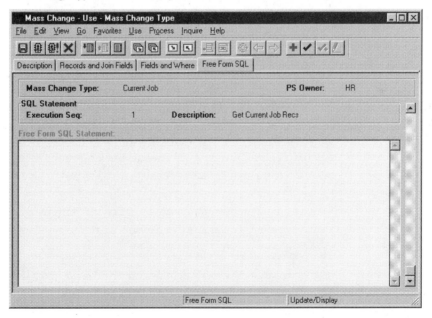

Figure 6.12 shows the Fields and Where panel. This panel allows you to further control the records to be accessed by the user. Any where clauses can be defined; they are attached to the records and join fields defined on the previous panel.

**FIGURE 6.12**   Mass Change Type–Fields and Where panel

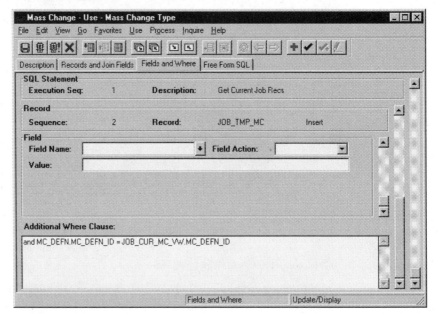

## Templates

Mass Change templates are used to identify the fields that will contain the where clauses of the SQL contained in the Mass Change type definitions. Again, a thorough understanding of SQL is required to define these fields. You have two choices when selecting fields to be used in the where clauses: Allow the users to enter criteria when they execute the change or establish default values for the fields that cannot be edited. Figures 6.13 and 6.14 show the panels that are used to define a Mass Change template. The Description panel allows you to set the owner of the template and also provides an area where you can enter text that explains the purpose and usage of the template.

The Criteria and Fields panel is where you specify the fields that will be used to control the data to be selected. Figure 6.14 shows the first SQL statement in the template. This is determined by looking at the execution sequence number, which is 1. This figure shows one criteria field, BARG_UNIT, for which the user can specify the value. There is also one default field, DEPTID, for which the developer specifies the value.

**FIGURE 6.13**   Mass Change Template–Description panel

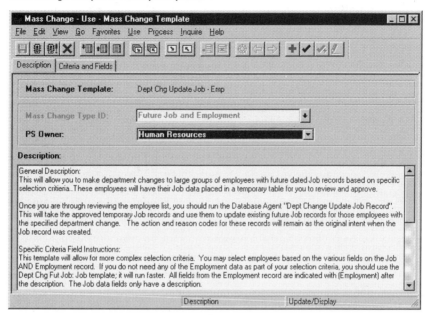

**FIGURE 6.14**   Mass Change Template–Criteria and Fields panel

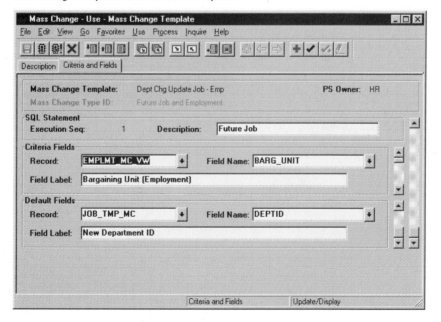

**N O T E** You must grant access to the template that you create before users can access it to create Mass Change definitions.

## Definitions

The Mass Change types and templates are typically defined by a PeopleSoft developer. You do not want your end users creating the types and templates. You want the end users to interact only with the definitions that they create for executing mass changes.

Mass Change definitions are the final step in preparing to run a Mass Change. Definitions are created by your end users using the types and templates that have been defined by the development team. To create a definition, select Use **>** Mass Change Definition **>** Description **>** Add to display the Mass Change dialog box shown in Figure 6.15. Select the template that you want to base the definition on. Specify the criteria and defaults that you will use with this definition. When defining the criteria, you can only use one SQL operator per field. You may have multiple values by creating additional rows.

**FIGURE 6.15**   Mass Change Definition–Description panel

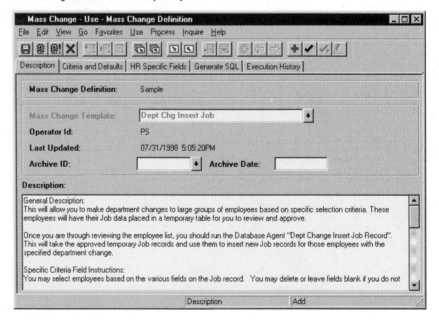

The next step is to generate the SQL to be used by the Mass Change you have defined. The SQL is generated and displayed in a read-only box for your review after you select the Generate SQL option.

You may also group definitions so that they can be run from one run control. To group definitions, select Use **>** Mass Change Groups **>** Add from the menu. Define an owner for the group and specify the definitions that you want to include in the group. You must specify the execution order before executing the Mass Change process. Figure 6.16 contains an example of a Mass Change Group.

**FIGURE 6.16**    Mass Change Group–Group Definition panel

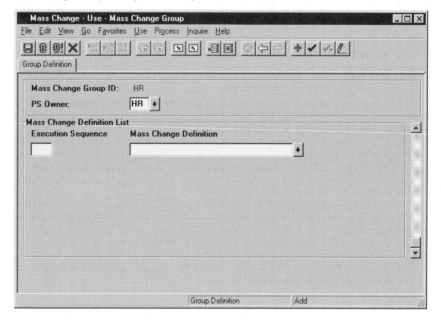

## Executing a Mass Change

Once you have created the definition or groups of definitions, you must then execute the Mass Change. Mass Changes can either be run online or in the background. To execute Mass Changes online, select the Execute SQL on Saving check box that is on the Generate SQL panel of the Mass Change Definition window. To execute Mass Changes in the background, use the Mass Change run panel. The Mass Change run panel is accessed by selecting Process **>** Mass Change **>** Add from the Mass Change panel. Select whether you want to run a single Mass Change process or a group that you have created. You then select the run location and time on the Process Scheduler request panel.

**TIP**   We recommend that only users with a good understanding of SQL be allowed to create their own Mass Change definitions. At my company, the technical staff builds all the steps when we build a Mass Change Process. In many cases, the technical staff also executes the Mass Change.

Let's now look at the Transaction Set Editor, which is used to apply PeopleSoft edits to high-volume batch processing.

# Transaction Set Editor

Transaction Set Editor (TSE) is a tool used to provide PeopleSoft edits to non-PeopleSoft tables for use in high-volume batch processing. It is designed to work with batch COBOL processes and is specifically designed for use with tables that are not subject to the normal panel edits of the online PeopleSoft applications. TSE is designed to help developers validate their data when writing their own custom COBOL code. This section provides an overview of the TSE functionality.

**NOTE**   TSE uses the concept of *transaction sets* that represent a transaction or groups of transactions that are executed from a single SQL process in the COBOL.

One function is the record edit. The record edit function must be integrated into the application that you are developing. There are several steps that must be completed for the record edit to work correctly:

▶ Verify that the record you want to work with is defined in both the PeopleSoft record definitions and the underlying database.

▶ Use the template for building an edit program provided by PeopleSoft.

▶ Define log tables if you intend to use them.

▶ Consider creating an application edit record definition if you intend to process multiple transaction sets from a single batch job.

The record edit process can provide edits for date ranges, prompt tables, required fields, and translate table values. The prompt table and translate table edits must have edit values defined for the data you are processing before the transaction set is processed or it will fail. The required field edit ensures that fields marked as required have data in them. Let's look at the processing modes that the record edit operates in.

The record edit can be implemented using update mode, log mode, or a combination of the two. Update mode uses a flag on the application record to mark errors for future online correction. Log mode writes a log transaction that can be used to automate error correction. The combination mode allows you to build a robust error correction process.

In addition, there are numerous environment variables that can be used to control the processing environment for TSE. The PeopleTools PeopleBook contains a detailed listing of all the possible environment parameters.

The TSE API provides additional services for formatting SQL, performing application-defined edits, and building SQL where clauses. The COBOL modules used to provide these functions are PTPTFLDW, PTPTSEDT, and PTPTSUSE.

Let's look at one more data management tool, the Cube Manager.

# Cube Manager

Cube Manager allows you to create templates for designing, building, and updating Online Analytical Processing (OLAP) cubes. These templates allow you to adapt quickly to field changes in your database or your cube. Cube Manager also provides the ability to establish default values for use with Arbor Essbase or Cognos Power-Play OLAP tools provided with PeopleSoft.

Before we explore Cube Manager and its uses, let's take a look at OLAP in more detail.

## Understanding OLAP

OLAP allows you to conduct detailed analysis of the transactional data in a relational database. This analysis is multidimensional in that you can look at the data from many perspectives, using different data elements and values.

The central concept of this multidimensional analysis is the cube. Unlike geometric cubes, OLAP cubes can have more than three dimensions; they typically have between three and eight dimensions. The dimensions of a cube are similar to a database field and can be thought of as the criteria used to identify discrete data elements.

# Metadata

Metadata is data that defines data. Metadata provides information about how data is formatted, structured, and stored. OLAP metadata includes the OLAP cube's dimensions, levels, and members. OLAP metadata is defined in PeopleSoft using trees and queries. Trees are used to summarize information for the particular element being defined. Queries are used to retrieve information that is used to populate the cube.

# Building Cubes

There are two primary steps in building a cube: First, design the cube, then build the cube.

## Designing the Cube

The first step in designing your cube is to identify what information you want to examine. Then, specify the level of granularity that you want to capture for further analysis. You must also determine the measure that you want to use for describing the results. For example, you may choose to show sales in dollars or units, or production in units.

The next step is to identify the dimensions. Dimensions are the criteria by which you want to view the data. The dimensions typically include time, location, department, or products.

When designing your cube, make use of the metadata stored in the PeopleSoft trees. The trees provide information that the Cube Manager can use to define the dimensions of the cube. Simply map the tree to the dimension in the Cube Manager Dimension panel and your data can then be summarized in the same way that the tree is defined. You may want to create additional trees that allow you to link the Cube Manager to your trees for this detailed summary.

You can also use subsets of existing trees if you do not need all the information provided by a given tree. Define a starting node on the tree, and the Cube Manager uses the tree from that point forward when building the dimensions.

There are three types of queries you can use with Cube Manager: dimension queries, attribute queries, and data source queries. They must all be defined as user queries and cannot be defined as role or database agent queries.

Use the dimension query to define dimensions instead of trees. You can also use the dimension query in conjunction with the tree to provide additional detail about the dimension. The most common use of the dimension query is when the data is hierarchical already and you do not want to define a tree. A single dimension query can return two levels of the dimension. You must define additional queries if you want more than two dimension levels in your cube. You must add one query for every additional level defined.

Use the attribute query to specify optional details about members. Many of the attributes that can be set are specific to either Essbase or PowerPlay but not both, except for the label attribute. The attribute query must return at least two columns, one for the member and the other for the attribute about that member. Refer to PeopleBooks for further details about the attributes that can be defined.

The data source query is used to populate the cube with data. Each row of your query populates a dimension and measure in the cube. The query must return one column for each dimension and one column for each measure that you have defined.

## Building the Cube

There are four basic components used to build the cube using Cube Manager: dimensions, analysis models, cube templates, and run control IDs.

**NOTE**  We will build a simple cube for gathering information contained in the PS_EMPLOYEES table as we discuss each component. In addition, we will show the elements of the query used to select the data.

**Dimensions**    The dimension is the fundamental building block for the cube. You must define the PeopleSoft metadata to be used to create this structure. As discussed in the previous section, the dimension is defined using trees, queries, or a combination of both. Dimensions are platform independent.

Figure 6.17 shows the Cube Manager Dimensions panel. To access this panel, select Design > Dimensions from the Cube Manager panel. In the Dimensions panel, enter a description of the dimensions and the member roll-up name and type. Be sure to specify which tree to use. This example uses the DEPT_SECURITY tree. You can also specify dimension queries on this panel to work with, or instead of, the tree.

The example in Figure 6.17 contains the DBTEST cube dimension defined as a Tree roll-up using the Department Security (DEPT_SECURITY) tree.

**Analysis Models**    The analysis model is used to define the basic structure of the cube. You specify the defined dimensions and measures to be used. You also specify the data source queries that will be used to populate the members and cube cells with data. Analysis models are platform independent.

**FIGURE 6.17**    Cube Manager–Dimensions panel

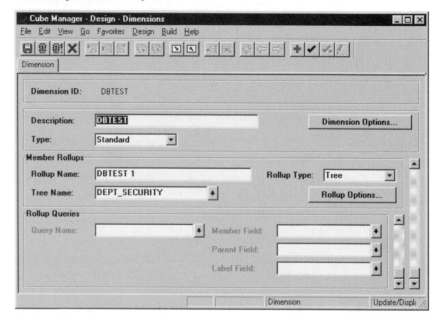

Figure 6.18 shows the Analysis Model panel where you define an analysis model for a cube. To access this panel, select Design **>** Analysis Models from the Cube Manager panel. This panel is used to specify the data sources and dimensions to be used in the analysis. You can specify multiple dimensions and measures. This panel allows multiple levels, which lets you specify the data field to be used with each dimension or measure. You can also specify a custom label to be used by Cube Manager when the cube is built.

Figure 6.18 shows the example analysis model DBTEST. We have populated the Description field; the Long Description field is optional. The Data Source Query Name is DBTEST, which is a query we defined using the PeopleSoft Query tool. Figure 6.19 contains the query DBTEST. The query *must* be defined before the analysis model can use it.

**Cube Templates**    Cube templates are platform dependent. You must specify whether the target platform for your cube is PowerPlay or Essbase. You must also specify the analysis model to be used to build the cube. Other options on this panel become available depending on your target platform.

**FIGURE 6.18**    Cube Manager–Analysis Models panel

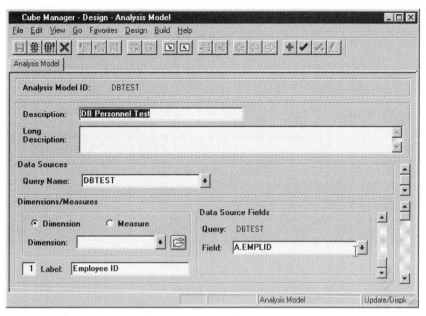

**FIGURE 6.19**    Query Designer–DBTEST query

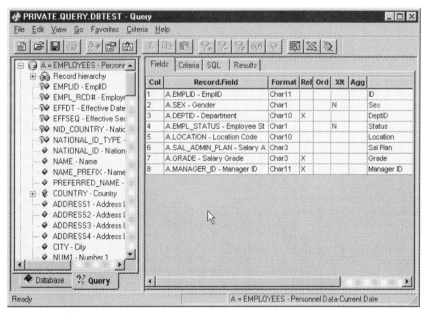

Figure 6.20 shows the Cube Template panel, which is used to create the template used in building a cube. To access this panel, select Build **>** Cube Template **>** General Settings from the Cube Manager panel. This panel has two basic options in addition to the description fields. You must specify the analysis platform, either Essbase or PowerPlay; the analysis model to be used; and any additional information that will be required on the Platform tab for the chosen target analysis platform.

**FIGURE 6.20**    Cube Manager–Template General folder

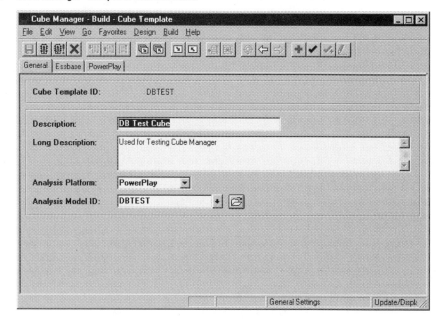

In the example in Figure 6.20, note that PowerPlay is the Analysis Platform and DBTEST is the Analysis Model ID.

Figure 6.21 contains the PowerPlay Template folder where the paths to the models and the data are configured for your network.

**Run Control IDs**    The cube is built using Process Scheduler, so you must define a run control ID to be used when building the cube. In the run control ID definition, specify the cube template to be used. You must also define whether this is a new build or a refresh of an existing cube. If the target platform is Essbase, you must define the post-build script that will run on the cube. You may also define bind variables to limit the data source queries during the build

Figure 6.22 shows the Build Cube run control panel that is used to initiate the process to build the designated cube. To access this panel, select Build **>** Build Cube from the Cube Manager menu. To initiate the build, you must specify the Cube Template ID, the Business Unit, and the As Of Date fields on this panel. You then have the option to create or update the metadata or the data.

**FIGURE 6.21**   Cube Manager–Template PowerPlay folder

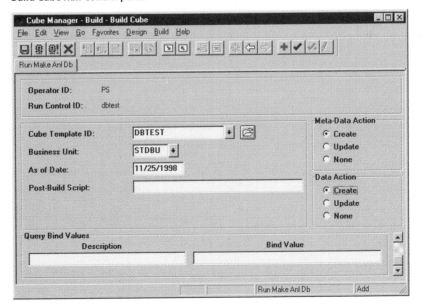

**FIGURE 6.22**   Build Cube Run Control panel

PART

II

PeopleTools

Let's examine a few troubleshooting tips that may help you when you have problems building a cube.

## Troubleshooting Problems with Cubes

No matter how well you have followed the procedures defined by PeopleSoft, when building your cube, errors may occur. The first place to check what went wrong with a build is the Process Monitor. Process Monitor may contain a message that can give you an idea of what may have happened.

The next step is the check the build log. This file is probably your best source of information on what occurred during the build process. This file can be found in the `temp` directory of your operating system. It is named `runcontrolid.log`. This file contains detailed information for each step performed during the build.

Verify that your Cube Manager settings are correct. Compare the settings you have with information contained in PeopleBooks, paying particular attention to platform-specific information.

Review the log files that are created by your OLAP tool. These logs will contain more specific information about the processes that occurred inside the build steps being performed by either Essbase or PowerPlay.

# Summary

PeopleSoft provides many data management tools that help you ensure the integrity of your database, perform conversions and transformations on your data, and move your data in and out of the database.

Data integrity tools include:

▶ SQL Alter, which verifies that the database tables are synchronized with the definitions defined in the Record Designer

▶ DDDAUDIT.SQR, an SQR report that validates the record definitions for tables, views, and indexes in the RDBMS

▶ SYSAUDIT.SQR, which searches for objects or code that refer to objects that no longer exist

Data Mover is a utility that updates database tables in your PeopleSoft system. The most common use of Data Mover is to load new data into your PeopleSoft System tables.

Import Manager helps you convert your data during implementation and can be used to validate data that you are importing against existing data already defined in your system.

Mass Change is a utility used for updating large amounts of data. Mass Change is particularly useful if the type of update you need to perform is required on a regular basis.

Transaction Set Editor (TSE) is a tool that provides PeopleSoft edits to non-PeopleSoft tables for use in high-volume batch processing. TSE is designed to work with batch COBOL processes and is specifically designed for use with tables that are not subject to the normal panel edits of the online PeopleSoft applications.

Cube Manager helps you create templates for designing, building, and updating OLAP cubes. These templates allow you to adapt quickly to field changes in your database or in your cube.

Chapter 7, "Development Tools," describes the tools that can be used by software developers to customize and enhance your PeopleSoft system.

PART

II

PeopleTools

# Development Tools

## FEATURING

▶ **APPLICATION DESIGNER**

▶ **BUSINESS PROCESS DESIGNER**

▶ **PEOPLECODE**

▶ **WEB APPLICATIONS**

▶ **APPLICATION ENGINE**

▶ **INTEGRATION TOOLS**

The development tools will be among the most commonly used components of your PeopleSoft system. As the system administrator, you need to have a good understanding of the development tools' functionality. You need to assist both developers and end users in troubleshooting problems that they encounter when using these tools. This chapter will not make you an expert at developing PeopleSoft applications, but you will become proficient enough to assist those who require support. Practical examples are provided to help you apply the functionality of these tools to real-life situations.

This chapter discusses the functionality of the most commonly used tools, beginning with the Application Designer. Other tools described in this chapter are the Business Process Designer, PeopleCode, Web applications, the Application Engine, and Integration tools.

**N O T E**   PeopleSoft uses the term "PeopleTools tables" to describe the database tables where information about the system is stored. This chapter sometimes refers to them as the "PeopleSoft system tables" to differentiate them from the system tables of the RDBMS.

# Application Designer

The Application Designer is the Integrated Development Environment (IDE) from PeopleSoft. The Application Designer is a new feature in PeopleSoft version 7 that incorporates the development tools that were separate in previous releases into one integrated, improved environment. To access the Application Designer, click the icon installed in the PeopleSoft group on the desktop or select Go **>** PeopleTools **>** Application Designer from any menu.

To understand how to use the Application Designer capabilities in your PeopleSoft environment, let's start with the component that is the basis of all PeopleSoft development: the record definition.

## Records

The first panel that you should become familiar with is the Record Definition Editor. This is your primary tool for defining PeopleSoft application tables. The definitions created in the Record Definition Editor are stored in the PeopleTools tables. In addition to defining tables, you can design views, dynamic views, working tables, and subrecords using the Record Definition Editor. You can also use the Record Definition Editor to define custom record definitions if you choose to add new functionality to your system.

The Record Definition window contains four panels that allow you to access various attributes of the existing fields: the Field Display, the Use Display, the Edits Display, and the PeopleCode Display. You move from one display to another by clicking on the icon in the toolbar or by selecting View and the desired display from the menu.

Let's describe some of the items found in the Record Definition Editor using the Field Display, illustrated in Figure 7.1. To access this panel, select File > Open and select the record type from the drop-down list. There are three ways to locate the desired record:

1. Enter the name of the desired record to access it directly.

2. Enter a partial record name to get a list of all records that begin with those characters.

3. Enter no information to get all the records and subrecords defined in your PeopleSoft system.

**FIGURE 7.1**    **Record Definition Editor–Field Display**

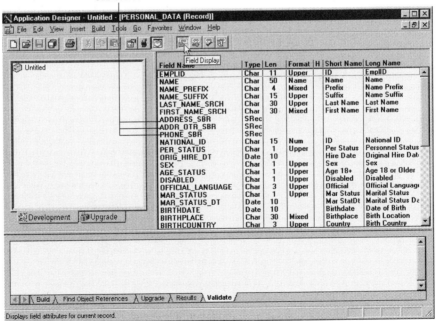

**N O T E**    Viewing the entire list of defined records will be slow if your PeopleSoft system contains a large number of records.

The Record Definition Editor allows you to define the fields to be used in your record definition. In the Field Display, simply select values that have been previously established, by you or by PeopleSoft, in the Field Definition Editor.

The Use Display of the Record Definition Editor, illustrated in Figure 7.2, allows you to set keys, define defaults, and specify whether a field is required or not.

**FIGURE 7.2**    Record Definition Editor–Use Display

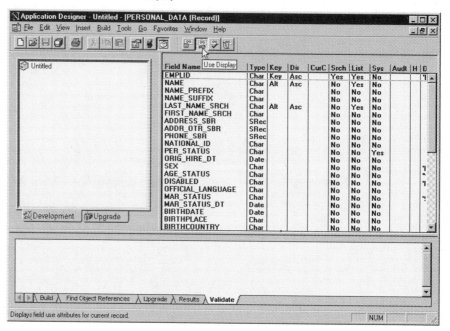

Figure 7.3 contains the Edits Display. The Edits Display allows you to determine the use of each field in the record, such as prompt table edits or translate table edits. Prompt table edits verify information in a field against a value in another table. For example, you cannot enter information about an employee unless that employee ID has been entered in the table you are prompting against.

**FIGURE 7.3**    Record Definition Editor–Edits Display

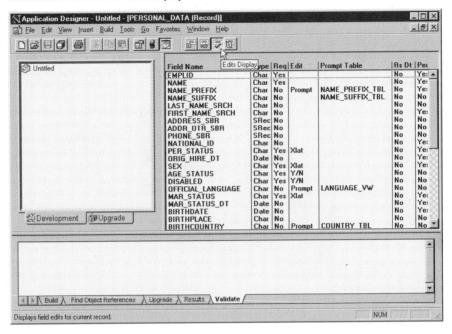

Translate values allow you to store information in the tables in a compact manner. The translate table is used to combine longer descriptions for fields throughout the system. The translate table also allows for concise storage in the system, with one full description being stored for each record. This table is used when there are no existing tables against which you can prompt the user for the description. For example, the ethnic group field from the personal data record uses the translate table to store the descriptions of all valid ethnic groups in your system. If the full meaning is needed, select the full description from the translate table, which is named XLATTABLE.

The PeopleCode Display, illustrated in Figure 7.4, depicts which PeopleCode has been added to each field. This display lists each field name. Each column lists a specific PeopleCode. The word "Yes" is displayed in the box if that PeopleCode exists for that field. PeopleCode is discussed in more detail later in this chapter.

## Subrecords

Note that the record definition in Figure 7.1 contains several subrecords, as the arrows in the figure illustrate. A subrecord is a convenient way for you to define, in one record definition, a particular set of data that may be used in multiple tables. Figure 7.5 contains a subrecord definition.

**FIGURE 7.4**   Record Definition Editor–PeopleCode Display

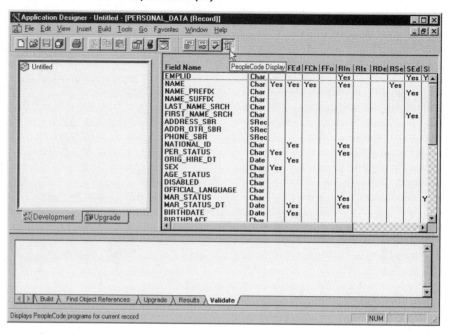

**FIGURE 7.5**   Subrecord definition

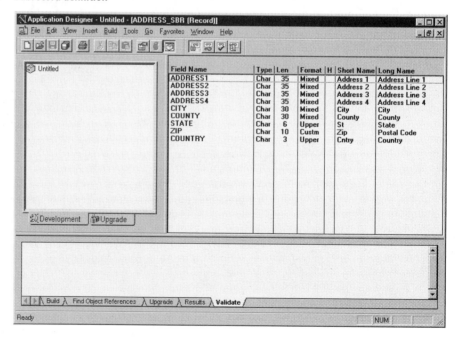

To add the subrecord to the record definitions where you need to use it, select Insert >
Subrecord from the menu. You are prompted for the name of the subrecord using the
familiar Open Object panel, illustrated in Figure 7.6.

**FIGURE 7.6**    Application Designer–Open Object panel

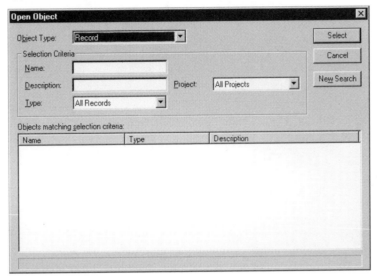

**NOTE**    The subrecord definition must be created and saved before it can be used in
other records.

**NOTE**    Subrecords are not created as independent tables in your database. The record
build process merges the subrecord definitions into one table for your database.

## SQL View

Another type of record definition that you can create is an SQL view, illustrated in
Figure 7.7. You create a custom SQL view to combine data from several tables so that
your end users can perform a query themselves. SQL views also allow you to perform a complicated join that cannot be accomplished using PeopleSoft Query.

PeopleTools

**FIGURE 7.7**    SQL view

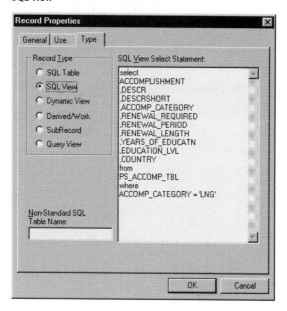

Create the SQL view record by defining the fields that you want to display in the initial record definition screen. Then select File **>** Object Properties from the menu. Select the radio button for the SQL view. The entry box where you enter the SQL view select statement for the new view appears. This statement is entered using standard SQL select criteria, listed in Figure 7.7. (View creation is described in Chapter 3, "Customization.")

The record definition cannot exist without the fields that make up the record. Let's examine in detail how to define your own fields in the system.

## Fields

The fields are defined using the Field Definition Editor. Figure 7.8 contains an example of a field defined in PeopleSoft. To open an existing record, select File **>** Open and select the field type from the drop-down list. You can also enter the first letters of the field name, which returns a shorter list from which to choose. Whichever you choose, you must select a specific field name to open the definition in the Field Definition Editor. If you are creating a new field, select File **>** New and select the field type from the drop-down list.

**FIGURE 7.8**    Field Definition Editor

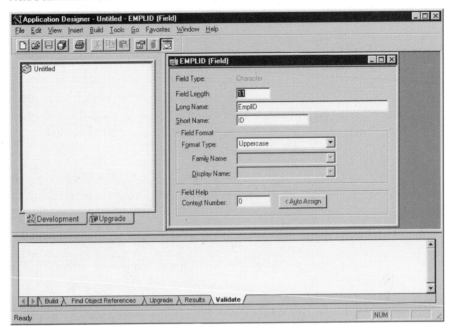

The Field Definition Editor allows you to define the properties of each field. Using the example in Figure 7.8, the following field characteristics are defined on this dialog box:

▶ The Field Type identifies the data type of the field being defined. This is specified at the time that you create the field. Many default attributes are initialized based on this value. In Figure 7.8, the Field Type is character.

▶ The Field Length is the maximum number of characters allowed in this field. In Figure 7.8, the Field Length is 11.

▶ The Long Name is used to specify a meaningful name for the field being defined. In Figure 7.8, the Long Name is EmplID.

▶ The Short Name is a concise name that is less than eight characters in length. In this example, the Short Name is ID.

▶ Under Field Format, the Format Type describes the final format of the field contents. Using the example in Figure 7.8, when this field is used in a panel, the data is converted to uppercase before storage and use. The Family Name and the Display Name are special fields that are used when defining custom fields. They allow you to set special formatting options for a custom field and they belong to format families. To define your own format family, select Tools **>** Miscellaneous Objects **>** Field Formats from the Application Designer menu. The Family Name specifies the family and the Display Name specifies the exact formatting option within that family.

▶ Define the Field Help, Context Number if you are creating a custom field and you want to generate a custom message when a user presses the F1 key. You can specify a number for this field or let the PeopleSoft system generate a number for you. This number refers to the message in the help file that you want to display when a user presses the F1 key.

The field formats that you define in the Field Definition Editor make developing applications much simpler when you begin to use the fields to define panels for your system.

## Panels

Panels are the user interface of your PeopleSoft system. The Panel Definition Editor is the tool with which you create new panels or modify the panels delivered by PeopleSoft. To access the Panel Definition Editor, select File **>** Open and select Panel from the Application Designer menu. If you are creating a new panel, select File **>** New and choose the panel type. Figure 7.9 contains a sample panel that shows most of the panel objects that are available with the Panel Definition Editor.

**FIGURE 7.9    Panel Definition Editor**

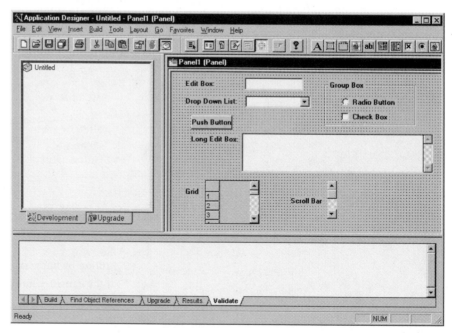

The most common objects found on a panel are the data entry and function controls. Figure 7.9 provides a visual representation of what the objects described in the following subsections will look like when used in a panel.

**N O T E** A detailed description of all panel objects is contained in the PeopleTools People-Book, Development Tools section.

## Data Entry Controls

The data entry controls are used to gather information from the user. They include:

▶ Edit boxes, which allow the user to enter information into the defined field.

▶ Drop-down lists, which allow a user to select information from a predetermined set of choices.

▶ Radio buttons, which also allow selection from a list of predetermined choices. Radio buttons occur in groups and only one can be selected at a time.

▶ Check boxes, which allow the user to turn a value on or off. Check boxes usually correspond to yes or no values.

## Function Controls

Function controls provide the user with the means to initiate some action. Function controls include:

▶ Command buttons, which activate Field Change PeopleCode for specified objects.

▶ Process buttons, which are used to activate a process using the Process Scheduler.

▶ Scroll bars, which allow the user to access data sequentially. Scroll bars are most often used to display effective date information from child records when using the parent record.

▶ Grid controls, which present the data to a user in a spreadsheet-like manner. Grid controls are used to display multiple occurrences of small amounts of information.

Panel objects must be linked to a record definition by filling in the information contained in the Panel Field Properties panel for the Panel Definition Editor, as shown

PART

II

PeopleTools

in Figure 7.10. To access the Panel Field Properties panel, right-click the panel object that you have defined in the Panel Definition Editor.

**FIGURE 7.10**   Panel Field Properties panel

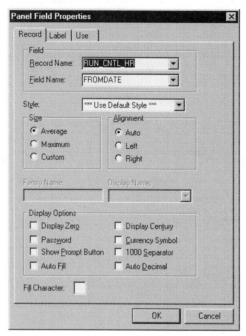

The properties that you can configure are found under the Record, Label, and Use tabs.

▶ The Record tab is where you define the record and field for the object.

▶ The Label tab is where you define the text that you want to display on the panel next to the object.

▶ The Use tab allows you to define the behavior of the object. The properties that can be defined vary with object type but may include such items as "hidden" or "display only."

The most common use of the Panel Definition Editor by the system administrator will be for troubleshooting once your system is in production. You can also use this functionality for developing customizations during your implementation. You can use the field properties to help you determine where the data is originating and identify any behaviors that have been established. To accomplish this, right-click the object that you want more information about and select Object Properties to display the Panel Field Properties panel. This panel will contain the record and field that is designated to hold the data for this panel field.

Once you have defined your panels, you may want to group similar panels into panel groups to allow your users to access the information more easily. You create and edit panel groups using the Application Designer. Let's look at panel groups in more detail.

## Panel Groups

Panel groups are used to collect transactions into logical groupings. You should include all parts of a single business transaction in a single panel group. The Panel Group Definition must be defined before a menu item can be added to access a panel that you have created.

Figure 7.11 contains the Panel Group Definition panel with the PERSONAL_DATA panel group from PeopleSoft HRMS displayed. In this panel, notice that two panels are associated with the group PERSONAL_DATA: PERSONAL_DATA_1 and PERSONAL_DATA_2.

PART

II

PeopleTools

**FIGURE 7.11**  **Panel Group Definition panel**

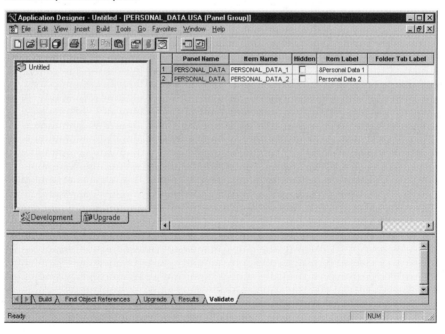

Use the Panel Group Definition panel to hide panels that you are not using while still leaving them associated with the panel group. By grouping the panels together, the tabs at the top of the window allow for easy selection of any panel in a panel group. An example of multiple panels in a group is shown in Figure 7.12. Notice that there is a tab for each Installation Table Panel.

**FIGURE 7.12**     **Panel group with multiple panels displayed**

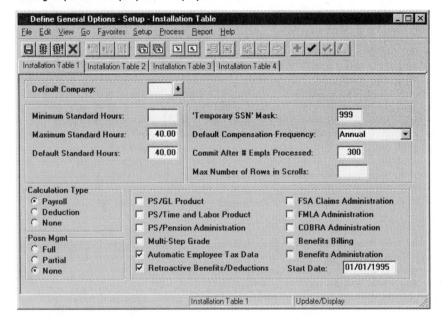

There are two important considerations when working with panel groups:

**1.** *All* panels *must* belong to a panel group.

**2.** When using multiple panels in a panel group, saving the record saves all the data on all panels, even if multiple records are involved.

## Menus

All panels and panel groups are accessed from menus. Let's look at the PeopleSoft menu definition.

PeopleSoft defines two types of menus: standard and pop-up. The most common menu is the standard menu, which allows you to create access to the panel groups that you have defined. When customizing your PeopleSoft system, I recommend that you create a custom menu to access your panel groups. At our company, we add a custom report menu item to those modules for which we have created our own reports.

Figure 7.13 contains an example of a menu design window. In this figure, the MANAGE_HUMAN_RESOURCES_[U.S.] menu definition is displayed.

**FIGURE 7.13** Menu design window

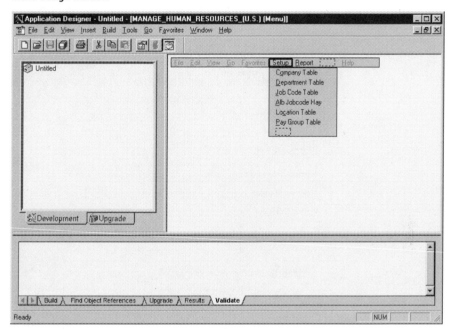

To add a menu item under the Setup menu bar label, for example, double-click the empty box represented by the dotted line under Pay Group Table. The Menu Item Properties panel appears, as shown in Figure 7.14.

**FIGURE 7.14** Menu Item Properties panel

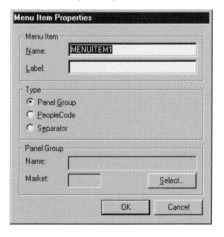

To add a new menu bar label, double-click the empty box to the right of the Report menu bar label in Figure 7.13 and fill in the Menu Item Properties panel as shown in Figure 7.14.

Occasionally, you might want to create an action that operates interactively with the end user and that is based on data in a single field. Create a pop-up menu for this purpose. The pop-up menu is used to execute PeopleCode or transfer to another panel when the user performs a right-click the panel field that has a pop-up menu associated with it. An example of the pop-up menu used in PeopleSoft is allowing the user to update information in the Electronic Data Interchange (EDI) panels from a panel field, which opens the pop-up menu for the user to initiate additional action.

**N O T E**   The pop-up menu is used infrequently in PeopleSoft HRMS. PeopleSoft delivers only 12 pop-up menus with version 7.5.

# Projects

The best enhancement in the new IDE from PeopleSoft is the project. Projects allow you to capture all the modifications from one programming effort into a single project that can then be easily migrated from your test database to your production database. The Project Definition window in Figure 7.15 contains the HR7UPG project. The Tree view is open as represented by the open folder in the left pane. The Upgrade tab in the lower pane displays the Upgrade Object type (note the window title).

To create a new project, select File **>** New and select the project type. Select Tools **>** Options to open the panel shown in Figure 7.16. This panel allows you to set the behavior of the project.

There are three basic options when setting the behavior of the project:

**1.** Add all objects to the project that you open, whether or not you modify them.

**2.** Add all modified objects to the project as you save them. (This is the real strength of the project concept in PeopleSoft.)

**3.** Manually add all objects to the project.

I recommend that you use the second option whenever possible. This allows you to automatically add any object to which you made a modification. The first option tends to add too many objects to a project, since it adds objects that you open whether you decide to modify them or not. The third option is too time-consuming.

**FIGURE 7.15**    Project Definition window

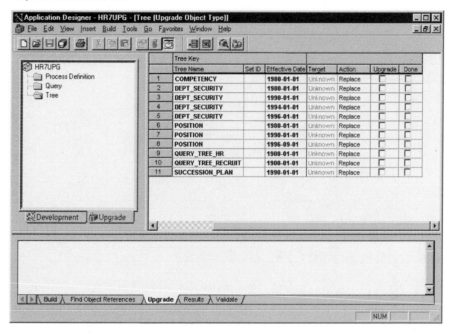

**FIGURE 7.16**    Project Options–Project tab

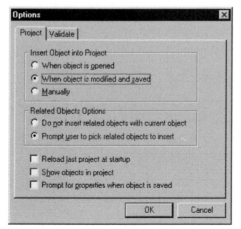

On this same panel, you can specify whether you want related objects added to the project. You can also specify that you want the project to reload at startup. Developers involved in a big project may find this useful.

To validate three-tier execution, Web client execution, or project integrity, select the Validate tab, shown in Figure 7.17.

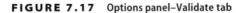

**FIGURE 7.17**    Options panel–Validate tab

# Business Process Designer

The fundamental part of automating your environment is defining the business processes that you want to automate. PeopleSoft provides the Business Process Designer to allow you to capture your processes in a graphical format. This tool allows you to connect various business activities into a single, defined process. The business activities can then be connected using workflow. Using the Navigator function, the end user can use the business process maps created by the Business Process Designer to graphically follow the business process flow through the system.

## Designing Processes

PeopleSoft provides a graphical design tool for assisting in the design of your business processes: a business process map. Figure 7.18 contains an example of a business process map for Human Resources that is delivered with your PeopleSoft system.

This map shows many business processes that are delivered by PeopleSoft, including Administer Training, Manage Competencies, Monitor Health and Safety, Plan Salaries, etc. This map can be used by your end users as a map of how business processes can be designed using your PeopleSoft system. As system administrator, you can control which items on this map your users are authorized to view.

The next item that the end user sees when using Navigator to execute a process is the actual business process itself. Figure 7.19 shows the Administer Training business process that was chosen from the Human Resources business map in Figure 7.18. To access the Navigator Display, select View > Navigator Display when you have any application panel open. Navigator is not accessible when using PeopleTools objects.

**FIGURE 7.18**    Business process map

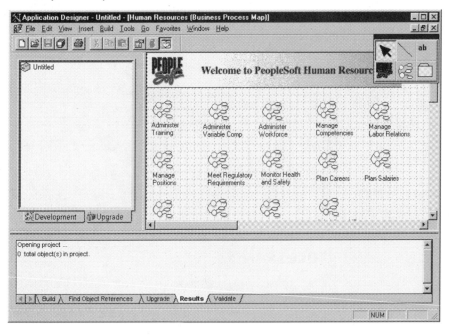

**FIGURE 7.19**    Administer Training business process

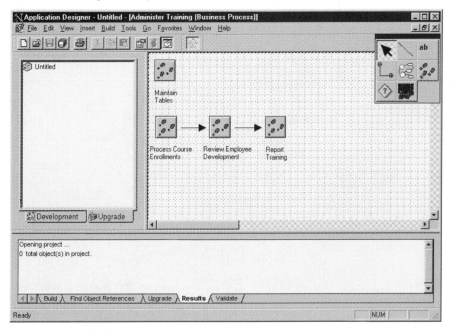

**PeopleTools**

PeopleSoft defines a business process as a complete business task that contains one or more business activities. Figure 7.20 shows the Process Course Enrollments business activity from the Administer Training business process.

**FIGURE 7.20**    Administer Training, Process Course Enrollments business activity

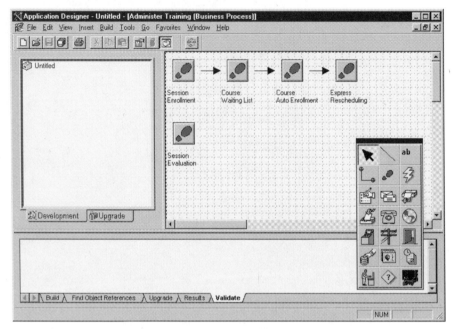

Business activities represent individual steps or groups of steps that together make up the business process. In Figure 7.20, the first activity to be performed is Session Enrollment. You then move sequentially to each step necessary to complete the Process Course Enrollments activity. Business activities can also be decision points, workflow routings, or approvals that have no application panels associated with them.

## Workflow

Workflow can be thought of as a combination of business processes that require multiple workers to complete a task and the flow of data between those workers. A combination of panels, records, e-mail, database agents, and message agents are used to enable the workflow that you design.

The first step in building your automated workflow is to capture the process in a graphical way. The typical process consists of access to one or more panels or panel groups to complete. Two examples of workflow are hiring a new employee or processing a purchase order.

## Components of Workflow

The components that make up a PeopleSoft workflow are as follows:

**Rules**   PeopleSoft defines rules as those actions that are required to process your business data.

**Roles**   Roles help you direct the process to specific types of people rather than to individuals.

**Routings**   Routings are the processes that connect the workflow together. They are used to specify how an action item is connected to the processes that make up your workflow.

## Using the Tools of Workflow

The tools of workflow include the Application Designer, which was discussed earlier in this chapter, and the Workflow Processor. Workflow Processor is the name People-Soft uses to refer to several online agents or tools that are used to create, modify, and administer workflow processes.

Workflow has several components: worklists, message agents, message definitions, database agents, application agents, and the Workflow Administrator.

**Worklists**   A worklist is an ordered list of tasks that need to be accomplished. Worklists are not agents but they are the basis for all action in a workflow.

**Message Agents**   Message agents allow you to extend access to PeopleSoft without installing an application for all users. Typically, a message agent takes data from a form and enters it into the system by automatically accessing the panel that a user has to use to accomplish a particular task. The PeopleSoft message agent is a Tuxedo service that runs on your application server beginning with PeopleSoft version 7.5.

**Message Definitions**   A message definition is used to define the mapping between the electronic document and the PeopleSoft panel fields where data is being entered using the message agent process.

**Database Agents**   Database agents are created to allow for automated triggering of workflow events. This allows you to automate processes in the workflow that normally require user intervention. Such processes might include, for example, a user having to run a query to determine overdue invoices or employees who need to update benefits information.

Database agents monitor tables in the database using queries to determine if a specified change has been made. When changes are made, the database agent triggers an action by the message agent.

PART

II

PeopleTools

**NOTE**   Database agents must have message agents defined to work properly. Beginning with PeopleSoft version 7.5, database agents must run in three-tier mode, since message agents are implemented through Tuxedo. See Chapter 5, "Application Tools," for more information about the three-tier architecture and Tuxedo.

Database agents are run on a periodic basis through the Process Scheduler, which is covered in more detail in Chapter 5, "Administration Tools." The Process Scheduler allows you to determine how often you want the database agent to execute and search for work.

**Application Agents**   Application agents monitor the data that is entered to determine if business rules have been triggered. If so, the agent then identifies which role has been defined to act on the condition that has been triggered. The work is then routed to the worklist of the person or group fulfilling that role. Application agents are triggered by the PeopleCode that is associated with a panel event, such as saving the panel.

**NOTE**   PeopleCode is discussed in more detail later in this chapter.

**Workflow Administrator**   The final component of the workflow system is the Workflow Administrator, which allows you to perform the following tasks:

- ▶ Control all aspects of workflow.
- ▶ Control the definition of rules.
- ▶ Control the assignment of individual users to roles.
- ▶ Communicate with workflow users.
- ▶ Schedule agents to run and monitor the flow of work through the system.

To access the Workflow Administrator, select Go > PeopleTools > Workflow Administrator. Figure 7.21 contains the Workflow Administrator panel.

The Workflow Administrator panel allows you to establish and manage your workflow processes. Figure 7.21 shows all the items under the Use menu. You can define:

- ▶ Approval rules
- ▶ Report delivery
- ▶ Roles
- ▶ Route controls

▶ Worklist e-mail

▶ Worklists

Let's look at how you can automate your business processes with the options available using the Workflow Administrator tools.

**FIGURE 7.21**    Workflow Administrator panel

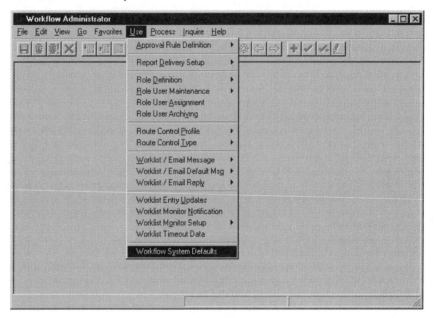

## Automating Processes

This section discusses how to automate processes using the workflow tools. The first step in automating the workflow is to create a message definition.

### Creating Message Definitions

To create a new business process, select File > New from the Application Designer. An empty Business Process Designer window appears, along with the Business Process palette. Select the object type that best fits the type of process you are trying to create. For example, to create a process for managing the flow of incoming electronic forms, place the InForm icon into the window, as shown in Figure 7.22. (The arrow in Figure 7.22 points to the InForm icon on the Business Process palette.)

PART

II

PeopleTools

**FIGURE 7.22**    Business Process Designer–InForm icon

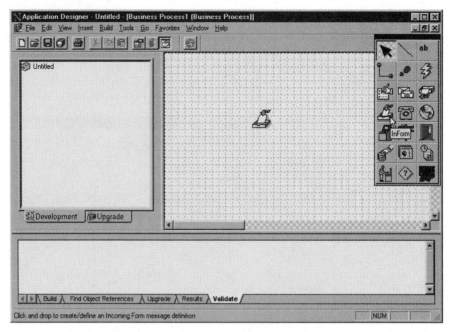

You are now ready to define the message agent definition for this process. Right-click the new business process icon you created. The Message Agent Definition panel appears, as illustrated in Figure 7.23.

**FIGURE 7.23**    Message Agent Definition panel

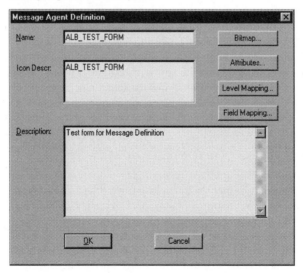

The following fields must be specified when you create the message agent definition:

**Name**   Enter a unique name for this process.

**Icon description**   Enter the label that you want to be visible in the business process when it is viewed using Navigator.

**Description**   Enter a description of this process's functionality.

**Bitmap**   If you click this button, you can specify a different icon to represent this object in the Business Process Designer.

**Attributes**   The attributes are the first step in mapping the electronic document to the panel. In the Message Agent Form Attributes panel, illustrated in Figure 7.24, you specify the Target Panel Group, Menu Name, Bar Name, Item Name, Action Name, and Search Record. When the attributes are for an electronic form, there are additional form attributes to specify. The Reply Method allows the message agent to automatically reply when the form has been processed or has errors. You probably want to select the Reply option for the When OK radio buttons. This specifies that the user be notified when that form has been satisfactorily processed. You can also select the Forward option for the When Error radio button. If an error occurs, this specifies that a message be forwarded to the originator that contains the original data submitted with the error.

**FIGURE 7.24**   Message Agent Form Attributes panel

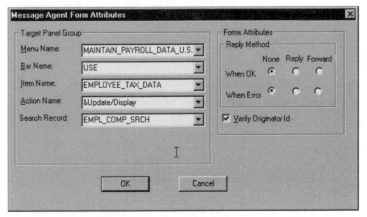

**Level mapping**   Level mapping allows you to control how the message agent handles fields that are at different scroll levels. If scroll levels are present, the record is displayed in the Record Hierarchy window of the Map Level Options panel, as shown in Figure 7.25. Highlight each record and set the desired action for when a row is found and for when a row is not found. You must set this for *each record* in the record hierarchy. The Delete Remaining Rows check box causes the message agent to remove any rows at scroll levels for which the external application or form does not provide data. The Output All Occurrences check box causes the message agent to return all rows from a scroll level. The external application must be capable of handling multiple rows; this option is *only* available for level 1 scroll bars. For example, PeopleSoft returns all the courses in which a student is enrolled.

**FIGURE 7.25**    Map Level Options panel

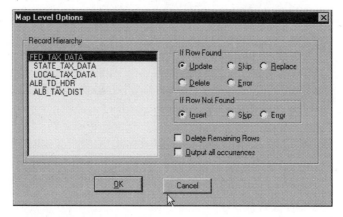

**Field mapping**    Field mapping is where the relationship between the data in the external application or form and PeopleSoft fields is defined. When creating a new message definition, you see a blank window to which you must add fields. Select the Add button to reveal the Map Field panel, illustrated in Figure 7.26. You must map the fields in the order of the key fields on the PeopleSoft record at each scroll level. Enter the external field name in the Field Name box, then select the record and field from the Value group. Do this for each field in your incoming electronic data. These records and fields are from the defined search records for your message definition. The Map Mode and Map When boxes are generally left with the default values of Copy and Input. You only change these values if the external application can handle output from the message agent.

When you click OK, the field that you just entered appears in the Message Agent Field Map panel, illustrated in Figure 7.27. This dialog box lists all the fields that you have mapped for the message agent process. You can also tell if the process is using just the value or displaying the translate value for a field; the example in Figure 7.27 is just using Copy. You can also see if this field is defined for input, output, or both with regard to data transfer. In this example, the field accepts input data only.

**FIGURE 7.26** Map Field panel

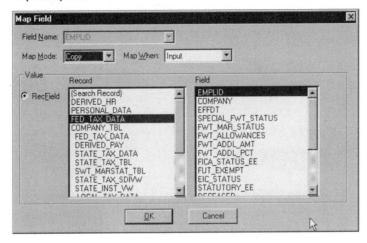

**FIGURE 7.27** Message Agent Field Map panel

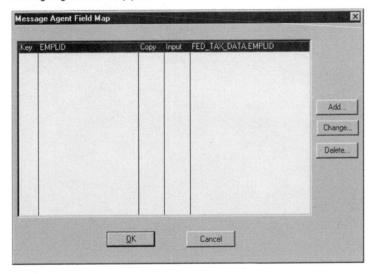

## Workflow Panels

Workflow panels are used to add the PeopleCode necessary to handle the workflow routings and actions. You must add workflow panels to the panel group that you are creating a workflow for. There are two workflow panels that are required by any panel group that uses the Virtual Approver or Virtual Router: WF_FUNCTIONS_01 and APPR_WRK_01.

You must add the appropriate workflow PeopleCode to a record that is being updated in the panel group that you are accessing. Specific information regarding workflow PeopleCode is described in the section on PeopleCode later in this chapter.

## Workflow Records

Workflow records are record definitions that are created to hold the worklist data until it has been processed. They are created just as you create any other record definition. Workflow records have workflow PeopleCode associated with them.

## Creating a Database Agent

Create the database agent in much the same way that you create message definitions. Insert the database agent icon into the Business Process Designer. Right-click the icon to open the Message Agent Definition panel, illustrated in Figure 7.28.

**FIGURE 7.28**    Message Agent Definition panel

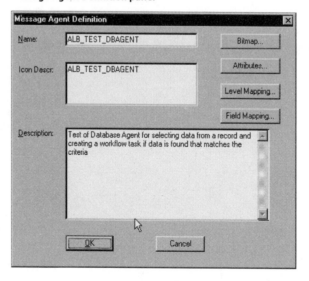

Enter all the information as discussed in the previous sections on creating message definitions. The major difference on this panel is the Attributes button. Click the Attributes button to get the Message Attributes panel shown in Figure 7.29. A new field appears; the Query Name field is the query that the database agent will be using. Note in Figure 7.29 that the Query Name is preceded by "[DBAG]" for database agent. This list box only allows you to select workflow queries for use by the database agent.

The query in this example, Monitor WL, must be defined before you create the database agent. Monitor WL is a workflow query created by someone with the authority to create workflow queries. As a result of this query, data is inserted into the record you defined and into its record definition. The panel and record must contain workflow PeopleCode in order for the workflow process to function properly.

**N O T E**   Chapter 8, "End-User Tools," contains a discussion of workflow queries.

**FIGURE 7.29**    Message Attributes panel–database agent

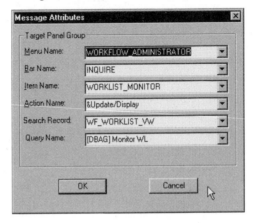

The message agent definition that is created as part of the database agent is what allows the message agent to perform its task. The database agent itself cannot perform any task other than executing the query that returns data for use by the message agent. Let's look at how to automate the execution of database agents.

## Running Database Agents with Process Scheduler

Define a Process Scheduler definition for each database agent that you create. The process definition controls how the database agent operates and is created just like any other process definition. After creating the process definition, create a run control panel that you can assign to a PeopleSoft menu to allow you to run the database agent.

**N O T E**   Creating process definitions is discussed in more detail in Chapter 5, "Administration Tools."

## Advanced Routing

PeopleSoft provides some advanced routing options to allow you to define a complex workflow process without using PeopleCode.

Route controls are used in conjunction with role definitions to allow you to define routing options more easily. The route controls allow you to assign an additional value that associates the data in your application to a role definition. This prevents you from having to design complex queries for routing workflow tasks.

First, create a route control type that is based on any prompt table value that you want. Figure 7.30 contains an example of a route control type definition.

**FIGURE 7.30**   Route Control Type panel

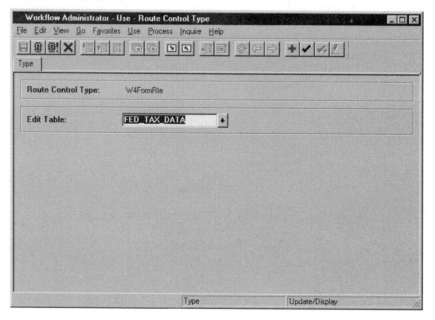

After creating the route control type, create a route control profile that is used to assign a value or range of values for each specific route control type defined in your system. Figure 7.31 contains an example of a route control profile.

**FIGURE 7.31**   Route Control Profile panel

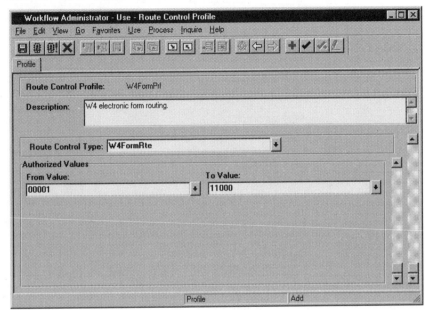

Route control roles give you the flexibility to have a dynamic query that is not hard-coded for use in your workflow. You pass bind values to the query at runtime. This allows you to change the behavior of the workflow by changing the values of your bind variables without having to update the PeopleCode or other workflow definitions in your business process.

## Virtual Approver

The Virtual Approver allows you to automatically approve those workflow tasks that use predefined processing rules. The business rules are defined in the approval rules table, allowing you to use the Virtual Approver and Virtual Router instead of writing complicated PeopleCode to perform the approval.

Workflow rules are defined using the Workflow Administrator. To access the rules definition panel, select Use > Approval Rule Definition > Step from the Workflow Administrator menu. Figure 7.32 contains an example of an approval rule definition.

**FIGURE 7.32**   Approval Rule Definition panel–Steps tab

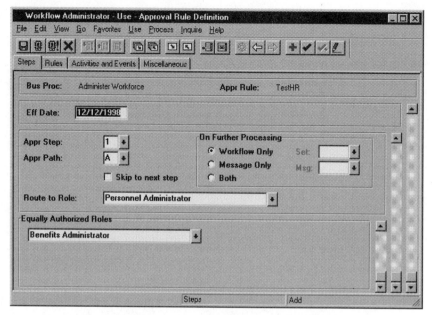

Specify the following options on the Approval Rule Definition panel:

**Bus Proc**   This field is the name of the business process for which you are creating the approval rule.

**Appr Rule**   This field is the name for the approval rule set that you are creating.

**Eff Date**   This field is the effective date for the approval rule set.

**Appr Step, Appr Path**   These fields should contain the approval steps and paths that are required by your approval rule definition.

**Route To Role**   This field is the role that processes the step.

**Equally Authorized Roles**   This field contains the roles that are authorized to process transactions.

**Skip To Next Step**   Check this box if the step can be skipped if further approval is required.

**On Further Processing**   Under this heading, you specify the response to the user if further approval is required. The default is to send a message to the user and trigger the business process event that has been defined. Enter approval authority for each user that can approve the business process.

Now you are ready to move on to the next panel used in creating the approval rule definition, the Activities and Events tab, shown in Figure 7.33. The options on this tab are as follows:

▶ The Pre-Approved Activity/Event specifies the action to take when the user approves the request.

▶ The Deny Activity/Event specifies the action to take if the request or transaction is denied.

▶ The Recycle Activity/Event specifies the action to take if the request is sent back to the previous step.

If any of these events are left blank, no automatic processes will occur; the status will change but no routing will occur.

**FIGURE 7.33**    Approval Rule Definition panel–Activities and Events tab

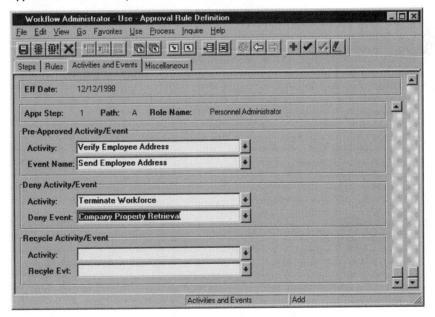

The final panel in the approval rule definition process is the Miscellaneous tab, shown in Figure 7.34.

**FIGURE 7.34**   Approval Rule Definition panel–Miscellaneous tab

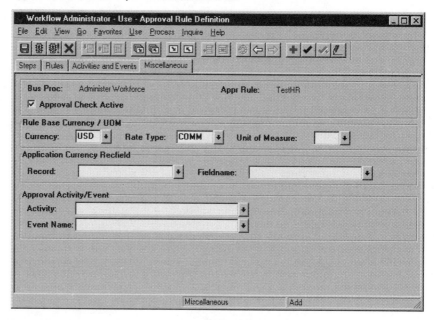

The options you can take on the Miscellaneous tab are:

▶ Enter the unit of measure (UOM) for the approval.

▶ Enter the event to be triggered upon approval.

▶ Suspend the use of this approval rule by removing the check next to the Approval Check Active check box.

**TIP**   The Virtual Approver makes extensive use of the roles for organizational levels. It is important that you verify that the roles match the structure of your company for accurate approval to occur. The roles are administered using the Workflow Administrator panels.

# Administering Workflow

There are several tasks that you need to perform to keep your workflow processes operating. First, you need to activate the workflow defaults.

## Activating Workflow Defaults

There are several defaults that you need to activate for your workflow system. To access the Workflow System Defaults panel, illustrated in Figure 7.35, select Use **>** Workflow System Defaults from the Workflow Administrator menu.

**FIGURE 7.35**   Workflow System Defaults panel

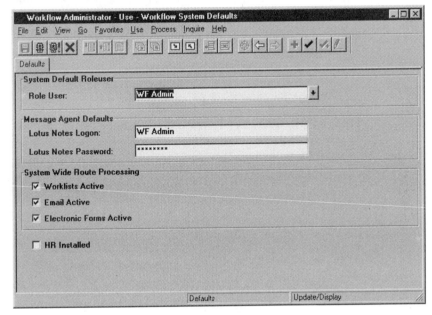

PART

II

PeopleTools

The options on the Workflow System Defaults panel are as follows:

▶ You must set a System Default Roleuser, especially if you are using query roles. This user receives any workflow tasks for which the system cannot determine the proper recipient. The person assigned to administer the workflow processes is the most likely candidate. This person should be knowledgeable about the PeopleSoft workflow process and should have the capability to correct the role that contains no role user.

**WARNING**   The System Default Roleuser must have a valid PeopleSoft operator ID, an e-mail address, and an electronic forms address. Otherwise, an error will be received by the application agent process.

▶ Under Message Agent Defaults, specify a user name and password for the message agent to access Lotus Notes if you are using Lotus Notes in your system.

▶ The System Wide Route Processing check boxes allow you to suspend the routing of a particular route type.

▶ Check the box next to HR Installed to specify if you are using PeopleSoft HRMS. If you are, checking this box allows the system to identify a role user's manager from the Personal Data table.

## Defining Roles

You must assign users to roles in order for them to receive work to process in their worklist. There are two basic types of roles: list roles and query roles.

**List Roles**   List roles are used when you want the same user or group of users to act on a task. The users are assigned to the roles and the work is routed to their worklist. You can define list roles as follows:

▷ List roles that let the first user select the task to complete it

▷ Simultaneous routing where multiple users act on a task at the same time

▷ List roles where only a single individual is assigned to carry out the task

**Query Roles**   Query roles are generated dynamically at runtime. Query roles are used when you want to make routing decisions based on information in the panel or based on who entered the data. For example, when an employee creates an expense voucher, it should be routed to his/her manager. The query role uses the results of a query to determine who that employee's manager is and then routes the expense voucher to the appropriate manager's worklist.

To define roles using the Workflow Administrator, select Use > Role Definition > Add from the menu. Enter a name for the role and click OK. The Role Definition panel appears (see Figure 7.36).

The following options are available on the Role Definition panel:

▶ Specify the Role Type as either a list or query role.

▶ Enter the list of role users or the role query name.

▶ Enter information in the Description field that describes what the role does and the type of user that will generally fill the role.

**FIGURE 7.36**    Role Definition panel

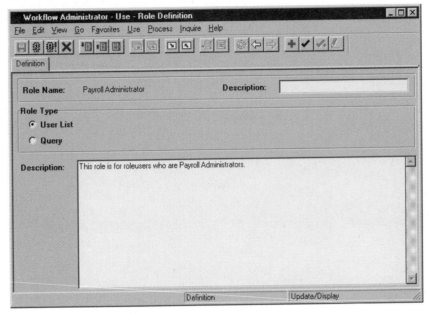

## Creating Workflow Messages

Workflow messages allow you to communicate information to your workflow users via e-mail or via their worklist. Create a default message that lists the users that you commonly send messages to. This prevents you from having to select each user individually each time you send a message.

To define a default message, select Use > Worklist/Email Default Message > Add from the Workflow Administrator menu. Figure 7.37 contains the Worklist / Email Default Msg panel.

The following options are available on the Worklist / Email Default Msg panel:

- ▶ Add a descriptive name for the message.

- ▶ Enter as much or little text as you want for the default message.

- ▶ Specify whether the message will be sent via e-mail or via a worklist.

To send ad hoc messages, select Use > Worklist/Email Message > Add from the Workflow Administrator menu. The panel that is displayed looks similar to the one for the default message shown in Figure 7.37.

**FIGURE 7.37**    Worklist / Email Default Msg panel

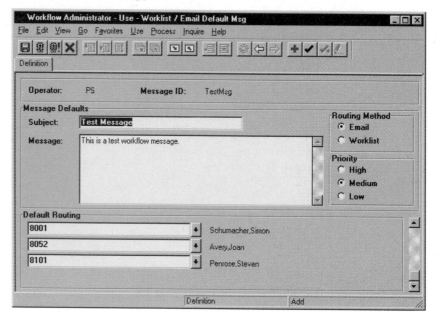

## Starting Workflow Agents

Although you define your workflow agents in the Process Scheduler process definition panels, you must still submit the jobs to the Process Scheduler. Designate when and how often the agents will be executed. All database agents must be scheduled in this manner. Schedule the application that looks for incoming forms from Lotus Notes, if you are using Lotus Notes. Schedule the execution of the predefined workflow monitoring agents that were delivered with your application.

The predefined workflow monitoring agents can be found under the Process menu item in Workflow Administrator. Chapter 8, "End-User Tools," describes how to submit jobs to the Process Scheduler.

Now that you understand workflow, let's take a closer look at PeopleCode, which is used extensively throughout your system.

# PeopleCode

PeopleCode is the structured programming language that is proprietary to People-Soft. PeopleCode is used to add new functionality to your PeopleSoft system by adding actions to an object that are carried out when certain events happen to the object.

# Implementations

All PeopleCode must be associated with both an object and an event. In PeopleSoft version 7 and higher, there are two classes of object for which you can define People-Code: records and menus. They are referred to as record PeopleCode and menu PeopleCode.

## Record PeopleCode

Record PeopleCode is defined on fields in a record definition. The code is not associated with the field but with the record field. In other words, any PeopleCode that you associate with a field is valid only in the record in which it is defined, not in all the records where the field is used.

PeopleSoft now uses the term "record field" to distinguish between the stand-alone field definition and the definition of a field as it is used in a record. In PeopleSoft 6 and earlier, record PeopleCode was referred to as "PeopleCode types." Beginning with version 7, PeopleSoft refers to these PeopleCode types as "record field events" or "People-Code events."

Some examples of events that can have record PeopleCode associated with them are RowInit, RowInsert, RowDelete, SaveEdit, and WorkFlow.

The record field events used in PeopleSoft are as follows:

▶ FieldDefault is used to set the default value of a field when it is displayed.

▶ FieldEdit is used to validate the contents of a field. FieldEdit is used to supplement the edits already on the field.

▶ FieldChange is used to recalculate panel values or change the formatting of the panel based on the change entered in the field.

▶ FieldFormula is an older event that was used to execute the PeopleCode on all the records and fields in the panel buffer. The FieldFormula event is being phased out by the RowInit and FieldChange events.

▶ RowInit is used to update panel group control each time a new data row is encountered.

▶ RowInsert is used when you want to apply some actions to a new row of data. The RowInit event is then triggered so do not use PeopleCode that is contained in RowInit in your RowInsert; it will be executed twice.

PART

II

PeopleTools

▶ RowDelete is used to apply actions to the deletion of a row of data. One application of the RowDelete event is to update a field that calculates a total on a panel that is dynamic based on multiple entries.

▶ RowSelect is an older PeopleCode event that can be used to filter data being presented. RowSelect is very inefficient because all of the data has to be sent to the client. Using search records and effective dates can provide much of the functionality of RowSelect.

▶ SaveEdit is triggered when the user attempts to save a record. SaveEdit is used to validate data in a panel group. Use SaveEdit also when saving a panel group with multiple panels; use FieldEdit when a panel group containing a single panel is saved.

▶ SavePreChange is used to provide one last validation or action point before the data is actually saved. SavePreChange events occur only after the SaveEdit event has completed successfully.

▶ SavePostChange is used to update tables that are not in the current panel group. This event executes after the successful database transaction has occurred.

▶ SearchInit is used to process events at the beginning of a search dialog. You can programmatically set key values for the search dialog using SearchInit events.

▶ SearchSave can be used to limit the amount of data returned in a search dialog by forcing the user to enter at least one key value. SearchSave can be very useful when searching tables that contain large amounts of data.

▶ WorkFlow is used when you want to trigger a workflow event. The WorkFlow event occurs just after the SavePreChange event.

▶ PrePopUp is used to execute code just before the display of a pop-up menu. PrePopUp can control the appearance of the pop-up menu.

## Menu PeopleCode

Menu PeopleCode is defined for menu items in a menu definition. Menu PeopleCode consists of a single event—ItemSelected. This means that any menu PeopleCode that has been created is executed when the user selects that menu item. For example, if you add menu PeopleCode to the Hire Workforce menu item, the PeopleCode executes before the panel group is processed. You can use menu PeopleCode to preload variables in a panel. Menu PeopleCode is not used much in PeopleSoft HRMS.

**N O T E**    The actual PeopleCode is not stored in the record or menu definitions. All PeopleCode is stored in binary format in the table PSPCMPROG.

## Workflow PeopleCode

There are three workflow-specific PeopleCode procedures that are used to activate events in the workflow process. These procedures, described in the following list, are executed after the panel has been saved:

**TriggerBusinessEvent**    This procedure must be used in every workflow People-Code program. There are three parameters required to activate a business event for workflow: the business process (BUSPROCESS), the business activity (BUSACTIVITY), and the business event (BUSEVENT). These three parameters must be included in the TriggerBusinessEvent PeopleCode.

The syntax for this procedure is:

```
TriggerBusinessEvent(BUSPROCESS."Business Process Name", BUSACTIVITY.
"Business Activity Name", BUSEVENT."Business Event Name").
```

You must use the actual names of the process, activity, and event and they must be enclosed in quotation marks.

**GetWLFieldValue**    This procedure returns the value from a field in the current worklist record. You must specify the field_name as a parameter when using this procedure.

**MarkWLItemWorked**    This procedure marks a worklist entry as worked when you access the panel group designated by the process. There are no parameters for this procedure.

You may want to use the following system variables in your workflow PeopleCode program:

**%BPName**    This variable identifies the business process you are currently working with. If the process was not opened from a worklist, this variable is blank.

**%MessageAgent**    This variable identifies a message definition when the message agent opens a panel. This function is useful if you want different functionality when the message agent opens a panel instead of a user.

**%WLInstanceID**    This variable identifies the instance number of the item you are currently working with. If the process was not opened from a worklist, this variable is blank.

**%WLName**    This variable identifies the worklist that you are processing a worklist item from. If the process was not opened from a worklist, this variable is blank.

# Application Processor

The Application Processor is the PeopleTools runtime engine. The Application Processor controls the processing that occurs with an application. Let's look at the flow of events through the Application Processor.

Looking at it from a high level, the Application Processor performs all the default processing required to populate the default panel, performs the RowInit event, and displays the returned data when a user requests a panel.

A more detailed examination reveals that the Application Processor looks for any blank fields in the panel or panel group, determines if there is default information defined for the field, and applies it. All rows of data in the panel group are processed in the same manner.

The RowInit event is triggered and if the user made the request in update mode, the SearchInit event is executed to determine if there are any restrictions on the key values that can be entered by the user.

The Application Processor also handles all the processing that occurs when the user changes data and elects to save it. The flow of these events was described in the "Record PeopleCode" section earlier in this chapter.

# PeopleCode Language

PeopleCode is the structured programming language used by PeopleSoft. It is similar to other structured programming languages with a few special features. You can access PeopleTools objects using special functions without having to hard-code the object name in your program. This section describes the PeopleCode language syntax.

## Data Types

A discussion of any structured programming language begins with the supported data types. The following data types are supported by PeopleCode:

- ▶ STRING
- ▶ NUMBER
- ▶ BOOLEAN

▶ DATE

▶ DATETIME

▶ TIME

▶ ANY

▶ OBJECT

ANY is a special PeopleCode data type that allows PeopleTools to determine the data type based on the variable's context. Undeclared variables are defined as ANY by default.

The OBJECT data type is used when working with external objects in PeopleCode programs.

## Comments

PeopleCode comments are like comments in other programming languages. They are used for informational purposes and are not executed. Comments are identified in one of two ways:

▶ The comment text is preceded by REM and terminated with a semicolon (;).

▶ The comment text is preceded by /* and terminated with */.

## Statements

Statements are used for the declaration and assignment of variables, program constructs, or subroutine calls. PeopleCode statements are generally terminated with a semicolon.

## Control Statements

Control statements are used for program control in PeopleCode programs. Table 7.1 outlines the syntax for the PeopleCode control statements.

**TABLE 7.1**   PeopleCode Control Statements

| Statement | Syntax |
|---|---|
| if... then... else | If condition Then<br>[statement_list_1]<br>[Else<br>[statement_list_2]]<br>End-if; |

**TABLE 7.1   (continued)**   PeopleCode Control Statements

| Statement | Syntax |
|---|---|
| evaluate... when | Evaluate left_term<br>When [*relational operator 1*] *right_term_1*<br>[*statement_list*]<br>.<br>.<br>.<br>When [*relational operator n*] *right_term_n*<br>[*statement_list*]<br>[When-other<br>[*statement_list*]]<br>End-evaluate; |
| for | For *count = expression1* to *expression2*<br>[*Step integer*];<br>*statement_list*<br>End-for; |
| repeat | Repeat<br>*statement_list*<br>Until logical_expression; |
| while | While *logical_expression*<br>*statement_list*<br>End-while; |

## Functions

PeopleSoft supports the use of functions that allow you to define code that can be called from many programs. These functions are provided for consistency and ease of maintenance. PeopleSoft supports four types of functions:

**Built-in functions**   Built-in functions are internal to the PeopleSoft system and can be called without being declared.

**Internal functions**   Internal functions are defined inside the same program that calls them.

**External functions**   External functions are defined outside the program that calls them. External functions are commonly stored in the FUNCLIB_ record definitions.

**External non-PeopleCode functions**   External non-PeopleCode functions are defined and stored in C libraries.

## Expressions

Expressions are statements that set the values of variables in any of the defined People-Code data types. PeopleSoft defines two additional expressions for handling values in the system:

**Metastrings or Meta-SQL**    Metastrings and Meta-SQL are used to store strings that are expanded by the system into SQL statements at runtime.

**Field references**    Field references are used to address record fields in the People-Code. The format is Record.FieldName.

## Operators

Operators are used to combine or modify values in expressions. The following operator classes are provided:

**Math operators**    Math operators perform standard mathematical operations, including addition (+), subtraction (-), multiplication (*), division (/), and exponentiation (**).

**String operators**    Two or more strings can be combined using the vertical bar ( | ) symbol to create a single string.

**Date operators**    Date operators allow you to perform mathematical operations on date and time expressions. Date-to-number comparisons return values in dates. Time and number comparisons return values in seconds. A date-plus-time operation yields a DATETIME expression.

**Comparison operators**    Comparison operators compare the values in expressions of the same data type. Comparison operators include equal, greater than, less than, and not equal.

**Boolean operators**    PeopleCode supports the Boolean operators True and False and the combinations using AND, OR, and NOT.

# Panel Buffer Data

The panel buffer is the area in memory where the data for the current panel group is stored. It is often necessary for PeopleCode to reference the data stored in the panel buffer. You can reference fields, rows of data, and scroll levels in the panel buffer using PeopleCode. Let's look at how to access panel buffer data.

## Contextual References

PeopleCode uses contextual references to access data in the fields and rows of current records. Contextual row references refer to a current row in scroll level 1 or lower in the current panel using the syntax RECORD.recordname. Contextual buffer field references refer to a specific buffer field using a record field name.

The following code excerpt uses a contextual reference in the PERSONAL_DATA table. This excerpt evaluates a value in the installation table to determine if action should be taken. Since this code affects only the PERSONAL_DATA table, the PERSONAL_DATA. prefix is not required.

```
/* if a change to a Personal_Data record was made that cold effect the
employee's eligibility for a benefit program, then BAS_DATA_CHG is
flagged. This flag is used in batch processing." */
if INSTALLATION.BENEFIT_ADMINISTRN = "Y" and
      BAS_DATA_CHG <> "Y" then
   If FieldChanged(BIRTHDATE) or
      FieldChanged(STATE) or
      FieldChanged(ZIP) then
      BAS_DATA_CHG = "Y";
   End-if;
End-if;
```

## Scroll Path References

PeopleSoft 7.5 has introduced a new type of reference for the panel buffer data, the scroll path reference. A scroll path reference has the syntax SCROLL.scrollname, where scrollname refers to the primary record name of the scroll level. This syntax is more strict in that it does not refer to any other scroll level. Scroll path references were introduced to reduce the chance of ambiguous statements being created.

A common use of the scroll path reference is to hide a scroll. The syntax for this is as follows:

```
HideScroll[Record.level 1 record name, level 1 row [Record.level 2
record name, level 2 row]] Record.target record name.
```

The examples provided in Chapter 3, "Customization," provide additional information on panel buffer data.

# Built-In Functions

PeopleSoft provides several built-in functions for your use. They are too numerous to describe fully in this chapter, but the following list describes the most commonly used functions:

**CurrEffDt** This function returns a date value for the effective date of the current scroll level.

**CurrEffSeq** This function returns the value of the effective sequence of the current scroll level.

**CurrLevelNumber** This function returns the current level number from which the function was called.

**CurrRowNumber** This function returns the current row number from which the function was called.

**DoCancel** This function cancels the current operation and behaves just like the user pressing the Esc key.

**DoSave** This function saves the current panel but delays the save until the end of the current PeopleCode program operation.

**Function** This function allows you to define a function in any PeopleCode module. This function must be placed at the top of the code.

**Gray** This function dims an object on a panel and does not allow data entry. This function is usually executed based on values in other objects on the panel.

**Hide** This function hides an object on the panel.

**UnGray** This function removes the dim on an object.

**UnHide** This function makes an object visible to the user again.

**HideMenuItem** This function hides menu items from the user. Execution of this function is usually based on properties of other objects or properties of the operator profile.

**InsertRow** This function inserts a row into the record in which the cursor is currently active.

**SetDefault** This function is used to set the field value to the default value defined in the record definition.

**UnCheckMenuItem** This function allows you to uncheck a menu item that is designed to act as a toggle.

PART

II

PeopleTools

**WinExec**    This function is designed to execute external Windows program files and then return control back to PeopleSoft.

**Year**    This function is used to extract the year from a PeopleSoft date value.

**SQLExec**    This function is used to execute SQL statements from within People-Code programs by passing a SQL command string to the SQLExec function.

The remaining built-in functions are defined in PeopleBooks, along with their syntax and examples of usage.

The next section discusses some of the special issues you will be dealing with when implementing PeopleCode for the three-tier environment.

# Three-Tier PeopleCode Issues

PeopleCode in the three-tier environment presents some special considerations, since not all PeopleCode events can occur on the application server. Some events must happen on the client. This section discusses where the events can occur and the validation process for PeopleCode that is targeted for deployment in a three-tier environment.

Let's first take a quick overview of the three-tier architecture and how it can be useful in your PeopleSoft system.

## Overview

The three-tier architecture is a modification of the traditional client-server, two-tier configuration. In a two-tier configuration, the data is contained in the database and all application code is executed on the client, as illustrated in Figure 7.38.

**FIGURE 7.38**    **Two-tier and three-tier client-server architecture**

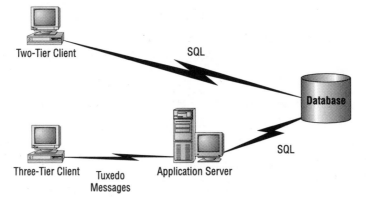

Two-Tier Client    SQL    Database

Three-Tier Client    Tuxedo Messages    Application Server    SQL

The three-tier architecture moves some of the most intensive program logic from the client to an application server that communicates directly with the database. With this approach, the client sends a request to the application server, the application server processes the request, and then executes the SQL on the database server. The application server receives the results of the request from the database server, and formats and interprets the results for the requesting client. The results are then sent to the client who displays the results for the user. This means that a single computer handles all the database connectivity for all the clients it services.

If you isolate this communication between the database server and the application server to an isolated LAN segment or co-locate these processes on the same computer, you can dramatically reduce the traffic on your network. Reduced traffic on the network benefits all users with better response times for all transactions—PeopleSoft and non-PeopleSoft.

Beginning with version 6, PeopleSoft provides a runtime version of the Bea Systems' Tuxedo online transaction processor software as the application server in a three-tier configuration. For most platforms, the recommended location for running the Tuxedo application server is on the database server. There are at least two exceptions:

▶ If you are using DB2/MVS as your database, you must implement Tuxedo on Windows NT.

▶ If you are using Microsoft SQL Server, PeopleSoft recommends that you run Tuxedo on a separate server. This configuration minimizes network utilization, since all communication then occurs internally on the server.

**N O T E**   The application server is discussed in detail in Chapter 5, "Administration Tools."

## Processing Groups

PeopleSoft defines the processing groups as mechanisms used in the partitioning of applications that generally run on either the client or the server. There are three primary processing groups that must be taken into consideration when attempting to move an application to three-tier mode: Panel Group Build, Panel Group Save, and FieldChange. All other processing groups must run on the client.

**Panel Group Build Processing Group**   The Panel Group Build processing group is responsible for getting the data and panel ready for the user to interact with

PART

II

PeopleTools

after a choice is made from a list of keys in a select window. The functions in this processing group are:

▶ FieldDefault

▶ FieldFormula

▶ RowInit

▶ RowSelect

▶ RowInsert

▶ RowDelete

Each of these functions corresponds to the PeopleCode in the Record Edits window, shown in Figure 7.39.

**FIGURE 7.39**    **Record Edits window**

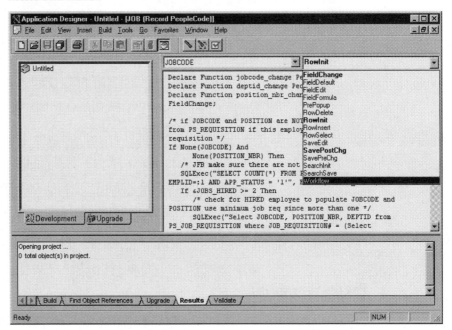

**Panel Group Save Processing Group**    The Panel Group Save processing group includes functions that are used after the user has saved the changes. The SaveEdit function must be completed successfully before the other functions can be executed. The other functions include SavePreChg, WorkFlow, and SavePostChg. Figure 7.40 contains an example of a SavePostChg routine that updates the union code on the pension union table when a JOBCODE change has been updated.

**FIGURE 7.40**    Panel Group Save processing group

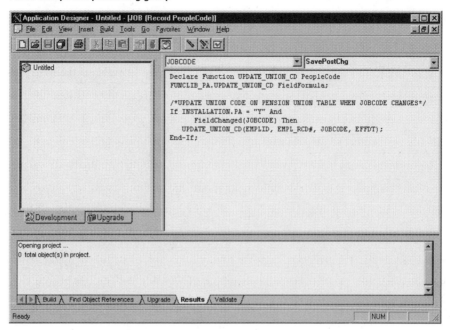

***FieldChange* Processing Group**    The FieldChange processing group includes events that occur after the user changes the data in a field, including processing changes that could have been created by a change to another field in the panel group. By default, FieldChange processing occurs on the client. The execution location can be changed to the application server for transactions that generate high SQL traffic to the database server. The FieldChange issues for a three-tier configuration are the same as described in the Record PeopleCode section earlier in this chapter.

## Process Locations

By default, all Panel Group Build processing is handled on the application server, all Panel Group Save processing is handled on the application server, and all FieldChange processing occurs on the client. The location at which a process runs can be adjusted by selecting the run location on the Panel Group Properties panel in the Panel Group Editor, illustrated in Figure 7. 41.

PART

II

PeopleTools

**FIGURE 7.41**    Panel Group Properties panel

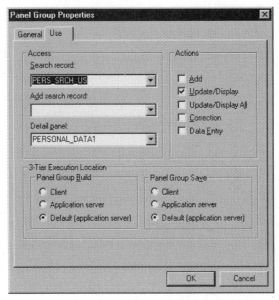

To access this panel, select File > Object Properties from the Application Designer window when you have a panel group open. Select the Use tab to access the 3-Tier Execution Location options. To change the run location, select the run location of your choice under Panel Group Build and Panel Group Save.

## Three-Tier Validation

When you create PeopleCode that you want to deploy using a three-tier configuration, the code must be validated using the PeopleTools validation process. The validation process checks for three-tier execution, Web client execution, and project validity. The process searches for client-only PeopleCode in the Panel Group Build, Panel Group Save, and FieldChange processing groups.

To validate PeopleCode to be used on a three-tier configuration, you:

1. Start the Application Designer.

2. Select > Tools > Options to open the Options panel, shown in Figure 7.42.

3. Choose the Validate tab and check the Validate 3-Tier Execution check box. If client-only PeopleCode is found, determine if the function can be moved to another process group or rewritten without the client-only function being used.

**FIGURE 7.42**    Options panel–Validate tab

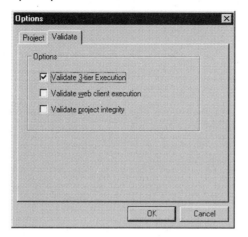

## PeopleCode in Web Development

It is important to realize that client-only functions cannot be used when developing applications for the Web. All processing should take place on the application server. Dynamic tree controls, for example, which allow you to program hierarchical, "drill-down" data access panels, are not supported on the Web client.

Minimize the use of FieldEdit and FieldChange in applications designed to run on the Web. Those events perform slowly since each action triggers a request from the application server. For more information on Web applications in PeopleSoft, see the section on Web applications later in this chapter.

# Application Reviewer

The Application Reviewer is a stand-alone Windows application that is used to trace the execution of PeopleCode. The Application Reviewer will be used extensively by your development staff. The system administrator should be familiar with its basic functionality and should have some information about starting it.

The Application Reviewer must be started *after* the panel group that you want to review is started. To start the Application Reviewer, select Go **>** PeopleTools **>** Application Reviewer from any menu. Figure 7.43 illustrates the Application Reviewer interface. Select Break **>** At Start from the Application Reviewer menu. This setting stops the execution of the first PeopleCode program encountered, allowing you to step through your PeopleCode program one line at a time. You can also monitor variable values as each PeopleCode program is executed.

**FIGURE 7.43**    Application Reviewer

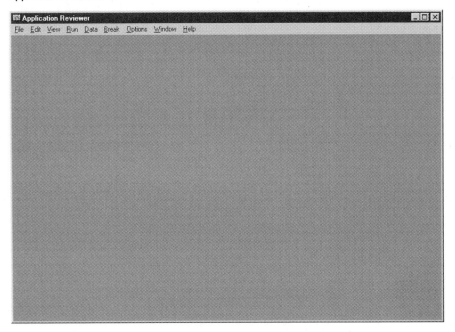

# Web Applications

Web applications are applications that are written to use the standards that are developed for the Internet. Web applications must have a Web server in place for the user to access the initial document that contains the references and loading instructions for the application. These documents are created in Hypertext Markup Language (HTML). PeopleSoft uses the Java language for delivering PeopleSoft functionality to the Web. Let's look at what functionality is delivered and how you access it with your own programs.

## Web Client Views

The Web client views are the PeopleSoft applets that are available for the Web client. You insert an applet tag to reference the specific view that you want to access into your HTML document. Let's look at the views or applets supplied by PeopleSoft.

**Panel view**    The panel view is used to display PeopleSoft panel groups. The client downloads specific panel group and panel information based on the specific panel group name, market code, menu name, and mode that you have specified in your applet tag.

**Query view**    The query view is used to display the results of predefined People-Soft queries to which the user has access. The applet tag can specify a query; only the results of that query are returned. If the applet tag is left blank, the user can choose any query to which access has been granted. Users *cannot* create new queries using the Web client.

**Worklist view**    The worklist view is used to display a user's worklist tasks. There are no specific parameters for the applet tag. You simply call the worklist and the user's operator ID allows the application server to retrieve the correct worklist. The user then double-clicks on a specific task and the corresponding panel group and information is retrieved.

# Developing Web Applications

Developing Web applications using PeopleSoft requires the same procedures that you use for developing any PeopleSoft application. The only additional task is the validation of the application for Web usage.

## Validating the Application

Once you have developed your Web application using the Application Designer, select Tools > Options. Choose the Validate tab, check the box Validate Web Client Execution, and click OK to validate your Web application. Verify that there are no messages in the Output Validate Window tab.

## Granting Access to the Application

Once your application is completed, it must be assigned to a menu. You grant access to a menu just as you grant access to any other PeopleSoft application using the Security Administrator, as described in Chapter 9, "Security." You may choose to define only the operator ID in PeopleSoft and have a third-party application monitor security for your Web development. You can use the security of some Web servers to provide access to your applications as well.

# Implementing Web Applications

When your development is completed, you are ready to implement your Web application. You must edit the HTML Web page and insert the PeopleSoft applet tag with the proper parameters. PeopleSoft provides NetObjects Fusion for use in creating and editing HTML documents that are needed to provide initial access to the PeopleSoft applets. You may already have a tool that you prefer to use; NetObjects Fusion is not required.

Let's take a closer look at the applet tag and the parameters that are used to activate the PeopleSoft applets.

## Applet Tag

The applet tag is a special HTML tag that is used to enclose the information needed for the applet to properly execute. The example below contains an example applet tag:

```
<applet
  CODE="psft.pt75.applet.PanelApplet.class"
  CODEBASE="/javaclient/"
  WIDTH=640
  HEIGHT=400
  ARCHIVE="javaclient.jar">
  <PARAM NAME="CABBASE" VALUE="javaclient.cab">
  <PARAM NAME="server_port" VALUE="9040">
</applet>
```

In this applet tag:

▶ The CODE statement references the Java class file that is required for the People-Soft transaction.

▶ The CODEBASE statement specifies the virtual applet directory on the Web server where the applets are stored.

▶ The HEIGHT and WIDTH statements specify the initial applet size.

▶ The ARCHIVE statement specifies the archive file that contains the Java class that the Netscape browser should download.

▶ The CABBASE statement specifies the archive file that contains the Java class that the Internet Explorer browser should download.

▶ The server_port variable is used to specify the port for the Jolt listener on the application server.

## Parameters

The parameters that activate specific PeopleSoft panels for the Web are inserted between the ARCHIVE statement and the end applet tag </applet>.

The following example uses a query parameter:

```
<PARAM NAME="query_name" VALUE="Personnel by Dept">
```

This query was defined using PeopleSoft Query before access was granted.

### Design Considerations

You may choose to hide or change the text on some of the default buttons that are delivered with the PeopleSoft Web applets. These can be changed by editing the parameters that are passed to the applet.

### Providing Help Documents

Providing help with Web applications requires you to build an HTML file containing the PeopleSoft documentation. You can do this with an HTML editor or you can use a word processing program and save it as an HTML file, if that is an option, or use a conversion program if your documentation already exists.

You must add a link from your application to your help file. This is accomplished by using the HTML anchor tag `<A HREF='filename'>Link Description</A>`.

PeopleTools

# Application Engine

The Application Engine development tool is designed to help you create powerful SQL programs without writing COBOL or SQR programs. To access the Application Engine, select Go > PeopleTools > Application Engine from any menu. The Application Engine is used in many of the new Financial modules for batch processing. Application Engine works on high-volume transactions; the PeopleCode described earlier is used to control the quality of data being entered and to provide additional online application functionality.

## Environment

The Application Engine can be a powerful replacement for COBOL or SQR programs, especially when you need the ability to add effective dates to your code or perform set processing. All code developed with the Application Engine is stored in the database. This means that you do not have to compile the code or interact with the operating system directly when using the Application Engine programs.

The effective date capability allows you to remove code from production without removing the code from your program. This allows for better archiving and gives you the ability to revert to a previous version of your program with little effort on your part.

The primary advantage of using the Application Engine to develop an application is that it reads the PeopleSoft record definitions and automatically adjusts to accommodate attributes when field definitions change.

The Application Engine programs contain sections, steps, and statements to accomplish their tasks.

## Sections, Steps, and Statements

Sections contain one or more steps. Sections are equivalent to COBOL paragraphs. Steps are the smallest units of work to be completed during a single commit to the database. The statements that make up steps are generally SQL statements, but statements can also be COBOL programs or a Mass Change process.

Application Engine programs are created from the Application Engine panel. To access the Application Engine panel, select Go > PeopleTools > Application Engine from any menu. Create your application, sections, steps, and statements using the panels found by selecting Use > Application Engine from the Application Engine menu.

# Integration Tools

PeopleSoft provides several tools such as the command line, Forms API, Message Agent, and EDI Manager to help you integrate your PeopleSoft application with other third-party applications.

## Command Line

PeopleSoft allows you to pass parameters on the command line at the startup of your PSTOOLS.EXE program. While the command line is not technically a tool but more of a method, it is the simplest way to integrate with third-party applications. The command line is also the least secure way to automate the execution of your PeopleSoft applications. If you have any security set, then the login information must be contained on the command line.

# Message Agent

The message agent is the recommended way to provide access to PeopleSoft panel groups outside your PeopleSoft system. The first object that must be created that uses a message agent is a message definition. You create message definitions using the Application Designer.

The next step when creating a message agent is to create the application that will pass the information needed by PeopleSoft using the message definition you created. PeopleSoft provides C and OLE/COM interfaces for use in programming the external application that you create. The API documentation must be used by your development staff to provide this access.

**N O T E**   I want to make you aware that you can link your PeopleSoft system to external systems. The implementation details are beyond the scope of this book.

# EDI Manager

The EDI Manager is used to transfer data electronically between your PeopleSoft system and business partners or other external sources. The linkages through which these transactions take place are provided by commercial EDI vendors or custom data exchange formats.

There are two basic types of transactions: inbound and outbound. Inbound transactions are translated into a format that is readable by the PeopleSoft agent and are then stored in staging tables. The data is then moved to the PeopleSoft database using load SQRs. The load SQRs can be started manually from a PeopleSoft menu or they can be scheduled.

Outbound transactions work in a similar manner. An SQR is run periodically that creates the outbound staging tables. The data is then converted into the EDI format and transmitted to the recipient.

Event codes that are specified in each transaction identify whether the transaction is new, updated, canceled, or a status request.

To access the EDI Manager, select Go **>** PeopleTools **>** EDI Manager. The Use menu, illustrated in Figure 7.44, allows you to define the elements of your EDI transactions, including Partner Profile definitions, Conversion Data profiles, Data Mapping profiles, and Action Code definitions.

**FIGURE 7.44**    EDI Manager–Use menu

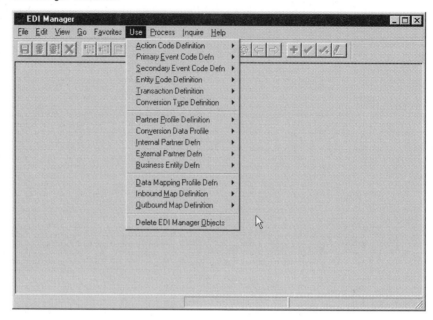

The Process menu, illustrated in Figure 7.45, allows you to execute outbound and inbound processes that have been defined.

**FIGURE 7.45**    EDI Manager–Process menu

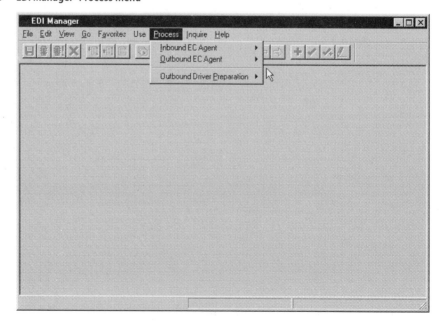

The Inquire menu, illustrated in Figure 7.46, allows you to execute reports that provide information about the transactions, any errors encountered, and summary log reports.

**FIGURE 7.46**    EDI Manager–Inquire menu

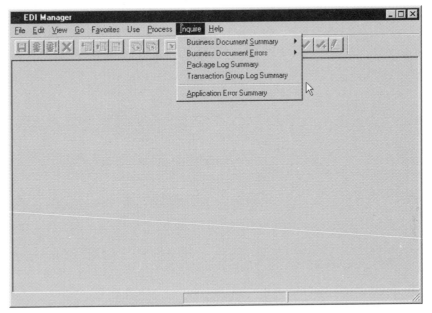

# Summary

This chapter provided an overview of the development tools available with your PeopleSoft system.

The Application Designer allows you to create and customize records, subrecords, fields, panels, panel groups, menus, and projects.

The Business Process Designer allows you to define business processes and represent them graphically using business process maps. The Business Process Designer also incorporates the concept of workflow, which is defined as a combination of the business processes and the flow of data among the workers in the given business processes.

PeopleCode is a structured programming language provided by PeopleSoft that allows the developers to write applications that add functionality to your PeopleSoft system.

The Application Reviewer is a stand-alone Windows application that allows the developers to trace the execution of PeopleCode.

The Application Engine is a development tool designed to help you create powerful SQL programs without writing COBOL or SQR programs. All code developed using the Application Engine is stored in the PeopleSoft database.

PeopleSoft provides several integration tools and methods that were discussed in this chapter, including:

▶ Using the command line at the startup of your PSTOOLS.EXE program is the simplest, but least secure way to integrate with third-party applications.

▶ The Forms API allows you to integrate business processes with third-party forms applications.

▶ Message agents provide access to PeopleSoft panel groups outside your PeopleSoft system.

▶ The EDI Manager is used to transfer data electronically between your PeopleSoft system and business partners or other external sources.

Now let's move on to the next chapter that describes the tools that allow your end users be more self-sufficient.

# End-User Tools

**P**eopleSoft provides many tools that enable the user to become more self-sufficient. The end-user tools described in this chapter are PeopleSoft components above and beyond the functionality contained in the panels and menus of the applications themselves. These tools allow end-users to decrease their dependency on technical support staff for routine tasks. For example, on many mainframe-based systems, an end-user has to make a formal request to a programmer to change the sort order or add a data element to a report. If this report is defined with a PeopleSoft query, the users can change the sort order or modify the query on their own, provided that they have been given sufficient authority to do so.

**N O T E**   This chapter assumes that you have a good understanding of SQL. The documentation that is provided with your RDBMS should contain detailed SQL information. In addition, there are many books dedicated to the subject of SQL.

## Query Tool

The PeopleSoft Query tool allows your end-users to perform ad hoc queries on data to which they have access. Query can also export report data to Crystal Reports for formatting or to Microsoft Excel for further analysis. Query provides a view of the tables and columns that is similar to Windows Explorer, as shown in Figure 8.1.

**T I P**   I recommend limiting your average user's use of Query to simple queries that use only one or two tables. If they have a more complicated query, show them how to do it or complete the query for them.

Query can also be a major headache for you. As users are trained in how to use the Query tool, they will begin experimenting with different queries. This is the point at which you should limit the functions that the users can perform. The PeopleSoft security view for the HRMS applications adds *six* tables to each query that is created. If your users attempt to join two tables that have different query views, they can quickly reach the join limit of your RDBMS, if it has a limit.

Use a phased plan for implementing Query on the desktop of your end-users that limits the users' capabilities until they are adequately trained. At my company, we add Query to our users' Object Security profiles only after they have completed the Query training. We are also selective about which users are given the ability to perform joins. An improperly defined query will result in slow system performance for all users. PeopleSoft provides reporting tables that are designed to provide much of the common information needed by queries, without having to do a join.

An example of a reporting table in HRMS is the PS_EMPLOYEES table. This table contains a single record for each active employee. The disadvantage of a single static table is that it must be refreshed to maintain current data. My company updates the PS_EMPLOYEES table daily with a scheduled job. (PER099.SQR is delivered by People-Soft for this task.)

**FIGURE 8.1**    The Query window

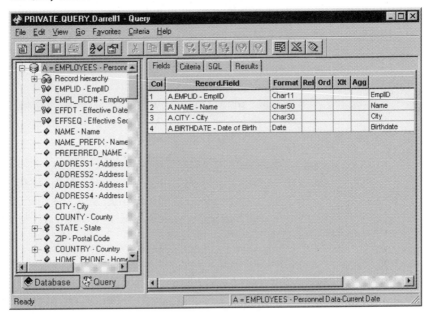

# Using Query

Here are the basics on how to create and run a query using PeopleSoft Query:

1. To access the Query window, select Go > PeopleTools > Query from the menu. Once the Query window is open, choose the table from which you want to retrieve data.

2. To add a table to your blank query, simply select the table from the component view, located in the left side of Figure 8.1. Another option is to select File > Open from the menu. The Component view has two tabs that can be selected by the user. The Database tab displays the available tables and the Query tab displays the tables that are included in the current query. The Database tab has two view options that can be set by changing your View Preferences. To do this, select View > Preferences. This option displays either an alphabetical list of tables to which you have access or it displays an access group view. The access group structure view is illustrated in Figure 8.2.

3. Once you have a table to query, select a field or fields from which you want to retrieve data. Select the Query tab from Component view and double-click or drag and drop the desired fields.

4. The fields that you selected should now be visible in the design view on the right. If they are not, make sure that the Fields tab is selected.

5. To limit the amount of data returned to a group that can be defined on a given field, enter the desired criteria by adding the field to the Criteria tab. To do this, select the Criteria tab and double-click the field or drag and drop the field into the Criteria list. Set the values or conditions for which you are searching. Figure 8.3 contains the Criteria tab. The query in this figure will result in a list of employees whose employee ID is between 09000 and 09400.

6. Other tabs that are visible in the Design view are the SQL and Results tabs. The SQL tab displays all the SQL statements associated with the current query. The Results tab displays the results of the query after you have executed it.

7. Another option that you can configure while building your query is setting the desired sort order for the query. Select the Field view and double-click the Ord column of the field you want to use as your primary sort. You may select additional fields if you want to specify a secondary sort order. You may also change the column heading for any field. You may display the translate description instead of the translate code for any field you have selected.

8. To run the query, select File > Run from the menu or click the Execute icon on the toolbar. The pointer in Figure 8.3 points to this icon.

**FIGURE 8.2**    Query Designer–Database tab

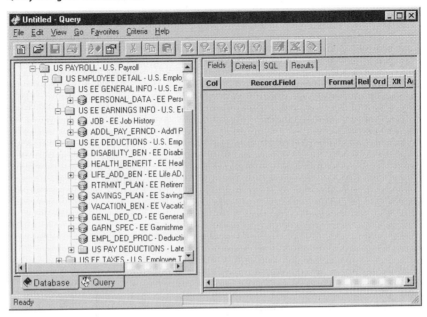

**FIGURE 8.3**    Query Criteria

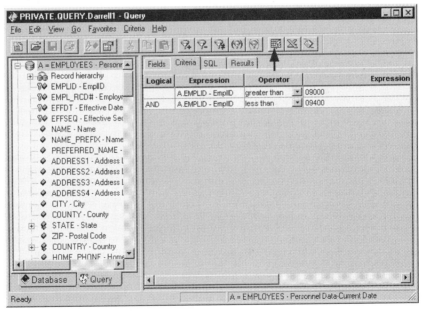

## Query Security

Now that we've established how to create a query, it is essential that you know how to keep these queries safe. Query security is an important aspect of the system because it allows you to restrict your users to the types of queries and the data that they can retrieve using Query. The first level of query security is access to the Query tool itself. This is established when the operator ID is created by granting or denying access to Query.

The next level of security restricts users to running queries that have been predefined; the users are not given the ability to create new queries. This can be established by editing the user's query security profile as follows:

1. Select Go > PeopleTools > Utilities.

2. Select Use > Query Security > Query Profile from the Utilities menu. This opens the Query Security window shown in Figure 8.4.

3. Use the check boxes to designate which Query functions a user or group may use.

**FIGURE 8.4**    **Query Security window**

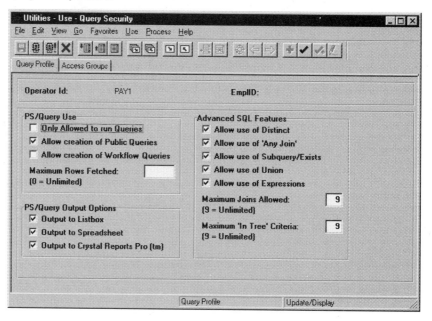

Figure 8.4 contains the profile for one of my company's payroll groups. This group has more rights than the average user since the users in the PAY1 group have had

more training on how to create and run their own queries. They cannot create work-flow queries. If you are not using Microsoft Excel for any of your groups, uncheck the box for Output To Spreadsheet to eliminate any possible errors.

In my company, one function that we limit is the use of database table joins, which are explained in more detail in the next section. Many of our groups do not have this access to minimize the chances that they will create queries that can seriously degrade the performance of the entire system. Users without SQL training have a unique ability to create Cartesian joins. Cartesian joins have a many-to-many rela-tionship and generate a tremendous number of table scans to complete. For these reasons, I recommend easing your users into the use of the PeopleSoft Query tool.

## Security Views

Security views are used to restrict your users to a particular subset of data. In the HRMS applications, two delivered security views are PS_EMPLMT_SRCH_US and PS_EMPLMT_SRCH_GBL. There are other views for other HRMS countries avail-able. These views link the operator security table (PS_SCRTY_TBL_DEPT) with PS_PERSONAL_DATA, PS_JOB, and PS_NID_TYPE_TBL to control the employees that each user has access to. PeopleSoft refers to this as row-level data security. Access to the data for each individual employee is controlled by these views.

For example, if you have a branch office that wants to restrict the local users to only the local employees, this is set using the Administer Security panels on HRMS ver-sion 7 and earlier. This functionality has been moved under the Administer HR Sys-tem, Maintain Data Security panels in HRMS 7.5. Version 7.5 also allows you to restrict access to countries. In addition, this functionality allows you to grant managers access to the employees in their department or departments underneath the Maintain Data Security panel in the Department Security Tree.

You can modify the PS_EMPLMT_SRCH_US and PS_EMPLMT_SRCH_GBL views to customize them for your company if the delivered security views are not sufficient. The recommended approach is to perform a Save As and designate a new name for your view. Then assign this view as the default security view. This allows you to revert back to the delivered functionality if you experience trouble with your custom secu-rity view.

**WARNING**    PeopleSoft recommends that you not modify the delivered security views but create your own custom security views.

PART

II

PeopleTools

## Advanced Options

Advanced query options are more powerful features that allow users with a good understanding of SQL to generate powerful queries. Some of the most useful options are:

**Workflow queries**    Workflow queries are designed to be part of automated business processes. There are two types of workflow queries: Role queries are used to determine who is to receive workflow tasks. Database agent queries are designed to search for predefined conditions in the database. These queries then trigger a workflow event.

**Aggregate functions**    Aggregate functions allow you to summarize data into fewer records for ease of understanding. The aggregate functions that are supplied with your PeopleSoft system are sum, count, min, max, and average.

> The sum function totals all records for a specified field based on the key field.

> The count function adds the number of rows returned.

> The min function displays the lowest value from a specified field.

> The max function displays the largest value from a specified field.

> The average function is equal to sum divided by count for the specified field.

**Expression option**    When you need to perform arithmetic operations on two or more fields, use the expression option. An expression also allows you to create a new column for output based on the execution of the arithmetic expression you have created. To create an expression, select the Expressions tab from the Query window, then define the data type that you want to create. Finally, enter the expression that you want to execute.

**Distinct option**    The distinct option is used to eliminate duplicate rows in the query. To enable the distinct option, select File **>** Properties from the menu to display the Query Properties panel. Then check the Distinct option and accept the change.

**Subquery option**    The subquery option is another advanced query option that is used to compare or return data based on data contained in the main query. To use a subquery, select subquery as a comparison type. Select the database record you want to query. The subquery is created using the techniques for a query.

**Join option**    The option that you should be most familiar with is the join. Joins are the heart of a relational database. They allow you to query data from multiple records and present it as a single output. Joins combine tables by linking on similar columns. The rows of both records are then compared in each column so that the desired data is returned. There are three types of joins used in a PeopleSoft Query:

▶ A hierarchical join is where a child table is joined with the parent.

▶ A related record join is where a table is linked to a prompt table that contains the values for the codes used in the first.

▶ An any record join is used when you want to join any two tables in the database.

**N O T E**   Child tables share the same key fields as the parent and have one or more additional key fields.

**Union**   Unions allow you to merge the data returned by two or more queries at the same time. To create a new union, select Edit **>** New Union from the Query menu. Create your query just like any other query. There are three rules that must be adhered to when creating unions:

▶ The queries that make up the union must return the same number of columns.

▶ The data types must match on all fields.

▶ The display order must be the same.

Now let's look at the SQL that is generated by the PeopleSoft Query tool during advanced queries. I use this feature when troubleshooting or assisting a user. It helps me understand the exact query syntax being executed. To view the underlying SQL statements, select the SQL tab, as shown in Figure 8.5. Notice that this is a display-only view. The generated SQL is not editable by any user. You can copy and paste this code into other applications for further analysis.

**N O T E**   The SQL shown in Figure 8.5 is an example that I quickly created. I select the fields EMPLID, NAME, CITY, and BIRTHDATE from the PS_EMPLOYEES table. Note that there is code in the WHERE criteria that uses the alias A1. This join is defined automatically by the PeopleSoft Query tool. This PS_EMPLMT_SRCH_US view is the security view that causes the query to return those employees for which I have been granted access.

PART

**II**

PeopleTools

**FIGURE 8.5**    Viewing SQL statements

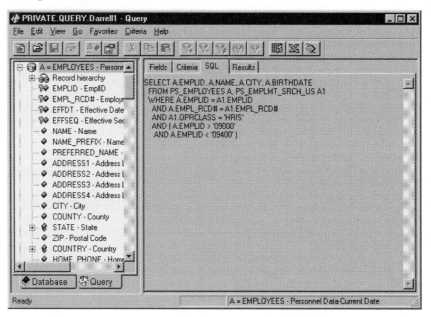

# Crystal Reports

PeopleSoft provides Crystal Reports, a report-formatting tool that produces high-quality, easy-to-read reports. The Crystal Reports tool has other capabilities but they are not recommended for use with PeopleSoft because PeopleSoft Security cannot monitor the query and control access to the PeopleSoft data.

## Running Reports

There are three ways to run a report using Crystal Reports. The first is to select a menu item from the online PeopleSoft application and launch the report using the Process Scheduler. This gives you the ability to run your report without having to exit the PeopleSoft application. You can schedule the report to execute at a later time if you are using a database platform that supports the Windows process scheduler. To specify a run time in the future, the report must be predefined and saved. The most common Crystal Reports that you might schedule this way are those delivered by PeopleSoft. Crystal Reports have a run control panel that is already defined that prompts you for run control parameters and allows you to schedule the time for running the query. An example of a run control panel used to delay the execution of a report is shown in Figure 8.6.

**FIGURE 8.6**    Run control panel

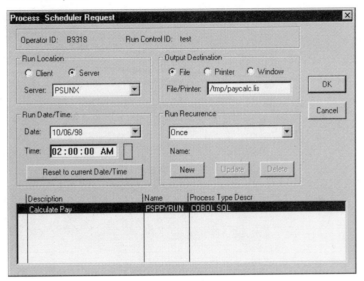

The second way to run a report is to launch Crystal Reports using PeopleSoft Query. This is the most common way to create a new Crystal Reports report. Follow these steps:

1. Launch PeopleSoft Query.

2. Define the query.

3. Execute it so that the output goes to Crystal Reports.

4. Define the format for this report and save the format.

5. Complete the execution of the query and verify the format of your data.

Let's look at how to format a report using Crystal Reports as noted in step 4. A report template opens automatically when you run your query to Crystal Reports. The report template contains three sections. The header, the footer, and the details sections contain all the columns and rows of data from your query. Figure 8.7 shows an empty template.

**NOTE**    If all your columns are not displayed, then you have too many columns defined for the page size and orientation that you have selected.

**FIGURE 8.7**    Crystal Reports template

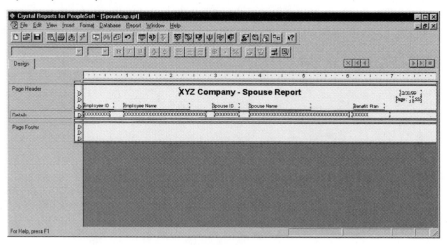

The header contains all the column names defined as the database field names. To change these to make it easier for the report user to understand, double-click the column heading you want to change, enter your new heading, and click anywhere on the screen outside the edit box for the column you are editing. You can also use this method to update the report title and other information that is contained in the page header or footer.

Once you are satisfied with the format of your report, save the report. I recommend using the same name for both the query and report so that it will be easier to identify. You will be able to rerun the report by simply rerunning the query to Crystal Reports and then printing the report.

The third way to run a report is to launch Crystal Reports in stand-alone mode. To do this, follow these steps:

1. Choose Start **>** Programs **>** Crystal Reports for PeopleSoft **>** 32-bit Crystal Reports for PeopleSoft from the Windows 95 or Windows NT Desktop.

2. Log on to the PeopleSoft PeopleTools server by selecting File **>** Log on Server from the Crystal Reports menu.

**WARNING**    You must log on to the PeopleSoft PeopleTools server *before* opening the report you want to run.

## Troubleshooting Crystal Reports

When troubleshooting problems with Crystal Reports, the most common errors will be problems with the Windows Registry. If you have a workstation that is working correctly, you can export the Crystal Reports registry entries to a file and then import them to other workstations to ensure that the registry is the same as a working machine.

Other possible errors may be tied to PeopleSoft Security and how the user tried to run the Crystal Reports application. For example, if the user fails to log on to the database using PeopleSoft PeopleTools ODBC-defined server, that user will not have access to his or her security profile in the database.

 **NOTE** The generated reports are stored in the \crw\reports subdirectory under the version directory on the file server. The reports have a *.rpt extension.

# nVision

PeopleSoft nVision is a PeopleTool that is used to create queries that populate Microsoft Excel spreadsheets for use in building reports or performing detailed data analysis. nVision allows your users to use all the functions of Excel that they may be more familiar with to perform detailed analysis of PeopleSoft data. Once you have defined an nVision report, you can use it over and over again to gather updated information.

 **NOTE** nVision is not to be confused with QueryLink that is used to export Query information into Excel. QueryLink uses an Excel template file called QUERY.XLT for its definition.

## Linking to Excel

PeopleSoft nVision and Microsoft Excel are closely intertwined. When you start nVision, Excel is started automatically and a special spreadsheet file named NVSUSER.XLM is opened, as shown in Figure 8.8. This spreadsheet has an nVision menu item from which all nVision commands are initiated.

**FIGURE 8.8**    nVision file Nvsuser.xlm

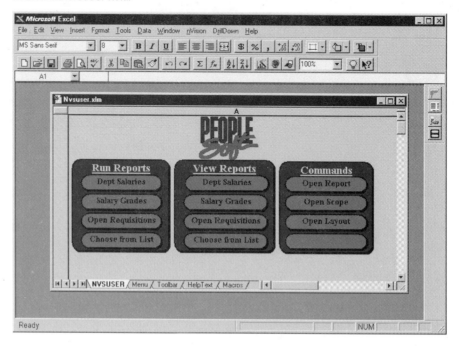

There are two types of reports that can be created using nVision: report instances and report layouts. Report instances contain the results of running the nVision query. Report layouts are the definitions for which nVision requests data to fill. Therefore, every time a report request is submitted using nVision, the data is retrieved into a report instance using the report layout that has been defined. This report instance can then be saved into a separate spreadsheet file for further analysis or printing. In addition to the special functions contained in the nVision menu item, you can use all the Excel functions in the created spreadsheet.

To run an nVision report, a report request must be created and submitted. To create a report request, select nVision **>** Report Request from the nVision/Excel menu. Before creating a report request, make sure that you have thoroughly defined the layout to be used. The first report requests you use are likely to be the delivered PeopleSoft layouts. (The next section describes how to create nVision layouts on your own.)

The report request contains information about the report, including the name, title, associated layout, and scope. The request is defined using the Report Request panel, as shown in Figure 8.9. To access this panel, select Use **>** Report Request from the nVision menu.

**FIGURE 8.9** PeopleSoft nVision Report Request panel

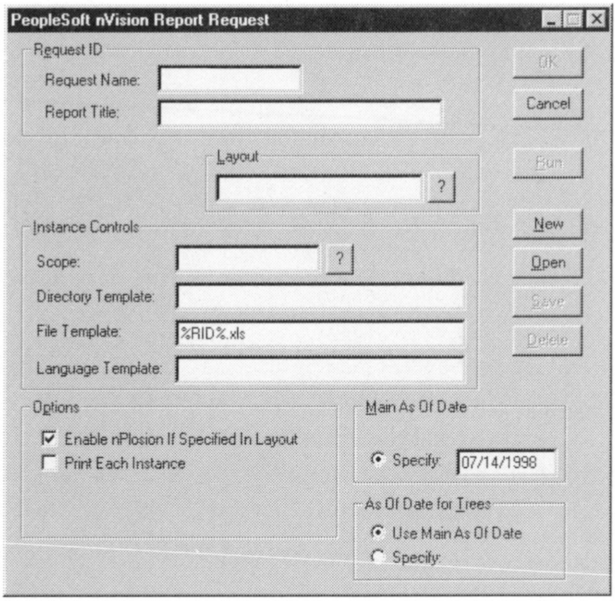

Enter the following information about your report request on this panel:

**Request Name** The name of the report is required.

**Report Title** The title of the request is used to define the title of the report.

**Scope** The scope of the report places limits on the report and also causes multiple instances of the report to be generated automatically when the request is executed.

**Layout** The layout that will be used by the request must be specified in the report request.

**Directory Template** The directory template is the target directory for the nVision report instance. If the directory does not exist, nVision creates it. This overrides the Configuration Manager setting. If you leave this blank, the directory defined with Configuration Manager is used.

**File Template** The file template is the filename that you want nVision to use when creating the report instance.

**Language Template** This field designates the output language for the report instance.

PART

II

PeopleTools

**Enable nPlosion If Specified In Layout**    If checked, this allows the use of nPlosion with the report. If this box is not checked, nPlosion will be disabled even if the layout definition specifies it. nPlosion is discussed in more detail later in this section.

**Print Each Instance**    Checking this box automatically sends each instance to the printer as it is created.

**Main As Of Date**    This field designates the reporting period for the nVision report.

**As Of Date For Trees**    This field is the effective date of any trees that are used in the report. You can use the Main As Of Date field or you can specify a different date.

Additional information that must be included is the directory and naming scheme to be used if you have multiple instances defined. If you use the same filename, the reports will overwrite each other and you will be left with only one instance of the report. You can use nVision directory templates and variables to create the unique directories when the report instance is being generated.

For example, let's assume that you have a report request named SALES that creates three instances. The simplest template is to use `%RID%%ICT%.XLS`, which specifies that the report will be named by the report ID, with the instance being used in the new filename. This template generates the following filenames: `SALES1.XLS`, `SALES2.XLS`, and `SALES3.XLS`. You can also specify directories in the template.

> **WARNING**    Designate your files so that no instances are named the same in the same directory. Otherwise, each successive report will overwrite the previous report when it is executed.

nPlosion is used to capture more detailed information about the row or column of data as the report is being run. Used in conjunction with the drill-down option, you can select a specific cell and expand it to include more detailed information than was used to create the summary information. nVision defines the nPlosion data in your generated report using the Microsoft Excel outline function. The outline function allows you to display or hide as much or as little of the detail as you want. An example of a use for nPlosion is on a regional sales report. Define the report to present the summary information but specify nPlosion. Then perform a more detailed analysis by selecting the cell that you want to return information about specific sales personnel, or return information by product, depending on your report definition.

# Layouts

The nVision layout is the power behind the nVision application. You can specify what data you want to retrieve and how you want it formatted in the layout definition that you create in Excel. This layout contains no actual data, just definitions of what data you want. There are two basic types of layouts that you can generate using nVision: tabular and matrix. Tabular layouts are used for general reporting; they generally return all information and include it in the report. Matrix layouts lend themselves to the summary of data and often contain aggregate functions. Both tabular and matrix layouts can be defined to use data retrieved using a PeopleSoft Query.

The tabular layout is the simplest to define. It represents data from a single query. The data is displayed with one data row in the database represented by one row in the Excel spreadsheet. Tabular layouts are limited to scope and query selection criteria, with no support for nVision variables, which allow you to define variables for heading or other information that could change from run to run. You can, however, define multiple layout sheets per report.

The matrix layout is much more powerful. You can integrate data from multiple queries. This allows you to represent multiple intersections of similar data using nVision variables. You select the data using a wide range of selection criteria, including business units, time spans, fields, labels, strings, and effective dates, in addition to the scope and query available in tabular layouts.

To create a new layout, follow these steps:

1. Select nVision > New Layout from the nVision/Excel menu. The nVision layout is basically a series of selection items that walk you through the creation of the layout. The first step is to name the layout. The name you choose must retain the default .XNV extension, but it can be as long as 50 characters.

2. The next prompt asks whether you are creating a tabular or matrix layout. If you choose a tabular layout, you are prompted for the query that you want to use to select the data.

3. Define which columns from the query you will be using in the layout.

4. Using the navigation buttons from the Layout Definition window, move your cursor to the column in which you want to place data from the query.

5. Once you have selected a column, click the Column button. The Query Result Column panel appears, allowing you to choose the desired column from the query.

6. Click the Apply button to finalize your selection.

PART

II

PeopleTools

7. Repeat steps 4–6 for each data element you want to use. When you're done, select the Close button.

8. Once all your data elements are defined, save your layout and close the Layout Definition window.

9. You are now ready to test your layout. To do this, create a report request using the steps outlined in the previous section and select your new layout.

**N O T E**   Column A and row 1 are hidden and reserved for use by nVision for control information.

**N O T E**   The matrix layout is used for summary reports. The data that is retrieved is generally derived from both row and column information from an Excel spreadsheet. This functionality is frequently used in financial reports. The complexity of matrix reports stems from the selection criteria that must be defined for the column and row information. Your programmers or sophisticated power users will most likely develop matrix layouts. Matrix reports can be useful, but you will probably have little involvement with them, other than troubleshooting the individual queries that make up the matrix. This chapter does not describe how to create a matrix layout because they are much more complicated than tabular layouts. Before you begin developing custom matrix layouts, review all the PeopleSoft documentation and, if possible, attend the nVision class.

As the system administrator, you should be concerned with the security of nVision reports. Let's take a look at the options available for the security of nVision reports.

# Security

PeopleSoft nVision provides security at both the data and operator level. Data security is obtained by granting access at the operator ID level, just as in normal PeopleSoft Security. This is accomplished through the use of a view called LED_AUTH_TBL, which can be customized, just as the PERS_SRCH_US security view can be modified in PeopleSoft HRMS.

Operator security is used to control which nVision functions a user has access to. Operator security is administered using the Select Menu Items functionality of the PeopleSoft Security Administrator. The two most important menu items for your end-users should be the ability to run reports and the ability to modify the scope of the reports. In the initial stages of your company's use of nVision, the technical staff should be involved in creating layouts and reports. Once your power users become more familiar with how nVision works, you may grant them specific access to define and create their own layouts and reports.

Performance of the system is critical to the success of nVision reports. Let's look at some of the factors that affect performance.

## Performance

There are several procedures that can cause performance problems when using nVision. The first and most important area is the efficient use of indexes for the queries that support nVision reports. You want to ensure that the queries are choosing the best index possible to support the query. Coordinate with your database administrator (DBA) to verify, by reviewing the query plans or other analysis tools, that any new queries designed for nVision are optimized.

The key to efficient use of your indexes is to define your query criteria in a manner that minimizes the number of records that must be searched for matching additional criteria. For example, if the account type is one of your criteria and is a primary key on the records, use the account type as your first criteria. This limits the processing to the subset of records meeting the account type criteria. This subset of records will then be used for any additional criteria that you define for the report. If you have multi-column indexes, as most PeopleSoft tables do, you can limit the scope of your search even more by ensuring that you define limiting criteria based on the key fields of the table you are querying.

The use of trees and security views in your nVision reports requires the extensive use of joins. The performance that your RDBMS experiences in processing joins is the most significant factor in determining the performance of your tree or security-controlled reports.

Now let's look at Process Scheduler, which can be used to automate many of your routine tasks.

PART

II

PeopleTools

# Process Scheduler

The PeopleSoft Process Scheduler is a powerful scheduling program that allows your end-users to run their own batch jobs. This capability gives the users the flexibility to schedule their jobs to run at a later time, when the system is less busy. At our company, there are several benefits reports that we have asked the users to schedule for periods after our nightly batches have completed. The users schedule their reports to start every hour after that time and the printouts are ready when they arrive the next day.

The system administrator can restrict the number of instances of a process type that can be running concurrently. For example, at our company, we allow only three SQR reports to be running concurrently. You can change this number dynamically as your system utilization and demands change. This prevents a single user from launching a series of reports that slow down the system excessively.

**N O T E**   Chapter 5, "Administration Tools," discussed the Process Scheduler from the system administrator's perspective. This section discusses the Process Scheduler from the user's perspective.

A utility called Process Monitor allows users to see the status of the processes they have submitted. Figure 8.10 illustrates a sample of the Process Monitor window with several completed payroll processes and one process that ended with an error status.

**FIGURE 8.10**   Process Monitor window

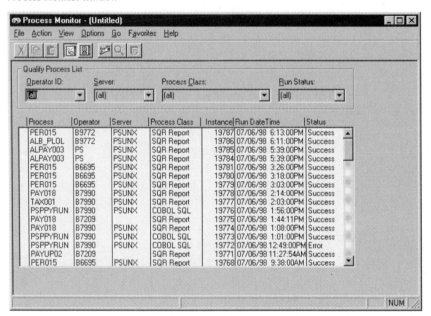

Users can see additional information about the processes they have submitted by double-clicking the desired process entry from the Process Monitor window. Figure 8.11 contains the Process Request Detail panel for process 19787 in Figure 8.10. This panel displays operator and run information for the process. You can determine the run location, the run control ID, and the process begin and end times.

**FIGURE 8.11**    Process Request Detail panel–Process Detail tab

Request parameters are the specific parameters that are passed to the program's command line at execution time. To view information on the request parameters for the process, select the Request Parameters tab in the Process Request Detail panel. Figure 8.12 displays this tab with the request parameters for process 19787. This panel is used for troubleshooting processes with errors to verify that all environment variables are correctly assigned and that the proper command-line information is being executed.

**FIGURE 8.12**    Process Request Detail panel–Request Parameters tab

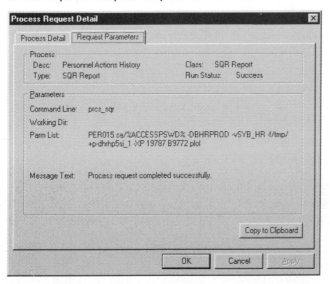

PART

**II**

PeopleTools

# Environment

The workstation environment is very important in the success or failure of processes being scheduled using the Process Scheduler. The processes, whether they are running on the server or the client, require valid environment information to succeed. The Configuration Manager on the workstations allows you to configure the options required by each program that uses the Process Scheduler services.

You can access Configuration Manager in two ways:

▶ Execute the program shortcut from the Windows Start menu.

▶ Select Edit > Preferences > Configuration from any PeopleSoft application window.

Valid environment parameters for your installation are described in the PeopleSoft Installation Guide for your RDBMS platform. Some of the environment parameters that must be configured include:

▶ The path to the temp directory on the workstation

▶ The Crystal Reports directory

▶ The database connectivity directory

▶ The PeopleTools directory

▶ The Microsoft Word directory

▶ Several parameters, called flags, that must be set for the SQR and COBOL programs

The panel that allows you to configure most of the environment parameters is the Process Scheduler tab in the Configuration Manager. Figure 8.13 contains this panel. The Configuration Manager establishes the environment parameters for the Windows operating system. Several of these parameters must also be set on the UNIX platform. You must specify the SQR directory and location of the database drivers. PeopleSoft provides the psconfig.sh and psconfig.csh files for you to use, depending on which UNIX shell you use. The other parameters are passed to Process Scheduler on the command line at execution time. Table 8.1 shows a list of the most common Process Scheduler parameters.

For a process to be scheduled using the Process Scheduler, that process must be submitted using a run control ID, or run ID for short. Let's discuss the use of run IDs when submitting processes to the Process Scheduler.

**FIGURE 8.13**    Configuration Manager–Process Scheduler tab

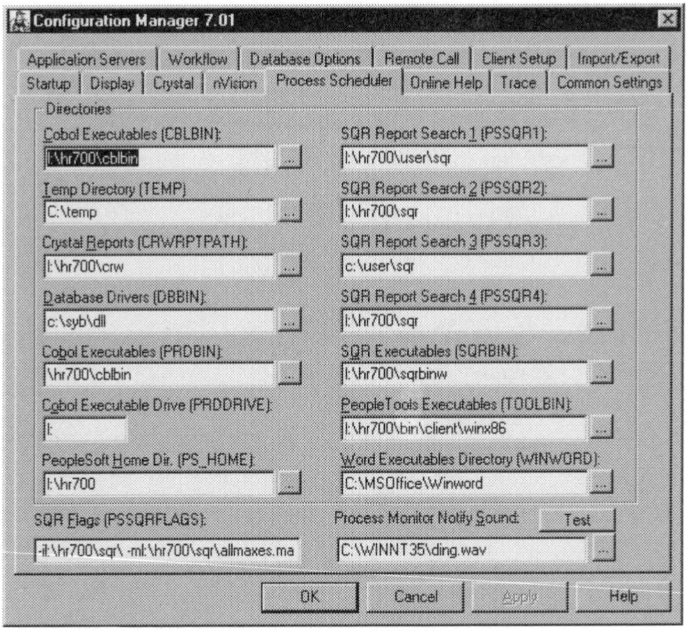

Configuration Manager 7.01

Application Servers | Workflow | Database Options | Remote Call | Client Setup | Import/Export
Startup | Display | Crystal | nVision | Process Scheduler | Online Help | Trace | Common Settings

Directories

Cobol Executables (CBLBIN):
I:\hr700\cblbin

SQR Report Search 1 (PSSQR1):
I:\hr700\user\sqr

Temp Directory (TEMP):
C:\temp

SQR Report Search 2 (PSSQR2):
I:\hr700\sqr

Crystal Reports (CRWRPTPATH):
I:\hr700\crw

SQR Report Search 3 (PSSQR3):
c:\user\sqr

Database Drivers (DBBIN):
c:\syb\dll

SQR Report Search 4 (PSSQR4):
I:\hr700\sqr

Cobol Executables (PRDBIN):
\hr700\cblbin

SQR Executables (SQRBIN):
I:\hr700\sqrbinw

Cobol Executable Drive (PRDDRIVE):
I:

PeopleTools Executables (TOOLBIN):
I:\hr700\bin\client\winx86

PeopleSoft Home Dir. (PS_HOME):
I:\hr700

Word Executables Directory (WINWORD):
C:\MSOffice\Winword

SQR Flags (PSSQRFLAGS):
-i:I:\hr700\sqr\ -m:I:\hr700\sqr\allmaxes.ma

Process Monitor Notify Sound:     Test
C:\WINNT35\ding.wav

OK     Cancel     Apply     Help

**TABLE 8.1**    Common Process Scheduler Parameters

| Parameter | Description |
|-----------|-------------|
| PS_HOME | Your PeopleSoft home directory. The location of all files required by clients. |
| DBBIN | The location of your database drivers. |
| TEMP | The designated temporary directory. |
| CBLBIN | The location of the compiled COBOL code. |
| WINWORD | The location on the client for your Microsoft Word executable file. |
| SQRBIN | The location of the SQR executable file. |
| PSSQR1 | The search order for SQR programs. You can also have three other search parameters: PSSQR2, PSSQR3, and PSSQR4. |

## Run IDs

Run IDs are used to track parameters that must be passed to a process to control the data that is being calculated or reported. The first time your users attempt to access a run control panel for a process, they must add a new run ID to the system. The user adds a run ID by selecting the Add menu item after choosing to open a menu item that is designated as a process run control panel. The user then fills in all the parameters that are required by the program. To execute the job, click the toolbar run process icon (it looks like a traffic light) or select File **>** Run from the menu. This run ID is used as the key in a table that stores run parameters.

The PeopleSoft run control tables are specific to each product they offer. For example, PeopleSoft HRMS has run control tables for each module. The run control table for Human Resources is RUN_CNTL_HR.

You can create your own custom run control table. I recommend that you do this if you are adding many custom reports that have more parameters than the standard PeopleSoft run control tables allow. You create this table using the Record Designer feature of Application Designer as described in Chapter 7, "Development Tools." In my company, we leave PeopleSoft's tables as delivered and customize our own as new processes because we need additional parameters.

## Working with Processes

There are several types of processes that can be executed using the Process Scheduler. Some examples are: COBOL SQL, SQR Reports, and Crystal Reports. Each of these processes can have errors during execution.

For example, when a COBOL SQL program causes an error, one of the first places you should check is the process log. Often, you can quickly determine the cause of the error. The following example shows the log from a payroll process that had an error. This log is located in the $PS_HOME/log/database_name directory on your UNIX machine if the process runs on UNIX. It is located in a similar location that you have defined on other operating system platforms.

A sample output from a process with an error follows:

```
PeopleSoft prcs_bat Started
Using RDBMS SYBASE
Database server SYB_HR
Database name HRPROD
Process instance 19772
PeopleSoft Payroll -- Version 6.00
Copyright (c) 1988-1997 PeopleSoft, Inc.
All Rights Reserved

DB Type:[SQLBASE | ORACLE | INFORMIX | DB2 |
```

```
DB2ODBC | DB2400 | DB2UNIX | SYBASE |
MICROSFT]:SYBASE

Server:[ ]:SYB_HR

Database:[ ]:HRPROD

Username:[ ]:B7990

Password:[********]:

Run Control ID[ ]: CHECKRUN

Process Instance:[0]:19772

SQL Trace:[0]:

Off-Cycle Calculation started for Run: 872
 at 12:49:31.29.
Calculation started for Company: BC1
 Pay Group: BW2
 Pay End Date: 1998-07-05
 Page#: 250
 at 12:49:34.78.
 50 check(s) to calculate.
Start employee processing at 12:49:36.68.
```

**Object Code error : file '/sybase/psoft/cblbin/PSPDEDLA.gnt'**
**error code: 153, pc=C0C0F0C3, call=29, seg=0**
**153 Subscript out of range**

```
HP/MF COBOL Version: B.11.25
HP-UX bcbshrhp B.10.20 E 9000/800
pid: 16094 gid: 3 uid: 102
Mon Jul 6 12:49:51 1998
 12:49pm up 20 days, 4:41, 2 users, load average: 0.41, 0.39, 0.41
Thread mode:No Threads
RTS Error:COBOL
Sync Signals:COBOL
ASync Signals:COBOL
cobtidy on exception:False

PeopleSoft prcs_bat Terminating
```

This process had an exception (shown in **bold**) that was not correctly handled by the COBOL program, so the process crashed as COBOL does when no error-handling routine is present. This particular type of error occurs most often when there is a version difference between the stored statements and the COBOL program being executed. Chapter 17, "Troubleshooting," covers this in more detail.

# PeopleBooks

PeopleBooks is the online documentation system delivered with your PeopleSoft system. It is built on the Folio Views platform. Folio Views (Folio) is a software application that is used by many software manufacturers, including PeopleSoft, to deliver online documentation. Folio has a powerful, full-text search capability to make it easy to find the information that you need. There are various Folio infobases that are used for each of the major products PeopleSoft delivers.

Figure 8.14 shows the main PeopleBooks window. You access PeopleBooks by selecting Help > PeopleBooks from the Application menu.

Note that the content list (or table of contents) is visible down the left side of the window. Each item annotated with a plus sign can be expanded to reveal more detailed information by clicking on the plus sign. The window on the right displays the full document with the cursor moved to the section you have selected from the content list on the left. A hit reference window is displayed underneath the content list and document windows. There are also tabs located across the bottom of the window that allow you to change your view to a single window view of any of the tab options.

**TIP**   You may also access the Advanced Search window by clicking on the binoculars in the lower left corner of the window.

## Using Advanced Query in PeopleBooks

The power of PeopleBooks is its ability to do full text searches and return a hit list by topic that allows easy selection of the appropriate section of the documentation. You can access the Advanced Query window in one of three ways:

▶ Select Search > Advanced Query from the PeopleBooks menu.

▶ Press F2.

▶ Click the binoculars in the lower left corner of the panel.

Figure 8.15 shows the PeopleBooks Advanced Query panel. The Advanced Query option allows users to build custom queries to find precisely the information they are looking for. Users can search for single words or phrases. To search for phrases, simply enclose the phrase in quotation marks. In Figure 8.15, the search phrase is "application server." There are several basic search functions, listed in Table 8.2.

**FIGURE 8.14**    The PeopleBooks window

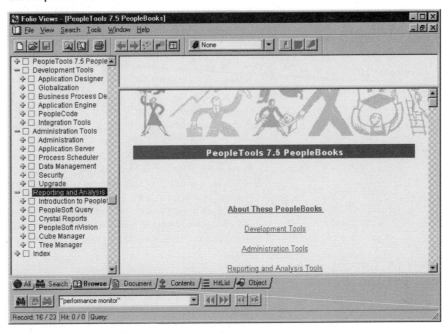

**FIGURE 8.15**    PeopleBooks Advanced Query panel

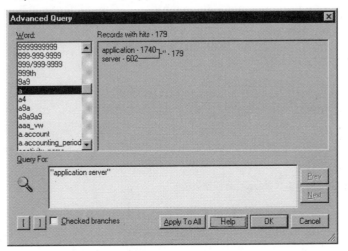

**TABLE 8.2**    Search Functions

| Function | Description |
|---|---|
| And | This function allows you to select text from PeopleBooks that contains both words or phrases for which you are searching. This function is used by either typing the word "and" or using the symbol "&" between the words or phrases. |
| Or | You can search for documents that contain either of the words or phrases for which you are searching. This function is used by typing the word "or" or using the vertical bar symbol "|" between the words and phrases. |
| Wildcards | Wildcard searches allow you to find words that match all of the characters except for those for which you have substituted the wildcard symbol. There are two types of wildcard characters. The single character wildcard ("?") is used to replace a single character. If you have two characters in a row that you want to use the single wildcard character for, you must type the symbol twice. The multiple character wildcard ("*") is used when you want to search for parts of words and do not care about suffixes or other additions. |
| Proximity | The proximity search is used when you want to find multiple words or phrases that are within the specified number of words of each other. For example, if you search for "ledger & error /5," the search will return any record in the infobase in which "ledger" and "error" are both found within five words of each other. This is extremely helpful in narrowing a broad search down to a smaller number of records for you to choose from. |

Suppose you wanted to find the phrase "application server." Open the query window as described above and enter the phrase as shown in Figure 8.15. The numbers of hits appear quickly as you type. As you can see, 1,740 records had the word "application" and 602 had the word "server," but only 179 had the phrase "application server." If you want to narrow the search even further and had another word or phrase that was involved, you enter it here as well.

Another topic that may be of interest is capturing your company's business processes in the same search so your users have only one place to search. Let's look at customizing PeopleBooks to meet the specific needs of your installation.

## Customizing PeopleBooks

PeopleSoft ships PeopleBooks with the ability to edit the infobase file. This allows you to insert your own documentation or provide examples that are specific to your installation.

There are several options for customizing. You can simply add notes or annotations to the infobase by placing your cursor in the document where you want to place the new text. Select Tools **>** Note and enter the desired text. You can also highlight specific text so your users can more easily see specific sections. To highlight a word or phrase, select Tools **>** Highlighter from the menu. The selected text is highlighted. You can assign specific highlighter colors or patterns to individual users so it is easy to see who highlighted the text. This is accomplished by creating custom highlighters and naming them. To create a custom highlighter, select Tools **>** Highlighter and choose New from the window. Name your highlighter and select the background color you want to use.

The other option you have for customizing your PeopleBooks is through the addition or deletion of text or objects. To add text, type the additional information just as if using your word processing package. If you have large amounts of information that you need to add and already have that information in another file, you can import that information. To import information from an external file, position the cursor where you want to place the document and select File **>** Import from the menu. Specify the document type and filename. A status bar appears that shows the status of the import. Once the import is complete, save the infobase. The new information becomes part of the original infobase.

I do not recommend that you give all users the ability to update PeopleBooks info-bases directly. The preferred method is to use the Folio shadow file functionality.

## Shadow Files

Folio has a capability called shadow files. Shadow files can be used to allow users or groups of users to have their own view into the infobase. This shadow file can contain extra comments, highlighting, or notes that are specific to that group of users. The shadow file stores these modifications in a separate file (the shadow file) to preserve the integrity of your master infobase.

The shadow file provides security for certain annotations that you want to add. Create the shadow file in a directory with limited access, and then only those users or groups that have access to this directory can see the contents of the shadow file and how it compares to the original documentation.

If you still have questions, additional information is available by selecting Help **>** Overview from the PeopleBooks menu. This opens the Folio Views help infobase, which contains descriptions and examples of all your available options.

# Summary

This chapter described the tools provided by PeopleSoft that can help your end-users become more self-sufficient. As the system administrator, it is your job to be familiar with these tools. But you also need to control the use of these tools. You need to prevent unauthorized access to files and you need to prevent users from running applications that might degrade the performance of your system.

The PeopleSoft Query tool allows your end-users to perform ad hoc queries on data to which they have access. The Query tool can also export report data to Crystal Reports for formatting or to Microsoft Excel for further analysis.

Crystal Reports is a report-formatting tool that produces high-quality, easy-to-read reports. Crystal Reports can be useful in troubleshooting problems in your People-Soft system.

nVision is a PeopleTool that creates queries that populate Microsoft Excel spreadsheets for use in building reports or performing detailed data analysis. nVision allows your users to use all the functions of Excel to perform detailed analysis of PeopleSoft data.

The Process Scheduler is a powerful scheduling program that allows your end-users to schedule the execution of their own batch jobs. The advantage of this feature is that CPU-intensive jobs can be run during off-hours.

PeopleBooks is the online documentation system delivered with your PeopleSoft system. The Advanced Query option allows users to narrow a search when looking for information in PeopleBooks. Users can customize PeopleBooks to reflect any changes made by your company. In addition, shadow files allow users or groups of users to have their own view into the infobase.

The next chapter discusses the security considerations you'll need to address while maintaining your PeopleSoft system.

# Security

**FEATURING**

▶ **ELEMENTS OF SECURITY**

▶ **PEOPLESOFT SECURITY TOOLS**

▶ **DEVELOPING A SECURITY PLAN**

▶ **PREPARING FOR A SECURITY AUDIT**

O ne of the most critical tasks of a PeopleSoft System Administrator is securing your system and data. Your challenge is to provide comprehensive system security without making access too unwieldy for your users. Security planning should be included in all steps of your implementation. The one question that you should constantly ask yourself and your team is: How can we make each access or change to the system as secure as possible?

There are countless books that have been written on the topic of system security. This chapter discusses several popular security ideas and describes some of the lessons that I have learned while dealing with PeopleSoft system security.

# Elements of Security

The elements of security can be thought of as those areas for which some form of authentication or verification can be implemented for your system. All systems and environments present unique challenges for implementing a security plan that is both effective and workable. For the PeopleSoft environment, there are three areas that need to be addressed by your security plan: the network; the database; and the application, which includes access to program functionality and data.

▶ The network is the foundation of the security system in which you operate any client-server application. It makes no difference whether you are in a Novell, Windows NT, or UNIX network environment; this is the first opportunity that you, the system administrator, have to control access into your system.

▶ The database is the heart of the PeopleSoft system. Most of the components of a PeopleSoft system, including employee data, panels, menus, PeopleCode, and other processing rules, are contained in the database. Proper security at the database level prevents unauthorized access into the system.

▶ PeopleSoft provides the Object Security capability for implementing security at the application level. This allows you to grant access to panels or menus for only those individuals or groups of individuals that truly need that access. Object Security is described in detail later in this chapter. PeopleSoft also provides methods for controlling access to individual rows of data using security trees and query security records.

The configuration for each of the three elements can be used to create layers of security for your PeopleSoft system.

# Network Security

In configuring your network for PeopleSoft, give each user the minimum amount of access necessary to do their job. For example, in a Novell 4.11 network, you control access to the PeopleSoft executable files and other files using two groups under Novell Directory Services (NDS). The first group is for end users. The second group is for administrators who have the authority to install and update the PeopleSoft files. The only subdirectory that an end user should need access to for creating or editing files is the directory designated for storing the Crystal Reports files. The same principles can be applied to Windows NT or UNIX environments.

Additionally, end-user access to the server on which your RDBMS is running should be strictly controlled. This rule can even be extended to the implementation partners who are working with you. It is a good idea to designate a member of your technical implementation team to control and move all files required for running batch jobs to the server. This policy helps you avoid confusion about the status of any customized files or updates that have been received from PeopleSoft.

PART

II

PeopleTools

# Database Security

Access to the database is a critical step in the security of your system. With the database, you have the built-in security of the RDBMS on which you are running the PeopleSoft applications. PeopleSoft provides a second level of security for the database. PeopleSoft users are defined inside the PeopleSoft system tables. When you create a new user, a user account is added to the database. That account has very limited rights when connecting directly to the database. The user has only the select right for three tables: PSDBOWNER, PSOPRDEFN, and PSLOCK. The PeopleSoft login process locates the user, determines the rights that the user has been granted, and then drops this connection and performs a login with PeopleSoft access account. The access account has full rights to the database, but uses the PeopleSoft security profile to control the individual user's access to data.

**NOTE** Microsoft SQL Server and Sybase do not use the PSDBOWNER table in the login process, so those users have only select rights to PSOPRDEFN and PSLOCK.

Limit the number of users to whom you grant direct access to the production database tables using the query tools. The query tools allow access to the data without going through PeopleSoft security. This direct access can be viewed as a security weakness during an audit, since these users can access all data in a table, not just that data to which they have been granted access using PeopleSoft security. You can provide query-only access to developers in your test database as the situation warrants.

# Application Security

PeopleSoft provides the system administrator with the ability to establish and implement security policies for both application functions and individual data rows (row-level security). You can restrict users to certain menu items. Access to specific menu items is controlled by the operator or class profiles that are administered by the Security Administrator program, which is discussed later in this chapter. The user can also be restricted to subsets of data, which is how PeopleSoft HRMS ensures that managers have access only to their own employees. Figure 9.1 shows a sample security tree diagram that identifies a manager's access to his employee's data.

**FIGURE 9.1**    Security diagram in Tree Manager

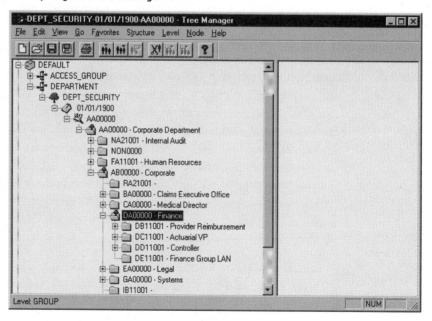

In the example in this figure, the manager of the Finance Department has access to all the employees below his level but has no access to the employees above his level.

The Tree Manager allows you to define the relationships that are hierarchical. The Tree Manager also helps you define data groupings to aid in data analysis. Figure 9.1 shows an example of a departmental security tree that is used by PeopleSoft HRMS. (The Tree Manager functionality is discussed later in this chapter.)

Access to the PeopleTools utilities is provided through the use of Object Security. Access to online panels and menus is provided through the Security Administrator PeopleTool. These security programs are discussed in detail later in this chapter. First, let's look at the Security Administrator.

# PeopleSoft Security Tools

PeopleSoft provides tools for use in administering the security of your system. Using these tools, you can control access to the data, menu items, and PeopleTools objects in your system.

This section discusses the security tools that are built into your PeopleSoft system: Security Administrator, Object Security, Query Security, and Tree Manager.

## Security Administrator

The Security Administrator is the PeopleTool that allows the system administrator to control data and application access in the PeopleSoft system. The Security Administrator is used to create user profiles, to control when and how the users can access the PeopleSoft system, and to control the objects that the users can access. In addition, you can create security groups and assign levels of access to each security group, allowing you to easily add or remove access to individuals by simply adding or removing them from the group. Let's take a closer look at the panels that make up the Security Administrator tool.

### Security Administrator Panels

The Definition window is where you establish and configure profiles using the Security Administrator. Figure 9.2 contains an example of the Definition window. Note that when you choose a view on the left side, the attributes for that view appear on the right side of the Definition window.

**FIGURE 9.2**   Definition window–General view

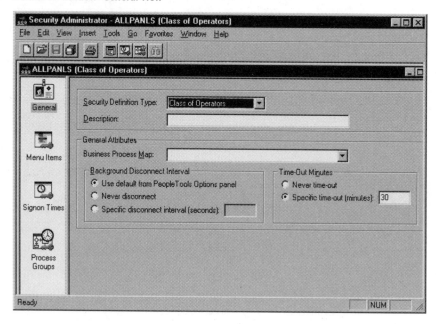

There are five views available when establishing or editing an operator or class profile: General, Menu Items, Process Groups, Classes, and Signon Times.

**The General view** (Figure 9.2)   The General view is the first view that is displayed.
Operator-specific information, such as employee ID and password is entered here.
The General view is also where you specify the following options:

▶ Whether the profile you are creating is an operator or a class

▶ The default language

▶ The access profile

▶ Whether this account can start the application server for your three-tier
environment, if applicable

**The Menu Items view** (Figure 9.3)   The Menu Items view displays all menu items
to which this operator or class has access. To grant access to a menu not on the list,
select Insert **>** Menu from the Security Administrator menu. To remove access,
highlight the menu item and press the Delete key. The menu items at this level are
equivalent to the menu bars that represent business processes. To grant access to
specific menu items for the items displayed in Figure 9.3, double-click a specific

menu item. The Select Menu Items panel appears. Figure 9.4 contains the Select
Menu Items panel and shows the first items under the Use menu item for Administer Workforce U.S. The Select Menu Items panel allows you to grant specific access
to panels and menu items. You can also grant Display Only access, as shown in the
Job Data 3 panel in Figure 9.4.

**FIGURE 9.3**   Definition window–Menu Items view

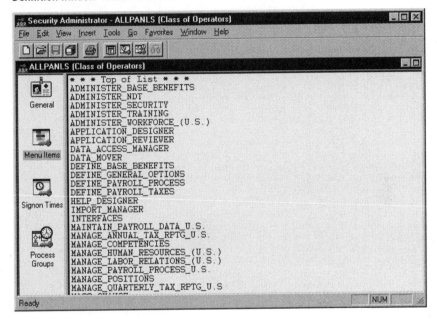

**FIGURE 9.4**   Select Menu Items panel

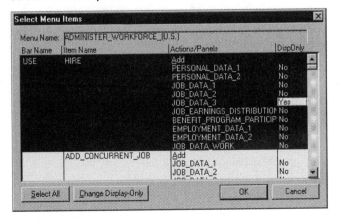

PART

II

PeopleTools

**The Signon Times view** (Figure 9.5)    The Signon Times view displays the times at which an operator or class can access the system. A single day can have more than one access period. The only requirement for multiple signon times is there must be an open period between each access time.

**FIGURE 9.5**    Definition window–Signon Times view

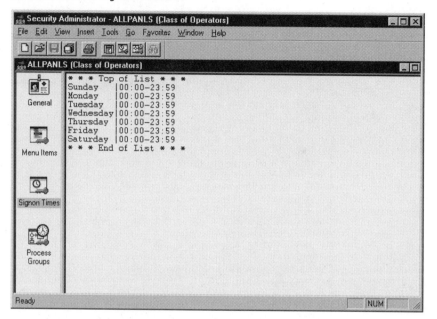

**The Process Groups view** (Figure 9.6)    The Process Groups view displays all processes for which the operator or class has access. These process groups are defined using the Process Scheduler menu item. You grant access to process groups by selecting Insert **>** Process Groups from the menu.

**The Classes view** (Figure 9.7)    The Classes view displays all classes to which an operator has been assigned. This view is available only for operator profiles. You must specify the primary access class for an operator if the user is assigned to more than one class. The Row-Level Security field allows you to specify the operator class to which this user belongs for access to individual rows of data in your system. This expands on the data access granted to the user with the use of a query security record. The security record that you use must include either the field OPRID, OPRCLASS, or RowSecClass for the Row-Level Security parameter to work. (The query security record and RowSecClass field are discussed later in this chapter.)

Each of these views has a separate attribute panel into which you edit the properties for the view.

**FIGURE 9.6** Definition window–Process Groups view

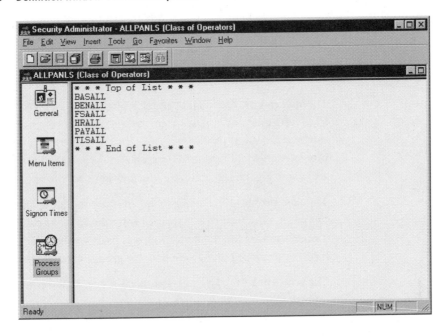

**FIGURE 9.7** Definition window–Classes view

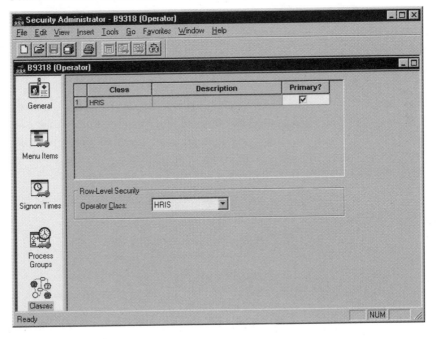

## Security Administrator Profiles

The Security Administrator profiles define the security access that has been granted. The actions that can be taken are based on the type of profile that is defined. There are three types of Security Administrator profiles that can be defined in the PeopleSoft system: operator, class, and access profiles. Let's look at each of them more closely.

**The operator profile** The operator profile will be used frequently in your system, since every operator in your system must have a defined operator profile. Operators can be stand-alone profiles with all access privileges directly associated with the profile, or they can belong to classes and inherit the rights of the class. Operators are able to log directly on to the system using a password.

**The class profile** The class profile can save you time by granting access security to a group once instead of having to grant the access to each individual operator. The class allows you to create groups of users with similar rights. Classes do not have login privileges; they are used for grouping users for security access.

**The access profile** The access profile is the most powerful profile in the system. This profile must have system administrator privileges set at the RDBMS level and is used to provide the secondary login access to the RDBMS. This is the account that is used for the direct database signon that occurs during the PeopleSoft login process.

**New Profiles** To create a new operator or class profile, open the Security Administrator and select File > New. Specify whether the definition type is an operator or class from the drop-down list, as shown in Figure 9.2. All process group and profile information for the new profile must be entered.

To create a new access profile, select Tools > Access Profiles and select the New button, as shown in Figure 9.8. Enter an access profile name and a password for this account. The access profile name must be an account with total access to your RDBMS.

**FIGURE 9.8**    Add Access Profile panel

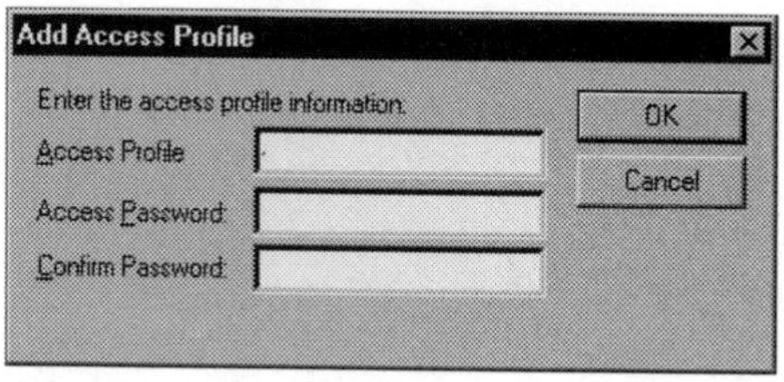

**Cloning Profiles**   Cloning profiles (creating a new profile based on an existing profile) has been simplified under PeopleTools version 7 and higher. To clone a profile, open an existing profile and select File **>** Save As. Enter the operator ID and password for the account into the Save Operator As panel, as shown in Figure 9.9, and a new profile, which is a clone of the profile you opened, is created.

**FIGURE 9.9**   Cloning profiles–Save Operator As panel

Save Operator As   [X]

Enter the operator profile information:

Operator Profile ID: [                    ]      OK

Operator Password: [                    ]      Cancel

Confirm Password: [                    ]

**Administering Profiles**   Each of the three profile types has unique features and uses.

### OPERATOR PROFILES

The administration of operator profiles is a critical part of the success of your security plan. You will update operator profiles to reflect personnel moves and the addition of new applications. The following tasks are required for administering operator profiles:

| TASK | HOW TO DO IT |
| --- | --- |
| Unlinking classes | Operators often move to other areas or change responsibilities. If this happens, you need to remove the access to certain classes of information. To remove a class, select the Classes process group, highlight the class that is no longer needed, and press the Delete key. Save the operator profile. |
| Changing passwords | Changing operator passwords is a simple process with the Security Administrator. Open the operator you are changing, enter the new password, and confirm the new password in the fields provided in the General process group. Then save the profile. |
| Changing access ID | The access ID is the account that is used by the PeopleSoft process to reconnect to the database after the initial signon. To create a new access ID, select Tools **>** Access Profiles from the Security Administrator window. Create a new access account and save it. |

PART

**II**

PeopleTools

| TASK | HOW TO DO IT |
|------|-------------|
| Changing access ID (continued) | Then open the operator profile for which you want to change the access ID. Select the desired access profile from the Access Profile drop-down list in the General process group. You need to change your access ID if the old ID had been compromised. You might also add an access ID to partition users into separate accounts to reflect business changes. If you are billing system time, you might look at the connection ID for tracking system usage. |

## CLASS PROFILES

The administration of class profiles will be less time-consuming than the administration of operator profiles. The most frequent updates to class profiles will occur during and after an upgrade as new functionality is added to classes, or if menu names are changed during the upgrade and security access for the class must be reactivated. The following tasks are required for administering class profiles:

| TASK | HOW TO DO IT |
|------|-------------|
| Updating class access | As you administer your PeopleSoft system, you will make new features available to your users. You may even have to remove access to other features, such as customizations. If you have given access to the class instead of to the operator, all you have to do is open the class profile and delete the menu item that you no longer want users of a particular class to access. |
| Managing the PSADMIN class | The PSADMIN class that is delivered with PeopleSoft has some special considerations. The purpose of this class is to give unrestricted access to most PeopleSoft objects as they are created. Therefore, it should only be used in a test environment. It should never be used in your production database because any operator that is assigned to this class has no verification performed on PeopleSoft objects. In other words, it bypasses all security settings that you are trying to enforce. |

## ACCESS PROFILES

Access profiles will require the least maintenance of all the security profiles. Access profiles should be established early in your implementation. The only routine change will be changing passwords. The following tasks are required for administering access profiles:

| TASK | HOW TO DO IT |
|---|---|
| Changing passwords | Changing access profile passwords requires a coordinated effort between several processes for certain RDBMS systems, especially if you have multiple databases on one hardware platform. Take the following steps: |

1. Change the password on the RDBMS.

2. Run a Data Mover script to update the access profile password on the PSOPRDEFN table using the encrypt_password command. Use the SQL update command to change the ACCESSPWD field.

3. Adjust your Process Scheduler configuration files so that the Process Scheduler application can log in to the database.

I recommend that you change the password for the access ID if the person filling your System Security Administrator role changes positions or leaves the company.

The Data Mover syntax for changing the access passwords is as follows:

```
Update PSOPRDEFN set ACCESSID = 'accessid', ACCESSPSWD
= 'accesspassword',
OPERPSWD = '0000000000000000'
Where OPRTYPE = 0;
Update PSACCESSPRFL
Set ACCESSID = ' accessid ',
ACCESSPSWD = 'accesspassword',
VERSION = 0,
ENCRYPTED = 0;
Encrypt_password *;
```

PeopleSoft also provides a Change Password dialog box for changing the access password. To access this dialog box, select Tools > Access Profiles from the Security Administrator menu. Enter your current password and then enter your new password twice to confirm the change.

Remember, this may require coordination if multiple databases are on the same server and use the same access ID.

| TASK | HOW TO DO IT |
|------|-------------|
| Deleting access profiles | Don't delete an access profile until you have created a new access profile to take its place. Every system *must* have at least one access profile defined. Without a defined access profile, no users can be granted access to any database object. |

Object Security extends your ability to control access to the development environment of PeopleSoft. Let's take a closer look at Object Security.

# Object Security

PeopleSoft provides the system administrator with comprehensive control over the PeopleTools themselves. Through the use of Object Security, the system administrator can control, for each database, the access rights for a user to change or update any object in the PeopleSoft system tables.

This feature is useful for allowing developers to have full access (except for security) to the development database. They can create procedures or test any part of the system. However, with access to the production database limited to view only, they cannot move or change the production environment outside of any change control processes you have in place.

Designate one person who moves the new objects or makes changes to existing objects into production. This ensures greater control over the updates to the production database. Make sure that person fully documents all changes to the production system. Change control is an important responsibility of the person you designate to supervise the process. This person should use the Application Upgrader tool discussed in Chapter 12, "Upgrading Your PeopleSoft System," to move new or updated objects from one database to another.

This person should also be responsible for moving new SQR reports or other code, such as modified COBOL programs, to your production environment. With PeopleSoft version 7, this becomes even more important because the Custom project should be updated with your customizations so they can be more easily recognized and preserved during an upgrade. The Custom project helps you complete your upgrade more quickly, since you do not have to manually update the upgrade project for your customized objects.

Let's move on to a discussion of object groups and their use in Object Security.

## Object Groups

Object groups allow you to establish groups of users and deny or grant access to specific objects in PeopleTools. When you have an object group loaded in the Object

Security window, there are icons across the top of the panel that let you select the types of objects that you want to work with. Figure 9.10 illustrates the Object Security panel with an object group loaded. To access this panel, select Go > PeopleTools > Object Security from any PeopleSoft menu.

**NOTE**  The numbers on the icons in Figure 9.10 are used for reference in the following paragraph, since PeopleSoft does not associate names with these icons in the online system.

In Figure 9.10, the globe icon (1) at the extreme left displays all the accesses that have been granted. The access list is sorted by type. The objects are displayed by name in a single window.

**FIGURE 9.10**    Object Security–Object Group panel

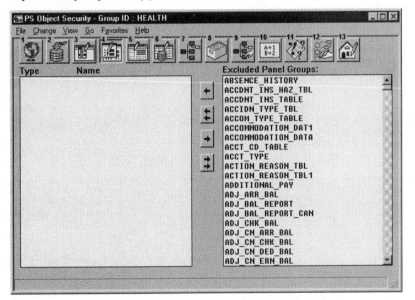

The other icons show the detail of included and excluded definitions for specific object types. If a group or operator has a specific item included in its list, then that group or operator has access; otherwise, the group or operator do not have access to the listed object type. The included objects are displayed on the left, and the excluded objects are displayed on the right. Once an exception exists, the Tree Definition view shows the included objects in the panel on the top and the excluded objects on the bottom.

The following object types can be displayed:

▶ Import definitions (2)

▶ Menus (3)

▶ Panel groups (4)

▶ Panels (5)

▶ Records (6)

▶ Tree structures (7)

▶ Projects (8)

▶ Tree definitions (9)

▶ Translate tables (10)

▶ Queries (11)

▶ Business processes (12)

▶ Business process maps (13)

Let's discuss how to establish the security of queries in PeopleSoft.

## Query Security

PeopleSoft delivers the Query tool to produce ad hoc or production queries that access data. In order to ensure that users can only access the same information that they have access to from the online panels, PeopleSoft implements Query Security. Query Security is used to limit a user's access to only those data records that are defined by the Query Security search record that is linked to the record definition. Query Security is generally implemented in the form of SQL views. PeopleSoft delivers some SQL views for your use, but you can modify them or create your own to customize the security of your system.

Query Security in PeopleSoft is implemented using security views that are associated with the record definition. If you link the JOB record to the PERS_SRCH_US security view, as shown in Figure 9.11, then the users that have access to query the JOB record can only access the information that they can see through the online panels. To access the Record Properties panel in Figure 9.11, select File > Object Properties from the Application Designer menu while the desired record definition is open.

Let's look at an example SQL statement showing the join to the query security record. This is the query that is illustrated in Chapter 8, "End-User Tools," in Figure 8.5. The code shown in **bold** represents the join to the query security record that is done automatically by PeopleSoft Query.

```
SELECT A.EMPLID,
A.NAME,
A.CITY,
A.BIRTHDATE
```

```
FROM PS_EMPLOYEES A, PS_EMPLMT_SRCH_US A1
WHERE A.EMPLID = A1.EMPLID
  AND A.EMPL_RCD# = A1.EMPL_RCD#
  AND A1.OPRCLASS = 'HRIS'
  AND (A.EMPLID > '09000'
    AND A.EMPLID < '09400')
```

In this example, the join to A1.EMPLID validates that the user has access to each employee who meets the criteria of greater than '09000' and less than '09400.' The PS_EMPLMT_SRCH_US query security record contains one record for each employee for each class or operator profile in your system. If you have 3,000 employees and 20 classes, then the resulting view contains 60,000 records.

**FIGURE 9.11**    Record Properties panel–Use tab

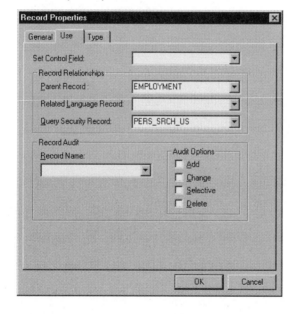

Now let's look at the SQL used to create the PS_EMPLMT_SRCH_US view that is defined as the query security record in this example.

```
SELECT
 A.EMPLID
,B.EMPL_RCD#
,C.OPRID
,A.NAME
,A.LAST_NAME_SRCH
,C.ACCESS_CD
,A.SSN
```

```
FROM PS_PERSONAL_DATA A
,PS_JOB B
,PS_SCRTY_TBL_DEPT C
WHERE C.ACCESS_CD='Y'
AND A.EMPLID=B.EMPLID
AND (B.EFFDT>=%CURRENTDATEIN
  OR B.EFFDT=
  (SELECT MAX(D.EFFDT)
  FROM PS_JOB D
  WHERE B.EMPLID=D.EMPLID
  AND B.EMPL_RCD#=D.EMPL_RCD#
  AND D.EFFDT<=%CURRENTDATEIN))
AND EXISTS
  (SELECT 'X'
  FROM PSTREENODE E
  WHERE E.SETID=' '
  AND E.TREE_NAME='DEPT_SECURITY'
  AND E.EFFDT=C.TREE_EFFDT
  AND E.TREE_NODE=B.DEPTID
  AND E.TREE_NODE_NUM
    BETWEEN C.TREE_NODE_NUM
  AND C.TREE_NODE_NUM_END
  AND NOT EXISTS
  (SELECT 'X'
  FROM PS_SCRTY_TBL_DEPT G
  WHERE C.OPRID=G.OPRID
  AND C.TREE_NODE_NUM<>G.TREE_NODE_NUM
  AND E.TREE_NODE_NUM
    BETWEEN G.TREE_NODE_NUM
  AND G.TREE_NODE_NUM_END
  AND G.TREE_NODE_NUM
    BETWEEN C.TREE_NODE_NUM
  AND C.TREE_NODE_NUM_END))
```

If you want to use the new functionality that lets operators belong to more than one class, you must replace OPRID or OPRCLASS with the field RowSecClass in the query security record that is being used, whether delivered by PeopleSoft or defined by you. The PeopleSoft online system is designed to look at information contained in this field when granting access to data executing a query.

**NOTE** The previous example for PS_EMPLMT_SRCH_US uses the PeopleSoft-delivered methodology where a user can only belong to one class.

Query Security will probably give you more troubleshooting problems than any other part of the system. Generally, when user queries exceed the table join limit imposed by your RDBMS, it is because the records that they are attempting to join use different Query Security views. The query must join to all the tables that are used in both views, in addition to the two records that they were attempting to join. This issue is covered in more detail in Chapter 17, "Troubleshooting."

# Tree Manager

The Tree Manager application is used to create and administer trees for your People-Soft system. Trees are objects that allow you to define groups or specify hierarchical relationships between values in your database. The example discussed previously is the departmental security tree for PeopleSoft HRMS. Once a tree has been created, it can be used for both reporting and security purposes. Trees are created using graphical representations and provide the system with a single source from which to gather summary information.

Let's look at some of the terminology associated with PeopleSoft trees:

**Categories**    Categories define the high-level grouping under Tree Manager. For example, PeopleSoft delivers the Default and Query categories.

**Nodes**    Nodes refer to the individual objects of the tree. For example, each department in a departmental security tree is a node.

**Relationships**    The relationships between nodes in a tree are referred to using terms used in a family tree. The parent is the higher level node. Parents have children below them. Children of the same parent are referred to as siblings. These terms are used when defining the relationships in Tree Manager.

PeopleSoft defines four types of trees:

**Detail**    Detail trees contain database values at the lowest level. The nodes at the higher levels that define the relationship do not exist as data in the database; they are known as arbitrary definitions.

**Summary**    Summary trees provide a means of grouping data in an existing detail tree in another tree structure. The detail level of a summary tree does not contain database values; it contains nodes in the detail tree that is being summarized.

**Node-oriented**    A node-oriented tree contains all the nodes of the tree defined by data in the database. The most common node-oriented tree in PeopleSoft applications is the departmental security tree.

PART

**II**

PeopleTools

**Query access**    A query access tree is used to define the query access groups of specific record definitions. Operator or class profiles are granted access to the specific Query Access groups that are defined. The operators or classes are then able to build queries using only the records defined in the access groups. An example of a Query Access group is shown expanded in Figure 9.12. To access the Tree Manager, select Go **>** PeopleTools **>** Tree Manager from any menu.

**FIGURE 9.12**    **Tree Manager–Workflow Access Group**

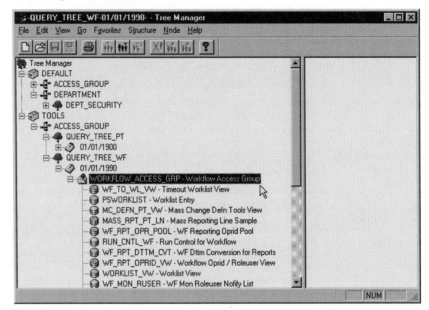

When working with existing trees, open the tree definition. Highlight the node for which you want to define additional children or siblings, right-click the object, and select Insert Child or Insert Sibling from the dialog box. When working with an node-oriented tree, enter  the database value that you want to use for this node. If the data exists, the node is inserted. If the data does not exist, the panel used for this data opens, and you can enter the new data. The node is created when you save the new data.

**T I P**    When creating a new Departmental Security Tree for HRMS, don't forget to run the process PER505.SQR to link the new effective date of the tree to the system.

In PeopleSoft HRMS, to tie the class profile to the specific tree node for which access is to be granted, select Go **>** Define Business Rules **>** Administer HR System from any menu. Then select Use **>** Maintain Data Security **>** Department and select the class that you want to update. Figure 9.13 contains the Department tab under Maintain

Data Security. Enter the department ID that represents the tree node. The class then has access to data rows that are in the specified department as well as access to all the branches of the tree below this node. Classes that required access to all personnel are granted access to the top node of the tree.

**FIGURE 9.13**    Maintain Data Security–Department tab

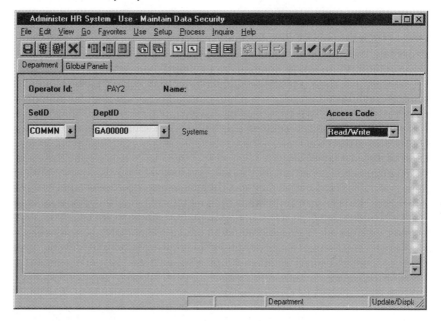

PART

II

PeopleTools

Let's look at how to tie this all together with a security plan.

# Developing a Security Plan

The first step in developing a security plan is to recognize the need for one. The second step is to develop the plan. Having a comprehensive security plan gives you the opportunity to be proactive and have a plan ready when your Corporate Security Officer asks you what you are doing about security. The security manager can be a good sounding board and source of information for what is expected and what is required from the security auditors.

## Evaluating the Threat

The first step in developing your security plan is to evaluate the threat. Threats to your system can be both internal and external. For example, if your company has direct access to the Internet, the external threat to your system is much greater than if direct Internet access does not exist.

The types of potential threats you are faced with include hackers, disgruntled employees, computer viruses, commercial espionage, and password disclosure. Let's take a quick look at each of these threats to gain a better understanding of how they can compromise your system.

The first threat that everyone talks about is a hacker. What is a hacker? The most common definition is someone who gains access to a system to which he or she does not belong. Hackers can be relentless in their attempts to break into your system if they believe that your system has information of value.

Internal threats can be a huge risk to your system. The disgruntled employee is often overlooked as a potential threat. Another common misconception is that only former employees are potentially dangerous. Former employees may become hackers and try to get back into your system to do damage. However, active employees may be a much greater threat. They can plant logic bombs (see note) in case they are terminated. They may be leaking information to sources outside your company for a variety of reasons.

**N O T E**  Logic bombs are programs that, if they don't receive a specific instruction within a specified amount of time, activate and begin to perform the programmed task, such as deleting files or deleting entire server disk volumes.

Computer viruses present a very real security threat. The most common sources of these viruses are from files downloaded from the Internet or from floppy disks that users exchange with other users. Some of the viruses that have been detected can cause significant damage to data files, by deleting or modifying them into unusable states.

Commercial espionage is a serious threat, especially in certain industries. Sometimes hackers are employed to gather and pass on company-confidential information. However, commercial espionage is not limited to electronic means. Sometimes commercial espionage entails searching through a company's trash for useful information.

Password disclosure is the most common security violation. Users give their passwords to coworkers. They write them down on "sticky notes" that are attached to their computer monitors. There have even been documented cases in which employees gave their passwords to a person on the phone who claimed to be from the LAN support group.

Let's discuss what you can do to meet the threats described here.

# Determining the Options Available to Meet the Threats

As the system administrator, you need to counter the threats described in the previous section. Proper password security provides a strong degree of security. Enforce password changes on a regular basis. Prevent password disclosure by synchronizing passwords between your systems, if possible. Many security experts believe that if you reduce the number of passwords a user has to remember, then you reduce the chances that the user will write the password down.

PeopleSoft does not currently perform password expiration to force users to change their passwords at a specified interval, although password expiration functionality is planned for a future release. You can use third-party tools for performing password expiration. For example, SQL<>Secure from Braintree Software is one product available if you are using Oracle as your database. DB2 mainframe users use the mainframe security (usually RACF) to provide this functionality.

You can discourage hackers from attacking your site by implementing a strong firewall policy if you are directly connected to the Internet. Another way to discourage hackers is to minimize the number of modems that are connected to your system. For those users who must have modems, provide additional security mechanisms by forcing a dial-back plan or by using smart cards.

The disgruntled employee is a tougher threat to counter. You must be vigilant to changes in your system, without appearing to be spying. Logic bombs can be detected by searching for files in unusual locations that are continually being updated by the employee. Concentrate on executable programs, including user-written macros. This is a sensitive area in some companies. Consult with both the security manager and (if available) the employee relations manager to work out a viable policy for monitoring your system that is not overbearing for employees.

A good virus prevention and detection program is critical. There are many ways for users to exchange programs and files that might include viruses. The best security measure that you can take is to implement active virus-scanning software that checks all inbound and outbound data on your system. Another effective security measure is to install an active monitoring agent on any workstation that accesses the Internet. For example, on my workstation, all files that are downloaded using the Web browser are scanned before they are stored on my system.

To counter the threat of commercial espionage, be vigilant to the way in which you present data. Implementing a firewall for your Internet access and limiting modem

PART

**II**

PeopleTools

connections into your system can reduce the electronic threat. If printed reports from your PeopleSoft system contain sensitive information, make sure those reports are shredded before discarding them.

The way to attack password disclosure is through employee education. Make your employees aware of the seriousness of disclosing their password to others. This will be your toughest task as a system administrator.

Now let's look at how profile groups can make administering your security plan easier.

## Establishing Profile Groups

Establishing profile groups in which you can group access to the system is an important step in making security administration easier. The groups should be configured based on functional responsibilities and/or departmental assignment.

Let's consider an example of a profile group. Suppose your company has a secondary Human Resources site that you want to restrict from viewing information for the entire company. Create a profile group and assign all the personnel in the secondary office to this group. Then give this group access to only those employees at their location.

## Publishing the Security Plan

Now that you have developed the security plan, you are ready to begin implementing it. The most important step in the implementation of your security plan is the establishment and publication of its security policies. You need to document the plan in written form and distribute the policy to the end users. Make sure that the users have a good understanding not only of the plan, but of why a plan is needed in the first place. Make them aware of the threats that you are trying to prevent. User education is critical to the success of a security plan.

## Training the Users

Poor end-user training is often blamed for security problems. This can be avoided by developing a plan that includes training new employees on security-related matters. In addition, schedule regular sessions to provide updates and reviews of security procedures for existing employees.

Once your security plan is in place, let's look at some ways to make a security audit of your system go more smoothly.

# Preparing for a Security Audit

One of the challenges that you will be faced with if you have either PeopleSoft Financials or Payroll installed is a security audit. Typically, your internal audit staff will conduct an annual security audit. The schedule will vary depending on your application and your corporate operating policies. If you have planned carefully and followed your procedures closely, the audit will be easier than if you did not prepare.

Let's look at some areas of potential concern that you will want to review in preparation for your audit.

## Documenting the Business Processes

One of the most important aspects of implementing your system is the documentation that you create. This is one of the most overlooked aspects of implementing a new ERP system, especially in the client-server environment. Careful planning and thorough procedures for documenting your system, the security configurations, and all the business processes will save you many headaches when the auditor arrives.

Make sure to document all security procedures. You should also document the access profiles and operator profiles that you create and modify. Document any other security-related changes that are made to your system. Chapter 14, "Documentation," provides more detail about how to document your PeopleSoft system.

## Spot-Checking Users for Compliance

Once your security plans are in place, do not become complacent. There is a natural tendency to put off reviewing the security plan; there is always another project that is more important. Take the time to review how well your security plan is working by spot-checking your users. You can formally test them, or you can use casual conversation to conduct this spot-check. Bring up an aspect of the plan, such as password protection, in casual conversation to see if the user reacts properly and knows the procedures.

It is important to determine if the end users know how to apply the security procedures or if they are merely quoting the plan. You might ask them questions like these:

▶ How often do you change your password?

▶ Who do you contact if you think someone else knows your password?

▶ What do you do with old reports that have sensitive information in them?

▶ What should you do if someone else tells you his or her password?

## Reviewing the Security Procedures Periodically

Your security plan should be a "living" document. Continually strive to improve your plan. New threats can spring up at any time. Coordinate with your corporate security administrator to ensure that you have the latest information on new threats. You may want your corporate security administrator to help with a periodic review of your security plan. This may help you identify potential weaknesses that you had not discovered.

# Summary

Managing the security of your PeopleSoft system is a major focus of your job as system administrator. There are three major elements on which to focus your attention: the network, the database, and the PeopleSoft applications.

PeopleSoft provides you with four tools to help you manage the security of your system:

- ▶ The Security Administrator allows you to create and modify operator, class, and access profiles.

- ▶ Object Security helps you manage the security of the development environment.

- ▶ Query Security allows you to prevent users from running queries on data to which they do not normally have access.

- ▶ Tree Manager allows you to define the hierarchical relationships that exist in the data contained in your system for reporting and security uses.

Make sure to develop a security plan in consultation with your company's security manager. In preparing this plan, evaluate the possible threats, such as hackers, disgruntled employees, computer viruses, commercial espionage, and password disclosure. Determine what options are available to you to meet these threats. Establish profile groups to simplify assigning access to employees with similar functions. Also, make sure to publish your security plan and train your users on the procedures required to implement the plan.

Finally, you may have to undergo an annual security audit. It is critical that you be prepared for such an audit so be sure to document all the business processes, spot-check your end users, and review and update the security plan on a regular basis.

Now that you know about security, you are ready to learn about the final tool available in the PeopleSoft system. Let's turn to Chapter 10 to learn about SQRs.

# SQR

The SQR program is a powerful production report tool that is used extensively in the PeopleSoft system, especially in HRMS. SQR is a third-party application from SQRIBE Technologies that is licensed for use with your PeopleSoft system. SQR can create standard production reports as well as production reports that contain graphics, form letters, table extracts to both tape and disk, and table update programs. SQR is often used to extend PeopleSoft's functionality substantially through front-end and back-end subsystems and interfaces. PeopleSoft's program for printing payroll checks is an SQR program. SQR can even call and print the MICR font required for the checks if your printer has the capability.

It is important that the system administrator become very familiar with the SQR tool. Let's take a look at what SQR is able to do for you.

## Overview of SQR

The SQR product comes with two programs that allow you to execute the reports that you create. The SQR program is the command-line interface that can be used from UNIX and is executed by the Process Scheduler when a SQR report or program is scheduled to run. The SQRW program is the Windows-based version of SQR that opens a dialog box for you to enter the report, user information, and run parameters.

One important characteristic of SQRs is portability. The same code can be run on multiple platforms and with multiple RDBMS systems.

**W A R N I N G**  If you hardcode directory paths into statements that open or close files in an SQR program, you lose some of the operating system portability because the directory paths may be different on different platforms.

Figure 10.1 contains the input window that allows you to start an SQR program manually from the Windows environment, without using the command line.

To run reports from the SQRW program, the user must have the proper RDBMS access to the data being used to create the report. When a user executes a program from SQRW, the security of your PeopleSoft system is bypassed, and SQRW relies only on the security of the RDBMS.

**FIGURE 10.1** The SQRW Start screen

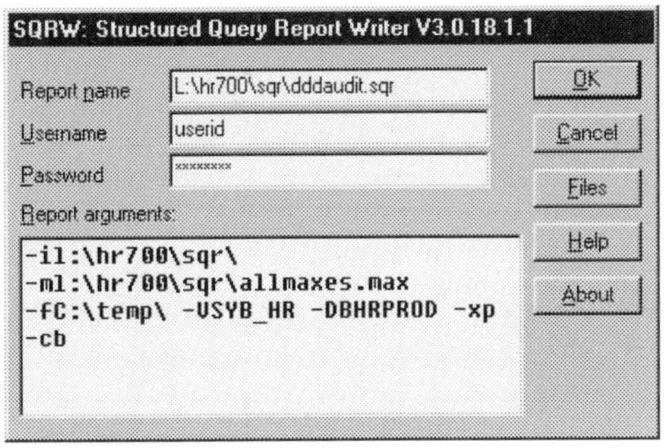

 **NOTE** My company restricts the usage of SQRW to technical staff. However, end users can run programs from the Process Scheduler that run on the client and use SQRW for Windows. All the security parameters are passed to the database without intervention by the user.

PeopleSoft provides two SQR programs that can help you move data from one database to another. The EXPORT.SQR and IMPORT.SQR programs can be found in the SQR directory on your file server. The SQR example directory under UNIX also contains some useful example code that you can use as guides for creating your own programs.

# The Five Elements of SQR Report Files

SQR report files consist of up to five sections, which are used to define the program. Of these five sections, only the REPORT section is required. The other possible sections are the SETUP, HEADING, FOOTING, and PROCEDURE sections.

## REPORT

The REPORT section is required and may contain all the elements needed for your report or program. Typically, you use the REPORT section to call all the other procedures using the do command and to control the flow of the report. The following example is taken from one of the examples later in this chapter; it represents a typical REPORT section.

```
begin-report
   do Get-Run-Values
```

```
    do Get-Sal-Form
    do Stdapi-Term
end-report
```

As you can see, the REPORT section is short and concise. Now let's look at the SETUP section.

**TIP**   I recommend that you define other sections in addition to the REPORT section in order to make your code easier to read and maintain by grouping specific actions and steps into separate procedures.

## SETUP

The SETUP section is used to specify the characteristics of the report. Common items defined in the SETUP section include the DECLARE-LAYOUT, DECLARE-PRINTER, and DECLARE-REPORT commands.

▶ The parameters of the DECLARE-LAYOUT command allow you to configure PAPER-SIZE, MARGINS, ORIENTATION, and FORMFEED information.

▶ The DECLARE-PRINTER command allows you to override the default settings of a printer. You specify the parameters that control how the report will look: the type of printer, the font, and the point size of the font. You can also specify if the printer has color capability.

▶ The DECLARE-REPORT command allows you to define more than one report. The DECLARE-REPORT command is required if you want to print multiple reports in a single SQR.

You can include a BEGIN-SQL section in your SETUP section as well. Be aware that any SQL you define in the SETUP section will be executed before any other SQL is validated when attempting to execute the program. You can use SQL in your SETUP section to create a temporary table for use in your report, as shown in the following example.

**NOTE**   This example is taken from *The SQR User's Guide.*

```
begin-setup
begin-sql on-error=skip
  drop table temptab;
```

```
      create table temptab (cnumb int, location char(30), tot float)
end-sql
end-setup
```

The printer is initialized using the PRINTER-INIT command. PeopleSoft uses this command to define the Hewlett-Packard LaserJet printer initialization and page size parameters by including the files SETUP01A.SQC for portrait mode or SETUP02A.SQC for landscape mode in the SQR setup routines. The following excerpt shows the printer-init string of the SETUP01A.SQC file.

```
printer-init
<27>E<27>(0N<27>&l00<27>&l8D<27>&l88F<27>(s16.66H<27>&a9L<27>&k2G
   !   |   |     |       |       |         |           |     |
   !   |   |     |       |       |         |           |    --> CR
   !   |   |     |       |       |         |           --> Left Margin
   !   |   |     |       |       |         --> Line Prntr font
   !   |   |     |       |       --> 88 text lines
   !   |   |     |       --> 8 lines per inch
   !   |   |     --> Portrait mode
   !   |   --> ISO 8859-1 symbol set
   !   --> Reset

page-size 79 125

!The above is the max page size for the HP LaserJet Series II printer.
!This allows for a left margin of 9 spaces (for 3-hole punched paper).
!Programs which use this SetUp are limited to 124 print positions.

#Define ColR 108   !Column # referenced by Standard Headings
```

**N O T E**   Comments in SQR code are annotated with an exclamation point (!).

In the previous example, each parameter is separated by the ASCII escape sequence <27>, which is required by the Hewlett-Packard Printer Control Language (PCL). The printer is being initialized for portrait mode printing using 8 lines of print per inch and 88 text lines per page. The line printer font is being set as the default and the left margin is being set at 9 characters.

You can create your own printer definition files using the PeopleSoft-delivered initialization routines as guidelines. Consult *The SQR User's Guide* for more details. You can also use the INIT-STRING parameter of the DECLARE-PRINTER command. This is the method recommended by SQRIBE Technologies.

Let's look at the HEADING and FOOTING sections.

## HEADING and FOOTING

The HEADING section contains all the information that you want to display at the top of each page of your report. Typical items are the date and report title. A sample HEADING section is as follows:

```
begin-heading 3                        !Reserves three lines per page
   date-time (1,1) MM/DD/YYYY          !Prints date in row 1 column 1
   print 'QR0100' (1,70)              !Report number - row 1 column 70
   print 'Quarterly Balances' (2) center !Report name - row 2 centered
end-heading
```

The FOOTING section contains all the information that you want to display at the bottom of each page of your report. Typical items might include the date and the report title. A sample FOOTING section is as follows:

```
begin-footing 2                        !Reserves two lines per page
   page-number (2) center             !Prints the date in row 2
end-footing                            !centered
```

The HEADING and FOOTING sections are created after a page has been filled. Their creation occurs when either a new-page command is issued or the maximum lines per page is achieved. This allows you to use variables that are defined by your main program in your headers and footers.

Now let's look at the heart of an SQR program, the PROCEDURE section.

## PROCEDURE

The PROCEDURE section starts with a begin-procedure statement. The procedure must be named and must be unique across all programs. You cannot duplicate a procedure name that is defined in a .sqc file included in your program. The PeopleSoft standard suffix for files that contain common procedures to be included in other programs is the *.sqc suffix.

Variables in SQR programs are not declared variables as in other programming languages. There are three data variable types used by SQR programs:

▶ The text variable, for which you use the $ symbol for the first character.

▶ The numeric variable, for which you use the # symbol for the first character. The second example in this section contains several numeric variables.

▶ The marker variable, for which you use the @ symbol in the first position. The marker variable is a special case that is used in the begin-document statement of reports that have varying output lengths. The marker variable denotes a relative position for inserting the value of the variable when the report is executed. For example, you might use the marker variable to insert a list of items purchased by a customer at the point annotated in the report. The following code shows how the marker variable might be used:

```
begin-document (1,1)
The following items were purchased:
.b
@items
.b
end-document

position () @items
begin-select
itemnr    (0,0,8)
quantity (0,0,6)
itemname (0,0,30)
itemcost  (0,+2,0) edit 999,999.99
totalcost  (0,+3,0 edit 9,999,999.99
from purchases order by cust_nr
end-select
```

SQR also uses runtime variables to alter report characteristics at execution time. SQR defines three types of runtime variables: bind, dynamic query, and substitution.

▶ The bind variable is used in SQL statements to control the data that is being accessed by using the results of a preceding query. For example, in the next code example, the column names ALB_SLOPE and ALB_INTERCEPT are assigning values to variables. The & symbol represents the bind variable and is placed in front of the column name from which you want to extract the value for further processing.

▶ The dynamic query variable is a text variable that is used to change the syntax of a query when that query is executed. Typically, you use a dynamic query variable to change the where criteria or the from table name when the query is executed. You can also use dynamic query variables to change column names. Use the syntax [$variablename] when representing the dynamic query variable.

▶ The substitution variable is used to change report specifications when the report is compiled. Use the ASK input command or the #DEFINE command to define

PART

II

PeopleTools

substitution variables. The most common use of substitution variables is in handling differences between platforms in the SQR. For example, suppose you have the statement #DEFINE col2 18. When the report is running, the command print $name (5, {col2}) places the value of $name variable in column 18 of the report.

The following code is an excerpt from a program example used later in this chapter. I use it here to discuss some of the elements of a PROCEDURE section.

```
begin-procedure Get-Sal-Form
begin-select
F.SAL_ADMIN_PLAN
F.ALB_SLOPE
F.ALB_INTERCEPT
  if &F.SAL_ADMIN_PLAN = 'NEX'
     move &F.ALB_SLOPE to #nexslope
     move &F.ALB_INTERCEPT to #nexintrcpt
  end-if
  if &F.SAL_ADMIN_PLAN = 'EXM'
     move &F.ALB_SLOPE to #exmslope
     move &F.ALB_INTERCEPT to #exmintrcpt
  end-if
  if &F.SAL_ADMIN_PLAN = 'OFF'
     move &F.ALB_SLOPE to #offslope
     move &F.ALB_INTERCEPT to #offintrcpt
  end-if
  let $fsalplan=&F.SAL_ADMIN_PLAN
  do get-ranges
from PS_ALB_SAL_FORM F
where F.EFFDT = $FromDate
end-select
end-procedure
```

In the first line of this code excerpt, note that this procedure is named Get-Sal-Form. The subsequent lines are the select statements that are used in this procedure. By evaluating the values that are returned by the steps in the select statement, the procedure is sequentially processing the data as it is retrieved from the PS_ALB_SAL_FORM table.

In addition, a second procedure, get-ranges, is called for each record that is retrieved. If the order in which the data is processed is important to the other procedures being called, you might add an order by statement to sort the data in the designated order.

In the PROCEDURE section, you can also declare parameters and then pass the parameters when the procedure is executed, as shown in the following example:

```
begin-procedure Calculate-percent-change(#beginvalue, #endvalue, [break
here]:#percchng)
  let #percchng = ((#endvalue-#beginvalue)/#beginvalue) * 100
End-procedure
```

This procedure is called using the following format:

```
do Calculate-percent-change(#PrevMonthSales, #CurrMonthSales,
#SalesPrct)
```

The value you are looking for is returned in the #SalesPrct variable for use elsewhere in your program.

Now let's look at how the SQR language is used.

**N O T E**    The sample directory on your UNIX server contains several examples of how to incorporate graphics and other objects into your SQR programs.

# Using the SQR Language

SQR can be used to create complicated reports more easily than with the PeopleSoft Query tool. In addition, you can use SQR to create programs to update tables in your system. The reports that you create can contain charts as well as data. You might find it useful to include charts to depict sales information graphically for monthly sales reports. SQR also provides functions to add bar-code information to your reports to allow for automated sorting or indexing of forms into a document management system when they are returned.

The print command writes data to the report. The values in the print command contain the row, column, and number of positions that the print command is to use in positioning the data on the page.

The following code excerpt, taken from an example later in this chapter, shows the print command in use. In this example, the literal Officer is printed on the current row at the column specified by the variable #col2. The variable #off is then printed on the same row in the column specified by the variable #col3. The edit mask is used to specify how the output should be formatted. For example, the edit mask *DD-MON-YYYY* prints the date 12/24/1998 in the following format: 24-DEC-1998. In the example below, the second print statement prints the value of the field #off as four numerals without commas.

```
print 'Officer'    (0,#col2)
print #off    (0,#col3,004) edit 9999
```

SQR stores one entire page of a report in memory. This allows you to place SQR code in a more logical order for concise coding, while giving you the flexibility to place the data anywhere on the page. You can print all the values from one array straight down a column and then start back at the top of the next column with the next array.

The code that follows is an excerpt from a program that I created to print data stored in an array. You can find the detailed syntax guide for the create-array command in *The SQR User's Guide*. First, take a look at the code to initialize the array using the create-array command:

```
create-array name=date1 size=7
    field=divis:char
    field=off:number
    field=mgr:number
    field=exm:number
    field=nex:number
    field=pt:number
    field=tot:number
```

To print data that has been stored in the array, simply use the following code:

```
begin-procedure Print-Report
move 0 to #j
let #col1 = 3
let #col2 = 30
let #col3 = 42
let #col4 = 54
let #col5 = 66
let #row = 7
print 'Employee Census' (4,38)
print $firstdate      (#row,#col3)
let #gtot = 0
while #j < 7
  get $divis #off #mgr #exm #nex #pt #tot from date1(#j)
  print $divis       (+2,#col1,20)
  print 'Officer'    (0,#col2)
  print #off         (0,#col3,004) edit 9999
  print 'Manager'    (+1,#col2)
```

```
          print #mgr          (0,#col3,004) edit 9999
          print 'Exempt'      (+1,#col2)
          print #exm          (0,#col3,004) edit 9999
          print 'Non-Exempt'  (+1,#col2)
          print #nex          (0,#col3,004) edit 9999
          print 'Part-Time'   (+1,#col2)
          print #pt           (0,#col3,004) edit 9999
          print 'Subtotal'    (+1,22)
          print #tot          (0,#col3,004) edit 9999
          let #gtot = #gtot + #tot
          add 1 to #j
          end-while
    print 'Grand Total' (+1,20)
    print #gtot       (0,#col3,004) edit 9999
    move 0 to #j
```

The preceding code produces the following report output:

```
                                        Employee Census


                                        1997-06-29


           Claims                    Officer       2
                                     Manager      52
                                     Exempt       55
                                     Non-Exempt  594
                                     Part-Time     5
                        Subtotal                 708

           Corporate Resources      Officer       2
                                     Manager      27
                                     Exempt      200
                                     Non-Exempt   83
                                     Part-Time    13
                        Subtotal                 325

           Finance                   Officer       2
                                     Manager      21
                                     Exempt      114
                                     Non-Exempt  147
                                     Part-Time     6
                        Subtotal                 290

           Special Claims            Officer       1
                                     Manager      22
                                     Exempt       62
```

PART

II

PeopleTools

```
                                   Non-Exempt    311
                                   Part-Time       0
                         Subtotal                396

            Marketing              Officer          4
                                   Manager         35
                                   Exempt         189
                                   Non-Exempt    391
                                   Part-Time      16
                         Subtotal                635

            Medical Director       Officer          1
                                   Manager          7
                                   Exempt          89
                                   Non-Exempt      23
                                   Part-Time        2
                         Subtotal                122

            Other                  Officer          6
                                   Manager         10
                                   Exempt          69
                                   Non-Exempt      48
                                   Part-Time        8
                         Subtotal                141
                      Grand Total               2617
```

**NOTE**   This is not the complete report output, only the first column of data.

SQR also makes use of command-line flags to further control the processing of your reports. These flags are set in your environment variables for use by the Process Scheduler but may be overridden at runtime by the process definition associated with the report. Table 10.1 describes the most commonly used SQR flags. Additional flags are defined in *The SQR User's Guide*.

**TABLE 10.1**   SQR Command-Line Flags

| SQR flag | Description |
| --- | --- |
| –A | Causes report output to be appended to existing copy of the report. The report is created if no previous copy exists. |
| –C | This command is used with SQRW to display a Cancel dialog box, making it easy to cancel execution of your SQR. |

**TABLE 10.1    (continued)    SQR Command-Line Flags**

| SQR flag | Description |
|---|---|
| −E`filename` | Specifies that an error file be created and allows you to specify the filename. |
| −F`filename/`<br>`directory` | Specifies a file or directory where the `*.lis` file should be created, instead of in the default location. |
| −I | Location of `*.SQC` or other `include` program files. |
| −M | SQR configuration file. Used to modify default SQR properties. |
| −RS | Creates a runtime version of your SQR. Creates a file with the `*.sqt` extension. PeopleSoft does not use runtime SQR programs. |
| −S | Displays the status of all cursors at the end of the run. This is used for troubleshooting SQR programs. |
| −T`nn` | Allows you to run the SQR in test mode for the specified (*nn*) number of pages. |
| −O`filename` | Filename for the log file. |
| −DEBUG | Used in conjunction with `#debug` command to display additional information when troubleshooting SQR programs. |

Once you have created an SQR that you want to move into production for use by your users, you can implement it into your PeopleSoft system. Let's look at how this is accomplished.

# Implementing an SQR

Once you decide to move a SQR into production, there are several steps required to make this to happen.

1. Create a run control panel using the Panel Designer. The panel that you create must allow you to enter any run parameters that you want to be changeable when initiating the program. When creating this panel, you may be able to take advantage of one of the run control tables that already exists. For example, if you want to compare values at two different times, simply prompt for the start date and the end date. (The Panel Design window is explained in more detail in Chapter 7, "Development Tools.")

PART

II

PeopleTools

**2.** After the run control panel is complete, assign the panel to a panel group and add it to the menu.

**3.** Assign the menu to the access profiles that need the capability to execute the program.

**4.** Create the Process Scheduler definition for your program. This definition helps the Process Scheduler determine how to execute this program. To access the Process Scheduler definition panel, select Go **>** PeopleTools **>** Process Scheduler from the menu. On the Process Definitions panel (Figure 10.2), specify the run location where the user can run the program: client, server, or both. This panel also allows you to specify the panel groups associated with this definition and the process security groups and process class to which this process belongs.

**FIGURE 10.2**    Process Scheduler–Process Definitions panel

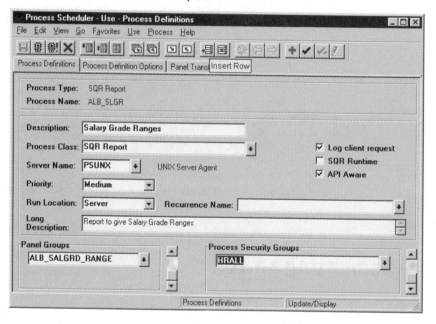

The Process Definition Options tab, shown in Figure 10.3, allows you to override or append to any system-wide parameters for SQR that have been established. This capability is useful if you need to pass specific command-line parameters to this program that are not pertinent to other SQR programs.

The Panel Transfers tab, shown in Figure 10.4, allows you to specify a destination for your program to take the user after the defined process is completed. This transfer is accomplished in conjunction with the Process Monitor.

**FIGURE 10.3**    Process Scheduler–Process Definition Options panel

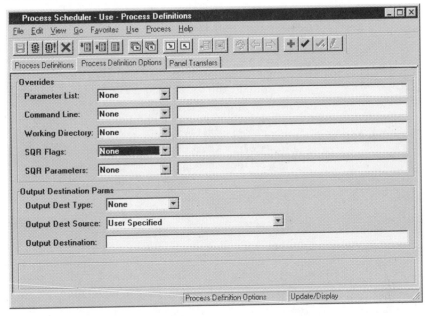

**FIGURE 10.4**    Process Scheduler–Panel Transfers panel

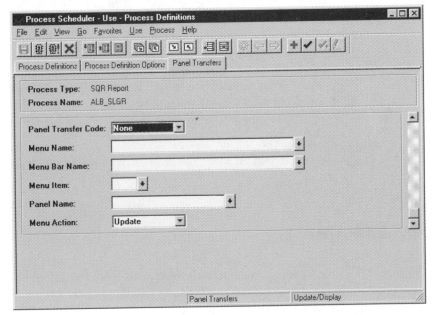

**WARNING**   The panel transfers are not automatically updated when menu and panel objects are moved or deleted.

**5.** Make sure that you have created steps in your SQR to select the needed parameters from the run control panel. The following excerpt from an SQR shows how to accomplish these steps:

```
if $prcs_process_instance = ''
    input $From_Check_Dt 'Enter from date (..Jan 01 1997)'type=date
    input $Thru_Check_Dt 'Enter thru date (..Jan 01 1997)'type=date
else
    do Select-Parameters
    let $From_Check_Dt = $RC_PAYRPT.START_DT
    let $Thru_Check_Dt = $RC_PAYRPT.END_DT
end-if
```

When the preceding program is executed, it prompts the user to enter the dates if the user is running the process from the command line. The program selects the dates that it needs when it has a process instance that has been assigned by the Process Scheduler program. This is accomplished by executing the Select-Parameters procedure, which is a procedure in a file that is listed in the #include definitions. Whichever method is used, the variables $From_Check_Dt and $Thru_Check_Dt should contain data when these steps are complete.

**TIP**   Configure your SQR so that it prompts for any run control parameters when executed from the command line. This allows you to run the program outside of the Process Scheduler when troubleshooting.

The next section presents examples of how to accomplish the steps described in this section.

# SQR Examples

The following two examples illustrate the power and flexibility of SQR. These examples can be modified for use in your company's environment, if your business processes follow the approach taken.

# Example 1: New Salary Ranges

The new salary ranges program is designed to calculate new pay scale ranges and insert them into the PS_SAL_GRADE_TBL table for use by Payroll group and the job panels. At our company, we created this program so that the Payroll functional users could implement a new pay scale with minimal effort and without assistance from our technical team.

The first step is to create a record definition for a new effective-dated table that will store the two pieces of the salary range formula that must be entered to create our pay ranges. Figure 10.5 contains the record definition for this table.

**FIGURE 10.5**    Salary formula record

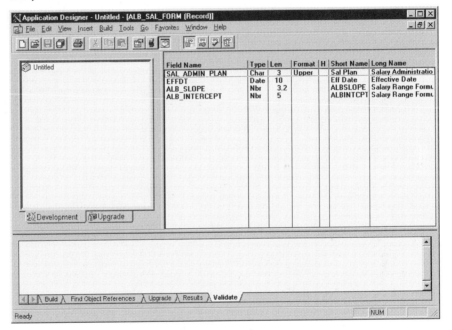

This record contains the effective date of the new scale, the salary administration plan for which the rate is to be calculated, the slope, and the intercept for use in calculating the ranges. The effective date and the salary administration plan fields are both designated as keys for the record. This allows the Payroll group to have no more than one rate change per day per salary administration plan.

A distinct panel group is created for this panel, since it is related to no other panels in the system. The panel is then added to the menu, as shown in Figure 10.6.

**FIGURE 10.6**    Salary Grade Range menu item

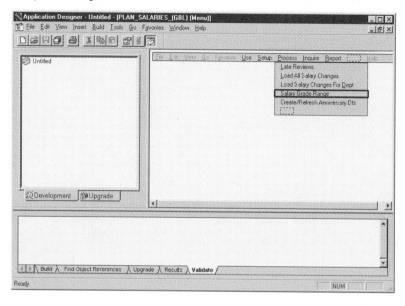

The next step is to create the run control panel that will be used to start the process. The only information that is needed is the effective date of the new change and the effective date of the previous salary ranges to be used as the baseline for the new ranges. Figure 10.7 contains this panel as it would appear at runtime.

**FIGURE 10.7**    Salary Grade Range run control panel

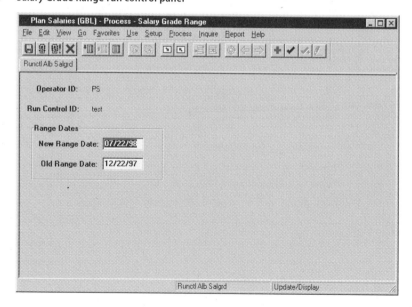

Now let's look at the SQR that was created to perform the changes. The SQR was originally created to run strictly from the command line for testing. This allowed one developer to build and test the program logic while the records and panels were being built for the production version. Excerpts from the program follow. The full program code can be found in Appendix A, "Sample Programs."

### ALB_SLGR.SQR

```
! alb_slgr.sqr   10/28/97   Create new salary grade ranges
#include 'setenv.sqc'     !Set environment

!*************************
begin-report
   do Get-Run-Values
   do Get-Sal-Form
   do Stdapi-Term
end-report

!**************************
begin-procedure Get-Run-Values
   do Stdapi-Init
   do Select-Parameters
   let $FromDate = RTRIM(&RC_BCBS.FROMDATE, ' ')
   let $ThruDate = RTRIM(&RC_BCBS.THRUDATE, ' ')
end-procedure

!**************************
begin-procedure Get-Sal-Form
begin-select
F.SAL_ADMIN_PLAN
F.ALB_SLOPE
F.ALB_INTERCEPT
   if &F.SAL_ADMIN_PLAN = 'NEX'
      move &F.ALB_SLOPE to #nexslope
      move &F.ALB_INTERCEPT to #nexintrcpt
   end-if
   if &F.SAL_ADMIN_PLAN = 'EXM'
      move &F.ALB_SLOPE to #exmslope
      move &F.ALB_INTERCEPT to #exmintrcpt
   end-if
   if &F.SAL_ADMIN_PLAN = 'OFF'
      move &F.ALB_SLOPE to #offslope
      move &F.ALB_INTERCEPT to #offintrcpt
```

```
    end-if
    let $fsalplan=&F.SAL_ADMIN_PLAN
    do get-ranges
from PS_ALB_SAL_FORM F
where F.EFFDT = $FromDate
end-select
end-procedure

!**************************
begin-setup
  page-size 1 100
  no-formfeed
end-setup
!**************************
#include 'rc_alb.sqc'      !Custom run control routines
#include 'datetime.sqc'    !Date Functions
#Include 'stdapi.sqc'      !Routines to Update Run Status
```

As you can see, several PeopleSoft-delivered modules are called from this program to format dates, set environment parameters, and update run information. The modules included in this program were designed to be shared by many PeopleSoft-delivered SQR programs. The PeopleSoft standard naming convention is to name these files with a suffix of .sqc. SQR will support any extension that you choose; however, I recommend using the PeopleSoft standard to avoid confusion and for easy identification. These files must be placed in your SQRDIR directory as defined by your environment variables.

Now let's look at the second example.

## Example 2: 401K Loan Report

This SQR is a report that we created at my company to generate a list containing 401K loan repayment information for employees whose balance remaining is less than their deduction amount. We use this information when running the biweekly payroll to ensure that the correct final deduction is taken for the loan repayment.

We took the following steps to automate this application:

1. We defined the run control panel, as illustrated in Figure 10.8. The only information we needed was the pay period ending date for the payroll. We added display fields for the operator ID and the run control ID. We also added a data entry box for the date that prompts against the PAY_CALENDAR table to validate the payroll ending date.

**FIGURE 10.8**  Run control panel for a 401K loan report

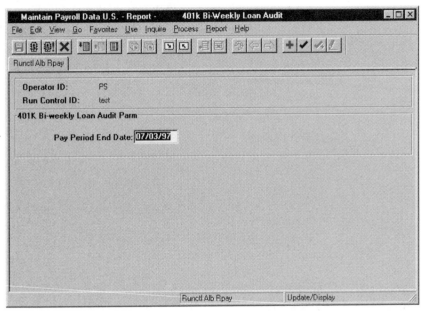

**2.** We created the panel group and process definitions, as outlined in Example 1.

**3.** We assigned access to the authorized users and groups.

The following excerpts from the SQR illustrate some of the unique procedures that have not been described earlier in this chapter. The code shown in **bold** shows how specifying operating system directories limits the portability of the program. We have not adjusted the hard-coded directory specifications since we run this only from the UNIX server.

```
!******************************************************************
!
!  Function: Open-Files
!  Description:  Open files and initialize accumulators.
!
!******************************************************************
begin-procedure Open-Files

    open '/sybase/psoft/extract/alb_rpay.log'   as   1
!   open 'c:\payderr.log'    as   1
        for-writing
        record=250:fixed
        status = #write1
```

```
                   if #write1 = -1
                       display 'Open for error log file failed'
                       stop quiet
                   end-if
                   lET #accum = 0
                   Let #page_cnt = 1
                   Let #line_cnt = 85
                   Let $error_flg = 'N'

           end-procedure Open-Files

           !*********************************************************************
           !
           !   Function: Data-Selection
           !   Description:   Joins PAY_EARNINGS and PAY_DEDUCTION on COMPANY,
           !                  PAYGROUP, PAY END DATE, OFF CYCLE, LINE# and PAGE#
           !                  and the maximum along with max ADDL# from PAY_EARNINGS.
           !                  The deduction class for company match (P, N, T) are
           !                  bypassed. The input parm of PAY END DATE is also
           !                  used as furthur criteria. Employee name is selected
           !                  from PERSONAL_DATA and the Deduction Code is used to
           !                  read GENL_DEDUCTION for goal amount and goal balance.
           !                  As each line is selected it is printed on a report.
           !
           !*********************************************************************
           begin-procedure Data-Selection
```

The following section of code contains the procedures for handling and notifying the user that an error has been encountered. The error-handling code is shown in **bold.** In this example, errors are handled by the procedure named format-sql-error. The error-handling procedure must be defined in your report or in one of your include files. The format-sql-error procedure provides the technical team with additional information to use in determining the cause of the error. Defining an error-handing procedure is just one means of stopping a program gracefully when an error occurs. You may use the commands STOP, WARN, and SKIP after the on-error command to specify how errors will be handled.

```
begin-SELECT on-error=format-sql-error
A.EMPLID
B.PAY_END_DT
B.DEDCD
B.DED_CUR
```

```
B.PAGE#
B.LINE#

    Let $DEDCD      = &B.DEDCD
    LET $EMPLID     = &A.EMPLID
    Let #PAGE       = &B.PAGE#
    Let #LINE       = &B.LINE#
    Let #DED_CUR    = &B.DED_CUR
    move '-' to $DDelimiter
    do Format-DateTime(&B.PAY_END_DT, $PAY_DATE, {DEFYMD}, '', '')
    do Get-Personal-Data
    do Get-Deduct-Data
    Let #accum      = #accum + &B.DED_CUR
    LET $DED_CUR    = TO_CHAR(&B.DED_CUR)
    LET $GOAL_B     = TO_CHAR(#GOAL_BAL)
    LET $GOAL_A     = TO_CHAR(#GOAL_AMT)
    LET $AMT        = edit($DED_CUR,'999,999.99MI')
    LET $GOAL_BAL   = edit($GOAL_B,'999,999.99MI')
    LET $GOAL_AMT   = edit($GOAL_A,'999,999.99MI')
    Let $loan_num   = to_char(#ALB_LOAN_NUM)
    Let #amount_left = #goal_amt - (#goal_bal + (#ded_cur * 2))
    If #amount_left  <= 0
       IF #line_cnt > 64
           do Print-Heading
       End-if
       do Print-Line
    End-if
 FROM PS_PAY_EARNINGS A,
      PS_PAY_DEDUCTION B
WHERE A.PAY_END_DT   =     B.PAY_END_DT
  AND A.COMPANY      =     B.COMPANY
  AND A.PAYGROUP     =     B.PAYGROUP
  AND A.PAGE#        =     B.PAGE#
  AND A.LINE#        =     B.LINE#
  AND A.OFF_CYCLE    =     B.OFF_CYCLE
  AND A.PAY_END_DT   =     $PAYDT
  AND B.DEDCD        like  'LOAN%'
  AND ((B.DED_CLASS <>     'N')
  AND  (B.DED_CLASS <>     'P')
  AND  (B.DED_CLASS <>     'T'))
  AND A.ADDL#        =
      (SELECT MAX(M.ADDL#)
       FROM PS_PAY_EARNINGS M
```

```
                  WHERE M.PAY_END_DT = A.PAY_END_DT
                    AND M.PAGE#      = A.PAGE#
                    AND M.LINE#      = A.LINE#
                    AND M.COMPANY    = A.COMPANY
                    AND M.PAYGROUP   = A.PAYGROUP
                    AND M.OFF_CYCLE  = A.OFF_CYCLE)
          Order By 1,3

      end-SELECT

      End-Procedure Data-Selection

      !********************************************************************
      !  Function: Format-SQL-Error
      !  Description:  Formats and writes log record. Also turns on error
      !                flag.
      !********************************************************************
      Begin-Procedure Format-Sql-Error
          Let $RECORD = $EMPLID || ' ' || $DEDCD || ' ' || $PAY_DATE || ':' ||
      $sql-error
          Write 3 from $RECORD
          Let $error_flg = 'Y'
          Display $sql-error
      End-Procedure Format-Sql-Error
```

**NOTE**   The full program code can be found in the ALB_RPAY.SQR program in Appendix A, "Sample Programs."

# Summary

This chapter described the versatility and flexibility of the SQR program to enhance your PeopleSoft system. SQR can create standard production reports and production reports that contain graphics, form letters, table extracts to both tape and disk, and table update programs. You can use SQR to create programs to update tables in your system and include charts in your reports to present the data. SQR is often used to extend PeopleSoft's functionality.

SQR report files have five major components. A REPORT section is required. SETUP, HEADING, FOOTING, and PROCEDURE sections are used to specify the characteristics of the report as well as to improve the readability of your code.

Once you have written and tested your SQR, you will want to move it into production by implementing it in your PeopleSoft system. The steps to accomplish this were described in this chapter.

Two major SQR examples were described in this chapter. The first example was an SQR program to calculate new pay scale ranges and insert them into the PS_SAL_GRADE_TBL for use by Payroll group and the job panels. The second example was an SQR program to generate a list containing 401K loan repayment information for employees whose balance remaining is less than their deduction amount.

Appendix A, "Sample Programs," contains the full code of the programs discussed in this chapter. In addition, Appendix A includes a few other examples for you to use as models.

Part III of this book describes all the tools and procedures you'll need for maintaining your PeopleSoft system.

PART

II

PeopleTools

# MAINTAINING THE SYSTEM

*Part III of this book explores the procedures that will help you maintain your system at peak operating levels using the PeopleSoft tools.*

*Chapter 11, "Performance Tuning," describes how to tune your PeopleSoft applications and databases for optimal performance. Chapter 12, "Upgrading Your PeopleSoft System," provides you with techniques to help you successfully upgrade your PeopleSoft system. Chapter 13, "Tax Updates," describes how the HRMS customer should implement the tax updates necessary to correctly calculate and withhold taxes from paychecks. Chapter 14, "Documentation," discusses the benefits of and techniques for properly documenting your PeopleSoft system. Chapter 15, "Disaster Recovery," discusses the design and implementation of a disaster recovery plan. Chapter 16, "Day-to-Day Administration," gives you some procedures and tips for monitoring your system on a routine basis. Chapter 17, "Troubleshooting," outlines some strategies for solving problems that you might encounter with your PeopleSoft system.*

# Performance Tuning

FEATURING

**P**erformance tuning is one of the most challenging tasks you will face as a system administrator. Performance tuning is taking an application that is already working correctly and making it run faster. Performance tuning also involves identifying bottlenecks in system performance and adjusting system parameters to clear up those bottlenecks so that they don't recur. My personal definition is that performance tuning is the "art" of balancing hardware and software configurations to provide the maximum output from the system. The hardware includes servers, workstations, and network hardware. The software includes the following:

▶ Operating system information for the client, the server, and the network

▶ Database configuration

▶ Applications configuration

Don't confuse performance tuning with troubleshooting. Troubleshooting is taking an application that is not working, uncovering the cause of the problem, and solving the problem.

**N O T E**  For more information on troubleshooting, see Chapter 17, "Troubleshooting."

Increased performance can be achieved in several ways. The following list identifies some of your options:

▶ Purchase additional (or faster) hardware.

▶ Modify the RDBMS parameters.

▶ Modify specific queries to take advantage of RDBMS-specific options.

Purchasing additional hardware can be a simple solution for situations where the current hardware is older or undersized for the task being performed. You should consider this option, but in some environments this will not be possible. For example, DB2/MVS users will probably not be able to purchase additional mainframe hardware as a first solution. Those users will need to spend time tuning the database and specific queries first. Adding additional processors to your server improves performance only if you are able to split a process and allow it to run in parallel on multiple processors. The PeopleSoft Payroll process is serial so you would have to create additional pay groups to take advantage of parallel calculations. In addition, if a query or program is performing poorly with the RDBMS, you may be better served to look at the query or the program. In these situations, you might be able to double or even triple your performance with additional hardware, when what you really need is to increase performance by a factor of ten.

 **N O T E**   This chapter will not provide you with hardware sizing guidelines. PeopleSoft and your hardware vendor are in a much better position to offer assistance on this issue.

This chapter covers some of the database options that can be critical to the initial performance of your PeopleSoft system. The most common performance problems found in the online system and in the batch environment are discussed, along with the tools that can help with performance tuning. The last section of the chapter describes two examples of performance tuning implemented at my company in PeopleSoft Payroll batch processing. While the examples discussed are specific to the PeopleSoft Payroll application, many of the tips can be applied to any PeopleSoft application.

Your first task is to develop a performance-tuning plan.

# Developing a Performance-Tuning Plan

The first step in developing a performance-tuning plan is to focus on the task of getting improved performance from PeopleSoft. Specifically, you need to determine how to improve performance as the number of records in critical database tables increases.

There are many approaches that can be used to increase the performance of your system. Begin by checking the PeopleSoft Customer Connection Web site (available only to PeopleSoft customers with a login name and password) at www4.people-soft.com/cc/. Download any information that may apply to your configuration.

Another source of information is your database vendor. I received several detailed white papers that were created as a result of my database vendor's benchmark tests of the PeopleSoft applications. These white papers include configuration recommendations for optimizing performance.

Once you have gathered this information, begin to develop a performance-tuning plan. My company's performance-tuning plan prioritized the parameters to be changed based on the performance gains the database vendor found in their benchmark tests. For example, one of the first items I tackled was increasing the temporary database space to a value approximately 25–30 percent of the size of my production database.

PART

**III**

**Maintaining the System**

**NOTE** The book uses the term "temporary database space" to refer to the area in the RDBMS that is designated to handle the temporary storage of table information either from specific SQL that creates temporary tables or from the use of sort and order by commands in your SQL.

As I added other test servers and database upgrade servers, I adjusted the size of the temporary database space even higher. PeopleSoft batch COBOL SQL statements contain many multiple sort queries, especially in the payroll processing stored statements, which also increase the size requirements of your temporary database.

**NOTE** The PeopleSoft stored statements are not database stored procedures. They are simply SQL statements that are stored in the database, which are called during batch execution, then compiled and executed.

Most PeopleSoft installations have a mixed online and batch environment. As with all performance tuning, there will be tradeoffs that are necessary to obtain adequate performance for both. These tradeoffs should be identified in the performance-tuning plan.

# Database Server Issues

Let's first look at some of the RDBMS issues that can affect the performance of your PeopleSoft application.

## Database Parameters

The tunable database parameters on your database are a good first start to improving both the online and batch performance of your PeopleSoft application. The temporary database is a potential bottleneck that should have adequate space allocated from the beginning. PeopleSoft uses many order by, group by, and descending order sorts and or processing statements in their SQL, which require large amounts of temporary database space. If you are running more than one database on the same server, allocating space equal to 50% of your largest database for temporary database space should be adequate. You can also increase the performance for the temporary database by allocating enough memory to load the temporary database entirely in cache or by using solid state disks (an expensive proposition).

# Disk I/O

Another area that is often overlooked in small to medium-sized databases is balancing disk I/O. You may experience satisfactory performance for your batch processes in a small database running on one disk. Monitor your disk I/O regularly and be prepared to add additional database devices, which can be a single hard disk or a RAID device to avoid bottlenecks. The PeopleSoft Payroll application has minimal I/O requirements due to the serial nature of the batch programs.

# Memory

Your PeopleSoft system creates a tremendous number of indexes. Plan on allocating enough memory to keep the data cache turnover rate on your database low. I performed some trial-and-error experiments initially, but once I moved to production, I had the "luxury" of being on a dedicated machine, so I gave my database engine a large percentage (65%) of the available memory on the server. I left enough space to allow for the UNIX kernel and the batch processes that run on UNIX to operate.

**NOTE** You cannot control the memory usage of your RDBMS. Check with your database administrator (DBA) or consult the documentation provided by your RDBMS vendor for more information.

If your database server is dedicated to PeopleSoft, one parameter that can be lowered is the amount of procedure cache. Since PeopleSoft does not use stored procedures or triggers, this can be set very low. A 3% procedure cache in PeopleSoft Financials is common; it can go even lower. I currently have my procedure cache at 10%, which provides good performance.

One parameter that requires trial-and-error experimentation to obtain a good performance tradeoff between batch and online processes is the user log cache size. The PeopleSoft Financials application post-process uses one large transaction, so a large user cache can reduce I/O. Remember that each user in the online system is also allocated this amount of cache. The parameters that have to be adjusted for the user log cache size vary with the RDBMS being used. Consult your DBA for the specifics of your platform. Performance tuning is a series of compromises that must be made to balance the performance of your batch and online transactions to best serve both environments.

PART

**III**

**Maintaining the System**

## Query Plan Analysis

Another process that you can undertake to tune specific transactions is to perform a query plan analysis. Generally, you do this after you have isolated a performance problem to a transaction or group of transactions. Make sure that you have at least one DBA who is familiar with how the query optimizer works for your database platform. This can be an invaluable asset when you begin to do query plan analysis to improve performance.

Query plan analysis is discussed in more detail later in this chapter.

# Two-Tier/Three-Tier Performance

Prior to version 6, PeopleSoft was strictly a two-tier online system. With PeopleSoft version 6, Tuxedo was delivered for the purpose of remote call three-tier processing. Most online performance tuning will improve the performance of both two-tier and three-tier systems.

PeopleSoft has been delivering the Query tool for ad hoc queries by end users for several versions. Beginning with the newer releases of PeopleSoft, you are not dealing only with the online programs and queries running against your database. As you move into the future, you will also be dealing with Online Analytical Processing (OLAP), Web access, and other forms of data access that are not even defined by PeopleSoft yet.

Performance of the online system is generally good. Most of the performance-related problems are related to the SQL views used by some of the online panels. I have not customized any of the views delivered by PeopleSoft since even the slowest SQL view executes in less than five seconds and is used infrequently. I felt it unnecessary to commit the resources to reviewing the SQL being used by the views with slow performance. The primary problem with the views has been poor optimizer choices by the RDBMS. I have not heard any complaints from the end users about the performance, except when an ad hoc query goes astray.

The performance of the client in a two-tier configuration can be improved using several methods:

1. Purchase a faster computer.

2. Provide adequate network bandwidth and run the maximum packet size that can be supported.

**3.** Use Windows NT Workstation for your power users. Windows NT provides a much more stable environment for running multiple windows and programs simultaneously than Windows 95 does.

The performance of the client in three-tier mode is directly related to the performance of the application server. An application server that is as fast as the database server is recommended. I run the application server on the same hardware as the database server, in what is known as a logical three-tier configuration. This eliminates network bandwidth as a performance issue. PeopleSoft recommends that you implement a logical three-tier configuration if your hardware platform is certified for both the database and application server.

**NOTE** Consult the RDBMS and operating system installation guides for specific configuration recommendations for your environment.

# Batch Performance

The performance of the batch jobs in PeopleSoft is critical to the success of your application. The batch programs will receive the most interest from both end users and management when they are performing poorly. One of the critical factors to successfully tuning these batch jobs is a thorough understanding of both the PeopleSoft data and the systems on which they are running.

If you are running Payroll, for example, make sure to educate your DBA about the payroll process. This allows the DBA to become familiar with the steps that must be executed to perform the payroll processing. With this knowledge, the DBA can build a test database that can be used to run tests of the payroll in an environment where stored statements and other parameters can be monitored and modified if necessary. Provide a controlled test environment that does not adversely impact other users or processes.

**TIP** Modification of the PeopleSoft stored statements is a customization and should be documented accordingly. Thorough testing should accompany any stored statement change.

One of your biggest allies in tuning PeopleSoft batch processes is the COBOL timings trace. The COBOL timings trace is a function delivered by PeopleSoft that allows you to gather statistics about the execution of the COBOL stored statements during

Maintaining the System

batch processing. This trace adds very little overhead to your normal processing, but if you periodically turn this trace on during production runs, you can get good benchmark statistics. This helps to identify when processes start slowing down. It is important to know what your system's normal performance is.

The values produced by COBOL timings trace generally apply for all RDBMS platforms. To initiate the COBOL timings trace, set the trace value to 128 (TraceSQL=128) in the pstools.ini file in the $PS_HOME/bin directory on your UNIX server, or check the COBOL Statement Timings check box for your client or Windows NT server.

The following is an example of an output of a payroll COBOL timings trace from my company's system:

```
PeopleSoft Batch Statistics
                           (All timings in seconds)

                 R e t r i e v e  C o m p i l e   E x e c u t e  F e t c h
Statement        Count   Time    Count   Time    Count   Time   Count   Time
PSPTCALC_S_AGG       5   1.00        5   0.00      212 334.00     212   2.00
```

Note that the execute time for the statement is greater than the execute count. An average time to execute that is greater than one second indicates a potential problem with the statement being executed. Resolving this and other problems is discussed in the Payroll examples section later in this chapter.

PeopleSoft considers tuning batch stored statements to be a customization issue. However, the performance that you are experiencing on your database platform may dictate that you make some minor modifications to some of the stored statements. Always test the changes carefully and monitor both performance and data integrity to ensure that you have not adversely impacted other programs or modules. These changes should be retested each time a new version of the stored statement is released by PeopleSoft. You should also test any modified stored statements each time you update your RDBMS version. I save all the scripts that I use for query plan analysis to make the testing easier. I have found that this enables me to remove some of the stored statement customizations after updating my RDBMS version.

For example, my company had a query that was performing slowly. We discovered this using the COBOL timings trace. I performed a plan analysis on the query and discovered that the query optimizer was having a difficult time choosing the correct index for the query. I modified the query to specify the index it should have used. Suddenly I had a query that had been taking over 1100 milliseconds (ms) to execute that was now taking only 3 ms. This may not sound significant until you notice that the query was being executed 2700 times for one batch cycle. We just saved 49 minutes on the batch process! Those kind of discoveries can make performance tuning exciting and make your users think you are a miracle worker.

# Tools for Performance Tuning

There are several tools that can be used to resolve performance problems and monitor your PeopleSoft system. This section first discusses the tools provided by PeopleSoft, then describes several techniques that I use at my company, and finally, talks about the third-party utilities that are available to help with performance tuning.

## PeopleSoft Tools

When you purchase a PeopleSoft system, PeopleSoft delivers several tools to help with performance tuning. These tools include:

- ▶ SQL Trace
- ▶ PeopleCode Trace
- ▶ Application Reviewer
- ▶ COBOL timings trace
- ▶ Process Scheduler logging
- ▶ SQR parameters
- ▶ Auditing utilities

### SQL Trace

The SQL trace functionality is used for both the client and the server. For the Windows client, the parameters that can be traced are found in the Trace panel of the Configuration Manager utility. Figure 11.1 illustrates this panel and some of the options that are available. You can select parameters for SQL Trace, PeopleCode Trace, the online trace file (the output file), and the Process Scheduler logging level from the Trace panel.

**FIGURE 11.1**  Configuration Manager–Trace panel

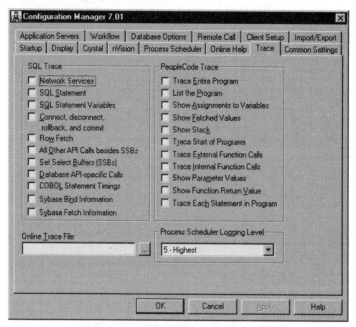

The SQL tracing functions allow you to capture the queries that are being executed and save them in a trace file. The trace file also captures the values of bind variables, connection status, and many other API- and database-specific parameters that are being executed. This information can help you identify the location and cause of your performance problems.

The same functionality can be found on the UNIX server by setting trace levels in the pstools.ini file. The options available for this are as follows:

```
;   TraceSql is implemented as a bit map with the following values
; 1=SQL Statements
; 2=SQL statement variables
; 4=SQL connect, disconnect, commit and rollback
; 8=Row Fetch (indicates that it occurred, not data)
; 16=All other API calls except ssb
; 32=Set Select Buffers (identifies that attributes of columns to be selected)
; 64=Database API specific calls
; 128=COBOL statement timings
; 256=Sybase Bind information
; 512=Sybase Fetch information
;
; So, If you want Statements and Row Fetch and COBOL timings, you would
; specify TraceSql=137  (1+8+128)
TraceSql=0
```

## PeopleCode Trace/Application Reviewer

PeopleCode tracing is not applicable for the batch environment and is generally used in troubleshooting problems with the online PeopleSoft application. You may want to use a PeopleCode trace to determine all the events that are occurring in an online transaction. These events may explain why a transaction is performing slowly. Be sure to use PeopleCode tracing if a custom record or panel is involved in a performance issue and the record has PeopleCode associated with it. PeopleSoft has left the PeopleCode Trace functionality in place but has replaced it with the more powerful Application Reviewer process, which gives you the ability to execute PeopleCode one statement at a time and set breakpoints in your code.

PeopleCode Trace is covered more extensively in Chapter 17, "Troubleshooting," and an overview of Application Reviewer is described in Chapter 7, "Development Tools."

 **NOTE** PeopleCode tracing seriously degrades the performance of the client performing the trace because all transactions are logged in the trace file.

## COBOL Timings Trace

The COBOL timings trace is an invaluable tool for establishing baseline performance parameters and discovering potentially weak queries. The COBOL timings trace is a function delivered by PeopleSoft that allows you to gather statistics about the execution of the COBOL stored statements during batch processing. The trace can be used in both the server and client environments. To initiate the COBOL timings trace, set the trace value to 128 (TraceSQL=128) in the pstools.ini file.

## Process Scheduler Logging

The Process Scheduler process creates log files for all processes that it initiates. These log files capture message outputs from normal operations and error messages from processes that terminate abnormally. If the process was a COBOL program, the log file contains information showing which stored statement was processing at the time of the error. The log file also contains the bind variable values for the transaction in process. This information can be used to check both the input data and the stored statement for accuracy.

The amount of data captured in the Process Scheduler log can be controlled with the LOGFENCE parameter. This value can be set on the client by setting the Process Scheduler Logging Level parameter on the Configuration Manager Trace panel (illustrated

PART
III

Maintaining the System

in Figure 11.1). On a UNIX system, this value is set in the `pstools.ini` file. The following excerpt shows the `LOGFENCE` section:

```
;Process logging controlled by the LOGFENCE parameter. Each message
;is assigned a "detail level" at compile time. Messages with a detail
;level of zero always show. Other levels show only if the fence is
;greater than the message level, e.g., if the fence is 2, level 0 and
;level 1 messages would show, but 2-4 would be supressed.
;
;Level
;  0  - Errors, "must show" msgs and connection header only.
;  1  - Critical events. For the Process Scheduler this would include
;         Process start attempts.
;  2  - Reserved.
;  3  - Reserved.
;  4  - Detailed messages about the operation of the process, including
;         sleeping messages.
;  5  - Show everthing. This is the default fence value.
LOGFENCE=5
```

When using SQR, the default `LOGFENCE` value is 5, which causes the display of errors, process start attempts, and other detailed messages specific to the process. Although this creates large log files, this is a very valuable setting. You can immediately begin troubleshooting problems without having to rerun a process just to get more detail.

## SQR Parameters

The SQR application, discussed in Chapter 10, "SQR," has command-line parameters that can be valuable in controlling and monitoring SQR Reports. PeopleSoft recommends two command-line parameters that can help with performance, `-XP` and `-S`.

**-XP**    The `–XP` parameter should always be used to prevent deadlocking issues. This parameter prevents stored statements from being created by SQR in your RDBMS. This parameter is not valid for all RDBMS platforms.

**-S**    The `–S` parameter allows you to produce a summary output file showing the frequency that SQL statements are compiled and executed, similar to the COBOL timings trace.

**N O T E**    PeopleSoft documentation also refers to SQR parameters as flags.

## Audit Reports and Utilities

PeopleSoft provides several tools that can be used to audit the integrity of your PeopleSoft databases. This section provides a quick summary of each. A more detailed explanation can be found in Chapter 6, "Data Management Tools."

**DDDAUDIT**    The DDDAUDIT is a SQR report that compares the data definition in the PeopleSoft system tables to the actual data objects that have been created in the database. While not used for performance tuning, the DDDAUDIT is a valuable tool for monitoring the database. It is especially useful in determining if a mismatch exists between the tables that are defined in the RDBMS and those defined in the PeopleSoft record definition tables. This utility can also provide comparisons in the development environment to ensure that data definitions have not been created and left unused by the developers.

**SYSAUDIT**    The SYSAUDIT is another SQR report that is used to compare PeopleSoft objects in the system. SYSAUDIT helps find objects that do not relate to any other objects in the system. If objects are found that do not reference any other objects, they can be deleted. They were probably left behind from a previous version after an upgrade.

Figure 11.2 illustrates the System Audit panel that allows you to determine what integrity checks are performed by SYSAUDIT. Unless you are looking for a specific problem, it's best to run SYSAUDIT with all audits except for Import Integrity. You can omit the Import Integrity check, because these are mostly used during the implementation process.

**FIGURE 11.2**    System Audit panel

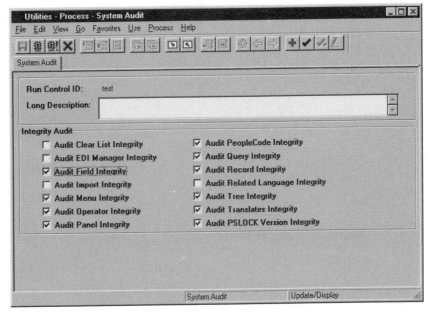

**NOTE**   SYSAUDIT is normally run with Process Scheduler, but can be run from SQRW.

**Alter Audit**   Alter Audit is an online process that compares the record definitions in the PeopleSoft system tables to the underlying RDBMS data definitions. The primary advantage of using Alter Audit over the DDDAUDIT program is that the Alter Audit process creates a script to correct any discrepancies that are found. This script is generated using the Data Definition Language of your specific database.

# Third-Party Tools

There are several tools provided by third-party vendors that can be useful in tuning and monitoring your database. This section contains a list of those vendors that provide certain types of tools. This information changes frequently, so I have listed some sources that can provide you with up-to-date information. I do not endorse any of these vendors, nor do I claim that this is a complete list. Your RDBMS vendor is also a good source of performance-tuning tools. They often deliver such tools with their RDBMS.

## RDBMS Vendors

- ► IBM
- ► Informix
- ► Microsoft
- ► Oracle
- ► Sybase

## Vendors of Database Monitoring and Query Performance Tools

- ► BMC Software
- ► Candle Corporation
- ► Cyrano
- ► Platinum Technology
- ► Savant

## Other Sources of Information

- ► *Intelligent Enterprise* (formerly *Database Programming and Design Magazine*)
- ► DBMS Magazine http://www.dbmsmag.com/

# Tuning the Network for Performance

The performance of the network on which PeopleSoft is running can play a critical role in the success of your PeopleSoft system. The response times that your users receive can be no greater than the maximum performance of your network. PeopleSoft offers several suggestions for network tuning in the performance tuning section of the People-Tools PeopleBook. Let's focus on the considerations that they do not address.

It is important to measure the impact that the PeopleSoft application is having on your network. To do this at our company, I generated a baseline of network performance statistics before the installation of PeopleSoft. I then went back and reran the same tests and compared the results after the PeopleSoft application was operational. The performance factors I monitored were peak utilization, average utilization, and error rate. I periodically go back and check to see if the network has experienced any significant changes from the original results. It is important to do this after an upgrade or after new users have been added to the system.

 **NOTE** The system administrator should seek the assistance of a LAN administrator when conducting the network performance tests. The LAN administrator should be familiar with the tools and concepts in this section.

Another aspect of network performance that will become more critical is the emergence of the Web-enabled PeopleSoft applications in PeopleSoft version 7 and beyond. As the system is extended to more users via Web browsers, the network utilization will climb. Make sure to give your power users the largest bandwidth available on your network. At my company, the Benefits and Payroll users are on the same LAN segment as the database server. This prevents problems with the routers and switches in the network from having an adverse impact on the availability of the PeopleSoft database.

Users that must connect over wide area network (WAN) links require special consideration. PeopleSoft provides the BEA Tuxedo application server to provide three-tier connectivity for your remote users. This access can be either from the traditional PeopleSoft Windows client or from a Web browser. The three-tier configuration results in less data being transmitted over the WAN link to the remote user, resulting in better performance.

PART

III

Maintaining the System

# Tuning the Operating System for Performance

Tuning the operating system is a complicated task that requires specific expertise to avoid problems. First, check the following items when tuning your operating system to ensure that they are not causing problems:

▶ Search any available documentation available from your operating system vendor for any patches that have been issued for your version of the operating system.

▶ Make sure that you have adequate hardware for the amount of data and desired performance level. This includes adequate memory and disks to reduce I/O contention.

▶ Tune the kernel parameters to maximize your use of the hardware.

Consider adjusting the following parameters if your operating system is HP-UX:

▶ Set up asynchronous I/O (absolutely necessary if using Sybase).

▶ Adjust the shmmax (shared memory) parameter to match your hardware memory.

▶ Make sure that the maxusers and maxfiles parameters are adequate for the number of expected users. Remember, the Process Scheduler is viewed as a user to the operating system so don't set the maxfiles so low that your batch processes have difficulty running. I suggest setting this to at least 2,000. It's safer to be too high than too low!

**NOTE**   This information is provided for background. Your UNIX or Windows NT system administrator should perform the tuning of the operating system.

Let's discuss how to monitor the performance of your PeopleSoft application.

# Performance Tuning–Payroll Examples

This section identifies some common performance problems using examples from my company. It outlines the steps we took to resolve them. These techniques can apply to similar situations that might arise with your PeopleSoft system.

**NOTE**   The COBOL timings trace shown in the examples are from much larger output files. I am showing only the lines in question for clarity.

# Example 1

This example is drawn from the example used in the *Batch Performance* section. At our company, this query is used for both on-cycle and off-cycle payroll calculations. This query loads tax information for each employee for which a check is being calculated.

## COBOL Timings Trace

The following is an extract of the initial test calculation of five checks. The batch statistics report is the output from the COBOL timings trace. The statement takes an average of 1.58 seconds (334 seconds/212 executions) to execute each time it is used.

| Statement | Retrieve Count | Retrieve Time | Compile Count | Compile Time | Execute Count | Execute Time | Fetch Count | Fetch Time |
|---|---|---|---|---|---|---|---|---|
| PSPTCALC_S_AGG | 5 | 1.00 | 5 | 0.00 | 212 | 334.00 | 212 | 2.00 |

PeopleSoft Batch Statistics
(All timings in seconds)

**TIP** Use the following rule of thumb when analyzing the COBOL timings trace: If the average time for a single execution of a statement is greater than one second and the statement is executing a large number of times during the process, then the statement is a strong candidate for performing a query plan analysis.

## Query Plan Analysis

The stored statement PSPTCALC_S_AGG was first found in the Data Mover script PSPTCALC.DMS. We created a script to execute the query found in PSPTCALC_S_AGG. The script uses both hard-coded values and variable passing to generate two query plans that can be compared.

**NOTE** Most RDBMS query optimizers can potentially generate a different query plan (and usually the most optimal plan) when values are hard-coded. I use the execution time from this hard-coded query as the standard for my analysis.

PART

III

Maintaining the System

**WARNING** The queries shown are designed to outline the methodology that can be used. This script contains Sybase-specific syntax that may need to be modified for your specific RDBMS.

The query I generated for this analysis was as follows:

```
use HRPROD
go
set showplan on
go
set statistics time on
go

declare @company     char(3)
declare @paygroup    char(3)
declare @pay_end_dt datetime
declare @emplid   char(5)
declare @balance_id char(2)
declare @state char(2)
declare @balance_yr smallint
declare @page        smallint

select @company="BC1",           @paygroup="BW1",
       @pay_end_dt="1997-11-23",  @emplid="00185",
       @state="$U", @balance_yr=1997

SELECT B.TXGRS_AGG ,
B.TAX_AGG ,
A.COMPANY ,
A.PAYGROUP ,
A.PAY_END_DT
FROM
PS_PAY_CHECK A ,
PS_PAY_TAX B ,
PS_PAY_CALENDAR C ,
PS_PAY_CAL_BAL_ID D
WHERE A.COMPANY=@company AND
A.PAYGROUP=@paygroup AND
A.PAY_END_DT<=@pay_end_dt AND
A.OFF_CYCLE='N' AND
A.SEPCHK=0 AND
A.EMPLID=@emplid AND
```

```
A.PAYCHECK_STATUS='F' AND
B.COMPANY=A.COMPANY AND
B.PAYGROUP=A.PAYGROUP AND
B.PAY_END_DT=A.PAY_END_DT AND
B.OFF_CYCLE=A.OFF_CYCLE AND
B.PAGE#=A.PAGE# AND
B.LINE#=A.LINE# AND
B.SEPCHK=A.SEPCHK AND
B.STATE=@state AND
B.LOCALITY=' ' AND
B.TAX_CLASS='H' AND
C.COMPANY=B.COMPANY AND
C.PAYGROUP=B.PAYGROUP AND
C.PAY_END_DT=B.PAY_END_DT AND
D.COMPANY=C.COMPANY AND
D.PAYGROUP=C.PAYGROUP AND
D.PAY_END_DT=C.PAY_END_DT AND
D.BALANCE_YEAR=@balance_yr
ORDER BY A.COMPANY ASC ,
A.PAYGROUP ASC ,
A.PAY_END_DT
go

SELECT B.TXGRS_AGG ,
B.TAX_AGG ,
A.COMPANY ,
A.PAYGROUP ,
A.PAY_END_DT
FROM
PS_PAY_CHECK A ,
PS_PAY_TAX B ,
PS_PAY_CALENDAR C ,
PS_PAY_CAL_BAL_ID D
WHERE A.COMPANY="BC1" AND
A.PAYGROUP="BW1" AND
A.PAY_END_DT<="1997-11-23" AND
A.OFF_CYCLE="Y" AND
A.SEPCHK=0 AND
A.EMPLID="00185" AND
A.PAYCHECK_STATUS='F' AND
B.COMPANY=A.COMPANY AND
B.PAYGROUP=A.PAYGROUP AND
B.PAY_END_DT=A.PAY_END_DT AND
```

PART

III

Maintaining the System

```
B.OFF_CYCLE=A.OFF_CYCLE AND
B.PAGE#=A.PAGE# AND
B.LINE#=A.LINE# AND
B.SEPCHK=A.SEPCHK AND
B.STATE="$U" AND
B.LOCALITY=' ' AND
B.TAX_CLASS='H' AND
C.COMPANY=B.COMPANY AND
C.PAYGROUP=B.PAYGROUP AND
C.PAY_END_DT=B.PAY_END_DT AND
D.COMPANY=C.COMPANY AND
D.PAYGROUP=C.PAYGROUP AND
D.PAY_END_DT=C.PAY_END_DT AND
D.BALANCE_YEAR=1997
ORDER BY A.COMPANY ASC ,
A.PAYGROUP ASC ,
A.PAY_END_DT
go

set statistics time off
go
set showplan off
go
```

**NOTE** You may have to update one or more fields in the database against which you are running the query, if the query looks for specific values that are present only during the batch processing cycle. In the above example, the field PAYCHECK_STATUS may not equal 'F' in the database on which you are testing. I created a query that updates this value. Once the testing was complete, I reset the value.

After executing this query, you should receive a detailed listing of the execution plan and optimizer choices used in executing the query. On my company's system, we discovered that a tremendous amount of time was spent trying to retrieve all the tax information for each individual for each pay period for the current tax year.

This query, when executed, yielded the following information:

```
Execution Time 11768.
Server cpu time: 1176800 ms.
Server elapsed time: 1556753 ms.
(39 rows affected)
```

The results received from both the hard-coded and variable-passing scripts were similar. The query optimizer was having a difficult time resolving this query efficiently.

The results of several attempts at forcing a query plan had only minimal impact on the final results. Therefore, I tried to gain a better understanding of the code being used to call the stored statement. I will not duplicate all the code used in this calculation, but I will outline the steps that I followed during this process.

First, I traced the COBOL modules being used by selecting the code calling the stored statement and working my way both forward and backward from that point in the code. After gaining a better understanding of how the results of this stored statement were used by the other COBOL routines used with the payroll calculation, I discussed our payroll processing procedures with the Payroll staff.

To better understand the Payroll process, I reviewed the COBOL programs to determine the order in which the program executed and the events that were occurring immediately before and after the stored statement that I was analyzing.

**N O T E**　You should have a COBOL programmer available to help with analyzing the PeopleSoft COBOL or consider using the services of PeopleSoft Services Group (PSG).

## Solution

As a result of my research, I determined that attempting to modify the stored statement would probably have minimal impact on our final results. However, at this point, the changes became a customization to the delivered stored statement. I modified the stored statement as follows:

**N O T E**　The code in **bold** indicates where the code is different.

### OLD CODE

```
...
WHERE A.COMPANY=@company AND
A.PAYGROUP=@paygroup AND
A.PAY_END_DT<=@pay_end_dt AND
A.OFF_CYCLE='N' AND
...
```

Maintaining the System

**NEW CODE**

```
...
WHERE A.COMPANY=@company AND
A.PAYGROUP=@paygroup AND
A.PAY_END_DT=@pay_end_dt AND
A.OFF_CYCLE='N' AND
...
```

This modification yielded the following results with a larger query set:

```
Execution Time 16.
Server cpu time: 1600 ms.
Server elapsed time: 6576 ms.
(4050 rows affected)
```

The COBOL timings trace that resulted from this change is as follows:

```
PeopleSoft Batch Statistics

                        (All timings in seconds)


                   R e t r i e v e   C o m p i l e   E x e c u t e   F e t c h
Statement          Count   Time     Count   Time     Count   Time     Count   Time
PSPTCALC_S_AGG     1211  290.00     1211    0.00     4528  322.00     4528    8.00
```

The resulting query saves 1,550,000 ms (1.5 seconds) each time the query is executed. This is a tremendous savings on a payroll calculation that may call this query as many as 40 times per check being calculated.

After conducting many tests myself, I had the Payroll staff conduct calculations of their own to further ensure that no other payroll data was being adversely impacted. I also asked the PeopleSoft Payroll engineers (via my account manager) if they could think of any other calculations that we should test. The PeopleSoft engineers reinforced that this was a customization and that we should proceed with caution. They stated that the results of this query were used for other calculations under specific circumstances, for example, processing special checks before a regular payroll check is calculated for an employee. Since we pay current and have a policy in which this does not happen, we felt safe in proceeding. Once both the Payroll staff and myself were satisfied with the results of the testing, the change to the stored statement was moved into production.

# Example 2

The second example involves a stored statement that is used to retrieve information from the paycheck table.

## COBOL Timings Trace

The following is an extract from a test calculation for one pay group that calculates 1,011 checks. The PSPEARRY_S_CALCRUN statement was taking an average of 1.25 seconds to execute each time it is used.

```
PeopleSoft Batch Statistics
                       (All timings in seconds)


                  R e t r i e v e   C o m p i l e   E x e c u t e   F e t c h
Statement         Count   Time   Count   Time   Count    Time   Count   Time
PSPEARRY_S_CALCRUN 1    0.00        1    0.00    1011  1260.00   1011    4.00
```

## Query Plan Analysis

I located the stored statement PSPEARRY_S_CALCRUN in the Data Mover scripts and created the following test script:

```
use HRPROD
go
set showplan on
go
set statistics time on
go

declare @emplid     char(5)
declare @company    char(3)
declare @runid      char(3)

select @company="BC1",          @emplid="00185",
       @runid="7B3"

SELECT C.RUN_ID
,A.COMPANY
,A.PAYGROUP
,A.PAY_END_DT
,A.OFF_CYCLE
```

```
     ,A.PAGE#
     ,A.LINE#
     ,A.PAYCHECK_OPTION
     FROM PS_PAY_CHECK A
     ,PS_PAY_CALENDAR C
     WHERE A.EMPLID=@emplid
      AND A.COMPANY=@company
      AND A.PAYCHECK_STATUS='C'
      AND C.RUN_ID=@runid
      AND C.COMPANY=A.COMPANY
      AND C.PAYGROUP=A.PAYGROUP
      AND C.PAY_END_DT=A.PAY_END_DT
     go
     set statistics time off
     go
     set showplan off
     go
```

## Solution

The output from the previous query yielded an unexpected result. As shown in the following excerpt from the output file, the two queries were selecting a different index to use when executed. The second version selects an index that contains a key field that is being used in the join.

**N O T E**   The code in **bold** indicates where the index selection lines are different.

```
QUERY PLAN FOR STATEMENT 3 (at line 7).
    STEP 1
        The type of query is SELECT.

        FROM TABLE
            PS_PAY_CHECK
        Nested iteration.
        Using Clustered Index.
        Index : PS_PAY_CHECK
        Ascending scan.
        Positioning by key.
        Keys are:
            COMPANY
```

Using I/O Size 2 Kbytes.
With LRU Buffer Replacement Strategy.

FROM TABLE
    PS_PAY_CALENDAR
Nested iteration.
Index : PSOPAY_CALENDAR
Ascending scan.
Positioning by key.
Index contains all needed columns. Base table will not be read.
Keys are:
    RUN_ID
    COMPANY
    PAYGROUP
    PAY_END_DT
Using I/O Size 2 Kbytes.
With LRU Buffer Replacement Strategy.

Parse and Compile Time 0.
Server cpu time: 0 ms.
Total writes for this command: 0

Execution Time 0.
Server cpu time: 0 ms. Server elapsed time: 0 ms.
(1 row affected)
...

QUERY PLAN FOR STATEMENT 1 (at line 2).
    STEP 1
        The type of query is SELECT.

    FROM TABLE
        PS_PAY_CHECK
    Nested iteration.
    **Index : PS1PAY_CHECK**
    Ascending scan.
    Positioning by key.
    Keys are:
        EMPLID
        COMPANY
    Using I/O Size 2 Kbytes.
    With LRU Buffer Replacement Strategy.

    FROM TABLE
        PS_PAY_CALENDAR

```
          Nested iteration.
          Index : PSOPAY_CALENDAR
          Ascending scan.
          Positioning by key.
          Index contains all needed columns. Base table will not be read.
          Keys are:
              RUN_ID
              COMPANY
              PAYGROUP
              PAY_END_DT
          Using I/O Size 2 Kbytes.
          With LRU Buffer Replacement Strategy.
     Parse and Compile Time 0.
     Server cpu time: 0 ms.
```

I modified the SQL contained in stored statement PSPEARRY_S_CALCRUN to force the query to use the index that was being used by the hard-coded test script. I created a custom Data Mover script containing the new stored statement. I then executed this script to load the statement in the PS_SQLSTMT_TBL table. The modified portion of the statement is as follows:

**OLD CODE**

```
…

FROM PS_PAY_CHECK A
,PS_PAY_CALENDAR C

…
```

**NEW CODE**

```
…

FROM PS_PAY_CHECK A (INDEX PS1PAY_CHECK)
,PS_PAY_CALENDAR C

…
```

The entire new statement is shown below:

---

**CUSTOM.DMS**

```
REM - Modified 2/19/1998 by Darrell Bilbrey
REM - Force the query to use index PS1PAY_CHECK
/
```

```
STORE PSPEARRY_S_CALCRUN
SELECT
 C.RUN_ID
,A.COMPANY
,A.PAYGROUP
,A.PAY_END_DT
,A.OFF_CYCLE
,A.PAGE#
,A.LINE#
,A.PAYCHECK_OPTION
FROM PS_PAY_CHECK A (INDEX PS1PAY_CHECK)
,PS_PAY_CALENDAR C
WHERE A.EMPLID=:1
  AND A.COMPANY=:2
  AND C.RUN_ID=:3
  AND A.PAYCHECK_STATUS='C'
  AND A.COMPANY=C.COMPANY
  AND A.PAYGROUP=C.PAYGROUP
  AND A.PAY_END_DT=C.PAY_END_DT
```

The adjusted stored statement yielded the following COBOL timings trace with a larger number of calculated checks:

```
PeopleSoft Batch Statistics
                      (All timings in seconds)

               R e t r i e v e   C o m p i l e   E x e c u t e   F e t c h
Statement       Count  Time    Count  Time    Count   Time    Count  Time
PSPEARRY_S_CALCRUN 3   0.00      3    0.00     4097  417.00     5309  14.00
```

The average execution time per transaction is now 0.1 seconds, a savings of 1.15 seconds per transaction. Unlike Example 1, this change resulted in no change to the data being returned. This change was moved into production without any further testing by the end users.

PART

III

**Maintaining the System**

# Summary

Performance tuning is critical to the success of your PeopleSoft system. The first step is to develop a performance-tuning plan. This plan should include a prioritized list of parameters that can be adjusted to improve the performance of your database. When developing this plan, incorporate any performance-tuning information provided by your database vendor.

When addressing performance issues on the database server, make sure to consider the tunable database parameters, disk I/O, and the amount of memory occupied by the indexes.

There are several areas you can address to try to improve performance in two-tier and three-tier configurations. In a two-tier configuration, you can upgrade the hardware, the software, and the network bandwidth. In a three-tier configuration, the performance of the application server directly impacts the performance of the client.

The performance of batch jobs will be very important to your end users. The COBOL timings trace can help by collecting statistics about the execution of COBOL stored statements during batch processing.

There are many tools available to aid you in performance tuning. PeopleSoft provides SQL Trace, PeopleCode Trace, Application Reviewer, COBOL timings trace, Process Scheduler logging, SQR parameters, and auditing utilities. In addition, many third-party vendors, including your RDBMS vendor, provide tools that can help you tune and monitor the performance of your database.

The network and operating system on which your PeopleSoft system is running can also be tuned to improve performance. Make sure to enlist the help of your LAN administrator or operating system administrator before making any changes.

Tuning performance is an ongoing responsibility of the system administrator. Make a checklist of performance-related issues to be checked periodically.

The two payroll examples in this chapter illustrated some real-life performance issues that my company had to address. In both examples, we used the COBOL timings trace and query plan analysis to isolate and resolve the problems.

# Upgrading Your PeopleSoft System

## FEATURING

A ll PeopleSoft installations will eventually face the daunting task of upgrading the system. This task can be mastered with careful planning and testing. This chapter discusses some of the options that should be considered, how to approach an upgrade, and some of the resources that you can use to make the process successful.

What makes a PeopleSoft upgrade process challenging? Unlike other applications your company may purchase, PeopleSoft applications are merely shell programs that must have some configuration information entered before using them. The data elements that have been configured during the implementation represent the heart of the PeopleSoft system. In addition, many of the delivered objects are stored in the PeopleSoft system tables. An upgrade involves merging your configured database with the database that contains the data objects that represent the new system. The upgrade consists of many SQL scripts and application upgrade projects that must be processed to complete the upgrade.

Make sure that when preparing for an upgrade, you consult the database administrator (DBA) of your PeopleSoft database. The DBA needs to help set up test databases and possibly run many of the scripts that must be executed on the server to accomplish the upgrade. The DBA should be included in the upgrade planning process to ensure that proper capacity planning and scheduling are accomplished. The DBA must also be informed of any version changes that will be required.

You should also involve the system administrator for your database server's operating system in the upgrade process. The system administrator should verify that all required patches and updates are in place prior to the beginning of the upgrade process. Be sure to consult the release notes and certification databases on Customer Connection for information regarding your specific environment.

Let's begin our look at upgrades by reviewing the tools that will be used to perform the upgrade steps.

## Tools for a PeopleSoft Upgrade

This section provides a brief summary of how each tool is used during the upgrade process. It is not my intent to make you proficient in the use of these tools. This section reviews the functionality of each tool; see Chapter 6, "Data Management Tools," for a more detailed description of each of these tools.

# Application Designer

Beginning with PeopleSoft version 7, the application upgrade functionality has been moved into the integrated Application Designer. To access the upgrade projects, select File > Open, choose the project type, enter the project name, and click Select. When the project is opened, additional menu items appear that allow you to perform the tasks of the upgrade such as Compare, Copy, etc. Figure 12.1 shows an upgrade project opened in the Application Designer panel.

**FIGURE 12.1** Application Designer panel

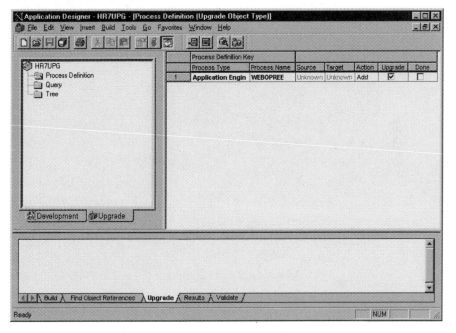

In Figure 12.1, note that there are several tabs along the bottom. These tabs represent different windows that display the output from processes that are being performed using the loaded project. Each tab's name represents the action being performed.

**The Build tab** When running a build process to create database script, the Build tab displays the tables that are being processed and indicates whether the table was built or skipped due to no changes.

**The Find Object References tab** The Find Object References tab is used to find references to the selected objects, such as records, panels, and menus.

PART

**III**

Maintaining the System

**The Upgrade tab**    The Upgrade tab displays the status of the copy process as it is running.

**The Results tab**    The Results tab displays the results of any processes that have been executed.

**The Validate tab**    The Validate tab displays information when you perform validation on a project after importing that project from another database.

The window in the upper left corner displays the objects in the project using two tabs, Development and Upgrade. Let's look at the information on both of these windows.

**The Development tab**    The Development tab displays the PeopleTools objects that can be opened and edited using Application Designer. The seven types of objects are as follows:

- Fields
- Records
- Panels
- Panel groups
- Menus
- Business processes
- Business process maps

**The Upgrade tab**    The Upgrade tab uses a Windows Explorer-like display to show the types of objects in the project. You can see specific objects in the project by expanding the Object Type folder. Figure 12.1 illustrates the Process Definition folder.

Let's look at the SQL tools that will be used during the upgrade.

## SQL Tools

The SQL tools are specific to each RDBMS. They are used to execute command-line or script-based SQL. PeopleSoft delivers some of the upgrade scripts in SQL format for use with the SQL tools for your RDBMS. Oracle uses SQL Plus. Sybase uses the ISQL utility. DB2 uses Data Mover. Check with the upgrade instructions to verify which SQL tool to use with your database. Your RDBMS vendor should provide extensive documentation on the use of their SQL tool, so I will not attempt to explain their use here.

PeopleSoft upgrade scripts that are delivered for use with your SQL tool are designed to modify the table structures of your database. The first script executed during an upgrade is usually executed with your SQL tool and is the PeopleTools upgrade. Once this script has been executed, the new functionality for the upgrade will be loaded in the subsequent steps.

For example, if PeopleSoft needs a new column in one of the system tables, the first task is to alter the current table to the new format. This alone does not affect the old functionality of the application. In the next step, the new data for the new column is populated by the release Data Mover script. The new version of PeopleTools can then log in to your copy of the production database, allowing you to perform the upgrade.

The next section provides a quick overview of Data Mover, which is used extensively during an upgrade.

## Data Mover

Data Mover is a PeopleSoft-delivered utility that loads database tables with data needed to populate the PeopleSoft system tables during an upgrade. Details of the Data Mover functionality are covered in Chapter 6, "Data Management Tools." Generally, the second script of the upgrade is a Data Mover script that loads the data required for the new version into the tables that were modified by the first script executed by the SQL tool. Data Mover is also used to populate data tables, such as tax tables. This functionality is generally used when performing tax updates, which are discussed in Chapter 13, "Tax Updates."

Figure 12.2 shows the Data Mover window. To start Data Mover, click the icon in the PeopleSoft release folder or in the PeopleSoft Installation folder. The window is split horizontally into two areas. The input area is on top and shows any loaded scripts. The output area is on the bottom and shows the results of each step of the process defined in the input area. All error messages are displayed in the output window and logged to the log file that you designate.

The upgrade process utilizes the audit scripts extensively. Let's quickly review the use of audit scripts.

PART

III

Maintaining the System

**FIGURE 12.2**    Data Mover window

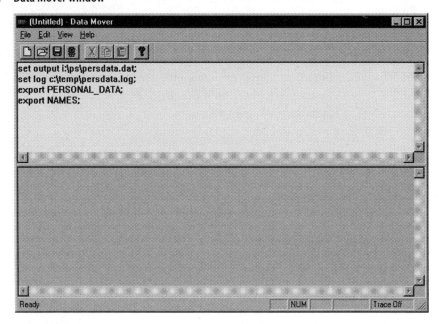

## SQR Audit Scripts

The two audit scripts that should be used extensively during the upgrade are DDDAUDIT.SQR and SYSAUDIT.SQR. The DDDAUDIT.SQR script compares the PeopleSoft system tables for records and indexes to the actual database tables and indexes. A resulting report lists any discrepancies that are found. SYSAUDIT.SQR searches the PeopleSoft system tables for orphaned data. The integrity of the following types of objects is checked by SYSAUDIT.SQR:

▶ Fields

▶ Records

▶ Queries

▶ Menus

The System Audit panel, shown in Figure 12.3, lists all of the objects whose integrity can be audited during the system audit run.

**FIGURE 12.3**    System Audit control panel

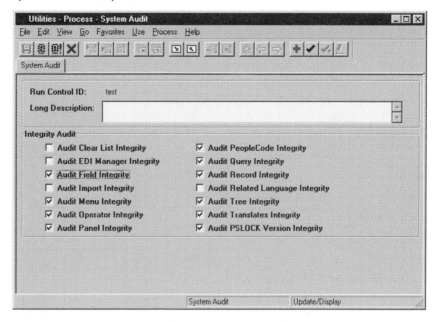

To access the System Audit control panel, select Go **>** PeopleTools **>** Utilities. To use this panel initially, you need to create a run control ID. Once you have selected the objects that you want to audit, click the Run button on the toolbar. You are then prompted for the run location and output settings. I generally run the system audit from the client, so I can do this without having the Process Scheduler running on the server.

Another process that is used in the upgrade process is the SQL Alter process.

## SQL Alter

As discussed in Chapter 6, "Data Management Tools," SQL Alter is used to build scripts for changing the database based on definitions in the PeopleSoft system tables. There is also an option for audit-only that can be used during an upgrade to get a list of discrepancies before or after a step is completed. I recommend that you create a project containing all tables for use during an upgrade. You only need to open this project each time an SQL Alter or other record comparison is needed.

To access the SQL Alter Build panel, illustrated in Figure 12.4, select Build **>** Project from the Application Designer window. You can build only the current or selected objects.

PART

**III**

Maintaining the System

**FIGURE 12.4**     SQL Alter–Build panel

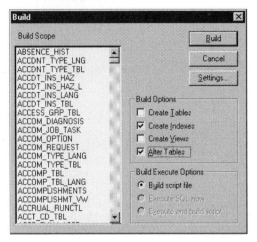

Figure 12.4 shows the Build Scope down the left side of this panel. The Build Scope lists all tables to be checked by the audit process. You must also select the type of build that you want to perform. For the audit, choose the Alter Tables check box. The Create Indexes box will automatically be checked. A radio button must be selected in the Build Execute Options group. I recommend that you always build to a script file so that you have a chance to review the changes before they are actually executed against your database.

Before clicking the Build button, select the Build Settings button. Figure 12.5 contains the Alter tab of the Build Settings panel. On the Alter tab, set the options that control which actions will be detected and scripted. You can decide if you want to drop columns that contain data or if you want to truncate the data if the new field definition is shorter than the existing definition and data. You also have the choice to limit the build with respect to additions (adds), changes, renames, or deletes.

When building a script, also select the Script tab, shown in Figure 12.6. On the Script tab, set the options that affect the script being generated. You can specify that comments be written to the script. You can also specify whether to create a single script or separate files. You must also designate the filename and location where you want the generated script file stored.

**TIP**   The upgrade procedures delivered with the upgrade specify the settings to be used for each step.

**FIGURE 12.5**    SQL Alter–Build Settings panel, Alter tab

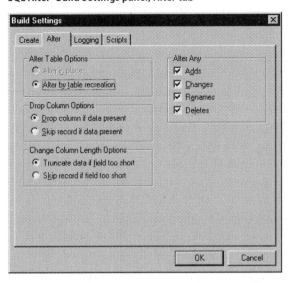

**FIGURE 12.6**    SQL Alter–Build Settings panel, Scripts tab

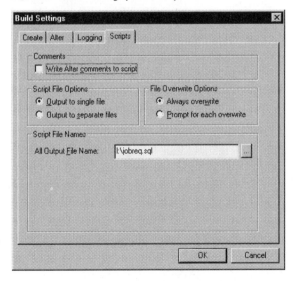

Let's look at the types of upgrades that can be performed on PeopleSoft databases.

# Upgrade Types

There are several types of upgrades. This section refers to them using the PeopleSoft version 7.5 nomenclature. Later in this section, discussion focuses on how each upgrade type has changed with the newer versions of PeopleSoft. There are three unique upgrade types:

- ▶ PeopleTools
- ▶ Application
- ▶ Custom

## PeopleTools Upgrade Type

A PeopleTools upgrade is probably the easiest upgrade to perform. A PeopleSoft upgrade is delivered as a set of scripts that first upgrade the table structures to support the new release. Then other scripts, usually Data Mover scripts, are executed to load the new PeopleTools object data to support the new release. PeopleSoft usually refers to these as the release scripts. Other items that may be updated during a PeopleTools upgrade include the Message table data and stored statements. The scripts for these are usually named `MSGTOOLS.DMS` and `STOREPT.DMS`.

In addition, there may be new COBOL code for any batch jobs or the Process Scheduler program that will have to be moved to the server and compiled. Application-specific COBOL is not affected during the PeopleTools upgrade.

In addition, you will receive PeopleTools maintenance releases that must be implemented. PeopleTools maintenance releases contain new software programs, scripts, and reports for the PeopleTools code; they contain no database changes. You may also receive updated code for third-party applications such as Crystal Reports, SQR, and the Tuxedo application server during a PeopleTools maintenance release.

## Application Upgrade Type

PeopleSoft splits the application upgrade type into two subtypes, application upgrade and application update, both of which are described in this section. The major differences between the two subtypes are the number of database changes involved and whether a PeopleTools release is involved.

### Application Upgrade

The application upgrade is performed when you want to upgrade to a new application release without losing any of your customizations. The application upgrade is always accompanied by a PeopleTools upgrade. This type of upgrade consists of two parts: the compare/report and the comparison copy.

First, you run a series of reports that compare a copy of the production database to the new demo database. These are SQR programs that build a report but also populate the defined project with objects that differ between the source and target databases. The compare/report processes evaluate differences between panels, fields, PeopleCode, colors, menus, records, and indexes. Once all the compare/report processes are run, open the project using the Application Designer (see Figure 12.1 earlier in this chapter) and verify that all the action codes are set properly. Some of the possible actions are add, replace, and delete. The Upgrade field should be checked for all actions that you want performed by the upgrade process.

You are then ready to run the comparison copy process to move all of the new application objects from the new demo database to your copy of the production database. Details of this process are described later in this chapter.

**N O T E**    The application upgrade was referred to as the comparison upgrade under earlier versions of PeopleSoft.

### Application Update

An application update is performed when you want to move only a limited amount of data between two databases. The most common application of this is an application maintenance release. An application maintenance release is similar to a PeopleTools maintenance release in that only minor changes are involved. You receive updated application object definitions, new batch programs, and new application data.

The application update replaces the selective upgrade defined in earlier versions of PeopleSoft.

## Custom Upgrade Type

All customizations are treated as upgrade projects using the Application Designer. You just add objects to a project, then use the application upgrade process to copy the customization to the other databases. PeopleSoft provides several ways to do this:

- ▶ You can add all the objects manually.

- ▶ You can have all changed objects added automatically.

- ▶ You can have all related objects added to the project.

If you select the option to add related objects to your project, PeopleSoft warns you to perform a comparison between the development and production databases before copying the new project to your production database. I concur with this and suggest you do comparisons to any project that has automatically added objects or related objects to ensure that no customizations are being overwritten. If you have more than one developer working on a PeopleSoft project, there is a chance that the same object may be included in more than one project. To control this at our company, one person is designated to perform any changes to the production database.

Let's discuss the necessary steps required to prepare for an upgrade to a new version.

# Preparing for an Upgrade

The first step in preparing for an upgrade is to download and distribute pre-release notes to both your technical and functional upgrade team as early as possible before a new version is released. The pre-release notes are generally available three or four months before a new release of the software is available. They can be found on Customer Connection. Your account manager should notify you when they are available.

The pre-release notes contain summary information about the changes that are included in the new release. The technical and functional area team members should review the pre-release notes in order to develop an impact plan and test schedule for the upgrade. Check your customization list to see if any new functionality can replace any customizations that you have made. This step can also be extended to translate values, which may have been added or updated. You should also verify the Action and Action/Reason codes from the ACTN_REASON_TBL, used by the Job table in PeopleSoft HRMS.

# Reviewing Customer Connection

Check the platform support database to determine what other upgrades must be undertaken as part of the upgrade process. The items to look for are:

▶ Database server operating system version—PeopleSoft usually certifies the latest versions so you may need to upgrade or apply patches to the database server operating system.

▶ RDBMS version—PeopleSoft certifies the latest version of the RDBMS, so you may be required to upgrade your RDBMS.

▶ Client connectivity version.

▶ SQR version (for the server).

The required versions for the first three items should be obtained from your server and database vendors. If you are using UNIX, request the new version of SQR for your server platform from your PeopleSoft account manager since you have no support directly from SQRIBE. The client version that you need is included on the CD-ROMs for the new version.

Customer Connection should also be reviewed frequently before and during the upgrade. Consider assigning someone this task for the duration of the upgrade and for some time afterwards. In addition, I also review Customer Connection during the upgrade process to see if any items required for the upgrade have been overlooked. This helps catch more items earlier, since multiple people are looking for the items. To ensure that duplicate items are not downloaded, a directory is designated to place any updates that are downloaded for the upgrade.

Another source of information that may help is your network of other PeopleSoft customers. Make sure to assemble a list of other PeopleSoft customers that have similarities to your installation. Check with them to see if they have encountered any problems with the upgrade. Don't forget to pass information that you discover on to them. Treat your relationship with other PeopleSoft customers like a bank account; do not continually withdraw information without making a deposit. There may also be a local PeopleSoft Users Group that can be useful for information sharing. Your account manager has information on local user groups, along with information on other customers with similar configurations or who are performing the upgrade at the same time.

The next step is to build checklists for your upgrade.

**PART**

**III**

**Maintaining the System**

# Building Checklists

Checklists are an important part of the PeopleSoft upgrade process. It is imperative that you closely monitor the steps you are performing to ensure that you do not execute any of them out of order.

PeopleSoft provides upgrade kits that help with building the checklists. Sometimes they even have scripts for specific RDBMS platforms to assist in the upgrade. Download any upgrade kits from Customer Connection. My company uses the Customer Connection scripts as the basis for custom checklists that we create for running the upgrade scripts and performing other upgrade tasks. The upgrade kits are usually available after the general release of the new installation version of the software and before the upgrade version is available.

At my company, the checklists usually look similar to the example in Table 12.1. I use the checklist provided in the upgrade kits on Customer Connection for the actual upgrade steps provided by PeopleSoft. This checklist matches the upgrade step numbers from the instruction manual.

**TABLE 12.1** Sample Checklist

| PeopleSoft Version 7 Upgrade Plan | | |
| --- | --- | --- |
| **Task** | **Date** | **Initials** |
| Upgrade RDBMS to the supported version. | | |
| Upgrade SQR to version 3.0.18.1 on the backup server. | | |
| Load UPGDMO with version 7 demo database data. | | |
| Do the first upgrade to version 7 on TESTDB using the upgrade procedures supplied by PeopleSoft. | | |
| Apply tax updates for version 7 to the test database. | | |
| Upgrade the database client connectivity software for the server to the supported version. | | |
| Apply the customizations to 7.0 COBOL. | | |
| Compile and link all code, including the application server code. | | |
| Configure Tuxedo for the test server. | | |

**TABLE 12.1  (continued)    Sample Checklist**

| PeopleSoft Version 7 Upgrade Plan | | |
|---|---|---|
| **Task** | **Date** | **Initials** |
| Test version 7—technical and functional users. | | |
| Modify the custom SQRs to handle the version 7 table definitions. | | |
| Load another copy of PRODDB to TESTDB. | | |
| Test the upgrade again (see the checklist for details). | | |
| Upgrade the production server operating system to the supported version. | | |
| Upgrade the production database to the supported version. | | |
| Upgrade SQR to version 3.0.18.1 on the production server. | | |
| Configure Tuxedo on the production server. | | |
| Schedule and perform the upgrade to the production database. | | |
| Move the version 7 source code to production—compile and link. | | |
| Apply the tax updates for version 7 to the production database. | | |

At my company, we also take this opportunity to create problem logs in which anyone testing the upgrade can log incidents or problems. Let's take a look at some of the things to consider when creating problem logs.

## Creating Problem Logs

Make sure to create problem logs on a network drive where the users who are performing the testing can enter any problems that they encounter. We generally maintain two logs: One log is for the technical team to record technical issues that they encounter during the upgrade. The other log is for the application issues. If the upgrade is extensive, consider adding a problem log for each major PeopleSoft function you are upgrading such as Financials, Manufacturing, or HRMS.

You are now ready to begin installing the new version of the software. Let's look at this process.

## Installing the Software

The first step in installing the software is to install PeopleTools and all the application modules to the file server. Once the files for each module have been extracted from the CD-ROM, you are ready to move any necessary files to the database server.

Create scripts and move the new version to the test area on the database server using the File Transfer program. The File Transfer program was described in Chapter 2, "Basic Implementation." I recommend that you create separate user IDs and directories that allow for complete compilation and isolation of updated code from the production code for testing. An example directory structure on UNIX might look like the following:

```
/psoft/hr70/
/psoft/hr75/
/psoft/fin70/
/psoft/fin75/
```

Let's now look at the upgrade instructions to determine where to go from here.

## Reviewing the Upgrade Instructions

Once you have installed the software to the file server, print and read the upgrade instructions, highlighting special sections that might be easily overlooked. At my company, we cross out sections that do not apply to our installation to prevent confusion when performing the tasks. We also add notes or steps to the upgrade instructions when we think of things that should be added for our specific installation. The most common items that we add are steps to backup the database. We tend to do backups more often than the prompts provided by PeopleSoft in the upgrade instructions.

We usually read and reread the upgrade instructions to become more familiar with the required tasks. Make sure to log on to Customer Connection and search for any needed patches or problems that have been reported. Also, look for any updates to the upgrade instructions themselves.

The next step is to create the databases to be used for the application update database and the copy of production for the first upgrade. Let's take a look at these databases.

# Setting Up the Databases

You need two databases: one to hold the demo database for the new version of People-Soft and an empty database sized to hold a copy of the production database. These databases are required to test and perform the upgrade. The new demo database contains the PeopleTools and application objects for the new PeopleSoft database. The demo database is created from Data Mover scripts that load only the required People-Soft tables. This database contains all of the new objects for both PeopleTools and the applications that are being updated. For multiple PeopleSoft products, I load all the new application information into a single demo database. I then have copies of each product line's production databases to which I apply the PeopleTools and specific application upgrades.

The second database should be sized to hold a full copy of your production database. This is required for performing an upgrade. This helps you discover any problems that are caused by your production data.

**TIP** I also record the execution time for each script that takes over two minutes. This allows me to better predict how long the final upgrade will take.

Beginning with PeopleSoft version 7.0, the log space of this second database must be significantly larger than previously used. I have a log space that is one-third to one-half the size of the database. This change is due to the new direction of the upgrade comparison steps. Version 7 and higher uses a push methodology where you first log in to the source and "push" (copy) the new data to the target database. Older versions of PeopleSoft used the pull methodology. The push methodology moves the transaction logging to the application update database and away from the database holding your copy of the production database.

The final step in preparing the databases is to execute the database integrity utility for your specific RDBMS. This ensures that you have no problems at the database level before beginning to run all the scripts for the upgrade.

Let's discuss the creation of your application update database in more detail.

PART

III

**Maintaining the System**

## Creating the Demo Database

As previously discussed, the demo database is used to store all the new PeopleTools objects that represent the new version of PeopleSoft. You must create a database to store these new objects. To build this database, take the following steps:

▶ Create an empty database using your RDBMS tools.

▶ Add the PeopleSoft data types, using the script discussed in Chapter 2, "Basic Implementation."

▶ Use Data Mover to import the demo database from the delivered raw data file.

You then have a database containing the new PeopleSoft release. You are now ready to proceed with building the copy of your production database.

## Building a Copy of the Production Database

The next step in preparing for the upgrade is to build a copy of your production database for each PeopleSoft application that you will be upgrading.

▶ Create an empty database using your RDBMS tools.

▶ Add the PeopleSoft data types using the script discussed in Chapter 2, "Basic Implementation," (not required for all databases).

▶ Load a copy of your production database. (I use this as an opportunity to test my backup system by doing a load from my database dumps.)

**WARNING** Once you have created the copy of the production database to use for the upgrade, you must stop new PeopleTools development, since the final step of the upgrade moves the PeopleTools tables from the copy of the production database to the production server.

Once you have created your databases, it's time to begin running the PeopleSoft upgrade scripts.

# Performing a Test Upgrade

You are now ready to perform the first step of the upgrade on your copy of the production database. Run through all the steps outlined in the upgrade procedures to get your first updated database. Document all problems or changes that have to be made. This is good information to pass back to your PeopleSoft account manager as feedback on the upgrade process, especially for problems that resulted from errone-ous PeopleSoft instructions or code. Having a record of these problems is also useful when the final upgrade steps are performed.

I cannot stress enough the importance of doing backups at several points through-out the upgrade process. PeopleSoft puts steps in to remind you to do this. I usually make backups more frequently than PeopleSoft recommends. I do a backup just prior to running any script that implements a lot of changes. Some examples of times I perform extra backups are before executing the table alter steps and before execut-ing the Data Mover scripts that load the new objects into the PeopleSoft system tables.

**TIP**   Make sure to assign someone the responsibility of continually checking Customer Connection to search for potential upgrade problems. In addition, I check two or three times per week during the upgrade process myself. Resolutions to problems that other companies have encountered during the upgrade are continually being posted to Cus-tomer Connection.

If many errors are found or the test upgrade takes a significant amount of time due to script errors, consider testing the scripts a second time. When you are satisfied with the performance of the scripts against the test upgrade, verify that all security is set to allow for end-user testing.

After running the upgrade scripts, apply any necessary tax updates if you are run-ning Payroll. Read the release notes carefully to determine the last tax update that is included in the new release. You may have to reapply some changes that are specific to the new version.

The next step is to make any customizations to the new COBOL that you want to carry forward from the current version to the new release. Load the new stored state-ments delivered with the upgrade using Data Mover. Make sure to reload any cus-tomized stored statements after loading the new PeopleSoft versions.

**WARNING**   Don't forget to reload any customized stored statements after loading the new PeopleSoft versions.

UNIX installations require that you compile all Payroll COBOL on the server using the `pscbl.mak file`. Link all code using the `psrun.mak` file. Make any necessary configuration changes and start the Process Scheduler and the Application Server if you are running on a three-tier configuration.

If all the steps have been successful, you are now ready to begin the test upgrade. If you encounter difficulty during any of these steps, verify that the previous steps completed successfully. If you are still experiencing problems, check the upgrade section of Chapter 17, "Troubleshooting," for more detailed steps to perform. Don't forget to use the Customer Connection databases as well.

Let's begin by discussing the steps required to upgrade PeopleTools.

## Upgrading PeopleTools

The upgrade to PeopleTools is your first step. The PeopleSoft system tables represent the building blocks of the applications delivered by PeopleSoft. If new functionality is being delivered with the upgrade, the system tables must be updated to accommodate these changes. You first run the SQL script, which makes any required structural modifications to the PeopleSoft system tables. This script adds new system tables or modifies the current tables so that the new definitions can be inserted into them. This script is generally named REL*XXX*.SQL, where *XXX* represents the PeopleTools release being implemented. This step is executed using the SQL tool for your RDBMS.

Once this script has executed successfully, you are ready to modify the data contained in the system tables.

**WARNING**   Upgrading PeopleTools and implementing the other steps that follow for the upgrade are examples of the procedures that you will perform. Follow the upgrade procedures delivered by PeopleSoft when performing an actual upgrade. These steps are provided to give you insight into the process and point out some potential problems.

## Modifying the PeopleSoft System Tables

The next step in upgrading your PeopleSoft database is to import the new version information into the PeopleSoft system tables. The script for this task is generally a Data Mover script that imports the new system table information. This file is usually named the same as the SQL script, with the `*.dms` extension that indicates that it should to be executed with Data Mover.

**WARNING**  The nature of the system tables and the way they are upgraded make it important for you to define a naming standard for the new objects that makes them easily identified and does not conflict with PeopleSoft-delivered objects. See Chapter 14, "Documentation," for recommended naming standards.

To modify your system tables, take the following steps in order:

1. Load any new system messages that have been changed for the new application.

2. Compile any update PeopleTools COBOL for use on your server platform.

3. Load the new PeopleTools stored statements for use by batch COBOL processes.

4. Copy the PeopleTools upgrade project to your test database.

5. Execute the build process to update any tables that have been changed by the new version.

6. Verify and update the operator security for the database.

Once you have successfully completed the steps required to upgrade the PeopleTools objects, you are ready to proceed with the upgrade to the new application version.

## Upgrading the Application

The first step in performing the upgrade to the new application version is to create an empty project. Then run the upgrade comparison reports to populate this project with the objects that have differences between the two databases. Reports are created for your review.

Understanding the comparison process will help you evaluate the information that is being produced in both the report and the project upgrade. The PeopleSoft comparison processes are mostly SQR programs that compare the copy of your production database to the objects contained in the demo database for the new version. There are several reports that look at specific PeopleSoft object types. For example, the panel comparison process determines which panels are different between the two databases. Other objects that are compared include the following:

▶ Records

▶ Menus

▶ Colors

▶ PeopleCode (both record and menu)

The PeopleCode comparisons are done online and are not executed using SQRW or the Process Scheduler.

When all the reports are complete, review the reports that were generated. Determine if you will accept the changes made by the new version or skip that update and continue with the older version. Usually, you want to skip the update to newer versions of objects only when you have made a customization to support a business process that cannot be handled by PeopleSoft.

Once you have determined the object copy status that you want to set for each object, open the project and set those copy parameters on the upgrade comparison project.

## Modifying the Application Tables

Once the upgrade comparison project has been copied into the test database, perform any required upgrades to the application tables. This ensures that both the record definitions and the underlying RDBMS are synchronized.

First, create any new tables that were added with the new release. Tables are created by executing the script that you generate using the Application Designer build process. You build an all-tables project and then execute the Create Tables build. Have the process create the SQL file. Execute the SQL to modify your tables.

> **NOTE**  At my company, I repeat the initial upgrade before end-user testing begins if many errors were encountered during the initial upgrade.

Once the tables have been edited, you are ready to test the new release.

# Testing the New Release

Now that the first database has been upgraded, it is time to begin testing the application to make sure that all the functions are working properly.

There are several issues to consider as you prepare to test the new version. First, at my company, the technical upgrade team and I perform many of the tests that the functional users will conduct before we begin end-user testing. Second, I have one member of my team trained in the Payroll process. This is critical in conducting our own tests of the batch processes (including Payroll).

Configure and set up workstations for end-user testing of the new version. This workstation must usually have other software upgraded as well. The primary compatibility issues are usually between the version of Microsoft Office and the links to PeopleSoft Query.

I have created a checklist that I use for each upgrade. In addition, my functional users have also created their own checklists for use during testing.

Consider a parallel operations period, especially for payroll if significant changes have been introduced by the upgrade. I generally run one payroll cycle to make sure that all programs are still working correctly. However, with a major release such as version 7.5, we are already planning to conduct more extensive testing that will probably cover one full month of payroll operations.

Don't forget to verify the customizations that you want to retain. You want to ensure that the upgrade process did not change them. I cannot stress this too seriously. There are many scripts that can impact your customizations. This verification step is a critical task on my checklist.

**TIP**   Don't forget to verify the customizations that you elect to retain to make sure that the upgrade process did not change them.

Before testing the batch environment, compile all the source code (COBOL) for the batch environment, including the code for the Process Scheduler (if you are on UNIX). Once all the code is compiled, you are ready to restart the Process Scheduler.

## Restarting Process Scheduler

As discussed in the previous section, make sure that all code has been successfully compiled before attempting to restart the Process Scheduler. In addition, make sure that all the new versions of the stored statements have been loaded before starting the Process Scheduler. You are now ready to restart the Process Scheduler using any new procedures that may have been introduced with the new version. The procedures for starting the Process Scheduler changed after both upgrades that we have performed.

There is one last step before your end users can begin their testing: verification of the security profiles.

PART

III

Maintaining the System

# Verifying the Security Profiles

When you are reviewing the security profiles, make sure to update them to reflect any new menu definitions. In some of the PeopleSoft upgrades, the names of menu items are changed slightly. These menu items must be reviewed to make sure that the users who had access before still have access to those menu items. This is a tedious process for the security administrator, but one that you should plan for in the schedule to minimize the complaints you receive from your end users when testing begins.

Let's discuss some of the tasks that you should test to ensure that the online functions are still working.

# Testing the Online Functions

Have your end-user upgrade team begin testing all the online functions listed in the checklists of critical business functions to be verified after the upgrade. If you created any workflow procedures, make sure that after the upgrade, they are still working as you designed. Queries may need modifying or roles may need to be redefined.

Test the delivered processes to ensure that they are working and to determine if there have been any changes in how they operate. An example of a process that we check closely at my company is the Hire process in PeopleSoft HRMS.

Verify that the application server is still operating without problems after the upgrade. This is very important if you have a large number of customized panels. Make sure that the customized panels work in three-tier mode if you will need them to.

One of the most common problems that you may discover in testing the online functions is that the upgrade adjusted a search view. Often, this is not discovered during the upgrade steps. Make sure to verify the syntax of the view and then drop the view and recreate it.

Another area that requires close testing is the interfaces both into and out of our PeopleSoft application.

# Testing the Interfaces

At my company, there are several interfaces between our Payroll system and external data sources. One of the steps that we perform during end-user testing is checking to see if the interfaces are functioning properly. If your interface table inserts new records or updates existing records in the database, it is imperative that you review the list of modified tables to ensure that your interfaces still function. The fastest way to identify quickly which programs (especially SQRs) contain a table that has been modified is to use the UNIX `grep` command to search all the files. We redirect this output to a file, which gives us a rough list of the programs we need to verify. The `grep` command is quite helpful in locating files.

For example, to search for any SQR that inserts records into the PS_JOB table, execute the following command:

```
grep 'INSERT INTO PS_JOB' *.sqr >job.out
```

This sends the output of the command to the `job.out` file. The output looks like the following:

```
cbn60a01.sqr:INSERT INTO PS_JOB
cbn60b01.sqr:INSERT INTO PS_JOB
cbn60c01.sqr:INSERT INTO PS_JOB
cbn70c01.sqr:INSERT INTO PS_JOB
chr60a23.sqr:INSERT INTO PS_JOB_RQMT_ACCOMP
chr60b23.sqr:INSERT INTO PS_JOB_RQMT_ACCOMP
chr60c23.sqr:INSERT INTO PS_JOB_RQMT_ACCOMP
chr70c23.sqr:INSERT INTO PS_JOB_RQMT_ACCOMP
cmp006.sqr:INSERT INTO PS_JOB
cmp006.sqr:INSERT INTO PS_JOB_EARNS_DIST
cmp007cn.sqr:INSERT INTO PS_JOB
cmp007cn.sqr:INSERT INTO PS_JOB_EARNS_DIST
cmp008cn.sqr:INSERT INTO PS_JOB
cmp008cn.sqr:INSERT INTO PS_JOB_EARNS_DIST
cmp009cn.sqr:INSERT INTO PS_JOB
cmp009cn.sqr:INSERT INTO PS_JOB_EARNS_DIST
cmp010cn.sqr:INSERT INTO PS_JOB
cmp010cn.sqr:INSERT INTO PS_JOB_EARNS_DIST
pos007.sqr:INSERT INTO PS_JOB_REQUISITION
```

## Custom Reports

The same issues that pertain to interfaces also pertain to the custom reports. If you are selecting data from a column in a table and the column name changes, then your SQL must be updated to the new column name. The `grep` command discussed in the previous section can be useful for this task as well. The data definition for a column could have been changed as well. For example, a decimal field may have added more precision. You must decide if you want to display this new definition in your reports.

PART

III

Maintaining the System

Once both your technical and functional staffs have completed their testing, you are ready to implement the final upgrade.

# Performing the Final Upgrade

Using the notes you made during the tests, first determine the amount of time required for the final upgrade. Choose a time window in which to perform your upgrade. At my company, we find it useful to look at the payroll schedule and give ourselves the maximum amount of time between regular payroll cycles in case of unforeseen problems.

Once you have scheduled your final upgrade, assemble the upgrade team and make sure that everyone understands the tasks that they must accomplish. While the DBA is running the database scripts, the LAN administrator is setting up access for the new client code on the server. The workstation setup must be performed on the PCs that will be running the new version. PeopleSoft has made this easier with version 7 by allowing multiple versions of the software to exist on the same machine. This allows some steps to be completed early.

One note of caution about upgrading the clients early: While the PeopleSoft application makes registry entries for each version, some of the third-party applications need some additional setup to allow multiple versions to coexist. SQR is one example. The SQR setup updates the registry to the latest version. To resolve this, start the Configuration Manager for the earlier PeopleSoft version and change the path of the SQR to the new executable files. This starts the SQR program that matches the registry entries when you run client SQRs.

Now let's look at what the DBA must accomplish during the upgrade.

## Applying the Upgrade to a Fresh Copy of the Production Database

Make your final move to production to a fresh copy of the production database. This allows the end users to continue entering data during our extensive test cycle. However, this often means more work for the technical staff during the final upgrade. Be sure that you have at least one, and preferably two, good database dumps before beginning the final move.

Next, execute the steps according to the PeopleSoft-delivered upgrade instructions to migrate all the new objects to the copy of the production database. Do this by running the Data Mover scripts to move the updated information into the PeopleTools tables. You will have to run many of the scripts that were executed earlier in the upgrade process.

**N O T E**  The production database will not be available to end users during this final move to production, so this task is typically scheduled over a weekend.

The next step to perform after all the scripts are completed is verifying the changes made during the test cycle.

## Verifying Database Changes Made During Testing

One of the final steps when performing application upgrades is to verify that any changes made during the testing cycle have been moved to the final copy of the production database. Some changes do not get moved properly. An example of this at my company was an update to a record definition that we made during testing to fix a search record. If we had forgotten to make sure that this object was contained in the project we were executing using Application Upgrade, then the object would not have been moved.

This may seem unnecessary, but our past experience caused us to include this step in our final checklist.

Now, let's look at the tasks being performed by the LAN administrator and PC specialists.

## Upgrading the Client

Upgrading the client software can be done simultaneously with your final move to the production database. The new icons and tools that you are delivering to the desktop must be installed. Beginning with version 7, PeopleSoft provides a method of building and exporting a profile. The technical team at my company creates several profiles that contain default settings geared for each functional area. The new Configuration Manager utility allows you to import this profile and then perform the installation. Figure 12.7 contains the Import/Export tab in the Configuration Manager that is used to import and export these profiles.

PART

**III**

Maintaining the System

**FIGURE 12.7**    Configuration Manager–Import/Export tab

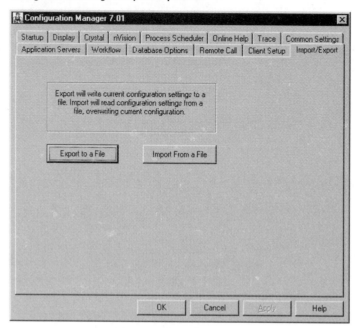

The technical team may also have to perform some preliminary steps to upgrade your client operating systems to supported versions or patch releases. This information can be found in the release notes and on Customer Connection.

Once your final move to production is completed and the application is deemed stable, it is time to perform a post-upgrade analysis.

# Post-Upgrade Analysis

Assemble your core upgrade team for a "lessons learned" session. The primary purpose of this session is to review any issues or problems that you encountered. Another purpose of this session is to update checklists and customization lists to ensure that they are updated with the latest information and ready for the next upgrade. The upgrade process may not get any easier, but you can make it flow more smoothly with a little planning and documentation.

## Reviewing the Logs

As part of the post-upgrade analysis process, review any error logs and notes that were made during the upgrade steps, including the test phase. Summarize the important facts into an agenda item to be discussed in the lessons learned session.

## Conducting the Lessons Learned Session

Use the experience gained during the upgrade to ensure the success of any future upgrades. The first step in this process is a formal lessons learned session, where the upgrade team reviews their checklists and problem notes. Discuss what went right and what went wrong.

At the lessons learned session, determine what changes will be necessary for the next upgrade to go more smoothly. At my company, we often decide that we may want to write some custom scripts to better utilize the capabilities of our RDBMS.

Consider sending an e-mail to your PeopleSoft account manager detailing any significant issues that were discovered during the upgrade.

## Updating the Checklists

After the lessons learned session, assign an employee the task of updating all the custom checklists with the agreed-upon changes. Place these checklists in a directory where they are ready to be used as templates for the next upgrade.

# Summary

This chapter was intended to give you a better understanding of the processes and tasks that must be accomplished in order to perform an upgrade to your PeopleSoft system.

PeopleSoft provides several tools to use during the upgrade process:

- ▶ Application Designer
- ▶ SQL tools
- ▶ Data Mover
- ▶ SQR audit scripts
- ▶ SQL Alter

There are three types of upgrades that you might perform:

1. PeopleTools

2. Application (both upgrade and update)

3. Custom projects (known as selective upgrades in previous versions of PeopleSoft)

To prepare for an upgrade, take the following steps:

1. Review the pre-release notes.

2. Review Customer Connection for information provided by other customers on similar upgrades.

3. Build checklists of tasks to accomplish during and after the upgrade.

4. Create problem logs for recording errors and other important information.

5. Install the new software on the file server.

6. Review the upgrade instructions.

When you're ready to start the upgrade, set up two databases: the new demo database and a second database to hold a copy of the production database. Then perform a test upgrade on the copy of the production database to make sure everything is working properly after the upgrade. This will also work out any problems with the upgrade process.

After the test upgrade, test the new release to make sure that all the functions are working properly. If all is well, continue with the full upgrade by applying the changes to a fresh copy of the production database, verifying the database changes, and updating the client software.

After the upgrade, conduct a post-upgrade analysis with a lessons learned session. This will help you learn from the problems that occurred and be better prepared for the next upgrade.

The next chapter discusses a special application update process that is specific to HRMS Payroll customers, the tax update.

# Tax Updates

## FEATURING

This chapter describes the steps required to implement a PeopleSoft tax update. This subject applies only to those companies using the PeopleSoft Payroll module. There are enough unique issues associated with tax updates to include a chapter in this book for system administrators who are trying to deal with PeopleSoft tax updates.

## What Are Tax Updates?

Tax updates are PeopleSoft-delivered updates to your PeopleSoft Payroll system. People-Soft generally delivers at least seven tax updates per year. PeopleSoft publishes a proposed list of tax updates and their anticipated release dates to allow you to prepare for them in advance.

**N O T E**   The updates delivered in the fourth quarter of every year are vital to your year-end tax and W-2 reporting processes. The information for the W-2 forms and SQR reports to print the W-2 forms are included with the tax updates. The tax table information for the following year is also included so that you can be ready for the first payroll of the new year.

The tax updates delivered by PeopleSoft may contain the following items:

- ▶ New or revised tax table entries for federal, state, or local taxes.

- ▶ If you are running multi-national payrolls, there may also be updates that are distinct from the North American tax updates.

- ▶ Panel changes that are required to support any new tax laws.

- ▶ Updated Payroll COBOL modules.

- ▶ Updated tax-reporting SQR programs for various U.S. states.

You have no choice about implementing these changes. They must be implemented for your PeopleSoft Payroll system to correctly calculate tax withholding from pay-checks. Additional tax updates may be required if PeopleSoft experiences delays in receiving information from any of the supported tax localities.

PeopleSoft Payroll customers must designate an individual to receive the notification that a tax update is available. PeopleSoft currently assumes that you will download the tax update from Customer Connection. However, you can receive tax updates on a CD-ROM instead. Downloading the update from Customer Connection became the default method in late 1998.

Let's look at the preparations required to implement a tax update.

# Preparing for a Tax Update

The first step in preparing for a tax update is to unload the new files for your version of the Payroll application onto your file server. I recommend creating a network directory where you can store each tax update version into subdirectories. Figure 13.1 shows an example of such a directory structure. Each tax update is indicated by the directory names that begin with "TAX", for example, TAX97t, tax97fix, and tax97g. The subdirectories contain certain PeopleSoft-delivered files, as follows:

▶ The Aup directory contains the application update data and the Data Mover scripts.

▶ The Cobol directory contains the updated COBOL programs.

▶ The Doc directory contains the documentation for the tax update.

▶ The Scripts directory contains the Data Mover scripts.

▶ The Sql directory contains the SQL scripts.

▶ The Sqr directory contains the updated SQR programs.

**FIGURE 13.1** Tax update directory structure

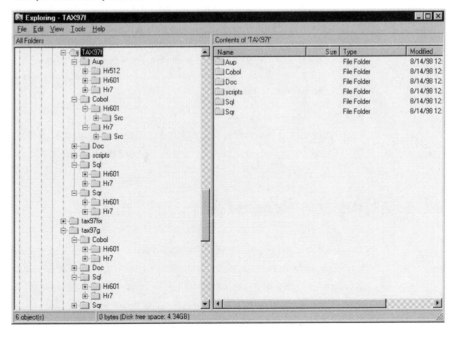

**PART**

**III**

**Maintaining the System**

The next step is to locate and print the instructions for the tax update. These instructions are delivered in Folio Infobase format and may be viewed online, but I have found it convenient to print the instructions. On a printed copy, you can annotate or highlight any important sections or steps in the printed document. You can also highlight or annotate the instructions online using the Folio Views product.

**TIP**   Remember to check Customer Connection for any updated instructions or files pertaining to the tax update you are installing.

Once you understand all the steps required to implement the tax update, you can finalize the preparations. This may require moving an application update project from the update directories into the application update database using Data Mover. The Data Mover application was discussed in Chapter 6, "Data Management Tools."

**WARNING**   Make sure that you don't overwrite any of your customizations when performing the tax update.

Copy the application update project to your demo database for your current version. Then compare the demo database to your copy of the production database to ensure that you are not overwriting a customization.

**TIP**   Follow the instructions provided for the specific steps that are required to complete the tax update.

Once all the preparations have been completed, you are ready to update your copy of the production database. Let's take a closer look at this process.

# Updating the Production Database

Following the instructions provided with the tax update, apply any changes to your copy of the production database. The instructions delivered by PeopleSoft recommend that you make the database changes before you execute any other procedures. Make any panel changes or record definition modifications as instructed.

PeopleSoft now delivers the tax updates using an application update project. An application update project allows you to implement changes made by PeopleSoft without having them labeled as customizations by your company. In the past, the instructions explained how to make the database changes yourself. Since the new change management functionality saves information about who made the changes, using the application update project ensures that the tax update changes will not show up as one of your customizations unless you subsequently change any database objects.

As in performing an upgrade, make a copy of your production database. At my company, I also use a copy of my payroll test database for testing tax updates since specific employee information is established in the test database to validate tax changes. In addition, create an empty application update database into which you will load the application update project. Once this database has been loaded, open the tax update project and run a validation to make sure that all the objects in the application update project are in the database. To perform the validation, select Tools **>** Validate Project, as shown in Figure 13.2.

**FIGURE 13.2**    **Project validation**

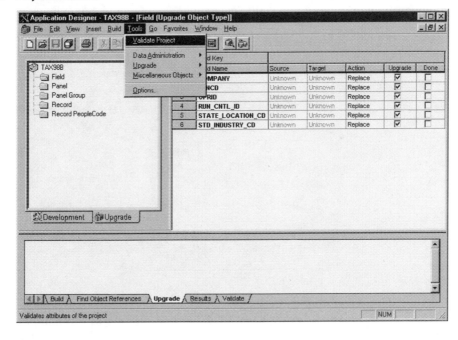

Using the application update project requires that you run comparison reports between the application update project and your copy of the production database. The difference between this comparison report and those discussed in Chapter 12, "Upgrading Your PeopleSoft System," is that in this case, you should run the comparisons in report-only mode. This prevents other objects from being added to the application update project.

Review the comparison report carefully and verify that the tax update changes will not overlay any customizations that you have performed. Adjust any action flags as required to copy the correct information into your test database, as shown in Figure 13.3. Note that in this figure, the Upgrade check boxes are checked for all objects. The action that will be taken for all these objects is to replace the existing object with the new object provided by the tax update. If the object is a customized object that you do not want to replace, remove the check from the Upgrade check box. You then have to make any necessary changes manually.

**FIGURE 13.3**    Identifying objects to be copied

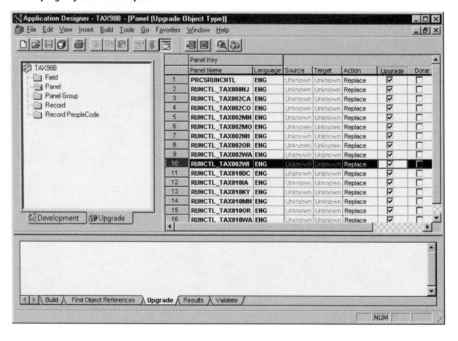

Once you have reviewed all the objects in the project, you are ready to perform the copy process. To copy from the demo database to your copy of the production database, select Tools > Copy from the Application Designer window with the application update project loaded. Select all the objects and run the copy process. Once the copy process completes, reopen the project and verify that all selected objects have been copied.

If any record definitions were changed, you need to alter the tables or recreate the views to apply the record definition changes to your underlying database tables. Run the project build process to create the scripts needed for altering your tables. To run the project build, select Build > Project from the Application Designer menu with the project open. The Build panel, illustrated in Figure 13.4, appears. Specify that you want to alter the tables and build a script file. Review the script before executing it on your database using the SQL tool for your RDBMS.

**FIGURE 13.4   Build panel**

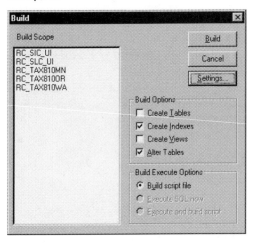

The next step is to run the Data Mover script to load the new tax table updates into your test database. To open the Data Mover project, select File > Open from the Data Mover window and open the update script that you extracted from the tax update directory created earlier. Verify that the paths are correct for the input and log files settings. Click the Run icon from the toolbar.

The tax update instructions contain a list of all tax table changes that have been made. Print this section and forward it to your Payroll manager. The Payroll manager will probably be anticipating these changes and may ask you when a particular change will be made before you receive the tax update from PeopleSoft. You should also give the Payroll manager the summary information that describes any changes in the tax calculation formulas for each tax locality.

The next step is to compile any updated COBOL programs and move them to your test COBOL directory. Execute the pscbl.mak process to compile each program. You

PART

III

Maintaining the System

can specify individual files by entering each filename on the command line in the UNIX environment. For example, to compile the PSPPYRUN.cbl program, execute the command pscbl.mak PSPPYRUN.

**TIP**   After the COBOL programs have compiled successfully, load any new stored statements that were delivered with the tax update using Data Mover. If you have modified any stored statements that have been updated, test the changes and reapply your customizations if necessary.

Move any new SQR files into your test directory. Check your customization log to determine if you have customized any of these programs. If you have, merge your customizations with the new program. Generally, these updated SQR programs relate to tax-reporting programs for the various tax localities. Do not modify them on your own except to correct a problem that you discovered.

**TIP**   Perform an impact analysis of any affected customizations or SQR reports when you alter a database table structure during a tax update.

Now that you have all your code in place, you are ready to test the changes introduced by the tax update.

# Testing the Changes

Testing the tax update is just as important as testing any other update delivered by PeopleSoft. At my company, we adapt our test plan to accommodate the issues that are unique to the tax updates. For example, if new COBOL modules are delivered, we run a test payroll calculation and examine the results to ensure that the new code is working and has not impacted other areas of the calculation process.

**TIP**   Do not forget to start your Process Scheduler if you are running your test pay calculation on your server. Make sure to stop the Process Scheduler while compiling any new code.

If panel changes have been introduced, make sure that the employees who are responsible for the use of that panel are advised of the changes. Test the new panel to ensure that the new functionality is still working properly.

# Implementing the Changes

Once you have completed testing, you are ready to move the tax update into your production database. Using the application update project that was copied to the copy of the production database used in testing, open the project, reset the copy flags to "Not Copied," and execute the copy process to move the tax update information to the production database.

**N O T E**  Follow the specific instructions provided with the tax update to complete the move to the production database.

**W A R N I N G**  Do not attempt to move the tax update changes to the production database during payroll processing. At other times, you should have no problems moving these changes to production while users are on the system. If there are many database table alterations, wait until users are off the system before updating the production database.

Remember to recompile any updated COBOL programs when you move the tax update into production.

**T I P**  I stop both the Process Scheduler and the Application Server when compiling (pscbl.mak) **and linking** (psrun.mak) **any new server source code.**

Remember to monitor your production database during the first payroll cycle that follows the move to production. The Payroll staff can also monitor specific tax calculations closely during the first production calculations that follow the update by using the notes about tax calculation changes and/or tax localities that you gave them.

**T I P**  Remember to back up your production database prior to implementing the tax update!

Now that we have reviewed the process, let's explain some of the problems you might encounter.

# Potential Problems

One of the first problems you may encounter is when you copy all the files to your directory structure. You may discover missing files. Usually the missing files are discovered quickly and are available from Customer Connection for you to download. At my company, the missing files are usually modified COBOL copy members. Be aware that these files may be missing in a tax update. The symptom for a missing file is an error message stating that a variable is undefined or not defined correctly when you attempt to compile your new COBOL program.

You may discover COBOL programs that do not compile. For example, at our company, we have had programs with syntax errors. A missing copy member is one cause of this problem. Again, Customer Connection should have an updated copy member available.

Running the table alteration scripts can potentially destroy your data if the scripts are not correct. For example, if a column is renamed and the script is not correct, the original data in the column can be lost. Always backup the database or the tables before altering any database tables. If you are running a script that updates multiple tables, consider a full database backup before you begin installing the tax update. For one or two tables or a group of small tables, at least create a Data Mover extract so you can recover your data if an error occurs.

Application update projects can potentially overwrite your customizations if you do not thoroughly review the objects being updated before you execute the copy step. I recommend that you maintain a copy of your modified objects in another database so that you have multiple copies of any customizations you have performed. The documentation of your customizations should always be kept current in case you have to rebuild them due to data loss.

You may encounter other problems; just remember to check Customer Connection to see if the problem has already been reported. I also double-check the update instructions to verify that I have not skipped a step.

**N O T E**    The tax update process has improved greatly since PeopleSoft version 7 began shipping. The number of problems that we have encountered has dropped significantly.

# Summary

Tax updates are PeopleSoft-delivered updates to your PeopleSoft Payroll system. PeopleSoft generally delivers at least seven tax updates per year.

To ensure the success of the tax update and to prevent it from overriding any customizations you've made to your PeopleSoft system, be sure to prepare carefully before every tax update. Create a directory structure to save the files that are delivered with the tax update. Review the instructions provided by PeopleSoft and check Customer Connection for any revisions to the installation.

To perform a tax update, take the following steps:

- ▶ Make a copy of your production database and create an empty application update database into which you will load the application update project.

- ▶ Validate the application update project.

- ▶ Copy the application update project from the application update database to your demo database.

- ▶ Run a comparison report between the project on the demo database and your copy of the production database to make sure that the changes do not overlay any customizations.

- ▶ Copy the tax updates into the production database.

- ▶ If necessary, alter the tables or recreate the views to apply any record definition changes. Run the project build to do this.

- ▶ Load the new tax table updates into the copy of the production database using Data Mover.

- ▶ Compile any updated COBOL programs.

- ▶ Load any stored statements that were delivered.

- ▶ Move new SQR files into the test directory.

- ▶ Test the changes.

- ▶ Recompile any COBOL programs.

- ▶ Move the changes to the production database.

PART

III

Maintaining the System

▶ Monitor your production database during the first payroll cycle following the update.

▶ Keep an eye out for potential problems like missing files, table alteration scripts (sometimes called alter scripts) that destroy your data, and application update projects that overwrite your customizations.

▶ Read and follow the PeopleSoft update instructions carefully.

Now that we have reviewed the tax update process, let's look at the documentation of your PeopleSoft applications.

# Documentation

## FEATURING

One of the most important tasks of the system administrator is making sure that your PeopleSoft system is properly documented. Proper documentation gives you a clear idea of what has been installed and customized in your system. This information will be extremely important during upgrades and for disaster recovery planning. Make every effort to ensure that your developers are thoroughly documenting all changes that they make to the system. This includes documenting any changes made to correct errors in delivered PeopleSoft code. The database administrator (DBA) should also be documenting modifications made to database objects; indexes and views are the most likely objects to be changed by the DBA for performance-tuning purposes.

This chapter discusses the reasons why you should document your system and describes some methods for documenting your system. PeopleSoft provides several tools to help with documentation that are discussed in this chapter. In addition, this chapter reviews the techniques for recording information in your program code to document the changes being made.

## Why Document?

Why document? This is an important question. I consider the documentation of my PeopleSoft system to be as critical as the blueprints for a building. If I make a change to the wiring or structure of my building, I modify the blueprints to reflect the change. Likewise, I modify the system documentation to reflect any changes that are made to my PeopleSoft system.

Good documentation is hard work so remember to spread the workload among your employees. Assign the maintenance of specific sections of the documentation to individual members of your team. For example, the LAN administrator is a good candidate to maintain any backup and restoration procedures for the file server and the workstations. Likewise, the DBA should maintain the documentation and disaster recovery plans for the databases. The DBA should also know how to recover the PeopleSoft environment that is running on the database server in a UNIX environment. This includes the Process Scheduler and Batch COBOL applications. The functional users should also document their procedures.

Any baseline performance measurements that were conducted as part of the implementation process should also be retained for future reference.

Let's look at the process of defining documentation standards for your PeopleSoft system.

# Defining Documentation Standards

Make sure to develop written standards for your documentation. Include topics such as how to document changes in source code and naming conventions for new objects and files. Consider implementing a version control system to track the source code for programs that you develop or modify. You can implement version control software that is available from third-party vendors or you may choose to manage source code changes by manually updating a master copy of your production code.

## Documenting the Code

Documenting your code with records of changes is a convention that you and your developers should strictly adhere to. Such records should provide a detailed history of how, when, and why a particular section of code was changed. Include the date, the person making the change, and a brief description of the change. You may even want to include a request number or some other cross-reference information that can point others to more information about the change. Two examples of other sources of information for source code changes are customization logs and change request forms.

The three code excerpts that follow demonstrate methods that you can use to document your code or changes to your code. Each example illustrates a method for documenting your code using remarks at the beginning of the program. You should include standard phrases or identifiers to allow programmers to locate any modified code easily.

 **N O T E**   The code example in this section reflects the recommendations of PeopleSoft and Cambridge Technology Partners and the standards used by my company.

PART

III

Maintaining the System

### Documenting SQR Programs

When documenting SQR programs, identify the filename, the author, the creation date, the purpose of the program, and the affected database tables. You should also identify any input or output from the program. The following example is excerpted from an SQR program:

```
!******************  Program  IDENTIFICATION  ******************
!
!  File Name:     ALB_SLGR.SQR
!  File Title:    New Salary Grade Ranges
!  Author:        Darrell Bilbrey
!  Date Written:  10/28/97
```

```
!  --------------------------------------------------------------
!  Functional Description:
!    This SQR reads the ALB_SAL_FORM table to get the new slope
!    and intercept for each sal_admin_plan for the new
!    effective date, select the information from the sal_admin_plan
!    table and alb_grade_pts table using the thru date
!    and inserts a record with the new range into the Sal_Grade_tbl.
!
!  Database Tables:
!      PS_ALB_SAL_FORM           - read
!      PS_SAL_GRADE_TBL          - read/Insert
!      PS_ALB_GRADE_PTS          - read
!
!  Input:
!      Database tables
!
!  Output:
!      ALB_SLGR.LIS
!**********************************************************************
!*****************Modification History*****************************
! Date        Log#Programmer
! ========= ==============
!    10/20/1998   001   D. Bilbrey
! Description of Change:
!
```

## Documenting COBOL Programs

When documenting COBOL programs, identify the filename, the author, the creation date, and the purpose of the program. The following example is excerpted from a COBOL program:

```
IDENTIFICATION DIVISION.

    PROGRAM-ID. PSPAGERT.

    ENVIRONMENT DIVISION.

    **********************************************************************
    *                                                                    *
    *              Confidentiality Information:                          *
    *                                                                    *
    * This module is the confidential and proprietary information of *
    * PeopleSoft, Inc.; it is not to be copied, reproduced, or          *
    * transmitted in any form, by any means, in whole or in part,       *
```

```
* nor is it to be used for any purpose other than that for which *
* it is expressly provided without the written permission of     *
* PeopleSoft, Inc.                                               *
*                                                                *
* Copyright (c) 1988-1997 PeopleSoft, Inc. All Rights Reserved   *
*                                                                *
******************************************************************
*                                                                *
*      $Date:: 9/06/97 3:16p        $                            *
*   $Revision:: 1                   $                            *
*   $Workfile:: PSPAGERT.CBL        $                            *
*                                                                *
******************************************************************

******************************************************************
*                                                                *
*                   PROGRAM DESCRIPTION:                          *
*                                                                *
* LOOKUP AND LOAD THE AGE RATE TABLE FOR THE EMPLOYEE            *
*                                                                *
******************************************************************

******************************************************************
*                                                                *
*           MODIFICATION HISTORY:                                *
*   DATE      LOG#    PROGRAMMER                                  *
*                                                                *
*   DESCRIPTION OF CHANGE:                                       *
*                                                                *
******************************************************************
```

**NOTE**  Remember that the maximum COBOL line length is 80 characters. This sample has been adjusted to fit the format of this book.

## Documenting PeopleCode

When documenting PeopleCode programs, identify the author, the creation date, the purpose of the program, and the affected database tables. You should also log and comment any updated PeopleCode programs. The following example is excerpted from a PeopleCode program:

```
/*        Modification History
   Date        Log#Programmer
   ======== =============
        10/20/1998    001    D. Bilbrey
   Description of Change:
*/
/* begin 001 */
updated program code
/* end 001 */
```

## File-Naming Standards

File-naming standards should be defined for all your custom COBOL programs, SQR reports, and queries. You may want to conform to the 8.3 (*XXXXXXX.XXX*) naming convention to be consistent with the delivered PeopleSoft files.

If you choose to adhere to the 8.3 naming convention, I recommend that you define a unique identifier to place at the beginning of each filename. My company uses AL as the unique identifier for all of our filenames. We could just have easily used AA. Avoid using PT, PS, or FS since PeopleSoft uses those prefixes in their file-naming conventions.

## Database Object Naming Standards

Database object naming standards should also be defined. You can use the same prefix that you are using for filenames or you may use something slightly longer, since the database object naming standards used by PeopleSoft are longer names. At my company, we use ALB_ as the prefix for database objects.

The database objects that follow this naming standard should include:

▶ Record definitions

▶ Field definitions

▶ Indexes

▶ Panels

▶ Panel groups

▶ Any other object defined using the Application Designer

**NOTE** At my company, we sometimes use the ALB_ prefix in our filenames for certain programs, especially if those programs update the database. The SQR example earlier in this section is such an example.

# Defining the Change Control Process

Define a set of procedures for controlling and monitoring the changes to your system. PeopleSoft sells their system promising how easy it is to customize the software to meet your company's unique requirements. However, if you don't control the changes and don't make sure that any changes are properly documented, the first upgrade to your PeopleSoft system will be a challenge.

The first step is to limit the number of people who can actually update your production code. Limit your developers to the test environment and implement a production control process for which a single person (or small group of people) is responsible for migrating any updated code and objects into production. This person should ensure that all changes have been properly documented using the defined documentation standards. At my company, this person also validates that testing has been accomplished and that end-user approval has been received before the change is migrated to production using the application upgrade process.

After a change is made to a COBOL program, move the code into place and compile it using the production account for the server platform if the code is designed to run on the server. Be sure to add the modified code to the master backup copy of your source code.

Beginning with PeopleSoft version 7.0, make sure to update your Custom project with any changes that you make. The Custom project is used by the upgrade comparison scripts to help identify your customizations and prevent them from being overwritten.

The final step in the change control process is to notify both the developer and the end user who requested the change that the new code has been moved into production. This notification should be performed by the person designated for moving changes to production.

**TIP** I strongly recommend that you create a directory on your file server where you store all the master code that is in production. You may want to create subdirectories for each file type that you are using.

One location for storing the documentation for your system is in the online People-Books. Let's look at how to customize PeopleBooks for your environment.

# Customizing PeopleBooks

PeopleSoft delivers PeopleBooks with your system and allows you to edit the infobase files that are included. You can insert your own documentation or provide examples that are specific to your installation.

There are several options for customizing the PeopleBooks:

▶ You can add notes or annotations to the infobase. To do this, place your cursor in the document where you want to place the note, select Tools > Note, and enter the desired text.

▶ You can highlight specific text so that your users can easily see the important sections. To highlight a word or phrase, select the text and choose Tools > Highlighter from the menu. The text will be highlighted. You can assign specific highlighter colors or patterns to specific users to identify who highlighted the text. To do this, create custom highlighters and name them. Each user who is highlighting text selects the designated highlighter. To create a custom highlighter, select Tools > Highlighter and choose New from the window. Name the highlighter and select the background color you want to use.

▶ Add or delete text or objects. To add text, enter the additional information as if you are using your word processing package. If you have large amounts of information to add and already have that information in another file, you can import that information. To import information into PeopleBooks, position your cursor where you want to place the document and select File > Import from the menu. Specify the document type and filename. A status bar appears showing the status of the import. Once the import is complete, save the infobase. The new information becomes part of the original infobase.

# Shadow Files

Be careful which users are allowed to update PeopleBooks infobases. The preferred method is to use the Folio shadow file functionality. You may even choose to make all your modifications in a shadow file, leaving the original PeopleSoft documentation untouched.

A shadow file allows users to create notes and annotations, or add their own text to the Folio infobase. Instead of directly editing the original, the edits are made on a file that points to the original, and the changes are stored in a separate file. I recommend that the shadow files be located in a directory where the users have update access. This allows you to disable update access on the directory where the original is stored.

To create a shadow file, open the PeopleBook that you want to update. Select File > New from the menu and define a directory and name as shown in Figure 14.1.

**FIGURE 14.1** Creating a shadow file

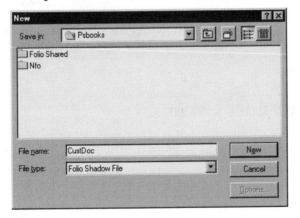

TIP   I recommend creating the shadow file in a directory that is separate from the original infobase. I create the shadow file in a directory where the users that need to update it have read, write, and update access. I leave the original infobase in a directory where they only have read access.

Note that once you have a shadow file in use, "(Shadow)" appears in the title bar to show that the file is a shadow file. Figure 14.2 illustrates this situation.

In addition to customizing PeopleBooks, you may find it helpful to create a procedures manual for your technical staff.

PART

III

Maintaining the System

**FIGURE 14.2**    Reading a shadow file

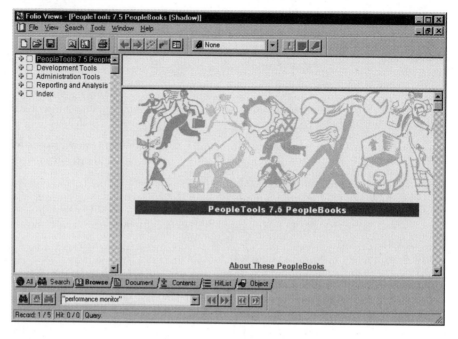

# Creating a Procedures Manual

The technical staff benefits greatly from having a procedures manual that they can use to reference company-specific policies and procedures for your PeopleSoft system. As a matter of fact, the idea for this book began as the procedures manual for my company.

The following list shows the outline for the procedures manual I developed for my company's PeopleSoft system. You may not need to create a procedures manual as detailed as this, but this list will give you an idea of the scope of information that should be included.

1. Create New Database for PeopleSoft

2. Client Setup

3. HP-UX Essentials

4. Testing and Upgrading the System

5. System Interfaces

6. Disaster Recovery

7. System Change Procedures

8. System Security Procedures

Let's look at the type of information that can be found in each of these sections.

**Create New Database for PeopleSoft**    This section describes in detail the procedures that are used to create a new database. It includes the following information:

- UNIX commands and procedures

- Sizing equations

- Sample database creation script

- Explanation about how to add PeopleSoft objects to the database

- Procedural checklist for creating the database

**Client Setup**    The client setup section provides detailed instructions on how to configure and establish connectivity for all two-tier and three-tier clients for each supported operating system. This section also describes how to establish database connectivity for each client. The directory paths to all software to be installed are listed here.

**HP-UX Essentials**    This section outlines the basic commands for the server operating system, which in my company's case is HP-UX. The file structure is explained for all root volumes. This section provides a detailed explanation about how the production and test directory structures are configured. The location of important log files is documented in this section.

**Testing and Upgrading the System**    This section describes the procedures for testing and upgrading the system. It documents and further emphasizes the testing procedures that we employ when adding to or updating our system. Included are the procedures that are carried out prior to both upgrades and payroll tax updates.

**System Interfaces**    This section provides detailed information about all the interfaces between our PeopleSoft system and other corporate systems. This section describes the procedures used to create a file extract to send to other systems.

**Disaster Recovery**    The Disaster Recovery section provides detailed information about the backup and recovery plans for the PeopleSoft system. These plans include backup schedules for the database, the file server, and the database server operating system. The order of recovery is outlined so that everyone involved knows what

PART

**III**

**Maintaining the System**

happens when. This section also describes a specific set of steps for recovering the database in the event of a hardware failure on the database server.

**System Change Procedures**   The system change control procedures that were outlined earlier in this chapter are defined in this section. This is the master document for the change control process. At my company, we distribute a copy of this section only to the power users and developers who submit changes to the system.

**System Security Procedures**   This section outlines the security procedures that are implemented for the PeopleSoft system. This section describes in detail the procedures that must be followed when granting a user access to the PeopleSoft system. Password expiration procedures are also discussed. This section was created to help document our security procedures so that our auditors can understand the processes and determine if they are adequate.

My technical staff finds this procedures manual to be very beneficial when performing new tasks. Their one complaint is the requirement that we update the procedures manual as new versions of PeopleSoft and the database are rolled out.

# Summary

This chapter described the importance of thorough documentation so that you have a record of what has been installed and customized in your PeopleSoft system. This information will be extremely important during upgrades and for disaster recovery planning.

As system administrator, it is your job to implement documentation procedures and make sure they are carried out. Assign a specific user in each functional and technical area to be responsible for ensuring that all changes are documented.

All code that your system uses should be well documented. When a change is made, the developers should indicate what change was made, who made the change, and the date the change was implemented.

Define naming standards for your files and database objects. Make sure the developers adhere to these standards.

Develop a change control process. Such a process should involve the following steps:

▶ Limit the number of developers who can change the production code.

▶ Compile and test any changes.

▶ Add the modified code to the master backup copy of your source code.

► Update your Custom project with any changes that you make.

► Notify the developer and the end user who requested the change that the new code has been moved into production.

Another method of documentation is to customize your PeopleBooks to reflect any customizations to your PeopleSoft system. You can do this by inserting notes, highlighting important text passages, or adding or deleting text or objects.

Finally, create a procedures manual that describes company-specific policies and procedures for managing and maintaining your PeopleSoft system.

Now that we have covered the topic of documentation, let's look at the process of creating and testing a disaster recovery plan for your system.

PART

III

Maintaining the System

# Disaster Recovery

## FEATURING

▶ **DEFINING THE REQUIREMENTS**

▶ **CREATING A DISASTER RECOVERY PLAN**

▶ **IMPLEMENTING THE PLAN**

▶ **TESTING THE PLAN**

**E**very computer system should have some form of disaster recovery plan. The more critical the system, the more detailed and robust the plan should be. I consider documentation and disaster recovery to be closely linked. As a matter of fact, you will probably read many of the same ideas in this chapter as you did in the previous chapter. I do this to stress how important documentation can be to a disaster recovery plan.

This chapter reviews the items that should be considered when defining the requirements for your disaster recovery plan. Using those requirements, you will learn how to create and implement the disaster recovery plan. Once the plan has been implemented, you must validate the plan by conducting tests. The final section discusses procedures for testing your disaster recovery plan.

**TIP**   If possible, contact your corporate disaster recovery coordinator for specific information and requirements that may already be defined. This person can be a valuable asset during your disaster recovery planning process.

**NOTE**   Disaster recovery planning is sometimes referred to as business resumption planning.

# Defining the Requirements

The requirements for your disaster recovery plan should include all the processes that management deems critical to your company's business operations. You should supplement the items important to management with critical technical issues. The technical issues should include all the systems necessary to run the critical processes.

The disaster recovery plan for your PeopleSoft system should also take into consideration the disaster recovery plans of other areas of your company. Add any processes that are needed to supplement critical areas of your company. For example, if one division provides an extract to a business process that another division deems critical, that extract is a critical process to both divisions and, as such, an item required for disaster recovery.

## Assembling the Team

The first task when defining the requirements for your disaster recovery plan is to assemble a team to participate in the disaster recovery process. This group should include:

▶ Management from the business units that are affected by the PeopleSoft system

▶ Technical and functional specialists that are familiar with both the PeopleSoft system and the business processes that use the PeopleSoft system

Once you have assembled the disaster recovery team, you are ready to begin prioritizing your business processes.

## Prioritizing the Business Processes

When prioritizing the processes in your PeopleSoft operations, use the critical processes that have been defined by management as your guideline. Validate that the management priorities fit the order in which you need to rebuild the system. For example, management may define payroll as their number one priority and interfaces as their number four priority. However, if one interface is needed to complete all payroll calculations, you must prioritize that interface ahead of payroll calculations in your disaster recovery plan.

You cannot develop the list of priorities in a vacuum. Consult with the functional managers and staff as well as with the managers of areas that are providers or recipients to your processes. For example, if you are working on a plan for restoring the inventory functions, make sure to include purchasing and manufacturing personnel in the meetings.

Make a list of all the business processes and allow the disaster recovery team to assign a priority to each process. Use a ballot to solicit the rankings from each member of the team. This gives you some idea of how each member views each process. It also gives each member a sense of participating. The team members can present the reasoning behind their choices and then you can conduct a final vote to determine the priorities.

## Specifying the Restoration Timeframe

An important issue that cannot be overlooked is the timeframe for the restoration of services, the time required to restore the system to normal operations. Management

PART

III

Maintaining the System

must clearly understand the cost implications of their decisions. While it may be desirable to immediately move the operations to a backup system, the cost associated with purchasing the required hardware may make it prohibitive.

For example, say the Payroll manager does not want any downtime during payroll processing. If he agrees to compromise on a three-hour maximum, this allows for flexibility when designing the disaster recovery steps for the payroll operations. You can reload a dump of your system and restore the transactions to a server that is available in another area. Normal payroll operations can resume once the last backup had been loaded. This plan allows you to share the costs of the backup hardware with other processes or divisions.

Upper management must participate in the decisions about the recovery timeframe. They are in the position to fund whatever recovery time they deem necessary. Conduct a disaster recovery needs assessment that includes a forecast for the costs associated with the system being down for various lengths of time. The longer the timeframe, the more soft factors may be introduced. A company that has many processes that rely on "just in time" delivery of inventory may experience a loss in sales or productivity in the event of a prolonged system outage. The needs of each company are different so do your homework when determining the timeframe for the restoration of services.

# Creating a Disaster Recovery Plan

Now that you have your requirements, a prioritized list of business processes, and the recovery timeframe required for each process, you can begin creating your disaster recovery plan by taking the following steps:

- ▶ Build a checklist of the business processes that must be included.

- ▶ Define all the hardware that supports each business process.

- ▶ List any interfaces in or out of each of the business processes. You need this information when coordinating with other areas that link to your corporate disaster recovery plan.

Outline several options for how the servers might be used during the disaster recovery process. When listing multiple options for the servers, allow for varying levels of redundancy and recovery time. This will help you when comparing the costs of each option.

Some possible options for your servers are:

▶ Complete mirroring of your server with full, real-time data replication between the servers

▶ A smaller server that you apply the transaction log from the production database to on a periodic basis—30 minutes or one hour

▶ A small server onto which you can load the previous day's backup and apply the transaction log manually to restore services

**N O T E**    Your test server is a good candidate for use during a disaster. My company uses a small server located in another location as our disaster recovery server.

Another consideration should be the physical location of your disaster recovery operations. There are three basic options: hot site, cold site, and multi-site.

**Hot site**    Hot site disaster recovery utilizes a dedicated site that is continuously operating and synchronized with the primary site. The hot site takes over immediately upon failure of the primary site.

**Cold site**    Cold site disaster recovery utilizes equipment that has been positioned at a site that is not continuously available to you. The cold site is activated and the latest data is loaded onto the standby systems to resume operations.

**Multi-site**    Multi-site disaster recovery is sometimes referred to as distributed processing. Companies that have multiple sites available may choose to use this method. Each site continuously updates segments of the functions of each of the other sites. When a disaster occurs, each remaining site becomes the primary source for the functions that they were synchronized with on the failed site. The multi-site option allows each site to assume some of the workload from the failed site without overloading any one site.

**N O T E**    Another consideration when using these options is the expected response time. If you require very little change in system response time, then you will need additional capacity when using the multi-site method. In other words, you don't want all of your sites operating at 90% capacity when no disaster is occurring.

**PART**

**III**

**Maintaining the System**

## Comparing Costs

It is important to look at the costs associated with each option for redundancy and recovery time. Gather the costs associated with each option. Then select the preferred option and get approval from upper management so you can create the disaster recovery plan.

At this point, it might be beneficial to create a Request for Proposal (RFP) to send out to selected vendors, soliciting price information for the hardware and software components that are required for your plan. Assemble the responses into a comparison spreadsheet for presentation to your management team. If you are considering a hot site or cold site solution, get estimates on the cost of leasing or purchasing space and include those figures in your cost estimates. If you are considering the multi-site solution, don't forget to verify that the other sites have the capacity to handle the additional workload.

**NOTE**   During this stage, gather pricing information based on purchasing and configuring the total disaster recovery on your own. The next section discusses the use of disaster recovery service bureaus with equipment leasing arrangements.

Once you have calculated the costs for doing all the disaster recovery on your own, explore the possibility of contracting for some of the services.

**NOTE**   If your company already uses a disaster recovery service or has other plans in place, maintain those plans while you gather price information for doing disaster recovery on your own.

## Contracting for Disaster Recovery Services

When contracting for disaster recovery services with outside vendors, consider some of the tips outlined in this section to help in the process.

Coordinate your disaster recovery plan with plans that are already in place for other areas of the company to save some money. For example, you may be able to add the services you need to an existing disaster recovery service agreement that another division has with an outside vendor. Compare the cost over three to five years between using the service bureau and purchasing and maintaining the disaster recovery equipment yourself.

There are vendors that specialize in operating and maintaining the hardware and software required for both cold site and hot site disaster recovery. These operations charge a leasing fee for the equipment and configuration that you require. For a cold site system, the pricing can be very competitive. Since the vendors that provide the services can spread their costs over several companies, it is less likely that every company will have a disaster at the same time.

If you use a service bureau for your cold site arrangement, be sure to request information about the geographic dispersion of the companies that are contracting for the same type of equipment as you. The greater the dispersion, the less likely it is that a natural disaster, such as an earthquake or hurricane, will affect all the companies at the same time. Do your homework and request reference contacts that have used the service bureau during a real disaster.

**TIP**   Don't forget to specify the amount of time that you want the service bureau to make the system available for disaster recovery testing during each year.

## Selecting the Options

You should now have all the information you need to select the recovery options (hot site, cold site, multi-site, internal, external) for each business process. Build your final list of the business processes, specify the recovery time required, and itemize the associated costs for final approval by management.

Once you have approval, you can begin developing your disaster recovery plan.

## Developing a Disaster Recovery Plan

Writing the disaster recovery plan should now be a straightforward process. You have the approved options. Use these options as the basis for your document. The disaster recovery plan should list all the business processes to be covered. Under each business process, list the following information:

▶ The function to be recovered

▶ The order in which the recovery should occur

▶ The individual (or role) responsible for the recovery of that business process

PART

**III**

Maintaining the System

For each function within a business process, define the individual or group of individuals who will have primary responsibility for the recovery of that function. This group may include:

▶ LAN administrators

▶ Database administrators

▶ Functional area experts

▶ UNIX administrators

▶ Business unit managers

Topics that should be covered for each function include:

▶ Backup procedures

▶ Recovery procedures

▶ Validation procedures

▶ Contingency plans

**N O T E**   Don't forget to provide contingency plans in case a function is delayed or unrecoverable (disasters during a disaster). Specify alternate methods to accomplish the function until the original method is restored.

# Implementing the Plan

You have identified the responsible individuals and written the disaster recovery plan. Now you must implement your disaster recovery plan.

The first step is to assemble all the individuals identified in the plan as having responsibility for recovery operations. Give each individual a copy of the disaster recovery plan. Conduct training for these individuals if they will be performing a task that is unfamiliar or not often used. Don't forget to plan for periodic refresher training.

Specify the date by which all implementation tasks must be completed. Once your plan is ready, implement the procedures as quickly as possible to reduce your vulnerability in the event of a disaster.

During a disaster, the individual with responsibility for each business process should verify that all the defined procedures are being carried out properly. As system administrator, you must monitor these individuals to make sure they are carrying out this task.

**T I P**   Since the plan includes the backup procedures required to recover your operations, it is important to implement the plan before a disaster occurs.

# Testing the Plan

It is important to test your disaster recovery plan periodically to verify that everything works as planned. Conduct at least one full recovery test for each business process each year. Some companies have a specified time period during which they test the corporate disaster recovery plan.

You may also want to occasionally conduct a verbal walk-through of the disaster recovery plan for specific business processes or functions.

**N O T E**   I know that all of this takes a great deal of time. Disaster recovery drills usually are low priority in a company, but make every effort to continuously ensure that your plan is ready.

**T I P**   Conduct lessons learned sessions after each recovery test to determine if adjustments in the plan are required. Keep the plan current!

## Quizzing Personnel

As part of the disaster recovery test, quiz your personnel on their roles and duties. Quiz them also on specific items from the plan. Some suggested questions are:

▶ What system gets restored first?

▶ Where are the backup tapes located?

PART

**III**

**Maintaining the System**

► How do you restore a database?

► How do you restore your server operating system?

► Where is your latest full backup?

**N O T E**   You are not necessarily looking for the correct answer as much as you are looking for the ability of the individual to tell you where to find the information that answers the question.

## Validating Backups

An important step is to periodically validate your backups to ensure that they are correct and usable. One way to accomplish this is to conduct the following test on a regular basis:

► Load a test database.

► Modify some information.

► Restore the database again using the same tape.

► Verify that the data is restored back to its original state.

There are utilities designed to perform database integrity checks on your backup tapes. These utilities are available from your database manufacturer or from third-party software companies.

One way that I test the backups is to use the latest backup tape to load a database that I have created for use in testing changes to the payroll programs or in troubleshooting payroll problems. Then I validate that the backup processes are working correctly and that the backup is usable.

**N O T E**   A good reference book for disaster recovery planning and other information systems-related topics for system administrators is *Managing Information Technology in Turbulent Times* by Louis Fried. I have found it very useful on many of the topics related to managing my PeopleSoft system.

# Summary

Comprehensive planning and documentation should ensure the success of your PeopleSoft disaster recovery plan. The first step is to assemble a team to define the requirements for the disaster recovery plan. This team should include the following members:

- ▶ Management
- ▶ Technical experts (database administrator, LAN administrator, operating system administrator, programmers)
- ▶ Functional experts
- ▶ Corporate Disaster Recovery Coordinator

The second step of disaster recovery planning is to define the plan and create the plan document. This step includes:

- ▶ Prioritizing business processes
- ▶ Determining recovery times for each process
- ▶ Calculating the costs to provide recovery
- ▶ Writing the plan document

Once the plan is prepared, the implementation occurs. Make sure that the responsible individuals have adequate documentation and training. Verify periodically that the plan is being carried out. Finally, conduct tests of the plan on a regular basis to ensure that all steps are working and, if necessary, adjust your plan based on the results of the testing.

The next chapter explains the day-to-day operations that keep your PeopleSoft system running smoothly.

PART

III

Maintaining the System

# Day-to-Day Administration

**FEATURING**

▶ **ESTABLISHING A ROUTINE**

▶ **MONITORING DATABASE OBJECTS**

▶ **MONITORING THE PROCESS SCHEDULER AND THE APPLICATION SERVER**

▶ **MONITORING SYSTEM LOGS**

▶ **MONITORING THE NETWORK**

▶ **CHECKING FOR UPDATED CODE**

The system administrator must make sure that the PeopleSoft system is operating properly at all times. It is important to establish a routine that you follow. You need to:

▶ Monitor space allocation in your database. Make sure that the index statistics are updated with the latest information so that the query optimizer for your RDBMS generates the best possible queries, if your RDBMS uses cost-based query optimization. (Your database administrator (DBA) will know if your RDBMS uses cost-based query optimization.)

▶ Monitor the log files from the scheduled processes, looking for errors or potential trouble spots.

▶ Monitor the network for congestion or other errors.

This chapter discusses how and when you should perform these tasks.

 **N O T E** Many of the tasks outlined in this chapter will probably be performed by your DBA. As system administrator, you should be aware of them so you can make sure they are being performed properly.

## Establishing a Routine

Establish a routine for both the support staff and yourself to check specific areas of the PeopleSoft application. Split the duties along the same lines as each team member's job function. For example, it makes sense for the DBA to monitor the database and for the LAN administrator to monitor the network.

The first step is to create a list of responsibilities for each job function. Make a checklist that helps you understand each team member's responsibilities. Table 16.1 contains an example of such a checklist.

You may want to add more specific details to your checklist, such as listing all the databases that should be backed up or identifying detailed steps to take with regard to tax updates.

**TABLE 16.1**   Responsibility Checklist

| Assigned to | Responsibility |
| --- | --- |
| DBA | Perform database dumps (backups). <br> Verify database integrity. <br> Monitor database performance. |
| LAN administrator | Monitor network utilization. <br> Backup the file server. |
| Change control coordinator | Verify that all PeopleSoft customizations are documented. <br> Migrate changes from the test database to the production database. <br> Implement tax updates in the payroll system. |
| Security administrator | Update security profiles. <br> Create new users. <br> Delete old users. |
| System administrator | Verify that all checklist items are being accomplished. <br> Audit the system tables. |

**NOTE**   The responsibilities of the change control coordinator may be added to one of the other functions.

Provide each team member with the proper training to carry out the assigned tasks. You may want to train team members on other tasks in order to provide for redundancy. This helps you retain team members and gives you flexibility when people are on vacation or when a member leaves the company.

**NOTE**   Many companies have found it hard to retain personnel once they get People-Soft experience. Remember to review the salaries of your most skilled individuals when they complete additional training and when salary survey information is available.

Let's look at how to monitor the database objects in your PeopleSoft system.

# Monitoring Database Objects

Monitoring the tables and indexes in the PeopleSoft database will usually be performed by your DBA. However, there are some things that the system administrator can check to ensure that all the tables and indexes are operating correctly. You can run the DDDAUDIT.SQR and SYSAUDIT.SQR reports to ensure that the underlying database matches the information stored in the PeopleSoft system tables. These reports are discussed in detail in Chapter 6, "Data Management Tools," and Chapter 12, "Upgrading Your PeopleSoft System." Samples of both audit reports can be found in Appendix B, "Sample Reports."

Execute the audit reports periodically on both your test and production databases. These reports can be useful after tax updates have been added to the HRMS databases or at any time to verify the database structures after customizations have occurred.

## Watching for Rapid Table Growth

Monitor your database and identify the tables that grow quickly. Run the UPGCOUNT.SQR report periodically to help identify the tables that are growing quickly. This report is located in the $PS_HOME\sqr directory. The UPGCOUNT.SQR report gives a record count for each table in your PeopleSoft database. Once you have identified the tables you need to monitor, create a new version of this script or write an SQL script to report the counts for just the selected tables.

The information you gather from monitoring table growth can be used for planning for additional database storage. You can also use this information to determine when you need to archive information in these tables.

PeopleSoft currently provides no archiving functionality, although there are discussions about adding archiving in a future PeopleSoft release. You must determine what archiving strategy works best for your environment. Implementing an archiving strategy probably requires customizing your PeopleSoft system by adding new records and panels if the end users need online access to the archived information.

When implementing an archiving plan, you must consider the legislated requirements for retention of the information that is being archived. For example, payroll information must be maintained for seven years. You are not required to maintain it online, but consider archiving records that can be queried for your W-2 records as a minimum.

## Updating Indexes on Key Tables

Every RDBMS maintains statistics about the tables and index structures of the databases. This is especially true of RDBMS systems that use cost-based optimization. These statistics should be updated periodically for tables that experience a large number of inserts, updates, or deletes. The updated statistics help the cost-based query optimizer make better choices when determining the best query plan to use for a database.

**WARNING**    Not every RDMS can use the cost-based optimization. Make sure yours is one of them.

Each RDBMS has specific syntax on how to update the statistics. Table 16.2 contains a list of the scripts for several RDBMS systems that can be used to either update the statistics or generate another script to do the update.

**TABLE 16.2**    RDBMS Scripts

| DBMS | Script |
| --- | --- |
| Oracle | ```dbmsutil.sql``` <br> ```execute``` <br> ```dbms_utility.analyze_schema``` <br> ```('ownerid', 'compute')``` |
| Informix | ```update statistics high``` |
| DB2/UNIX | ```sqr runstats.sqr``` |
| Sybase | ```\PS_HOME\scripts\updstats.sql``` |

Your RDBMS may also have some utilities or stored procedures that can be used to determine when the statistics should be updated for these indexes.

## Reorganizing Tables

Some database tables in your system will require a periodic reorganization. This reorganization modifies the structure and indexes to align the data in the correct order. Such a reorganization can reduce the amount of I/O required to retrieve the data. The manufacturer of the database most likely has provided tools to determine when a reorganization is required and to carry out the reorganization. Reorganization of the database tables should be done by your DBA.

## Validating Database Integrity

Validate the integrity of your database on a regular basis. Your RDBMS should provide a utility to do this. This should be a regularly scheduled process that your DBA performs for all databases, not just the PeopleSoft database.

At my company, I execute a full integrity check weekly using a scheduled cron script that I have created. In addition, I perform checks on the most used tables

PART

**III**

**Maintaining the System**

more frequently. The available utilities and the transaction volume for the database affect the frequency with which the integrity checks can be performed. If the utilities take a lot of time to run or your transaction volume is low, you won't have to run the validation as frequently.

# Monitoring the Process Scheduler and the Application Server

Monitor both the Process Scheduler and Application Server applications to ensure that they are operational. Beginning with PeopleSoft version 7.5, the PeopleSoft Server Administration (PSADMIN) process is used to control both the Process Scheduler and the Application Server.

PSADMIN allows you to control many of the functions for both servers. You can:

- ▶ Start a server.
- ▶ Stop a server.
- ▶ Delete a server.
- ▶ Add a server.
- ▶ Configure a server.
- ▶ View the log files.
- ▶ View the status of the server.

Make sure to monitor the log file for each server. I recommend stopping and restarting a server when the log file grows greater than 10MB. The log files can get quite large when the trace options are activated.

**WARNING**   Do not leave trace options that capture detailed SQL information running continuously on your production server or you will quickly run out of disk space.

**NOTE**   Not all companies will be using both the Process Scheduler and the Application Server applications.

The PSADMIN menus for UNIX are shown as follows. The initial menu is accessed by executing psadmin from the $PS_HOME\appserv directory on your UNIX server.

## INITIAL MENU

```
--------------------------------
PeopleSoft Server Administration
--------------------------------

    1) Application Server
    2) Process Scheduler
    3) Web Components
    q) Quit

Command to execute (1-3, q): 1
```

## APPLICATION SERVER MENU

```
--------------------------------------------
PeopleSoft Application Server Administration
--------------------------------------------

    1) Administer a domain
    2) Create a domain
    3) Delete a domain
    q) Quit

Command to execute (1-3, q): 2
```

## PROCESS SCHEDULER MENU

```
------------------------------------------
PeopleSoft Process Scheduler Administration
------------------------------------------

    1) Start a Process Scheduler Server
    2) Stop a Process Scheduler Server
    3) Configure a Process Scheduler Server
    4) Create a Process Scheduler Server Configuration
    5) Delete a Process Scheduler Server Configuration
    6) Edit a Process Scheduler Configuration File
    7) Show Status of a Process Scheduler Server
    8) Kill a Process Scheduler Server

    q) Quit

Command to execute (1-3, q): 3
```

PART

**III**

Maintaining the System

```
WEB COMPONENTS MENU

-----------------------------------------
PeopleSoft Web Components Administration
-----------------------------------------

    1) Web Server Administration
    2) Tuxedo Web Monitoring Facility Administration
    3) PeopleSoft starter page Administration
    4) Generate Web Components configuration files
    q) Quit

Command to execute (1-4, q):
```

# Monitoring System Logs

Monitoring the system logs for your PeopleSoft system is an important part of the routine administration of your system. The following list shows many of the logs that you should check on a regular basis:

**RDBMS log**    The RDBMS log contains information about the operations of and errors encountered by your RDBMS.

**Database server operating system logs**    These logs record information about any errors encountered by the operating system.

**Process Scheduler logs**    The Process Scheduler logs contain routine information and error messages about the operation of the Process Scheduler.

**Individual process logs for critical processes**    These logs contain routine information and any errors encountered for individual processes. The files use the naming convention *process name_<instance_number>*.log.

**Application Server logs**    The Application Server logs contain routine information and error messages about the operation of the Application Server application.

## Analyzing Batch Process Logs

Examine the log files from your batch processes periodically. One item you may want to track is performance data. For example, with batch payroll jobs, the log file contains the start time, stop time, and the number of checks processed. Create a spreadsheet to store this information and calculate a checks-per-hour number. This number allows you to compare different batch processes with each other. You may be able to identify performance degradation before your users notice it. You can then initiate performance-tuning measures to regain the previous performance numbers and prevent problems in the future.

## Monitoring the Network

Your LAN administrator should establish procedures to periodically monitor and compare the network performance. These results should be compared to a baseline number that you have recorded.

Statistics that should be captured are:

▶ Average utilization for a specified period

▶ Peak utilization during the same period

▶ Number of collisions (on an Ethernet network)

▶ Errors

You can use these statistics to plan for increased utilization when you are introducing new users or functionality. Careful monitoring of these statistics can also help you choose the proper LAN segmentation and bandwidth. If your utilization is increasing steadily, you should be able to predict when you will need to add more bandwidth.

## Checking for Updated Code

One procedure that is required for the administration of your PeopleSoft system is applying patches or code updates. You, or one of your staff, should check the People-Soft support Web site, Customer Connection, frequently. To use this Web site, Customer Connection requires that you be a PeopleSoft customer and that you have an access account. Your account manager can help you establish this if you are a new customer. Schedule the Customer Connection check on your calendar just like you would schedule other appointments.

PART

III

Maintaining the System

Remember to check for updated code in the "Updates and Fixes" section. People-Tools maintenance roll-up releases are posted there. PeopleTools maintenance releases are available on a periodic basis. The maintenance releases contain updated PeopleTools software. They are identified by adding a value of .01 to the PeopleTools version. For example, PeopleTools maintenance release 7.52 is the second mainte-nance release for PeopleTools 7.5. The maintenance releases are called roll-up releases because each release contains all the code found in previous maintenance releases. Using the above example, you must install PeopleSoft release 7.51 before installing release 7.52.

At Customer Connection, you will also find application-specific patches that may apply to your system. Patches are for specific problems that have been corrected by PeopleSoft. PeopleSoft is moving away from releasing so many patches. Their goal is to incorporate as many patches as possible into a single maintenance release.

You will receive regular maintenance releases for both PeopleTools and PeopleSoft applications in CD-ROM format. The files posted to Customer Connection are updates between these releases.

 **TIP**   I recommend that you load all updated code to your test database before updating your production database.

Another source of information regarding updated code is the PeopleSoft Plugged-In e-mail mailing list. This is a new service that delivers weekly e-mail that explains the Custom Connection postings. Again, your account manager can help you subscribe to this service. There is also a mailing list available for accounts that are in produc-tion, depending on which applications your company has licensed. I know there is a mailing list for HRMS.

# Summary

This chapter discussed processes that you should monitor on a regular basis. These processes are:

- ▶ Database objects
- ▶ System logs

▶ Process Scheduler

▶ Application Server

▶ Network operation

This chapter also discussed the importance of locating and applying updated code for your system. Information about these updates is available from Customer Connection or via an e-mail mailing list.

I realize that you cannot check everything everyday. Be realistic, and with diligence, you will develop a routine that works best in your environment. Be sure to remain flexible because events beyond your control can wipe out the best planning. Chapter 17, "Troubleshooting," describes the procedures for solving problems that occur in your PeopleSoft system.

PART

III

Maintaining the System

# *Troubleshooting*

## FEATURING

▶ **IDENTIFYING THE PROBLEM**

▶ **ARRIVING AT A SOLUTION**

▶ **PREVENTING PROBLEMS**

▶ **TROUBLESHOOTING PEOPLECODE**

▶ **TROUBLESHOOTING TWO-TIER CONNECTIVITY PROBLEMS**

▶ **TROUBLESHOOTING THREE-TIER PROBLEMS**

▶ **TROUBLESHOOTING EXAMPLES**

One of the most time-consuming and challenging tasks that you will face as a system administrator is troubleshooting problems that occur in your PeopleSoft system. If your company has a small to medium-sized PeopleSoft installation, you may have one or two people available for troubleshooting. If your installation is large, you may have a team of employees dedicated to troubleshooting. No matter which scenario describes your organization, this chapter is designed to help you resolve any problems with your PeopleSoft implementation swiftly and efficiently.

This chapter presents one approach to troubleshooting. It is not intended to be a comprehensive troubleshooting guide. You will encounter problems that have not been described here, but you should be able to apply the methods in this chapter to your specific problem. This chapter provides you with guidelines and tips on how to troubleshoot your system, but remember that there is no replacement for experience. As you become more familiar with your system, you will be able to resolve problems more quickly.

## Identifying the Problem

The first task is to identify the problem. This chapter discusses methods for identifying the problems using information provided by process logs, users, and PeopleSoft tools. If the problem is with a batch process, the log file may contain information about the problem. If the problem is with the online system, the user should be able to provide information from an error message. Often, the reports you receive from users are only symptoms of the real problem. You must then use the PeopleSoft tools to help isolate and identify the real problem.

Here are some questions that you can ask to help you isolate the problem:

▶ What is the problem?

▶ Which users are affected?

▶ Which systems and/or processes are affected?

▶ What *data* is involved with the process?

**N O T E** *Verify the data!* In my experience, a large percentage of problems (I estimate 70–80 percent) are caused by errors in the data. Either data was entered incorrectly or an interface process did not update a record correctly. Incorrect data can cause problems for both online and batch programs.

As system administrator, you will also have to prioritize multiple problems. To do this, consider how critical a problem is. A payroll problem that is preventing the paychecks from being processed is more critical than a user who is having trouble running an ad hoc query. Other problems may not be so easy to prioritize.

# Soliciting User Help

Involve your users in the troubleshooting process as much as possible. Have them provide you with a screen shot of any error message or of the panel that contains the erroneous data. Ask your users detailed questions about the steps that were performed when the error occurred.

## The Advantages of Screen Shots

For problems involving the online panels or functions, an image of the exact error message, called a screen shot, can be valuable to the troubleshooting process. There are several advantages that the screen shot has in the troubleshooting process. One advantage is that you have an exact copy of the error message. The users at my company know how to capture a screen and paste the screen into Microsoft Word to get a sample of the error message. The users then send the technical team the file via e-mail or they print it and deliver it to us. These Microsoft Word files, however, can get quite large if many screens are involved. You can also use third-party screen-capturing software to capture single windows or the entire screen.

To capture a screen using Microsoft Word, press the Print Screen key on your keyboard. Then open Microsoft Word and select Edit > Paste from the menu. The captured screen is pasted into the Word document, as shown in Figure 17.1. You can then save and/or print the document.

When the end user captures the error message with a screen shot, you save time because you do not have to replicate the problem yourself. The second advantage of screen shots is that you have the information at hand if you need to send it to Customer Support at PeopleSoft for help in resolving the problem. You also have a record you can save for future reference if the problem occurs again.

**FIGURE 17.1**    Screen capture in Microsoft Word

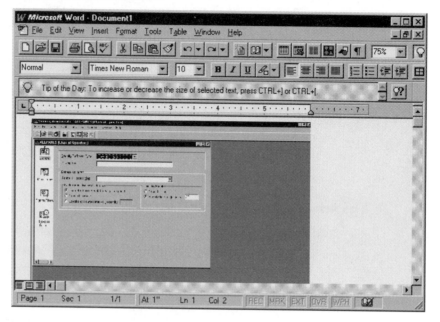

## Seeking Information from the User

Now that you have the information gathered from the screen shot, solicit the following information from the user:

▶ Identify the process being performed.

▶ Identify the panel being accessed.

▶ Identify the record being accessed.

▶ Identify the field being accessed.

▶ Identify the data that the user was attempting to update.

▶ Determine if this is a new function for the user or if the user has performed the function before.

▶ Ask the user if any other information can be provided.

**NOTE**    The user may not be able to provide all this information, but get as much as you can.

## Using the Application Designer to Isolate a Problem

 **NOTE** The scenario in this section assumes that you are experiencing an error message related to a specific field on a panel.

With the information collected from the user, begin looking at the specific People-Soft objects involved. I recommend that you identify the record involved and look at the specific data being entered. First, in the Application Designer, open the panel definition that is returning the error message.

Verify the field that is being used by the panel. Remember that there may be more than one record on a single panel. To identify the field and record, right-click the field object on the panel and select Panel Field Properties. In Figure 17.2, the Department field is selected. The Panel Field Properties panel opens (illustrated in Figure 17.3), showing a Record Name of JOB and a Field Name of DEPTID for this panel field object.

Now you have the record and field that you can use to select information about the data in the record.

**FIGURE 17.2** Application Designer–Panel definition

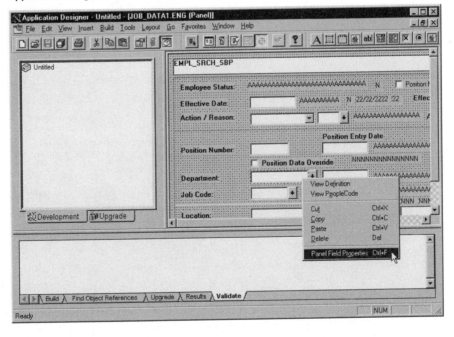

PART

III

Maintaining the System

**FIGURE 17.3**    Panel Field Properties panel

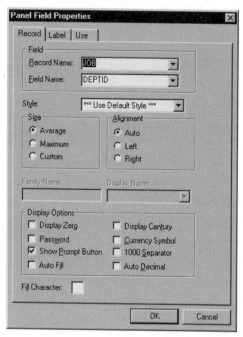

Using the SQL Query tool, look at the data in the table. I prefer to do this using a tool other than PeopleSoft Query so I can look directly at the data in the database without the security filters being applied.

If you determine that the error is from PeopleCode, then open the record definition and look at the PeopleCode associated with the field causing the error message. People-Code errors that stop processing will

▶ Display an error message stating that a PeopleCode error has occurred.

▶ Provide information about the error.

Other PeopleCode errors can corrupt the data or change the behavior of panels but processing does not halt. You can access the record definition directly from the panel definition by right-clicking the field and selecting the View Definition option. Press the PeopleCode display icon on the toolbar, as shown in Figure 17.4, to reveal the fields and the PeopleCode types associated with each field.

Double-click the Field Change box for the DEPTID field, as shown in Figure 17.4, to reveal the Record PeopleCode, illustrated in Figure 17.5. This scrollable window allows you to browse and change the PeopleCode associated with this field. Locate the code that is causing the error message to determine which actions are being taken and where the inputs are coming from.

**FIGURE 17.4**    PeopleCode display

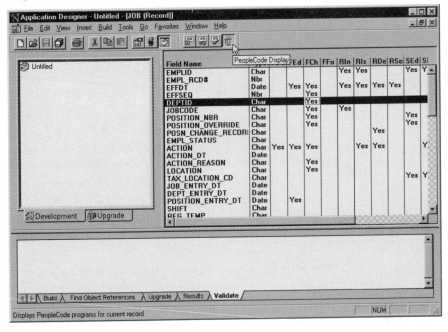

**FIGURE 17.5**    DEPTID–record PeopleCode

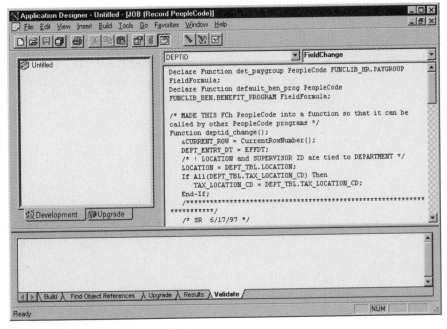

If the problem is not immediately apparent, continue troubleshooting the People-Code using information found in the *Troubleshooting PeopleCode* section later in this chapter.

# Arriving at a Solution

Now that you have isolated the problem, the next step is to determine how to solve the problem. There are many different paths that you can take to get to a solution. This section describes the steps you can take to help you arrive at a solution to your problem. With experience, you should be able to skip some of these steps when searching for a solution.

## Researching Solutions

PeopleSoft has several sources of information available that can suggest solutions to problems you may encounter and problems encountered by others. This section reviews the three most common sources: Customer Connection, PeopleBooks, and the Global Support Center.

### Customer Connection

One source of information is Customer Connection. This is the Internet-based online support center. You can search discussion groups, looking for other customers with the same environment or who have the same questions as you. Most importantly, you can find documents to help you resolve problems that have been reported by others using the following sections of Customer Connection:

▶ Updates and Fixes

▶ News and Information

▶ Continuous Documentation

PeopleSoft has introduced a new search tool for the Customer Connection site. This search tool allows you to search multiple categories for information that you have entered as the search criteria. Figure 17.6 illustrates the search panel from Customer Connection.

**FIGURE 17.6**    PeopleSoft Customer Connection search panel

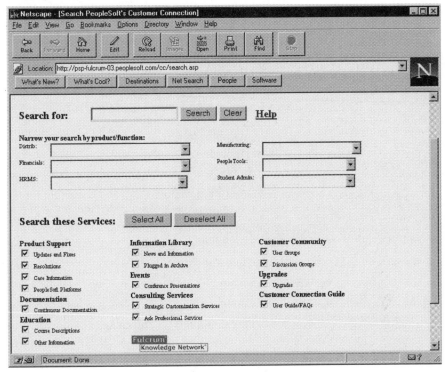

**NOTE**    Remember that customizations may affect how you can resolve a problem that another company resolved in a completely different way. You may have to adapt a solution found on Customer Connection to your environment.

Enter your search criteria in the Search For box. Narrow your search to a specific product or function by selecting from the available drop-down list boxes. You can limit the search to specific categories on Customer Connection. For most problems, I recommend that you limit the search to the Product Support, Documentation, and Information Library categories. If the problem occurs during an upgrade, include the Upgrades category in your search. If you receive hundreds of possible solutions, narrow your search using the provided options or add more search criteria.

PART

III

Maintaining the System

## PeopleBooks

The PeopleBooks for your PeopleSoft applications have some specific information on problems that have error codes associated with them. One example is the Payroll error messages. These messages can be viewed online. Use the error message number to locate further information in PeopleBooks about the error.

## Reporting the Problem to PeopleSoft's Global Support Center

If you have researched the information available to you and are still experiencing the problem, it's time to open an incident with the Global Support Center. When you report a problem, specify if you want the problem classified as "production critical." This should be used *only* if your production system is down. Do not report incidents as critical unless they are; it only slows down the response for everyone. Have the information you have gathered ready. Make sure you know which versions of People-Tools, PeopleSoft application modules, the RDBMS, and the server operating system you are using. After you report the problem, keep searching for a resolution or a work-around to resolve the problem while waiting for an answer from PeopleSoft.

PeopleSoft has recently announced a new policy regarding problem resolution. This policy is still being refined, but the current information can be found on Customer Connection under News and Information–Problem Resolution. The new policy is designed to reduce the length of time that it takes to get a problem resolved. This policy lays out specific procedures for you to follow to help set the priority of your problem. Procedures are defined if you want to appeal the priority that was assigned to your problem or to request escalation of your problem if you are not seeing results.

You can log and monitor your cases with the Global Support Center from Customer Connection. If you have been unable to find a resolution to your problem, you can report it online.

# Using Trace Functions to Solve Problems

Be prepared to provide trace files or other information in response to questions from the Global Support Center. If you have not already performed a trace to isolate the problem, the Global Support Center may ask that you perform a trace with particular settings. Figure 17.7 contains the PeopleSoft trace panel introduced in Chapter 5, "Administration Tools." The PeopleCode options are discussed in detail in the *Troubleshooting PeopleCode* section of this chapter.

**FIGURE 17.7**  PeopleSoft trace options

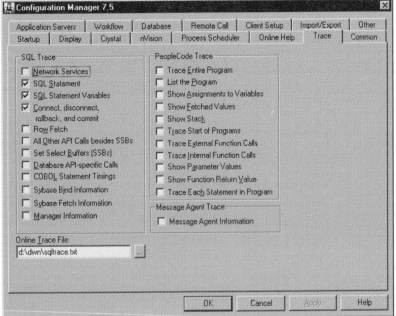

The trace file is useful for understanding the processes that are occurring. The Global Support Center uses the trace file to verify that an application is operating properly.

## Approaches to Solving the Problem

First, attempt to duplicate the problem. If the problem is with the online system, it may be easy to duplicate the problem. Use your test and development databases when trying to find a solution. If the problem is with a batch process, create some procedures to help. Consider using another database for testing batch processes.

When trying to troubleshoot batch process problems, I create a test database into which I load a current copy of the production database. This allows me to conduct concurrent testing with a full copy of the database in which the problem is occurring. I change the parameters and test solutions without fear of impacting production data.

Using a copy of the production database also guarantees that I closely match the database setup that existed when the problem initially occurred. It also saves me the time

PART

**III**

**Maintaining the System**

required to run interface programs to load data that may not be in my normal test database. I can zero in on the problem more quickly. Once I have a backup of the production database, I continue to look for a work-around to get the batch process running again while waiting for the load process for the test database to complete.

When you are using the test or other non-production database, you can comment out program lines or add display statements to allow you to better understand where the problem is occurring. If you are working in the test database, you may want to get a fresh database backup before altering any online panels or programs. This makes it easier to reset the database back to its original state when you identify the problem.

Look at all the records associated with an employee or account. Some PeopleCode is designed to validate all records when it is executed. An older record may be causing the problem when the system tries to save a new record. This is especially true of the HRMS job panels. If you have an employee that was terminated, rehired, and then terminated again, make sure that all the fields concerning termination date and date last worked on the Employment panel and record are accurate.

## Testing the Solution

Once you have arrived at a possible solution to the problem, it is important to test it before implementing the solution. It is tempting to implement the solution directly if your production system is down. Try to avoid this temptation.

There is one exception to this rule: If the problem has been isolated to the data in a table, then you must update the production database. The test database may not have the same data. Make sure to take some precautions before you update or delete any production data. Write the SQL statement to capture just the record that you want. Select the information that is currently in the record you are updating for use as a reference if you have to delete the record and start over.

Update the data and verify that the problem is solved. Have the users validate the function and advise them if you had to alter or remove data to resolve the problem.

# Preventing Problems

There is no surefire method to completely eliminate problems in your PeopleSoft system. You can be proactive by testing and applying maintenance releases for your version of PeopleSoft as they become available. The PeopleTools maintenance releases often solve many problems without impacting your application data. However, application maintenance releases should be applied using the full upgrade procedures, since you risk losing your customizations if you apply them without performing all the required comparisons.

**T I P**   I do not recommend rushing to implement an application maintenance release to fix a problem. Application maintenance releases require thorough testing before implementation.

Subscribe to the mailing lists that apply to your environment. This ensures that you are notified when problems occur in environments similar to yours. At a minimum, subscribe to the following mailing lists if available:

▶ PeopleSoft Plugged-In

▶ RDBMS problem notification

▶ Server operating system

**N O T E**   Your PeopleSoft account manager should be able to help with the Plugged-In mailing list. I recommend checking the Web sites of your RDBMS and server operating system vendors for any mailing lists available to customers. For example, I subscribe to two mailing lists available from Hewlett-Packard (HP): Patch Digest for HP-UX and HP Security Bulletins.

Build a network of colleagues who have similar PeopleSoft systems and business processes that you can exchange information with. Keep an open line of communication with other PeopleSoft customers by passing on information that you have discovered. Another option is to join a local or regional users group. This gives you additional opportunities to exchange ideas with other PeopleSoft users and provides an avenue for building your troubleshooting network.

Customer Connection also has a library of white papers that can be found in the News and Information section. The topics are varied, but are designed to help you better manage your system. If you are new to PeopleSoft or are considering implementing the PeopleSoft Application Server, I highly recommend the "Three-Tier Answerbook" white paper.

PART

III

Maintaining the System

# Troubleshooting PeopleCode

Troubleshooting PeopleCode problems may require the use of the PeopleCode Trace options that you specify in the Configuration Manager Trace folder. Beginning with version 7.5, the Application Reviewer process performs all the functionality found in the PeopleCode trace, with several additions. PeopleSoft has left the PeopleCode Trace in place for your use.

Let's first look at the PeopleCode Trace and what it can do for you. Then we will discuss the Application Reviewer functionality.

## PeopleCode Trace

Figure 17.8 illustrates the SQL Trace and PeopleCode Trace options.

**FIGURE 17.8**    **SQL Trace and PeopleSoft Trace options**

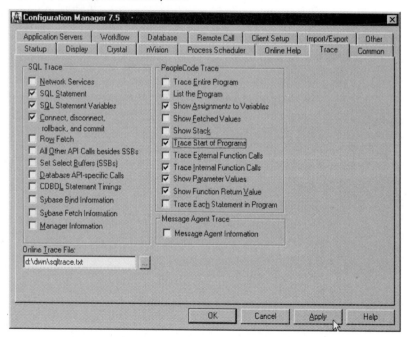

The PeopleCode Trace options are as follows:

**Trace Entire Program**    This option traces the operation of the entire program and includes two additional functions: Trace Internal Function Calls and Trace External Function Calls.

**List the Program**    This option is used mostly by PeopleSoft developers to return a listing of the program being executed. No tracing is performed.

**Show Assignments to Variables**    This option lists the variables and the values that have been assigned to them.

**Show Fetched Values**    This option lists the variables and the values that have been returned to them by other functions.

**Show Stack**    This option returns internal program stack information. It is not usually selected except by PeopleSoft developers.

**Trace Start of Programs**    This option provides timing information for the program start, the program completion, and the program duration.

**Trace External Function Calls**    This option traces calls to external PeopleCode programs; these calls are usually contained in the FUNCLIB records.

**Trace Internal Function Calls**    This option traces calls to other functions contained in the same PeopleCode module.

**Show Parameter Values**    This option records the values of parameters that are passed to another function.

**Show Function Return Value**    This option records the values returned by a function.

**Trace Each Statement in Program**    This option records the text and line number for each statement being executed. This option is different from the List the Program option in that only executed statements are recorded.

To create a PeopleCode Trace for troubleshooting a problem, take the following steps:

1. Make sure that all the PeopleSoft windows are closed.

2. Select the options that you want to trace in the Configuration Manager Trace panel.

3. Apply the configuration.

4. Start the PeopleSoft application and perform the operation that is having the problem. The program will run more slowly when the trace is on, since all activity is being monitored and logged.

5. When the error message displays, close the application.

6. Open the trace file in a text editor and review the information that was captured. I usually start at the bottom of the file, since the information that I am

**PART**

**III**

**Maintaining the System**

most interested in should be at the end of the file if I stopped the application immediately after the error occurred.

The trace file should provide you with the information necessary to help identify the source of the problem. If you are still unable to locate the problem, check Customer Connection or contact the Global Support Center.

# Application Reviewer

The Application Reviewer has replaced the PeopleCode Trace utility. Application Reviewer is a stand-alone application that features a step execution function that allows developers to step through a PeopleCode program one line at a time during development. You can use this functionality for troubleshooting purposes. The Application Reviewer should be executed after you open the panel group with the problem. Start the Application Reviewer by selecting Go > PeopleTools > Application Reviewer from the menu. Select Break > Break at Start to prepare to trace People-Code execution. Select the menu item that you want to trace.

The Application Reviewer stops the program execution when the first PeopleCode program begins to execute. The program display in the PeopleCode Program window of the Application Reviewer appears. You can now step the program through execution. You can view local and global variable information. You can also turn on logging to capture the information. Figure 17.9 contains the PeopleCode Log Options panel. To access this panel, select Options > Log from the Application Reviewer menu.

**FIGURE 17.9**    Application Reviewer–PeopleCode Log Options panel

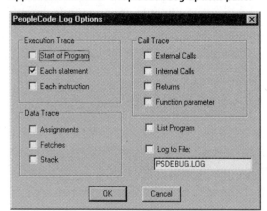

Note that many of the same options are available in the Application Reviewer as are available with the PeopleCode Trace utility. The log options are grouped into three categories: Execution Trace, Call Trace, and Data Trace. Let's look at each of these categories.

## Execution Trace

The following options are available with Execution Trace:

**Start of Program**    This option provides timing information for the program start, the program completion, and the program duration.

**Each Statement**    This is the default setting. This option records the text and line number for each statement being executed.

**Each Instruction**    This option traces each instruction being executed.

## Call Trace

The following options are available with Call Trace:

**External Calls**    This option traces calls to external PeopleCode programs; these calls are usually contained in the FUNCLIB records.

**Internal Calls**    This option traces calls to other functions contained in the same PeopleCode module.

**Returns**    This option records the values returned by a function.

**Function Parameter**    This option records the values of parameters that are passed to another function.

## Data Trace

The following options are available with Data Trace:

**Assignments**    This option lists the variables and the values that have been assigned to them.

**Fetches**    This option lists the variables and the values that have been returned to them by other functions.

**Stack**    This option returns internal program stack information. This option is not usually selected except by PeopleSoft developers.

PART

III

Maintaining the System

### Additional Options

The following options are also available through the Application Reviewer for tracing PeopleSoft applications:

**List the Program**   This option is used mostly by PeopleSoft developers to return a listing of the program being executed. No tracing is performed.

**Log to File**   This is the filename of the log file.

For analysis purposes, the Application Reviewer trace file should provide you with the same information as the PeopleCode trace file. The advantage of the Application Reviewer is that it provides you with the ability to analyze the execution of the PeopleCode program one line at a time.

**NOTE**   You will not receive support from the Global Support Center for your custom PeopleCode. They will refer you to the PeopleSoft Professional Services Group. If you intend to write custom PeopleCode, send at least one developer to PeopleCode training. Training is a good idea, even if you have no intention of creating your own PeopleCode.

# Troubleshooting Two-Tier Connectivity Problems

Troubleshooting connectivity problems with two-tier PeopleSoft clients will be a common task for the system administrator and the technical staff. Typically, you will receive calls from your users saying that they cannot connect to the database. Probably the most common connectivity problem involves the user's password. Users will forget their passwords. On systems that have case-sensitive passwords, users may be attempting to enter a password in the wrong case. Indications that the error is with the password are generally quite specific; the error message says that the user ID is not authorized or has failed to connect.

There are two other areas that you should check when troubleshooting connectivity problems: the network and the client.

**TIP**   If the problem is isolated to a single user, verify that the password is correct and start your search at the client. However, if you have several users reporting the problem, begin searching on the database server and then move back to the network.

# Network

In the two-tier environment, there are two common problems:

▶ The user is not connected to the network. This prevents the user from being able to start the PeopleTools executable file and access the PeopleSoft login screen.

▶ The network is not functioning properly between the user and the client. This can be caused by improper configuration or malfunctioning network hardware.

To verify network connectivity from the client to the database server, create a guide similar to the following steps created by my company:

1. Attempt to ping the database server by name. If successful, then network connectivity exists. If this test fails, continue to step 2.

2. Attempt to ping the database server by IP address. If successful, then the client cannot access a Domain Name Server (DNS). Check the settings to make sure that the client has the proper settings for the DNS server. If this test fails, continue to step 3.

3. Attempt to ping the router that is local to the user by address. If successful, then there is a network connectivity problem between the client workstation and the database server. Contact the network support staff for resolution. If this test fails, continue to step 4.

4. Attempt to ping the local host by name. This is commonly called a loopback test. If this test is successful, then the problem is on the user's local LAN segment. Contact the network support staff for resolution. If this test fails, the problem is either with the LAN adapter on the user's machine or with an improper configuration. Check both.

Now let's look at some tasks you need to perform when troubleshooting on the client.

# Client

One of the first tasks that you should perform after verifying that the client is connected to the network is to make sure that the database connectivity software is loaded correctly and that any path statements to the software are correct. You can use the Configuration Manager to help determine if there are problems with these paths. Update any erroneous directory paths and click the Apply button in Configuration Manager. If you are using profiles that you have exported, reload the profile for the client workstation.

PART
III

Maintaining the System

**N O T E**   Configuration Manager was discussed in Chapter 5, "Administration Tools."

Verify that the client is using the correct database connectivity driver and the correct version of that driver. This may be the native connectivity driver for the database or Open Database Connectivity (ODBC) driver, which is the primary method of connectivity for some databases, including Microsoft SQL Server.

Another fix that may solve the problem is to purge the PeopleSoft cache directories on the client. This is accomplished by selecting the Purge Cache Directories button from the Configuration Manager Common panel. This helps solve problems that occur immediately after the application of a PeopleTools maintenance release, when the client workstation begins the login process but cannot start the application.

Now let's look at some special considerations when troubleshooting three-tier problems.

# Troubleshooting Three-Tier Problems

Troubleshooting problems in a three-tier configuration can be difficult, since the primary users of three-tier connectivity are likely to be remote users. The complexity of the configuration can contribute to the types of problems you might encounter. This section looks at the factors that can affect the three-tier environment, such as the network, the client, the application server, the RDBMS, and PeopleCode.

## Network

The most common problems you will find in a three-tier configuration will be linked to the network and the ability of the client to connect to the application server. Be prepared to walk your remote users through a quick checklist to determine if the network is causing the problem. Network problems are not PeopleSoft problems, but you should be aware of potential network problems. The following is a quick guide that my company uses to determine if our remote clients have network connectivity problems:

**N O T E**   This guide is similar to the two-tier list shown in the previous section.

1. Attempt to ping the application server by name. If successful, then network connectivity exists. Check the workstation configuration manager settings for the application server (discussed later in this chapter). If this test fails, continue to step 2.

2. Attempt to ping the application server by IP address. If successful, then the client cannot access a DNS. Check the settings to make sure that the client has the proper settings for the DNS server. If this test fails, continue to step 3.

3. Attempt to ping the router that is local to the user by address. If successful, then there is a network connectivity problem between the corporate office and the remote location. Contact the network support staff for resolution. If this test fails, continue to step 4.

4. Attempt to ping the local host by name. This is commonly called a loopback test. If this test is successful, then the problem is on the user's local LAN segment. Contact the network support staff for resolution. If this test fails, the problem is either with the LAN adapter on the user's machine or with an improper configuration. Check both.

# Client

If you have network connectivity but the client cannot connect and only one user has reported any problems, verify the configuration settings on the client workstation. Using Figure 17.10 as a guide, verify that the port number for the application server is correct.

If multiple clients cannot connect, then verify that your application server is running.

**FIGURE 17.10**     Configuration Manager–Application Servers panel

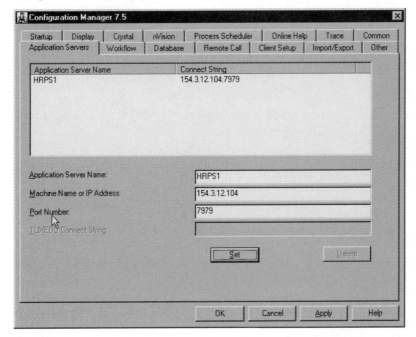

PART
III

Maintaining the System

# Application Server

The application server is a critical component of a three-tier configuration. If users are experiencing problems using three-tier mode and you have verified the client connectivity issues outlined previously, then you need to verify the operation of the application server itself by taking the following steps:

1. Start the PSADMIN utility that is used to administer the application server. PSADMIN in the UNIX environment utilizes a character-based menu system.

2. Select Administer a Domain from the Application Server Administration menu.

3. Select the domain that is experiencing problems from the menu.

4. Check the domain status. If the domain is up and running, as shown in the Server Status output, then verify that the connectivity between the application server and database server is working. A connectivity problem is more likely to occur when using a physical three-tier environment. Use the tmadmin command to verify connectivity.

5. Check the application server log file for error messages. If there are error messages, check the Customer Connection Web site for possible solutions or updates to the application server code that might fix the problem.

To help you visualize these tasks, the application server menus for a UNIX server follow. This menu is the first menu of the PSADMIN utility:

---

**INITIAL MENU**

```
--------------------------------

PeopleSoft Server Administration

--------------------------------

   1) Application Server
   2) Process Scheduler
   3) Web Components
   q) Quit

Command to execute (1-3, q): 1
```

---

The Application Server Administration Menu allows you to manage the domains on the application server:

## APPLICATION SERVER ADMINISTRATION MENU

```
--------------------------------------------
PeopleSoft Application Server Administration
--------------------------------------------

    1) Administer a domain
    2) Create a domain
    3) Delete a domain
    q) Quit

Command to execute (1-3, q): 2
```

The Domain Administration Menu allows you to control a specific domain, which corresponds to a connection to a database. You can start, stop, and configure the application server from this menu.

## DOMAIN ADMINISTRATION MENU

```
--------------------------------
PeopleSoft Domain Administration
--------------------------------

       Domain Name: HRPS1

    1) Boot this domain
    2) Domain shutdown menu
    3) Domain status menu
    4) Configure this domain
    5) TUXEDO command line (tmadmin)
    6) Edit configuration/log files menu
    q) Quit

Command to execute (1-6, q) [q]:
```

The Domain Status Menu allows you to view the status of both the server and client connections.

PART

**III**

Maintaining the System

**DOMAIN STATUS MENU**

```
------------------------------
PeopleSoft Domain Status Menu
------------------------------

      Domain Name: HRPS1

  1) Server status
  2) Client status
  q) Quit

Command to execute (1-2, q) [q]:
```

The following example shows the results of selecting the Server Status option from the Domain Status Menu. This sample output shows that there are five processes running. The current status for all services is idle.

**SERVER STATUS**

```
Portions * Copyright 1986-1997 RSA Data Security, Inc.
All Rights Reserved.
Distributed under license by BEA Systems, Inc.
TUXEDO is a registered trademark.
```

| > Prog Name | Queue Name | Grp Name | ID | RqDone | Load Done | Current Service |
|---------|----------|--------|----|------|---------|----------------|
| BBL | 33331 | SITE1 | 0 | 1 | 50 | ( IDLE ) |
| PSAPPSRV | APPQ | APPSRV | 1 | 1927 | 96350 | ( IDLE ) |
| PSAUTH | 00001.00001 | BASE | 1 | 54 | 2700 | ( IDLE ) |
| PSSAMSRV | SAMQ | APPSRV | 100 | 0 | 0 | ( IDLE ) |
| WSL | 00001.00020 | BASE | 20 | 0 | 0 | ( IDLE ) |

The Edit Configuration/Log Files Menu allows you to update and view the configuration and log files for the application server.

**EDIT CONFIGURATION/LOG FILES MENU**

```
---------------------------------------------
PeopleSoft Edit Configuration/Log Files Menu
---------------------------------------------

  1) Edit psappsrv.cfg (current configuration file)
  2) Edit APPSRV.LOG  (current application server log file)
```

```
       3) Edit TUXLOG       (current Tuxedo log file)
       q) Quit

   Command to execute (1-3, q) [q]:
```

The Domain Shutdown Menu allows you to control the shutdown of a specific domain on the application server.

### DOMAIN SHUTDOWN MENU

```
--------------------------------
PeopleSoft Domain Shutdown Menu
--------------------------------

      Domain Name: HRPS1

   1) Normal shutdown
   2) Forced shutdown
   q) Quit

Command to execute (1-2, q) [q]:
```

If you determine that the application server is not working and selecting the Boot This Domain option in the Domain Administration Menu fails to start the application server, reconfigure the application server and attempt to restart it. The configuration of the application server is discussed in Chapter 5, "Administration Tools." The "Three-Tier Answerbook" white paper available on Customer Connection is an invaluable tool in configuring and troubleshooting the application server.

If you have gotten this far with your three-tier troubleshooting and still do not have a solution, check your database.

## RDBMS

Although it is unlikely that the database is causing a three-tier connectivity problem, make sure to check the database server when users report problems. Check to see if the database server is operating properly by taking the following steps:

▶ Verify that the server is operational.

▶ Verify that the listener ports are operational.

▶ Verify the network connectivity of the server.

PART

III

Maintaining the System

When a three-tier problem is specific to a single process or function, you may have a PeopleCode problem. Let's examine how to troubleshoot PeopleCode in a three-tier environment.

## PeopleCode in a Three-Tier Environment

You can trace PeopleCode on the client just like you can in a two-tier environment. You also have the capability to trace PeopleCode running on the application server if your application server is running on Windows NT. PeopleCode tracing is *not* supported on UNIX application servers.

Remember that client-only PeopleCode cannot run on the application server. The application receives an error if a processing group attempts to use client-only People-Code on the application server. Validating your PeopleCode for three-tier execution should prevent this problem.

# Troubleshooting Examples

This section discusses several situations that may occur with your PeopleSoft system. It also provides some tips and checklists that we use at my company to help isolate and solve these types of problems.

## Login Error

**Scenario**: A common error that your users will encounter is with the login process. Figure 17.11 shows the SQL Access Manager panel that your users see when they attempt to log in using the wrong user ID or password.

**FIGURE 17.11**    SQL Access Manager: Error 30022, login failed

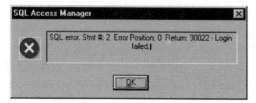

 **NOTE**    The error code 30022 is a Sybase-specific message; the exact message will vary from database to database.

**Problem Isolation**: Verify that the user has connectivity to the proper database using the troubleshooting steps outlined earlier in this chapter. Have the user attempt to log in again if you made changes to the connectivity configuration.

**Solution**: Fix the database connectivity problem, if necessary. Then have the user log in with the correct password. If the user has forgotten the password, have the security administrator reset the password. Have the user log in and change their password.

**Prevention**: This is not easily prevented because users will forget their password on occasion.

Make sure that your users contact the technical staff if other software that requires database access is to be loaded on their workstation. This can prevent the corruption of the database connectivity information or drivers for the PeopleSoft application.

## Process Scheduler Will Not Restart

**Scenario**: The Process Scheduler has stopped or you stopped the Process Scheduler to perform maintenance and it will not restart. At my company, we saw this problem with earlier versions of PeopleSoft, but we have not seen it recently.

**Problem Isolation**: Attempt to isolate the problem.

We never completely isolated the cause of this problem. In earlier versions of PeopleSoft, we noticed that the Process Scheduler did not purge deleted records until a restart. As a result, we had processes that our users had deleted but the processes were still in the database. We also had processes that had aborted and had no completion time.

**Solution**: For the stopped process, we deleted all the records in the PSPRCSRQST table and the Process Scheduler started properly.

For the maintenance release, we reloaded all the stored statements.

**Prevention**: If the new maintenance release includes updated COBOL modules, you may have to execute a new Data Mover script to load the new stored statements into the PS_SQL_STMT table. This is especially true if you have new COBOL modules that begin with the name PT*, which indicates PeopleTools COBOL code.

## Improper Security View Set for Record

**Scenario**: The user is trying to perform a query that joins two tables. When the user attempts to execute the table, the maximum number of joins for a query for the RDBMS is exceeded, resulting in a database error message.

**NOTE**   The maximum number of joins does not apply to all database platforms.

**Problem Isolation:** Identify the tables that are involved in the query. Then open the record definition for each table and determine the query security record that is being used by each record. This is accomplished by taking the following steps:

**1.** Open the record definition in the Application Designer.

**2.** Select File **>** Object Properties to display the Record Properties panel.

**3.** Select the Use tab, as illustrated in Figure 17.12.

**FIGURE 17.12**   Record Properties panel–query security view

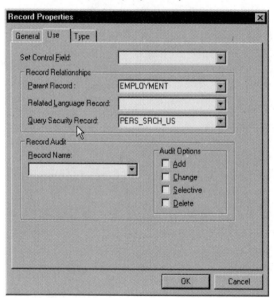

**Solution:** Set both records to the same query security record and have the user attempt to execute the query again.

**Prevention:** At my company, we verify that all of the database tables that are frequently used in queries use the same query security record. We do this each time we perform an upgrade. This prevents the users from having these problems.

## Batch COBOL Errors

**Scenario:** A batch COBOL program encounters an error during execution and stops processing.

**Problem Isolation**: Review the process logs for this program. If a COBOL process caused the error, there should be information in the log to help you identify the process that encountered the error. Remember, a COBOL program stops processing if it encounters data that it has not been programmed to deal with, either by program code or error handling code. Do not initially rule out bad data as a source of the error.

Another possibility is a mismatch between the COBOL program and the stored statement versions. This can be caused by not executing the script that accompanies an update containing new COBOL programs.

**Solution:** If data was causing the error, correct the data. To correct version mismatches, reload the latest stored statements using the Data Mover script that matches your current release level of PeopleTools and the PeopleSoft application.

**Prevention**: Reload your stored statements to match the version of the COBOL programs when updated COBOL programs are implemented. For example, if a tax update changes the PSPPYRUN.cbl program, make sure to load the stored statement in the included PSPPYRUN.dms.

## Example COBOL Errors

The following examples illustrate how to fix two common COBOL errors.

**Error Code 114**    Error code 114 problems can usually be resolved by reloading stored statements.

```
Execution error : file 'PTPSQLRT.gnt'
error code: 114, pc=0, call=2, seg=0
114 Attempt to access item beyond bounds of memory (Signal 10)

HP/MF COBOL Version: B.11.25
HP-UX bcbsalh2 B.10.20 A 9000/777
pid: 10885 gid: 3 uid: 102
Thu May  1 10:45:55 1997
 10:45am  up 14 days,  2:51,  4 users,  load average: 1.10, 1.08, 1.07
Thread mode:          No Threads
RTS Error:            COBOL
Sync Signals:         COBOL
ASync Signals:        COBOL
cobtidy on exception: False
```

PART

III

Maintaining the System

**SQLRT Errors**    SQLRT errors are returned when the SQL handling program PTPSQLRT has a problem with the stored statement or with database connectivity.

To fix this problem, reload the stored statements contained in PSPEARRY.dms. The discussion in the next paragraph explains how to determine which program contains the initial error. SQLRT errors with a code other than error code 114 are fixed by reloading the database connectivity modules and relinking the PSRUN file using the psrun.mak program.

You can identify which stored statements may be causing the problem by looking at the routine that calls the FETCH and looking at the first COBOL program name found after the error, which in the following code example is PSPEARRY, shown in **bold.**

```
Start employee processing at 14:48:36.66.
SQLRT: DA000-FETCH                              30022 ct_fetch():
user api layer: internal common library error: The bind of result set
item 35 resulted in truncation.
SQLRT: SQL-CONNECT                              30009 ct_fetch():
user api layer: internal common library error: The bind of result set
item 35 resulted in truncation.
PTPSQLRT - CURSOR=ZERO PASSED
SQLRT: SQL-CONNECT
FETCH-OTHER-EARNS(FETCH)

PAGE#=8224,LINE#=24,SEPCHK=4,EMPLID=               ,EMPLRCD#=224,
NAME=              LOAD-ERN-ARRAY(PSPEARRY)
MAIN(PSPPYCAL)
MAIN(PSPPYWKS)
MAIN(PSPPYWK6)
MAIN(PSPPYWK5)
MAIN(PSPPYWK4)
MAIN(PSPPYWK3)
MAIN(PSPPYWK2)
PROCESS-PAY(PSPPYWK1)
Calculation did not finish at 14:48:37.30 !!!!!
PeopleSoft prcs_bat Terminating
```

# New Employee Record Cannot Be Accessed

**Scenario:** An Employment user entered the information into the PeopleSoft system for a new employee. A Compensation and Benefits user attempted to open the employee's record to add tax and benefits information but the record could not be retrieved. The Employment user attempts to insert the employee again, thinking that the record was not saved successfully. An error message about a duplicate Social Security Number (National ID with PeopleSoft 7.5) appears.

**Problem Isolation**: Our technical staff determined that the employee information was present when using the SQL tool. Upon questioning the Employment user, we discovered that the new employee was the first person hired in a new department. First, we went to the online department table setup to verify that the information was correct. Then we went to the departmental security tree to verify that the new department was set up correctly. We discovered that the department ID had not been added to the security tree. This prevented the user from accessing the data, since the employee ID was not in a department to which the user had access. Search records are discussed in more detail in Chapter 9, "Security."

**Solution**: We added the department ID to the security tree and executed the SQR to link the new tree to the online security. The SQR, PER505.SQR, is executed by selecting Process > Update Security > Department Table menu item from the Administer Workforce panels. Select the designated language and enter the effective date of the change you made in the run control panel shown in Figure 17.13. Execute the process to complete the update.

**FIGURE 17.13**    **Security update report run control panel**

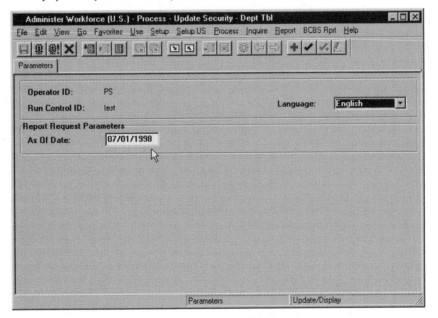

**Prevention**: PeopleSoft lets you place an employee into a department ID that you do not have access to if you have Hire authority. Ensure coordination between the individual responsible for department table and the individual responsible for the departmental security tree.

# Processing Pay Reversal for the Wrong Pay Group

**Scenario:** A user reports processing a pay reversal but cannot locate the check.

**Problem Isolation:** The user is usually looking in the wrong place or entering the wrong criteria for the information. The online panel sorts checks by pay group first, then by date. The check may be at the top of the list and the user expects it to be at the bottom. Use the SQL tool to find all the information that pertains to the employee for which the check was being processed.

**Solution:** At my company, we generally update the rows involved in the table to reflect the proper pay group. We have seen this several times and have saved a series of SQL scripts to fix the problem. First, we execute statements to capture the record as it exists. Then we update the information to the correct data. This is done to get the information back in to the correct pay group.

**Prevention:** The best prevention for this is user attention. At my company, we created checklists that prompt the user to verify items before calculating or confirming a paycheck. PeopleSoft allows a paycheck to be processed in a different pay group because you can process reversals for employees who have been moved to a new pay group since the original check was written. The problem is that the delivered PeopleSoft check-printing SQR will not print a check for an employee if it was processed in the wrong pay group.

# Printing Errors

Printing errors will be a big item on your troubleshooting checklist. This section discusses two categories of printing errors: paycheck printing errors and general printing errors.

## Paycheck Printing Errors

There are several types of printing errors. Table 17.1 lists the errors along with common symptoms and their potential solution(s).

## General Printing Errors

There are two general printing problems that you will encounter. Table 17.2 lists the general printing problems and their potential solutions.

**TABLE 17.1** Paycheck Printing Problems and Solutions

| Problem | Solution |
|---|---|
| No checks printed when the job ran. | 1. Verify the run control parameters.<br>2. Ensure that the checks were confirmed.<br>3. Check the log to ensure that the paycheck printing job ran. The paycheck SQR records the number of checks and amount in the log file.<br>4. Verify that the printer is online. |
| The signature did not print when using the electronic signature cartridge. | 1. Verify that the cartridge was properly inserted into the printer.<br>2. Make sure that the paycheck printing program references the cartridge correctly. |
| All checks did not print. | 1. Verify the run control parameters.<br>2. Verify that all the paychecks were confirmed.<br>3. Verify the log file to make sure that the confirmation process completed before the paycheck printing program was executed. |
| Bank routing codes were printed with default printer font after the printer lost power. | 1. You must run the program to reload the MICR font that is required by the bank to the printer. |

**TABLE 17.2** General Printing Problems and Solutions

| Problem | Solution |
|---|---|
| The SQR completed on the server but the report did not print. | Check the run parameters in the Process Monitor to determine the settings that were used by the user. If user printed to a file, then simply print the file. If the user selected a printer but did not code the correct printer information, the user may have to rerun the report if no *.lis file was generated. For UNIX servers, remember that the printer syntax should look like this:<br>/tmp +p-d*printerdevicename* |
| The SQR completed but only one line printed when running on a UNIX server and printing to a Hewlett-Packard LaserJet. | Modify the SETUP01A.SQC and SETUP02A.SQC printer definition files to add a carriage return/line feed code to the end of each line. (See the UNIX printing section that follows in this section for additional information.) This problem occurred with older PeopleSoft versions, but the printer definitions should be correct with newer version (7.x). |

PART

III

Maintaining the System

## UNIX Printer Configuration

If you are using Hewlett-Packard LaserJet printers when SQR reports are printed from your UNIX server and are experiencing the second problem described in Table 17.2, you need to modify the following two printer setup files to include the carriage return and line feed in order for the printing to be correct:

SETUP01A.SQC   This file is used for reports to be printed in portrait mode. Append the following HP-PCL string to the printer definition file:

<27>&k2G

SETUP02A.SQC   This file is used for reports to be printed in landscape mode. Append the following HP-PCL string to the printer definition file:

<27>&k2G

> **N O T E**   PeopleSoft now includes the carriage return/line feed code in the printer setup files beginning with version 7.

# Summary

This chapter discussed techniques that you can use when troubleshooting problems with your PeopleSoft system. The procedures discussed were:

- ▶ Identifying the problem
- ▶ Arriving at a solution
- ▶ Preventing problems
- ▶ Troubleshooting PeopleCode
- ▶ Troubleshooting two-tier connectivity problems
- ▶ Troubleshooting three-tier problems

This chapter also provided several examples of troubleshooting that were encountered at my company. The resolution and prevention of these examples was also discussed.

There are two kinds of printer problems that you'll likely experience: paycheck printing problems and general printing problems. This chapter provided checklists of issues to check in troubleshooting both of these types of problems. This chapter also discussed the modification of two printer setup files for use with Hewlett-Packard LaserJet printers.

This book cannot provide examples for every problem that you may encounter with your PeopleSoft system. This chapter gave you some guidelines to follow when troubleshooting problems with your system.

Part IV, "Expanding the System," looks at techniques and software to help you extend your PeopleSoft system to other parts of the enterprise. Part IV will also look at some of the PeopleSoft strategic initiatives to help you plan for the future with your PeopleSoft system.

PART

III

Maintaining the System

# EXPANDING THE SYSTEM

*Chapter 18, "Extending PeopleSoft to the Enterprise," discusses how PeopleSoft is developing Web-enabled applications that allow the PeopleSoft applications to interface with the Internet. This chapter also describes how to add new functionality to your People-Soft installation. Chapter 19, "Planning for the Future," discusses how to control the customizations that you implement on your PeopleSoft system, how to monitor PeopleSoft's development strategies, and how to use PeopleDollars to influence what new functionality PeopleSoft decides to develop.*

# Extending PeopleSoft to the Enterprise

## FEATURING

▶ WEB-ENABLED PEOPLESOFT

▶ ADDING NEW FUNCTIONALITY TO YOUR
PEOPLESOFT SYSTEM

This chapter discusses some of the PeopleSoft functions that are designed to extend your PeopleSoft system to your company's entire enterprise. Many of the projects and applications described in this chapter require coordination between the business units throughout your company.

The first topic is the Web-enabled functionality of PeopleSoft. This chapter discusses the components and processes that make up this new technology and the advantages of implementing the Web-enabled applications in your organization.

Many companies need to add new functionality to their PeopleSoft system. The second part of this chapter addresses this topic and also discusses how to integrate your PeopleSoft system with third-party applications that add new functionality.

# Web-Enabled PeopleSoft

Beginning with version 7.0, PeopleSoft began shipping tools and Web applets for operation in a browser-based configuration. The Web-enabled applications are made possible by PeopleSoft's adoption of a three-tier architecture. There are, however, a few new components that make the applications function using Web technology. This section describes the components that make this possible and describes the applets that are available with PeopleSoft version 7.5. Using the Web technology, PeopleSoft began referring to this configuration as an *n*-tier client-server configuration. This chapter describes the *n*-tier configuration in detail.

**NOTE** The Web-enabled PeopleSoft applications do not require you to have Internet connectivity for them to work. You are simply using technology developed for use on the Internet to provide connectivity to large groups of users without needing to visit each individual workstation.

## The Components

The application server is a critical component of a three-tier configuration and is discussed in detail in Chapter 5, "Administration Tools." Two additional features of the three-tier application server must be activated for the Web applications to function: Jolt, and possibly Jolt Internet Relay and Jolt Relay Adapter, depending upon your configuration.

**Jolt**   Jolt is a product designed to communicate with Web clients for Tuxedo. Jolt takes the place of the workstation listeners and handlers for Web clients.

**Jolt Internet Relay and Jolt Relay Adapter**    The Jolt Internet Relay and Jolt Relay Adapter are products that are required to transfer Web client requests from your Web server to the Jolt listeners on your application server, if both servers are located on separate machines.

You must have a Web server to provide the initial connection to the PeopleSoft Web applets. PeopleSoft provides a Web server to run on your application server if you do not already have one available. Use your existing Web server if possible. PeopleSoft provides instructions on how to move the files to your Web server.

Now let's discuss the other components that are necessary for the Web-enabled People-Soft applications.

**Firewall**    A firewall is a device designed to prevent unauthorized access into your network or into portions of your network. There are two general types of firewalls: host-based and router-based. A host-based firewall is software-based and uses information about the application to validate access to the network. A proxy server is an example of a host-based firewall. A router-based firewall operates at the network level and screens TCP/IP header packets to determine if access should be granted.

**N O T E**    The source for much of this firewall information is the book *Network Security* by Fred Simonds.

**Web server**    A Web server is a specialized server that is designed to respond to requests from HTTP. A Web server may include provisions for FTP services.

**Internet browser**    The Internet (or Web) browser is the client module that allows the user to use documents and other programs that were designed with standard formats, such as HTML, so that the Internet browser can properly display the information, no matter what operating system the browser operates on. The two most widely known browsers are Netscape Navigator and Microsoft Internet Explorer.

Other functionality that goes beyond the Internet standards can be achieved through the use of programs designed to interpret the additional functionality. These programs are called plug-ins. For example, the new Adobe Acrobat plug-in launches the Acrobat Reader whenever a .pdf file is accessed.

Each Web client should have an Internet browser installed. The preferred browser with PeopleSoft version 7.0 is Microsoft Internet Explorer (IE). IE is the required browser for PeopleSoft version 7.5. PeopleSoft has stated that Netscape will again be supported with the release of version 8.

PeopleSoft provides functionality in PeopleTools to allow the Web client to run the applications that you develop on your own. For more information on PeopleTools, see Chapter 7, "Development Tools."

Let's take a closer look at the PeopleSoft Web architecture.

## The Architecture

This section discusses how all the components described in the previous section fit together to form a Web-enabled application. Refer to Figures 18.1 and 18.2 during this discussion. Figure 18.1 illustrates the components and communication paths for the logical *n*-tier PeopleSoft configuration. In this figure, the Web server, the application server, and the database server are all running on the same physical machine.

**FIGURE 18.1**    **PeopleSoft Web architecture–logical *n*-tier**

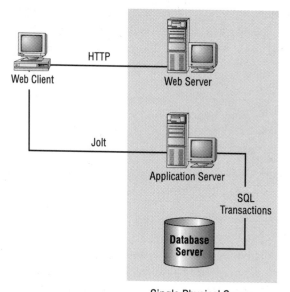

Single Physical Server

**1.** The Web client requests the application startup page from the Web server using the HTTP protocol.

**2.** The Web server sends the application startup page, along with the Jolt communicator application, back to the Web client.

**3.** The Jolt communicator application has configuration information that specifies the port number with which to access the application server's Jolt handler.

**4.** The transaction request is sent to the Jolt handler on the application server.

**5.** The application server translates this request into SQL and requests the proper information from the database server.

**6.** The database server executes the query and returns the results to the application server.

**7.** The application server returns the results directly back to the Web client.

---

**NOTE**  Notice that after the initial request for the Jolt client module, the Web server has no other function.

---

Now look at Figure 18.2, which contains the physical *n*-tier model. In this diagram, the Web server, application server, and database server are on separate servers. This figure also contains a firewall to illustrate how the communications look if you are using the Internet to connect some of your users.

**FIGURE 18.2**    PeopleSoft Web architecture–physical *n*-tier

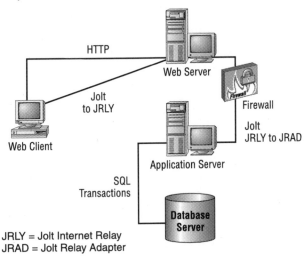

JRLY = Jolt Internet Relay
JRAD = Jolt Relay Adapter

**1.** The Web client requests the application startup page from the Web server using the HTTP protocol.

**2.** The Web server sends the application startup page, along with the Jolt communicator application, back to the Web client.

**3.** The Jolt Relay Adapter (JRAD) starts on the Web server.

**4.** The Jolt communicator application has configuration information that specifies the port number with which to access the JRAD on the Web server.

5. The transaction request is forwarded to the Jolt Relay (JRLY) handler on the application server.

6. The application server translates this request into SQL and requests the proper information from the database server.

7. The database server executes the query and returns the results to the application server.

8. The JRLY handler on the application server returns the results back to the JRAD adapter on the Web server.

9. The JRAD sends the results back to the Web client.

**NOTE**   In this example, the Web server is involved in all the transactions between the Web client and the application server.

This configuration is used when you have a full physical *n*-tier configuration, where the Web server, the application server, and the database server are on separate machines. It can also be used when the Web server is running separately from the logical three-tier application server and database server.

## The Functionality

PeopleSoft delivers several applications for Web deployment as part of the standard product, including the following applications:

▶ Employee Self-Service

▶ Expense Reporting

▶ Purchasing

▶ Course Enrollment

PeopleSoft will continue to introduce other applications with each new release. The PeopleSoft Web site (`http://www.peoplesoft.com`) contains additional and current information about the latest functions that are available.

## Advantages of Adopting the Web Applications

There are two major advantages to adopting Web-enabled applications for widespread deployment in your company:

**Ease of deployment**   Web applications can be deployed easily. Simply place a link that starts the application on a standard HTML page on your Web server. All subsequent users have the option to select this link.

**Ease of administration**    The administration of Web applications takes place primarily on the Web server and on any underlying application servers and databases. Program updates happen once, relieving the administrative staff from visiting each workstation.

In addition, many companies are implementing intranets for delivering information and internal applications to end users. The new PeopleSoft Web applications allow these companies to develop a consistent application delivery method.

# Adding New Functionality to Your PeopleSoft System

Most companies find it necessary to add functionality or to integrate their PeopleSoft systems with other applications. This section discusses the advantages of three possible approaches that the system administrator can take to implement new functionality.

## Implementing Additional PeopleSoft Applications

One way to add functionality to your PeopleSoft system is to purchase the additional functionality from PeopleSoft. When researching a request for new functionality, check with PeopleSoft to determine if the functionality exists in a current or future PeopleSoft product. The advantage of choosing additional PeopleSoft applications is that the in-house knowledge of the PeopleSoft applications will ensure that the new functionality is implemented properly and used effectively. It will also integrate smoothly with your existing PeopleSoft applications. You may be able to share some of the same equipment when running the new functionality.

## Developing Your Own Applications

You may choose to develop your own applications that integrate with your existing PeopleSoft application. There are two basic paths that you can take: building the applications using PeopleTools or building the applications using other development tools.

### Building the Application Using PeopleTools

You can use PeopleTools to develop your new application and integrate the entire application into the data model and structures of your existing PeopleSoft system. This option gives you close integration, and it gives you support for new operating systems as the PeopleTools versions are updated. This is especially important for an application that needs tight integration with the online or batch PeopleSoft processes. For example, my company added a panel to the Jobcode panel group to track the evaluation information for each position. We did this so that we could track the information used for evaluating each position using the Hay Compensation Study.

> **N O T E**   Your PeopleSoft licensing agreement may restrict the types of applications that you can develop. Check that agreement carefully.

## Building the Application with Other Development Tools

You can develop new applications with other development tools with which you are familiar, such as Visual Basic or PowerBuilder. This option is attractive if you want the new application to have some level of isolation from your existing PeopleSoft system. For example, my company is in the process of implementing a new timecard system. We wanted a Web-based timecard system that could be linked to the PeopleSoft data model for easier transfer of hours worked for payroll purposes. The current PeopleSoft Time and Labor modules did not contain the functionality that we needed, so we decided to build the new functionality using tools other than those supplied by PeopleSoft.

You may also choose this option if the deployment of the new application will be widespread and you don't want to continually upgrade and test this application as new PeopleTools and PeopleSoft application upgrades are implemented.

## Choosing Your Approach

You have reviewed the options; now you must make the choice. No two situations are exactly alike. However, there are a few basic considerations that can help you decide:

**Support**   The level of programming and end-user support that you have companywide is important in deciding whether to build with PeopleTools or not.

**Data ownership**   The owner of the data that must be accessed or updated by the new application may have policies or opinions about how their data should be accessed.

**User platforms**   The target platforms of the primary users of the new application may dictate which method you choose. If all the users have Web browsers, you may choose to implement a new application using the Web-enabled *n*-tier approach. If the users do not have Web browsers or your company has development standards, you may choose to develop the application using third-party development tools.

# Implementing Third-Party Applications

The third option for adding new functionality is the use of PeopleSoft partners and the applications they have developed to integrate with your PeopleSoft applications. Let's look at a few of the categories in which applications have already been developed.

**NOTE** If your company already has a third-party application that you would like to integrate with PeopleSoft, check with the vendor to see if they already provide this integration. They may be willing to work with you to provide one if you can convince them that other PeopleSoft customers might be interested in the same functionality.

## Voice-Response Systems

You may choose to implement some of your employee self-service, such as benefits enrollment, using integrated voice-response systems. Implementing a voice-response system provides your users with easy access to information. All that is required is a touch-tone phone and the user can register for benefits or change existing benefits without requiring that a PeopleSoft client be installed. The systems that are available link directly into your PeopleSoft tables to give you control over what a user can and cannot change. One vendor offers similar capabilities for remote entry of expense reports using a voice-response system.

Several vendors have voice-response systems currently available that integrate with PeopleSoft applications. Consult the Alliance Partners section of the PeopleSoft Web site for the latest information.

## Imaging/Document Management

There are at least two different ways to integrate imaging with your PeopleSoft system. The first method includes solutions for document management where the information is business documents integrating with the PeopleSoft HRMS or Financial applications.

The second path is integrating with PeopleSoft Manufacturing for the management of engineering documents and drawings using document management.

An example of one integration is with the HRMS applications. The vendor adds a button to several of the HRMS panels. When the user wants to select documents that reference the employee whose data is displayed, the user simply selects the Document button. The document management application starts (if it is not already running) and pulls up the information for the selected employee that the user has access to. This allows your users to move back and forth easily between the documents associated with an employee and the online data maintained by PeopleSoft.

There are vendors that can provide each of these solutions. Again, the latest information is on the PeopleSoft Web site.

## Light Directory Access Protocol (LDAP)

Lightweight Directory Access Protocol (LDAP) is a protocol defined by RFC 1777 that defines access to a subset of X.500 directory information. LDAP can provide easy access to information about objects that are defined in the directory server database. Employee information is the most common type of data being used with LDAP.

LDAP is a new integration for PeopleSoft that has recently been announced. Netscape has developed a product for the integration of the PeopleSoft Security and HRMS systems with the Netscape LDAP directory server. This product is called Netscape PerLDAP for PeopleSoft and automatically populates the Netscape Directory Server with information contained in the PeopleSoft database. This allows the sharing of this information for security access to other Web-enabled applications that can read the Netscape Directory Server.

Netscape has also released a product called the Netscape Application Server for PeopleSoft. This product is designed to provide Web access to PeopleSoft panels using the Message Agent API. This product provides functionality similar to the Jolt-enabled Tuxedo application server delivered by PeopleSoft. If your company is already using the Netscape Application Server for other processes, this product could be worth investigating.

**N O T E**   More information on the Netscape products discussed here is available on the Netscape Web site (http://home.netscape.com/).

## Network Domains

Plans are also in place to integrate PeopleSoft Security with the Windows NT domain structure to allow security access information to be configured and controlled from the Windows NT domain. The latest information shows that Windows NT integration is targeted for PeopleSoft version 8. Specific details of this functionality have not yet been released.

Novell has developed an integration tool called NDS (Novell Directory Services) Integration for PeopleSoft that links the hire process of an employee in PeopleSoft HRMS to the creation of a network account. For example, when a new employee record is created, a network account is automatically created for the new employee. If you use Novell GroupWise for e-mail, GroupWise can also create the e-mail account for the new employee. An added benefit of using NDS Integration for PeopleSoft is that when employee information—such as a work phone number—is changed in PeopleSoft, NDS is synchronized automatically. This can streamline the process of creating user accounts for all employees for self-service applications, since the information is only entered once.

You can also use NDS as the single point of authentication for casual users. Once a user has been authenticated by NDS, access is granted to PeopleSoft information for that user without the user having to login again. The PeopleSoft system administrator maintains full control over what access is granted using the NDS Integration tool.

NDS Integration for PeopleSoft is currently available from the Novell Consulting Group.

**N O T E**  You can visit the Novell Web site (`http://www.novell.com/`) for more information about the NDS Integration for PeopleSoft product.

# Summary

Once you have your basic PeopleSoft applications implemented, you will probably need to provide access to more users throughout your enterprise. You have two options available to help you do this.

Web-enabled PeopleSoft allows you to deliver PeopleSoft access using standard Web browsers. You can use delivered PeopleSoft tools and Web-based applets to accomplish this. These Web-based applications are made possible by PeopleSoft's adoption of a three-tier architecture.

In addition, you can add new functionality to your PeopleSoft system by adding new PeopleSoft functionality, developing your own applications, or purchasing applications from third-party vendors.

Chapter 19, "Planning for the Future," will provide guidance to help you continue to make your PeopleSoft applications successful.

# Planning for the Future

## FEATURING

- ▶ CONTROLLING CUSTOMIZATIONS

- ▶ PEOPLESOFT STRATEGY

- ▶ PEOPLEDOLLARS BALLOTING

**T**his chapter reviews some of the concepts introduced earlier in this book. This chapter will give you some ideas to apply as you take your PeopleSoft system into the future. I will also discuss ways that you can influence the direction in which PeopleSoft takes their applications in the future.

# Controlling Customizations

As you move into the future with your PeopleSoft applications, you may have a tendency to introduce more and more customizations into your PeopleSoft system. These customizations may be the result of increased familiarity with the product combined with your users' desire to implement new functionality. As the developers become more familiar with the PeopleSoft applications and tables, they are more likely to attempt customizations.

Review the information in Chapter 3, "Customizations." This chapter will remind you about the considerations that should be addressed when customizing your PeopleSoft application.

Continue to monitor the customization requests carefully. Remember to review the PeopleSoft sources of information, such as Customer Connection, to determine if the requested new functionality is available in other modules or is planned for a future release.

Monitoring the customizations you perform should position you well for future PeopleSoft upgrades. While PeopleSoft provides scripts to help migrate your customizations to the new release, reviewing the upgrade comparison reports can become quite tedious if you have implemented several upgrades without removing any of them.

One final word on customizations: Review your current customizations with each upgrade to determine if the new release provides the same or similar functionality as the customization. Compare the functionality provided by the PeopleSoft upgrade to the functionality of your customization and ask yourself the following questions:

▶ Does the new PeopleSoft functionality better meet the needs of the end users?

▶ How will the customization affect future PeopleSoft upgrades?

▶ How hard will it be to train the end users to use the functionality provided by the PeopleSoft upgrade?

▶ Can the current business processes be adapted to fit the new PeopleSoft functionality?

Review and select the best option for your environment: adopting the PeopleSoft functionality and deleting your customization or keeping your customization and not implementing that part of the PeopleSoft upgrade. If you choose to implement the new PeopleSoft functionality, define any setup parameters and enable access for your users. Migrate the required information from your current process to the tables that support the new functionality. Once the users are satisfied with the new process, delete all the PeopleSoft objects (panels, records, menus) that supported the old functionality and/or the customization.

**NOTE** I recommend that you initially remove the PeopleSoft objects from your users' security access profiles, in case you need to compare information, then delete the objects at a later date.

# PeopleSoft Strategies

The PeopleSoft strategies for applications and support are continually evolving as the computing and business environment changes. Make yourself aware of the strategies that PeopleSoft is pursuing using the following techniques:

▶ Attend the PeopleSoft Users' Conference. This is a good opportunity to hear presentations on the PeopleSoft strategy.

▶ Attend any meetings or participate in any teleconferences that are available to help you better understand PeopleSoft's strategy.

▶ Review Customer Connection, looking for information that announces new functionality or strategies being developed by PeopleSoft.

▶ Subscribe to mailing lists from PeopleSoft that provide information ranging from fixes to upcoming conference calls.

▶ Locate and join your local users' group. This can provide you with a list of contacts with whom to share ideas.

▶ Get involved with the special interest groups (SIGs) that cover topics of interest to your company. Some examples of SIGs are the Financial Services SIG, Production Account Management, and the Large HRMS SIG.

▶ Visit the PeopleSoft Web site, http://www.peoplesoft.com, on a regular basis. The information on the public Web site is updated on a regular basis and may contain information not found on Customer Connection.

Information from these sources will help you in planning for the future of your own PeopleSoft system.

When PeopleSoft was originally conceived, many companies conducted business quite differently than they do today. Some of these changes include the following:

▶ Companies are implementing electronic commerce systems on the Internet.

▶ Industries are also becoming more specific in their computing needs. They need software that carries out specific business functions in their organizations.

▶ Companies are more willing to purchase business software than to invest the resources to develop the product themselves, as they might have done in the past.

▶ Multinational companies are demanding that ERP providers, such as People-Soft, and other high-technology companies provide better methods for managing their global corporations.

Let's look at the actions being taken by PeopleSoft to adjust to these business demands.

## e-Business

PeopleSoft has just introduced an e-business strategy. This initiative focuses on both external and internal business customers. The goal of PeopleSoft's e-business strategy is to enable customers to conduct commercial transactions and exchange information over the Internet. e-business integrates the PeopleSoft system of applications with the Internet. The e-business strategy moves toward a universal desktop from which the end users carry out routine tasks using a desktop that can be customized for each individual user's job duties and personal desires.

The components of PeopleSoft's e-business strategy are:

**Backbone**    The e-business backbone allows users of the e-business applications to use their everyday PeopleSoft applications from their desktop. Many of the People-Soft applications will be adapted for e-business users. The backbone also provides integration points for third-party applications.

**PeopleSoft Business Network (PSBN)**    PSBN allows organizations to identify network content, both internal and external, that their end users require to do their job. This enables users to work more productively. Customers will be able to install e-business communities, which are groups of applications that perform a specific role in the organization. Some examples of e-business communities that PeopleSoft plans to make available over time are:

- Affinity Programs
- Asset Management
- Communications
- Employee Benefits
- Payroll - Procurement
- Profile Management
- Recruitment & Training
- Telecom Services
- Time & Labor
- Travel & Expense Management
- Workforce Management

**Extensions**  e-business extensions are applications that expand the number of business processes that can be conducted over internal and external networks. e-business extensions include PeopleSoft-delivered applications and products developed by third-party vendors.

**NOTE**  The information in this section came from the PeopleSoft Web site (http://www.peoplesoft.com). More detailed information about e-business can be found there.

## Industry-Specific Applications

PeopleSoft has transitioned their sales and support infrastructure to align with industries. The Industry Business Unit (IBU) structure has been in place for just over a year. PeopleSoft defines 11 distinct business units and designs groups of applications to meet the unique needs of each business unit. The 11 business units are:

- Communications
- Federal Government
- Financial Services

▶ Healthcare

▶ Higher Education

▶ Manufacturing

▶ Public Sector

▶ Retail

▶ Service Industries

▶ Transportation

▶ Utilities

The focus of the PeopleSoft effort is now turning to similarities between companies in the same industry. The goal is to introduce application modules that are specific to an industry (or sub-industry). For example, PeopleSoft has acquired Intrepid systems to provide retail management solutions to the retail industry and TriMark Technologies for the insurance industry. PeopleSoft plans to continue this trend of adding industry-specific functionality.

The Enterprise Solution Assembly diagram, shown in Figure 19.1, shows the Industry and Sub-Industry focus that is being implemented.

**FIGURE 19.1**    **Enterprise Solution Assembly**

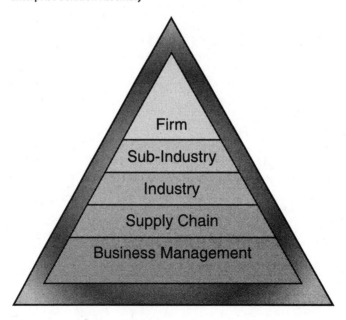

PeopleSoft has three approaches to delivering applications to meet the requirements of each category:

▶ Develop the applications at PeopleSoft and integrate them with existing applications.

▶ Buy the applications from third-party vendors and integrate them with existing applications.

▶ Partner with third-party vendors whose products can interface with People-Soft applications.

The recent acquisition of TriMark Technologies, developer of software for the insurance industry, represents one of the first steps in the move to this strategy.

PeopleSoft also continues to develop Alliance Partners that can provide additional functionality for their customers. Some examples of PeopleSoft's Alliance Partners are discussed in Chapter 18, "Extending PeopleSoft to the Enterprise."

# Globalization

PeopleSoft has been working toward the globalization of their entire product line. Their goal is to be a single source for the ERP systems that manage your company's business worldwide. PeopleSoft wants to provide an integrated system that can translate currency on demand or schedule manufacturing in one country based on the demand in another country from a single system. The goal of globalization is an integrated system that works in multiple languages and integrates data from several different financial systems.

The HRMS product line is being marketed in numerous countries. The Payroll application is being delivered for various countries and can support a multinational payroll, with employees being paid in different currencies and on different schedules.

PeopleSoft has also announced support for the European Monetary Unit (EMU). The new European currency will be supported by all Financial applications as well as by the Payroll application in the participating countries.

PeopleSoft's globalization goal is that a single global product can allow companies to reduce internal support costs. The global architecture is designed to give you the flexibility to implement the PeopleSoft applications in countries that are not even targeted by PeopleSoft by adding the localization yourself. PeopleSoft's globalization strategy is an advantage to your company if you do business internationally, or if you anticipate doing business internationally in the future.

# PeopleDollars Balloting

Each year, PeopleSoft customers are given the opportunity to cast their ballot for new functionality to be added to the PeopleSoft products. PeopleSoft uses the term "dollars" to define your votes. You are given a set amount of fictitious dollars with which to vote on proposed functions. You can place all your "money" on one function or spread them across several functions. Each customer receives "money" for People-Tools and for global functionality. You are given an additional amount based on the other modules purchased by your company.

PeopleDollars balloting allows each customer to influence the direction that People-Soft pursues in developing new functionality. This system also allows users' groups or special interest groups to rally behind specific functionality by "block" voting to push for new functionality that meets the needs of a particular group of users. For example, a group of insurance companies might pool their PeopleDollars to push for a critical application enhancement that can improve the processing of certain transactions.

# Summary

This chapter briefly outlined processes that you need to monitor to help take your PeopleSoft system into the future.

Continue to control and review your customizations as new PeopleSoft versions become available. Maintain a detailed customization log to refer to as new releases are delivered. Some of your customizations may no longer be necessary if PeopleSoft has implemented the changes in a new release.

Continually monitor and update yourself on the strategies that PeopleSoft is pursuing for its applications. You might want to assign this task to a specific employee. Monitor Customer Connection, the PeopleSoft Web site (http://www.peoplesoft.com), and keep in touch with other customers via mailing lists and users' groups.

Participate in the PeopleDollars process. It is your opportunity to influence the functionality that PeopleSoft adds to future releases.

# PART V

# APPENDICES

*Appendix A, "Sample Programs," contains the source code for example programs used throughout this book. Appendix B, "Sample Reports," contains excerpts from the two types of reports described in Chapter 6, "Data Management Tools." Appendix C, "The Parse-Name Function for Microsoft Excel," contains the source code for a Microsoft Excel function called The `ParseName` that parses the PeopleSoft name field into its various parts.*

# *Sample Programs*

**FEATURING:**

▶ **NEW SALARY RANGES PROGRAM EXAMPLE**

▶ **SQR PROGRAM EXAMPLES**

▶ **INCLUDE FILES**

# New Salary Ranges Program Example

This appendix contains the code for program examples discussed in this book. The examples are organized by the chapter that describes their use. Refer to the appropriate chapter for more detailed information.

## Chapter 3, "Customization"

### ALB_SLGR.SQR

```
!****************** Program IDENTIFICATION ******************
! File Name:    ALB_SLGR.SQR
! File Title:   New Salary Grade Ranges
! Author:       DB
! Date Written: 10/28/97
! --------------------------------------------------------------
! Functional Description:
!   This SQR reads the ALB_SAL_FORM table to get the new slope
!   and intercept for each sal_admin_plan for the new effective
!   date, selects the information from the sal_admin_plan table
!   and alb_grade_pts table using the thru date, and inserts a
!   record with the new range into the sal_grade_tbl.
!
! Database Tables:
!     PS_ALB_SAL_FORM          - read
!     PS_SAL_GRADE_TBL         - read/insert
!     PS_ALB_GRADE_PTS         - read
!
! Input:
!     Database tables
!
! Output:
!     ALB_SLGR.LIS
!
!*****************************************************************
! Update 6/16/1998 by SB
!     Update to use run control panel.
!*****************************************************************
!
#include 'setenv.sqc'    !Set environment
```

```
begin-report
do Get-Run-Values
  do Get-Sal-Form
  do main
  do Reset
  do Stdapi-Term
end-report

begin-procedure Get-Run-Values
   do Stdapi-Init
   if $prcs_process_instance = ''
    do ask-from-thru-date
   else
    do Select-Parameters
   end-if
   let $FromDate = RTRIM(&RC_ALB.FROMDATE, ' ')
   let $ThruDate = RTRIM(&RC_ALB.THRUDATE, ' ')
end-procedure

begin-procedure Get-Sal-Form
begin-select
F.SAL_ADMIN_PLAN
F.ALB_SLOPE
F.ALB_INTERCEPT
  if &F.SAL_ADMIN_PLAN = 'NEX'
     move &F.ALB_SLOPE to #nexslope
     move &F.ALB_INTERCEPT to #nexintrcpt
  end-if
  if &F.SAL_ADMIN_PLAN = 'EXM'
     move &F.ALB_SLOPE to #exmslope
     move &F.ALB_INTERCEPT to #exmintrcpt
  end-if
  if &F.SAL_ADMIN_PLAN = 'OFF'
     move &F.ALB_SLOPE to #offslope
     move &F.ALB_INTERCEPT to #offintrcpt
  end-if
from PS_ALB_SAL_FORM F
where F.EFFDT = $FromDate
end-select
end-procedure

begin-procedure main
begin-select
```

```
A.SAL_ADMIN_PLAN
A.GRADE
A.EFFDT
A.EFF_STATUS
A.DESCR
A.DESCRSHORT
A.SALARY_MATRIX_CD
A.RATING_SCALE
A.MIN_RT_HOURLY
A.MID_RT_HOURLY
A.MAX_RT_HOURLY
A.MIN_RT_MONTHLY
A.MID_RT_MONTHLY
A.MAX_RT_MONTHLY
A.MIN_RT_ANNUAL
A.MID_RT_ANNUAL
A.MAX_RT_ANNUAL
A.STEP_INCREM_TYPE
A.STEP_INCREM_ACCUM
B.POINTS
   move &B.POINTS to #grpts
   move &A.SAL_ADMIN_PLAN to $salplan
   do Calculate-New-Range
   do Insert-New-Range
   do Print-New-Midpoints
from PS_SAL_GRADE_TBL A, PS_ALB_GRADE_PTS B
where A.EFFDT = $ThruDate
and B.SAL_ADMIN_PLAN = A.SAL_ADMIN_PLAN
and B.GRADE = A.GRADE
end-select
end-procedure

begin-procedure Calculate-New-Range
   if $salplan = 'NEX'
     let #tempmid = (#nexslope * #grpts) + #nexintrcpt
     let #minannual = round(#tempmid * .8,0)
     let #maxannual = round(#tempmid *1.2,0)
   end-if
   if $salplan = 'EXM'
     let #tempmid = (#exmslope * #grpts) + #exmintrcpt
     let #minannual = round(#tempmid * .8,0)
     let #maxannual = round(#tempmid *1.2,0)
   end-if
```

```
    if $salplan = 'OFF'
      let #tempmid = (#offslope * #grpts) + #offintrcpt
      let #minannual = round(#tempmid * .8,0)
      let #maxannual = round(#tempmid *1.2,0)
    end-if
    let #midannual = round((#minannual + #maxannual)/2,0)
    let #minmonth = round((#minannual/12),2)
    let #midmonth = round((#midannual/12),2)
    let #maxmonth = round((#maxannual/12),2)
    let #minhrly = round((#minannual/2080),3)
    let #midhrly = round((#midannual/2080),3)
    let #maxhrly = round((#maxannual/2080),3)
end-procedure

begin-procedure Insert-New-Range
begin-SQL
Insert into PS_SAL_GRADE_TBL
(SAL_ADMIN_PLAN,
GRADE,
EFFDT,
EFF_STATUS,
DESCR,
DESCRSHORT,
SALARY_MATRIX_CD,
RATING_SCALE,
MIN_RT_HOURLY,
MID_RT_HOURLY,
MAX_RT_HOURLY,
MIN_RT_MONTHLY,
MID_RT_MONTHLY,
MAX_RT_MONTHLY,
MIN_RT_ANNUAL,
MID_RT_ANNUAL,
MAX_RT_ANNUAL,
STEP_INCREM_TYPE,
STEP_INCREM_ACCUM)
Values
(&A.SAL_ADMIN_PLAN,
&A.GRADE,
$FromDate,
&A.EFF_STATUS,
&A.DESCR,
&A.DESCRSHORT,
```

```
                    &A.SALARY_MATRIX_CD,
                    &A.RATING_SCALE,
                    round(#minhrly,4),
                    round(#midhrly,4),
                    round(#maxhrly,4),
                    round(#minmonth,2),
                    round(#midmonth,2),
                    round(#maxmonth,2),
                    round(#minannual,0),
                    round(#midannual,0),
                    round(#maxannual,0),
                    &A.STEP_INCREM_TYPE,
                    &A.STEP_INCREM_ACCUM)
                    end-SQL
                    end-procedure


                    ! The users want a report to see what is being inserted.
                    begin-procedure Print-New-Midpoints
                    print &A.SAL_ADMIN_PLAN    (0,0,3)
                    print &A.GRADE             (0,+3,3)
                    print #tempmid             (0,+3,8) EDIT $999,999
                    print #minannual           (0,+4,8) EDIT $999,999
                    print #midannual           (0,+4,8) EDIT $999,999
                    print #maxannual           (0,+4,8) EDIT $999,999
                    print #grpts               (0,+3,4) EDIT 9999
                    end-procedure


                    begin-setup
                      page-size 1 63
                      no-formfeed
                    end-setup
                    #include 'rc_alb.sqc'     !Company specific run control routines
                    #include 'datetime.sqc'   !Date handling routines
                    #Include 'stdapi.sqc'     !Routines to update run status
                    #include 'askftd.sqc'     !Ask from/thru date – command line execution
                    #Include 'reset.sqc'      !Reset printer procedure
```

**NOTE**   An example of an include file is at the end of this appendix in alphabetical order.

# SQR Program Examples

The three examples in this section correspond to the three examples of SQR program at the end of Chapter 10.

## Chapter 10, "SQR"

### Example 1: New Salary Ranges

See the code for ALB_SLGR.SQR in the previous section.

### Example 2: 401K Loan Report

This SQR generates a list containing 401K loan repayment information for employees whose balance remaining is less than their deduction amount.

---

**ALB_RPAY.SQR**

```
!****************** Program IDENTIFICATION *************************
!
!  File Name:    ALB_RPAY.SQR
!  File Title:   401k LOAN REPAYMENT
!  Date Written: 01/07/97
!  ----------------------------------------------------------------
!  Functional Description:
!    This SQR joins the PAY_EARNINGS and PAY_DEDUCTION tables to pull
!    data based on pay end date. The data is sorted in EMPLID order
!    and a report is created with employee name and the amount of the
!    deduction for the loan, loan number. A total for the deduction
!    code is produced at the end.
!
!  Database Tables:
!      PS_PAY_EARNINGS        -  read
!      PS_PAY_DEDUCTION       -  read
!      PS_PERSONAL_DATA       -  read
!      PS_GENL_DEDUCTION      -  read
!
!  Input:
!      Database tables
!
```

```
!  Output:
!      ALB_PAYD.LIS
!
!************************************************************************

#include 'setenv.sqc'        !Set environment
#Include 'setup01.sqc'       !Printer and page-size initialization

begin-report
  do Init-DateTime
  do Init-Number
  do Get-Current-DateTime
  do Init-Report
  do Process-Main
  do Reset
  do Stdapi-Term
end-report

begin-heading 7
  #Include 'stdhdg03.sqc'
end-heading


!************************************************************************
!
!  Function: Init-Report
!  Description:  Set up report titles, handle asking for parms when
!               running outside Process Scheduler, handle getting
!               parms when running thru Process Scheduler.
!
!************************************************************************
begin-procedure Init-Report

  move 'Bi-Weekly 401k Loan Audit' to $ReportTitle
  move 'ALB_RPAY' to $ReportID
  display $ReportTitle
  do Stdapi-Init

  if $prcs_process_instance = ''
    do Get-E-Date
  else
    do Select-Parameters
```

```
      do Get-Values
   end-if

end-procedure


!*********************************************************************
!
!  Function: Get-Values
!  Description:  Get input parms into program variables.
!
!*********************************************************************
begin-procedure Get-Values

   do Get-Pay-End-Dt

end-procedure


!*********************************************************************
!
!  Function: Process-Main
!  Description:  Main driver.  Opens files, gets data, and ends report.
!
!*********************************************************************
begin-procedure Process-Main

  do Open-Files
  Let $AsOfDate = $PAYDT
  do Data-Selection
  do Setup-Report

end-procedure


!*********************************************************************
!
!  Function: Open-Files
!  Description:  Open files and initialize accumulators.
!
!*********************************************************************
begin-procedure Open-Files

!  open '/sybase/psoft/extract/alb_rpay.log'   as   1
   open 'c:\payderr.log'    as    1
```

```
                    for-writing
                    record=250:fixed
                    status = #write1
                    if #write1 = -1
                        display 'Open for error log file failed'
                        stop quiet
                    end-if
                    lET #accum = 0
                    Let #page_cnt = 1
                    Let #line_cnt = 85
                    Let $error_flg = 'N'


end-procedure Open-Files


!*********************************************************************
!
!  Function: Data-Selection
!  Description:  Joins PAY_EARNINGS and PAY_DEDUCTION on COMPANY,
!                PAYGROUP, PAY END DATE, OFF CYCLE, LINE# and PAGE#
!                and the maximum along with max ADDL# from PAY_EARNINGS.
!                The deduction class for company match (P, N, T) are
!                bypassed.  The input parm of PAY END DATE is also
!                used as furthur criteria. The Employee name is selected
!                from PERSONAL_DATA and the Deduction Code is used to
!                read GENL_DEDUCTION for goal amount and goal balance.
!                As each line is selected it is printed on a report.
!
!*********************************************************************
begin-procedure Data-Selection


begin-SELECT on-error=format-sql-error
A.EMPLID
B.PAY_END_DT
B.DEDCD
B.DED_CUR
B.PAGE#
B.LINE#

      Let $DEDCD     = &B.DEDCD
      LET $EMPLID    = &A.EMPLID
      Let #PAGE      = &B.PAGE#
```

```
        Let #LINE       = &B.LINE#
        Let #DED_CUR    = &B.DED_CUR
        move '-' to $DDelimiter
        do Format-DateTime(&B.PAY_END_DT, $PAY_DATE, {DEFYMD}, '', '')
        do Get-Personal-Data
        do Get-Deduct-Data
        Let #accum      = #accum + &B.DED_CUR
        LET $DED_CUR    = TO_CHAR(&B.DED_CUR)
        LET $GOAL_B     = TO_CHAR(#GOAL_BAL)
        LET $GOAL_A     = TO_CHAR(#GOAL_AMT)
        LET $AMT        = edit($DED_CUR,'999,999.99MI')
        LET $GOAL_BAL   = edit($GOAL_B,'999,999.99MI')
        LET $GOAL_AMT   = edit($GOAL_A,'999,999.99MI')
        Let $loan_num   = to_char(#ALB_LOAN_NUM)
        Let #amount_left = #goal_amt - (#goal_bal + (#ded_cur * 2))
        If #amount_left  <= 0
           IF #line_cnt > 64
               do Print-Heading
           End-if
           do Print-Line
        End-if
     FROM PS_PAY_EARNINGS A,
          PS_PAY_DEDUCTION B
    WHERE A.PAY_END_DT  =       B.PAY_END_DT
      AND A.COMPANY      =      B.COMPANY
      AND A.PAYGROUP     =      B.PAYGROUP
      AND A.PAGE#        =      B.PAGE#
      AND A.LINE#        =      B.LINE#
      AND A.OFF_CYCLE    =      B.OFF_CYCLE
      AND A.PAY_END_DT   =      $PAYDT
      AND B.DEDCD       like   'LOAN%'
      AND ((B.DED_CLASS <>     'N')
      AND  (B.DED_CLASS <>     'P')
      AND  (B.DED_CLASS <>     'T'))
      AND A.ADDL#        =
          (SELECT MAX(M.ADDL#)
           FROM PS_PAY_EARNINGS M
          WHERE M.PAY_END_DT = A.PAY_END_DT
            AND M.PAGE#      = A.PAGE#
            AND M.LINE#      = A.LINE#
            AND M.COMPANY    = A.COMPANY
```

```
                    AND M.PAYGROUP    = A.PAYGROUP
                    AND M.OFF_CYCLE   = A.OFF_CYCLE)
        Order By 1,3


end-SELECT


End-Procedure Data-Selection


!**********************************************************************
!
!  Function: Setup-Report
!  Description:  Checks error flag. If it has been set, then a
!                message is displayed for the user to get the error
!                log printed.
!
!**********************************************************************
Begin-Procedure Setup-Report


If $error_flg = 'Y'
    display '**********************************************************'
    display '**********************************************************'
    display '***            ERRORS HAVE BEEN DETECTED              ***'
    display '***          PLEASE HAVE ERROR LOG PRINTED            ***'
    display '**********************************************************'
    display '**********************************************************'
End-if


end-procedure Setup-Report


!**********************************************************************
!
!  Function: Print-Heading
!  Description:  Checks line count for paging.  Prints headings for
!                report.
!
!**********************************************************************
Begin-Procedure Print-Heading
  If #line_cnt < 80
      new-page
  End-if
  Let #line_cnt = 10
```

```
        print ' 401k Loan Repayment for Biweekly ' (+1,33,34)
        print $PAYDT (,67,12)
        print ' Payroll' (,79,8)
        print ' ' (+1,11,70)
        print ' EMP ID        Name                        SSN '   (+1,4,54)
        print 'Deducted Amt    Balance        Goal     Loan Num  '  (,66,58)
        print '--------      ------------------------  --------'   (+1,4,55)
        print '------------  ------------  -----------  --------- '  (,66,58)
End-Procedure


!*********************************************************************
!
!   Function: Print-Line
!   Description:  Prints each data line.
!
!*********************************************************************
Begin-Procedure Print-Line
    print $EMPLID (+1,5,5)
    print $NAME (,17,30)
    print $SSN (,50,9)
    print $AMT (,64,11)
    print $GOAL_BAL (,80,11)
    print $GOAL_AMT (,96,11)
    print $LOAN_NUM (,114,3)


    LET #line_cnt = #line_cnt + 1
End-Procedure


!*********************************************************************
!
!   Function: Get-Personal-Data
!   Description:  Uses EMPLID from the data selection to read
!                 PERSONAL_DATA for SSN and Employee Name.
!
!*********************************************************************
BEGIN-PROCEDURE Get-Personal-data
Let $SSN   = ' '
Let $NAME  = ' '

BEGIN-SELECT on-error=format-sql-error
C.NAME,
```

```
C.SSN
  Let $SSN    = &C.SSN
  Let $NAME   = &C.NAME
 from PS_PERSONAL_DATA C
where C.EMPLID  = $EMPLID
End-SELECT


End-Procedure Get-Personal-Data


!**********************************************************************
!
!  Function: Get-Deduct-Desc
!  Description:  Uses the Deduction Code from the data selection
!                to read GENL_DEDUCTION for goal amount and goal
!                balance.
!
!**********************************************************************
BEGIN-PROCEDURE Get-Deduct-Data

BEGIN-SELECT on-error=format-sql-error
D.DED_ADDL_AMT
D.GOAL_AMT
D.GOAL_BAL
D.ALB_LOAN_NUM

    Let #DED_ADDL_AMT  = &D.DED_ADDL_AMT
    Let #GOAL_AMT      = &D.GOAL_AMT
    Let #GOAL_BAL      = &D.GOAL_BAL
    Let #alb_loan_num       = &D.ALB_LOAN_NUM

  from PS_GENL_DEDUCTION D
where D.DEDCD  = $DEDCD
  AND D.EMPLID = $EMPLID
  AND D.EFFDT =
      (SELECT MAX(H.EFFDT)
       FROM PS_GENL_DEDUCTION H
      WHERE H.EFFDT <= $PAYDT
        AND H.EMPLID = $EMPLID
        AND H.DEDCD  = $DEDCD)
End-SELECT


End-Procedure Get-Deduct-Data
```

```
!***********************************************************************
!
!  Function: Format-SQL-Error
!  Description:  Formats and writes log record.  Also turns on error
!                flag.
!
!***********************************************************************
Begin-Procedure Format-Sql-Error
    Let $RECORD = $EMPLID || ' ' || $DEDCD || ' ' || $PAY_DATE || ':' ||
$sql-error
    Write 3 from $RECORD
    Let $error_flg = 'Y'
    Display $sql-error
End-Procedure Format-Sql-Error


#include 'rc_alb.sqc'     !Company-specific run control routines
#include 'askeffdt.sqc'   !Ask From/Thru Date
#Include 'getjobtl.sqc'   !Get-Job-Title procedure
#Include 'datemath.sqc'   !Routines for date arithmetic
#Include 'reset.sqc'      !Reset printer procedure
#Include 'curdttim.sqc'   !Get-Current-DateTime procedure
#Include 'datetime.sqc'   !Routines for date and time formatting
#Include 'number.sqc'     !Routines to format numbers
#Include 'stdapi.sqc'     !Routines to Update Run Status
```

## Example 3: Census Report

This report currently runs from the command line only. It has not been implemented into a PeopleSoft menu to be run from the Process Scheduler.

### ALCENSUS.SQR

```
!  alcensus.sqr   06/10/98   Create Company Census Report.  Time
!                            comparison between 2 points in time.
!  Created by Darrell Bilbrey

begin-report
  do Get-Input
  do Initialize-Variables
  do Set-First-Date
```

```
          do main
          do Set-Second-Date
          do main
          do Compare
          do Print-Report
      end-report

      ! Get run parameter either from prompts (if on command line) or
      ! from run controls established inside PeopleSoft
      begin-procedure Get-Input
        if $Prcs_Process_Instance = ''
          display 'Enter Dates for Comparison: (YYYY-MM-DD)' noline
          input $firstdate maxlen=10 'Enter earlier date:' type=char
          input $secondate maxlen=10 'Enter later date:'
        else
      end-if
      end-procedure

      !  Establish parameter for first pass through PS_JOB table
      begin-procedure Set-First-Date
        move $firstdate to $calcdate
      end-procedure

      !  Establish parameter for second pass through PS_JOB table
      begin-procedure Set-Second-Date
        move $secondate to $calcdate
      end-procedure

      !  Create and initialize the arrays for the calculation
      begin-procedure Initialize-Variables
      create-array name=date1 size=7
          field=divis:char
          field=off:number
          field=mgr:number
          field=exm:number
          field=nex:number
          field=pt:number
          field=tot:number

      create-array name=date2 size=7
          field=divis:char
          field=off:number
```

```
            field=mgr:number
            field=exm:number
            field=nex:number
            field=pt:number
            field=tot:number

create-array name=compdate size=7
            field=divis:char
            field=off:number
            field=mgr:number
            field=exm:number
            field=nex:number
            field=pt:number
            field=tot:number

!  Initialize date1 array
put 'Claims',0,0,0,0,0,0 into date1(0)
put 'Corporate Resources',0,0,0,0,0,0 into date1(1)
put 'Finance',0,0,0,0,0,0 into date1(2)
put 'Special Claims',0,0,0,0,0,0 into date1(3)
put 'Marketing',0,0,0,0,0,0 into date1(4)
put 'Medical Director',0,0,0,0,0,0 into date1(5)
put 'Other',0,0,0,0,0,0 into date1(6)

!  Initialize date2 array
put 'Claims',0,0,0,0,0,0 into date2(0)
put 'Corporate Resources',0,0,0,0,0,0 into date2(1)
put 'Finance',0,0,0,0,0,0 into date2(2)
put 'Special Claims',0,0,0,0,0,0 into date2(3)
put 'Marketing',0,0,0,0,0,0 into date2(4)
put 'Medical Director',0,0,0,0,0,0 into date2(5)
put 'Other',0,0,0,0,0,0 into date2(6)

!  Initialize compdate array
put 'Claims',0,0,0,0,0,0 into compdate(0)
put 'Corporate Resources',0,0,0,0,0,0 into compdate(1)
put 'Finance',0,0,0,0,0,0 into compdate(2)
put 'Special Claims',0,0,0,0,0,0 into compdate(3)
put 'Marketing',0,0,0,0,0,0 into compdate(4)
put 'Medical Director',0,0,0,0,0,0 into compdate(5)
put 'Other',0,0,0,0,0,0 into compdate(6)

end-procedure
```

APP.

**A**

Sample Programs

```
!    Main processing procedure that will select the data and
!    update the correct array
begin-procedure main
move 0 to #totrec

move 1 to #cntfld
move ',' to $pholder
move ' ' to $emailfld
begin-select
A.EMPLID
A.DEPTID
A.SAL_ADMIN_PLAN
A.EMPL_STATUS
Z.ETHNIC_GROUP
A.FULL_PART_TIME
H.MANAGER_LEVEL
A.LOCATION
  move &A.EMPLID to $emplid
  move &A.LOCATION to $locate
  if &A.SAL_ADMIN_PLAN <> 'NEX'
    do Check-Dept-ID
    if $deptid = ' '
      move &A.DEPTID to $deptid
    end-if
  else
    move &A.DEPTID to $deptid
  end-if
let $divid = substr($deptid,1,2)
  do Get-Division-Category
  if &A.FULL_PART_TIME = 'P'
    move 'Part Time' to $emplevel
  else
    if &A.SAL_ADMIN_PLAN = 'NEX'
      move 'Non-Exempt' to $emplevel
    end-if
    if &A.SAL_ADMIN_PLAN = 'OFF'
      move 'Officer' to $emplevel
    end-if
    if &A.SAL_ADMIN_PLAN = 'EXM'
      move 'Exempt' to $emplevel
      if &H.MANAGER_LEVEL = 'B3'
```

```
                    move 'Manager' to $emplevel
            end-if
          end-if
       end-if
       if $calcdate = $firstdate
         do Create-Totals-Date1
       end-if
       if $calcdate = $secondate
         do Create-Totals-Date2
       end-if
! do Write-File ! Create download file
       add 1 to #totrec
       move ' ' to $deptid
       move ' ' to $divid
from HRPROD..PS_JOB A, HRPROD..PS_JOBCODE_TBL H,
HRPROD..PS_PERSONAL_DATA Z
where A.COMPANY='BC1'
!and A.EMPL_STATUS <> 'T'
and A.EMPL_STATUS in ('A','P','L')
and Z.EMPLID = A.EMPLID
and A.EFFDT = (select max(K.EFFDT)
              from HRPROD..PS_JOB K
                where K.EMPLID = A.EMPLID
                and K.EFFDT <= $calcdate)
and A.EFFSEQ = (select max(L.EFFSEQ)
               from HRPROD..PS_JOB L
                 where L.EMPLID = A.EMPLID
                 and L.EFFDT = A.EFFDT)
and H.JOBCODE = A.JOBCODE
and H.EFF_STATUS = 'A'
and H.EFFDT = (select max(I.EFFDT)
              from HRPROD..PS_JOBCODE_TBL I
               where I.JOBCODE = H.JOBCODE
                  and I.EFFDT <= A.EFFDT)
end-select
end-procedure

! Changes department ID of managers to their correct department
begin-procedure Check-Dept-ID
begin-select
```

```
B.DEPTID
B.MANAGER_ID
  move &B.DEPTID to $deptid
from HRPROD..PS_DEPT_TBL B
where B.MANAGER_ID = $emplid
and B.COMPANY='BC1'
and B.EFF_STATUS = 'A'
and B.DEPTID = (select min(D.DEPTID) from HRPROD..PS_DEPT_TBL D
                 where D.MANAGER_ID = B.MANAGER_ID
                 and D.DEPTID = B.DEPTID)
and B.EFFDT = (select max(E.EFFDT)from HRPROD..PS_DEPT_TBL E
                 where E.DEPTID = B.DEPTID
                 and E.EFFDT <= getdate())
end-select
end-procedure

! Captures the correct division category for census reporting
begin-procedure Get-Division-Category
begin-select
M.DESCR
  move &M.DESCR to $divcat
from HRPROD..PS_ALB_CENS_DV_TBL M
where M.ALB_DIV_ID = $divid
end-select
end-procedure

begin-procedure Create-Totals-Date1

evaluate $divcat
  when = 'Claims'
    if $emplevel = 'Officer'
      array-add 1 to date1(0) off
    end-if
    if $emplevel = 'Manager'
      array-add 1 to date1(0) mgr
    end-if
    if $emplevel = 'Exempt'
      array-add 1 to date1(0) exm
    end-if
    if $emplevel = 'Non-Exempt'
      array-add 1 to date1(0) nex
```

```
              end-if
           if $emplevel = 'Part Time'
              array-add 1 to date1(0) pt
           end-if
           array-add 1 to date1(0) tot
      when = 'Corporate Resources'
           if $emplevel = 'Officer'
              array-add 1 to date1(1) off
           end-if
           if $emplevel = 'Manager'
              array-add 1 to date1(1) mgr
           end-if
           if $emplevel = 'Exempt'
              array-add 1 to date1(1) exm
           end-if
           if $emplevel = 'Non-Exempt'
              array-add 1 to date1(1) nex
           end-if
           if $emplevel = 'Part Time'
              array-add 1 to date1(1) pt
           end-if
           array-add 1 to date1(1) tot
      when = 'Finance'
           if $emplevel = 'Officer'
              array-add 1 to date1(2) off
           end-if
           if $emplevel = 'Manager'
              array-add 1 to date1(2) mgr
           end-if
           if $emplevel = 'Exempt'
              array-add 1 to date1(2) exm
           end-if
           if $emplevel = 'Non-Exempt'
              array-add 1 to date1(2) nex
           end-if
           if $emplevel = 'Part Time'
              array-add 1 to date1(2) pt
           end-if
           array-add 1 to date1(2) tot
      when = 'Special Claims'
           if $emplevel = 'Officer'
```

```
      array-add 1 to date1(3) off
   end-if
   if $emplevel = 'Manager'
      array-add 1 to date1(3) mgr
   end-if
   if $emplevel = 'Exempt'
      array-add 1 to date1(3) exm
   end-if
   if $emplevel = 'Non-Exempt'
      array-add 1 to date1(3) nex
   end-if
   if $emplevel = 'Part Time'
      array-add 1 to date1(3) pt
   end-if
   array-add 1 to date1(3) tot
when = 'Marketing'
   if $emplevel = 'Officer'
      array-add 1 to date1(4) off
   end-if
   if $emplevel = 'Manager'
      array-add 1 to date1(4) mgr
   end-if
   if $emplevel = 'Exempt'
      array-add 1 to date1(4) exm
   end-if
   if $emplevel = 'Non-Exempt'
      array-add 1 to date1(4) nex
   end-if
   if $emplevel = 'Part Time'
      array-add 1 to date1(4) pt
   end-if
   array-add 1 to date1(4) tot
when = 'Medical Director'
   if $emplevel = 'Officer'
      array-add 1 to date1(5) off
   end-if
   if $emplevel = 'Manager'
      array-add 1 to date1(5) mgr
   end-if
   if $emplevel = 'Exempt'
      array-add 1 to date1(5) exm
```

```
            end-if
            if $emplevel = 'Non-Exempt'
              array-add 1 to date1(5) nex
            end-if
            if $emplevel = 'Part Time'
              array-add 1 to date1(5) pt
            end-if
            array-add 1 to date1(5) tot
       when = 'Other'
            if $emplevel = 'Officer'
              array-add 1 to date1(6) off
            end-if
            if $emplevel = 'Manager'
              array-add 1 to date1(6) mgr
            end-if
            if $emplevel = 'Exempt'
              array-add 1 to date1(6) exm
            end-if
            if $emplevel = 'Non-Exempt'
              array-add 1 to date1(6) nex
            end-if
            if $emplevel = 'Part Time'
              array-add 1 to date1(6) pt
            end-if
            array-add 1 to date1(6) tot
  end-evaluate
  end-procedure

  begin-procedure Create-Totals-Date2
  evaluate $divcat
       when = 'Claims'
            if $emplevel = 'Officer'
              array-add 1 to date2(0) off
            end-if
            if $emplevel = 'Manager'
              array-add 1 to date2(0) mgr
            end-if
            if $emplevel = 'Exempt'
              array-add 1 to date2(0) exm
            end-if
```

```
        if $emplevel = 'Non-Exempt'
          array-add 1 to date2(0) nex
        end-if
        if $emplevel = 'Part Time'
          array-add 1 to date2(0) pt
        end-if
        array-add 1 to date2(0) tot
    when = 'Corporate Resources'
        if $emplevel = 'Officer'
          array-add 1 to date2(1) off
        end-if
        if $emplevel = 'Manager'
          array-add 1 to date2(1) mgr
        end-if
        if $emplevel = 'Exempt'
          array-add 1 to date2(1) exm
        end-if
        if $emplevel = 'Non-Exempt'
          array-add 1 to date2(1) nex
        end-if
        if $emplevel = 'Part Time'
          array-add 1 to date2(1) pt
        end-if
        array-add 1 to date2(1) tot
    when = 'Finance'
        if $emplevel = 'Officer'
          array-add 1 to date2(2) off
        end-if
        if $emplevel = 'Manager'
          array-add 1 to date2(2) mgr
        end-if
        if $emplevel = 'Exempt'
          array-add 1 to date2(2) exm
        end-if
        if $emplevel = 'Non-Exempt'
          array-add 1 to date2(2) nex
        end-if
        if $emplevel = 'Part Time'
          array-add 1 to date2(2) pt
        end-if
        array-add 1 to date2(2) tot
```

```
when = 'Special Claims'
  if $emplevel = 'Officer'
    array-add 1 to date2(3) off
  end-if
  if $emplevel = 'Manager'
    array-add 1 to date2(3) mgr
  end-if
  if $emplevel = 'Exempt'
    array-add 1 to date2(3) exm
  end-if
  if $emplevel = 'Non-Exempt'
    array-add 1 to date2(3) nex
  end-if
  if $emplevel = 'Part Time'
    array-add 1 to date2(3) pt
  end-if
  array-add 1 to date2(3) tot
when = 'Marketing'
  if $emplevel = 'Officer'
    array-add 1 to date2(4) off
  end-if
  if $emplevel = 'Manager'
    array-add 1 to date2(4) mgr
  end-if
  if $emplevel = 'Exempt'
    array-add 1 to date2(4) exm
  end-if
  if $emplevel = 'Non-Exempt'
    array-add 1 to date2(4) nex
  end-if
  if $emplevel = 'Part Time'
    array-add 1 to date2(4) pt
  end-if
  array-add 1 to date2(4) tot
when = 'Medical Director'
  if $emplevel = 'Officer'
    array-add 1 to date2(5) off
  end-if
  if $emplevel = 'Manager'
    array-add 1 to date2(5) mgr
  end-if
```

```
              if $emplevel = 'Exempt'
                array-add 1 to date2(5) exm
              end-if
              if $emplevel = 'Non-Exempt'
                array-add 1 to date2(5) nex
              end-if
              if $emplevel = 'Part Time'
                array-add 1 to date2(5) pt
              end-if
              array-add 1 to date2(5) tot
          when = 'Other'
              if $emplevel = 'Officer'
                array-add 1 to date2(6) off
              end-if
              if $emplevel = 'Manager'
                array-add 1 to date2(6) mgr
              end-if
              if $emplevel = 'Exempt'
                array-add 1 to date2(6) exm
              end-if
              if $emplevel = 'Non-Exempt'
                array-add 1 to date2(6) nex
              end-if
              if $emplevel = 'Part Time'
                array-add 1 to date2(6) pt
              end-if
              array-add 1 to date2(6) tot
      end-evaluate
      end-procedure


      ! Compare the two arrays and put difference in the third array
      begin-procedure Compare
      let #j = 0
      while #j < 7
        get $divis1 #off1 #mgr1 #exm1 #nex1 #pt1 #tot1 from date1(#j)
        get $divis2 #off2 #mgr2 #exm2 #nex2 #pt2 #tot2 from date2(#j)
        let #off3 = #off2 - #off1
        let #mgr3 = #mgr2 - #mgr1
        let #exm3 = #exm2 - #exm1
        let #nex3 = #nex2 - #nex1
        let #pt3 = #pt2 - #pt1
        let #tot3 = #tot2 - #tot1
```

```
      put $divis1 #off3 #mgr3 #exm3 #nex3 #pt3 #tot3 into compdate(#j)
      add 1 to #j
end-while


end-procedure

! File creation procedure - Creates semi-colon delimited file
begin-procedure Write-File
print $divcat           (0,0,030)
print $pholder          (0,0,001)
print $minoritydes      (0,0,012)
print $pholder          (0,0,001)
print $emplevel         (0,0,010)
print $pholder          (0,0,001)
print #cntfld           (0,0,001)
end-procedure

begin-procedure Print-Report
move 0 to #j
let #col1 = 3
let #col2 = 30
let #col3 = 42
let #col4 = 54
let #col5 = 66
let #row = 7
print 'Employee Census' (4,38)
print $firstdate      (#row,#col3)
let #gtot = 0
while #j < 7
  get $divis #off #mgr #exm #nex #pt #tot from date1(#j)
  print $divis (+2,#col1,20)
  print 'Officer'    (0,#col2)
  print #off   (0,#col3,004) edit 9999
  print 'Manager'    (+1,#col2)
  print #mgr   (0,#col3,004) edit 9999
  print 'Exempt'     (+1,#col2)
  print #exm   (0,#col3,004) edit 9999
  print 'Non-Exempt' (+1,#col2)
  print #nex   (0,#col3,004) edit 9999
  print 'Part-Time'  (+1,#col2)
  print #pt    (0,#col3,004) edit 9999
  print 'Subtotal'   (+1,22)
```

```
                        print #tot    (0,#col3,004) edit 9999
                        let #gtot = #gtot + #tot
                        add 1 to #j
                        end-while
                  print 'Grand Total' (+1,20)
                  print #gtot      (0,#col3,004) edit 9999
                  move 0 to #j
                  move 0 to #gtot
                  print $secondate      (#row,#col4)
                  while #j < 7
                     get $divis #off #mgr #exm #nex #pt #tot from date2(#j)
                     print #off (+2,#col4,004) edit 9999
                     print #mgr (+1,#col4,004) edit 9999
                     print #exm (+1,#col4,004) edit 9999
                     print #nex (+1,#col4,004) edit 9999
                     print #pt  (+1,#col4,004) edit 9999
                     print #tot (+1,#col4,004) edit 9999
                     let #gtot = #gtot + #tot
                     add 1 to #j
                  end-while
                  print #gtot      (+1,#col4,004) edit 9999
                  move 0 to #j
                  move 0 to #gtot
                  print 'Difference'      (#row,#col5)
                  while #j < 7
                     get $divis #off #mgr #exm #nex #pt #tot from compdate(#j)
                     print #off (+2,#col5,004) edit 9999
                     print #mgr (+1,#col5,004) edit 9999
                     print #exm (+1,#col5,004) edit 9999
                     print #nex (+1,#col5,004) edit 9999
                     print #pt  (+1,#col5,004) edit 9999
                     print #tot (+1,#col5,004) edit 9999
                     let #gtot = #gtot + #tot
                     add 1 to #j
                  end-while
                  print #gtot      (+1,#col5,004) edit 9999
                  end-procedure

            begin-setup
              page-size 60 85
            !  no-formfeed
            end-setup
```

# Include Files

The following file is an example of an include file referenced by the programs shown in this appendix. The other include files used by programs in this appendix are provided by PeopleSoft.

### RC_ALB.SQC

```
! RC_ALB: Retrieves parameters from the RC_ALB run-control record.
!
!      $Date:: 11/04/96           $
!   $Revision:: 4                 $
!   $Workfile:: RC_ALB.SQC        $
!
!Select-Parameters

begin-procedure Select-Parameters

begin-select

RC_ALB.OPRID
RC_ALB.RUN_CNTL_ID
RC_ALB.CALENDAR_YEAR
RC_ALB.EMPLID
RC_ALB.MONTHCD
RC_ALB.RERUN
RC_ALB.DEDCD
RC_ALB.PAY_END_DT
RC_ALB.PREV_PAY_END_DT
RC_ALB.LOCATION
RC_ALB.LOCALITY
RC_ALB.OFF_CYCLE
RC_ALB.CYCLE_SELECT
RC_ALB.RUN_ID
RC_ALB.PLAN_TYPE
RC_ALB.BENEFIT_PLAN
RC_ALB.ASOFDATE
RC_ALB.FROMDATE
RC_ALB.THRUDATE
RC_ALB.ACTION
```

```
            RC_ALB.ACTION_REASON
            RC_ALB.UNWAY_EXP_DT
            RC_ALB.UNWAY_NEW_DT
            RC_ALB.DEPTIDBEG
            RC_ALB.DEPTIDEND
        from PS_RC_ALB RC_ALB
        where RC_ALB.OPRID = $prcs_oprid
         and RC_ALB.RUN_CNTL_ID = $prcs_run_cntl_id
        end-select

        end-procedure
```

# Sample Reports

## FEATURING

▶ DDAUDIT.SQR

▶ SYSAUDIT.SQR

his appendix contains excerpts from two types of reports described in Chapter 6, "Data Management Tools." That chapter contains more detailed information about these reports and how to run them.

# Example 1: *DDDAUDIT.SQR*

This example contains the report generated by the DDDAUDIT.SQR program. This report has been shortened, but the example shows the typical output from each of the defined queries.

```
Report ID: DDDAUDIT              DATA DESIGNER/DATABASE AUDIT REPORT

          (TABLE-1) SQL Table Names defined in the
          Data Designer that are not blank and not the
          same as the Record Name:         .                 No rows found.

          (TABLE-2) SQL Table defined in the Data
          Designer and not found in the Database:            No rows found.

          (TABLE-3) SQL Table defined in the Database
          and not found in the Data Designer:

             SQL Table Name
             ------------------
             PS_CLOSE_EARN_TMP
             PS_CLOSE_LEDG_LOG
             PS_CLOSE_LEDG_TMP


          (TABLE-4) Tablespace not defined for SQL
          Table in the Data Designer:

             Record Name
             ---------------
             ALB_PE_SCORES
             ALB_REP_DEDCD
             ALB_REP_ERNCD
             3 Total Rows

          (VIEWS-1) Views defined in the Data Designer
          and not found in the Database:

             Record Name
             ---------------
             ALB_PE_SCR_VW
```

```
            IMAGE_VW1
            IMAGE_VW2
            IMAGE_VW3
                        4 Total Rows
```

(VIEWS-2) Views defined in the Database and
not found in the Data Designer:

```
    View Name
    ------------------
    PS_SKILLS
    PS_SRCH_PTS_LICENS
    PS_SRCH_PTS_SKILL
    PS_SRCH_PTS_TEST
```

(INDEX-1) Index defined in the Data Designer
and not found in the Database:

```
    Record Name         Index ID
    ---------------     --------
    SET_CTL_REC_TMP     A

            1 Total Rows
```

(INDEX-2) Index defined in the Database and
not found in the Data Designer:

```
    SQL Table Name      Index Name
    ------------------  ------------------
    PS_CLOSE_EARN_TMP   PS_CLOSE_EARN_TMP
    PS_CLOSE_LEDG_LOG   PS_CLOSE_LEDG_LOG
    PS_CLOSE_LEDG_TMP   P$_CLOSE_LEDG_TMP
```

(INDEX-3) Uniqueness or the number of keys
in the Index Definition do not match between
the Data Designer and the Database:

```
                                    Unique   Key Count
    Record Name         Index ID    DD  DB   DD    DB
    ---------------     --------    ------   ---------
    ALB_PE_SCORES          _        U   U    2     3.00
    ALB_RC_PAYINFAC        _        U   U    2     3.00
    ALB_RC_PAYRPT          _        U   U    2     3.00
    ALB_REP_DEDCD          _        U   U    1     3.00
    ALB_REP_ERNCD          _        U   U    1     3.00
```

# Example 2: *SYSAUDIT.SQR*

This example contains the report generated by the SYSAUDIT.SQR program. This report has been shortened, but the example shows the typical output from each of the defined queries.

```
Report ID:  SYSAUDIT                      PS SYSTEM TABLE AUDIT REPORT

        (AUTHS-1) Authorized Signon Operator does
        not exist in Operator Definition table:          No rows found.

        (AUTHI-1) Authorized Item Operator does not
        exist in the Operator Definition table:          No rows found.

        (OPRDF-1) Operator Definition Signon count
        does not match count from Authorized Signon
        table:                                           No rows found.

        (OPRDF-2) Operator Definition Signon does
        not exist in Authorized Signon table:            No rows found.

        (OPRDF-3) Operator Definition Signon count
        does not match count from Authorized Signon
        table:                                           No rows found.

        (OPRDF-4) Operator Definition AuthItem does
        not exist in Authorized Item table:              No rows found.

        (PNLDF-1) Panel Definition Field count does
        not match the record count in Panel Field
        table:

                            Lang    Field   Record
            Panel Name      Code    Count    Count
            ------------------  ----  ------  ------
            BAS_PARTIC_ENT2     ENG     46       48

        (PNLDF-2) Panel Definition Field does not
        exist in the PanelField table:                   No rows found.

        (PNLDF-3) Panel Definition SubPanel does not
        exist in the PanelField table:                   No rows found.

        (PNLFD-1) PanelField table Panel does not
        exist in the Panel Definition table:             No rows found.
```

(PNLFD-2) PanelField table SubPanel does not
exist in the Panel Definition table:                No rows found.

(PNLFD-3) PanelField table Record/Field does
not exist in the RecordField table:                 No rows found.

(PNLGR-1) Panel Group Name in Panel Group
table was not found in Panel Group
Definition table:                                   No rows found.

(PNLGR-2) A Panel Group contains a Panel
Name that does not exist in Panel Definition
table:

| Sub Panel Group | Panel Name | Item Name | Item Num |
| --- | --- | --- | --- |
| RUN_ALPAY004 | RUNCTL_ALPAY004 | RUNCTL_ALPAY004 | 1 |

(PNLGR-3) Panel Group Definition contains
Search Panel Name that does not exist in
Panel Definition table:

| Panel Group Name | Search Panel Name |
| --- | --- |
| RUN_PER003M | RUNCTL_PER003M |

(PNLGR-4) Panel Group Definition contains
Search Record Name that does not exist in
Record Definition table:                            No rows found.

(PNLGR-5) Panel Group Definition contains an
Add Search Record Name that does not exist
in the Record Definition table:                     No rows found.

(RECDF-1) Record Definition Field count does
not match the number of records in Record
Field table:                                        No rows found.

(RECDF-2) Record Definition Fields do not
exist in Record Field table:                        No rows found.

(RECDF-3) Record Definition Parent Record
does not exist in Record Definition table:          No rows found.

(RECDF-4) Record Definition SubRecord does
not exist in Record Definition table:               No rows found.

(RECDF-5) Record Definition Query Security
Record does not exist in Record Definition
table:                                              No rows found.

(RECFD-1) Record Field definitions contain
Record names that do not exist in the Record
Definition table:                                   No rows found.

(RECFD-2) Record Field Program count does
not match record count from ProgramName
table:                                              No rows found.

(RECFD-3) Record Field Program references do
not exist in the Program Name table:                No rows found.

(RECFD-4) DBField records do not exist for
the following RecField table Fields:                No rows found.

(RECFD-5) Record definitions do not exist
for the following RecField table SubRecords:        No rows found.

(VIEWT-1) View Text definition contains
Record name value that does not exist in
RecDefn table:                                      No rows found.

(DBFLD-1) Record Field definition does not
exist for the following DBField table
fields. *** This Audit is informational
only. Base Language Fields are not required
to be associated with a record. ***

   Field Name
   ------------------
   PAYGROUP98A

(DBFLD-2) Record Field definition does not
exist for the following DBFieldLang table
fields. *** This Audit is informational
only. Related Language Fields are not
required to be associated with a record. ***        No rows found.

(PRGNM-1) PeopleCode Program definition
contains Record/Field value that does not
exist in RecField table:                            No rows found.

(PRGNM-2) PeopleCode Program Name table
contains Program name that does not exist in
PcmProg table:                                          No rows found.

(PRGNM-3) PeopleCode Program Name table
contains Program name references used more
than once:                                              No rows found.

(PCMPR-1) PeopleCode Program table contains
Program name not currently in use:

| PeopleCode<br>Program Name | Name<br>Count |
| --------------- | ----- |
| PCM55050 | 18 |

(PCMPR-2) PeopleCode Program table contains
Program name that does not exist in PcmName
table:                                                  No rows found.

(PCMPR-3) PeopleCode Program table Name
count does not match record count in PcmName
table:                                                  No rows found.

(PCMNM-1) PeopleCode Name table contains
Program name that does not exist in
PcmProgram table:                                       No rows found.

(PCMNM-2) PeopleCode Name table contains
Record/Field name that does not exist in
ProgName table:

| PeopleCode<br>Prog Name | Record Name | Field Name |
| --------------- | --------------- | ------------------------- |
| PCM55050 | RC_PAYINIT | COMPANY |

(MENUD-1) Menu Definition Item does not
exist in MenuItem table:                                No rows found.

(MENUI-2) Menu Item table contains Panel
Group type with invalid Panel Group name:               No rows found.

(MENUI-3) The Menu Item table contains Panel
Group that does not exist in the Panel Group
Definition table:

| Item Menu Name | Number | Bar Name | Item Name | Panel Group Name |
|----------------|--------|----------|-----------|------------------|
| Plan &Careers  | 12     | &Use     | &Skills   | SKILLS1          |

(MENUI-4) Menu Item table PeopleCode type contains PanelGroup name that does not exist:                                                   No rows found.

(MENUI-5) Menu Item contains PeopleCode Program name that does not exist in PcmProg table:                                                No rows found.

(TREED-1) Tree Definition Level count does not match record count in Tree Level table:    No rows found.

(TREED-2) Tree Definition Node count does not match record count in Tree Node table:      No rows found.

(TREED-3) Tree Definition Leaf count does not match record count in Tree Leaf table:      No rows found.

(TREED-4) Tree Definition contains Structure ID that does not exist in Tree Structure table:                                                 No rows found.

(TREED-5) Tree Definition contains Query Access Group structure with undefined levels and leaves:                                           No rows found.

(TREED-6) Tree Selector Control contains Tree name that is not defined in Tree Definition table:                                             No rows found.

(TREEB-1) Tree Branch Node count does not match record count in Tree Node table:          No rows found.

(TREEB-2) Tree Branch Leaf count does not match record count in Tree Leaf table:          No rows found.

(TREEB-3) Tree Node Num, Node Num End, or Level Num is invalid in Tree Branch table:      No rows found.

(TREEL-1) Tree Level does not exist in Tree Definition table:                               No rows found.

(TREEL-2) Tree Node does not exist in Tree Definition table:                                No rows found.

(TREEL-3) Tree Leaf does not exist in Tree
Definition table:                                          No rows found.

(TREEL-4) Tree Leaf ranges not valid in Tree
Definition table:                                          No rows found.

(TREEL-5) Tree Leaf does not have parent
Tree Node in Tree Definition table:                        No rows found.

(TREEL-6) Tree Branch does not exist in Tree
Branch table:                                              No rows found.

(TREEL-7) Tree Branch does not exist in Tree
Branch table:                                              No rows found.

(TREES-1) Tree Structure table contains
Level Record name that does not exist in
Record Definition table:                                   No rows found.

(TREES-2) Tree Structure table contains
Level Panel name that does not exist in
Panel Definition table:                                    No rows found.

(TREES-3) Tree Structure table contains Node
Record name that does not exist in Record
Definition table:                                          No rows found.

(TREES-4) Tree Structure table contains Node
Field name that does not exist in
RecordField table:                                         No rows found.

(TREES-5) Tree Structure table contains Node
Panel name that does not exist in Panel
Definition table:                                          No rows found.

(TREES-6) Tree Structure table contains
Detail Record name that does not exist in
Record Definition table:                                   No rows found.

(TREES-7) Tree Structure table contains
Detail Record name that does not exist in
Record Definition table:                                   No rows found.

(TREES-8) Tree Structure table contains
Detail Panel name that does not exist in
Panel Definition table:                                    No rows found.

| | |
|---|---|
| (TREES-9) Tree Structure table contains Summary Tree that does not exist in Tree Level table: | No rows found. |
| (TREES-10) Tree Structure table contains Level Menu-Menu Bar combination that does not exist: | No rows found. |
| (TREES-11) Tree Structure table contains Node Menu-Menu Bar combination that does not exist: | No rows found. |
| (TREES-12) Tree Structure table contains Detail Menu-Menu Bar combination that does not exist: | No rows found. |
| (TREES-13) Tree Structure table contains Level Menu-Panel combination that does not exist: | No rows found. |
| (TREES-14) Tree Structure table contains Node Menu-Panel combination that does not exist: | No rows found. |
| (TREES-15) Tree Structure table contains Detail Menu-Panel combination that does not exist: | No rows found. |
| (QRYDF-1) Query Definition Select count does not match record count in the Query Select table: | No rows found. |
| (QRYDF-2) Query Definition Expression count does not match record count in the Query Expression table: | No rows found. |
| (QRYDF-3) Query Definition Bind count does not match record count in the Query Bind table: | No rows found. |
| (QRYRC-1) Query Definition Record name does not exist in the Record Definition table: | |

| Oper ID | Query Name | Record Name |
|---------|-----------------------------|---------------|
| BJones | Skils | SKILL_TBL |

(QRYRC-2) Query Definition Record JoinRecord
name does not exist in the Query Record
table:                                                     No rows found.

(QRYRC-3) Query Definition Record JoinField
name does not exist in the Query Field
table:                                                     No rows found.

(QRYFD-1) Query Definition Record name does
not exist in the Record Definition table:

| Oper ID | Query Name | Record Name |
|---------|-----------------------------|---------------|
| BJones | Skils | SKILL_TBL |

(QRYFD-2) Query Definition Field name does
not exist in the Field Definition table:

| Oper ID | Query Name | Record Name | Field Name |
|---------|-----------------------|---------------|-------------------|
| BJones | earn | EARNINGS_BAL | MONTHCD |

(QRYSL-1) Query Selection Record count does
not match record count in Query Record
table:                                                     No rows found.

(QRYSL-2) Query Selection Field count does
not match record count in Query Field table:   No rows found.

(QRYSL-3) Query Selection Criteria count
does not match record count in Query
Criteria table:                                            No rows found.

(QRYSL-3A) Query Selection Criteria having
count does not match record count in Query
Criteria table:                                            No rows found.

(QRYSL-4) Query Selection Parent select
number does not exist in Query Select table:   No rows found.

(QRYCR-1) Query Criteria Selection-Left does
not exist in the Query Selection table:              No rows found.

(QRYCR-2) Query Criteria Selection-Right1
does not exist in the Query Selection table:         No rows found.

(QRYCR-3) Query Criteria Selection-Right2
does not exist in the Query Selection table:         No rows found.

(QRYCR-4) Query Criteria Field-Left does not
exist in the Query Selection table:                  No rows found.

(QRYCR-5) Query Criteria Field-Right1 does
not exist in the Query Selection table:              No rows found.

(QRYCR-6) Query Criteria Field-Right2 does
not exist in the Query Selection table:              No rows found.

(QRYCR-7) Query Criteria Expression-Right1
does not exist in the Query Selection table:         No rows found.

(QRYCR-8) Query Criteria Expression-Right2
does not exist in the Query Selection table:         No rows found.

(QRYBN-1) Query Bind definition contains
Fieldname that does not exist in Query Field
table. *** This Audit is informational only.
Make sure the prompt Field Name in PSQRYBIND
exists in PSQRYFIELD for a given Query. ***

|          |                                | Bind |            |
| Oper ID  | Query Name                     | Num  | Field Name |
| -------- | ------------------------------ | ---- | ---------------- |
| BJones   | TUITNRE                        | 2    |            |

(XLATT-1) Translate table Field does not
exist in DBField table:                              No rows found.

(XLATT-2) Translate table Field not unique:          No rows found.

(IMPDF-1) Import Definition Field count does
not match the Record count in ImportField
table:                                               No rows found.

(IMPDF-2) Import Definition Field does not
exist in ImportField table:                          No rows found.

(IMPDF-3) Import Definition Record name does
not exist in RecDefn table:                              No rows found.

(IMPDF-4) Import Definition Field name does
not exist in RecField table:

| Import Name | Field Name |
| ------------------ | ------------------ |
| CW_BEN_PGM | RESPONSE_DUE_DT |

(IMPDF-5) Import Definition Field name does
not exist in ImportField table:                         No rows found.

(IMPFD-1) ImportField table contains Import
name that does not exist in Import
Definition table:                                       No rows found.

(IMPFD-2) Import Field Translate count does
not equal the number of Records in
ImportTranslate table:                                  No rows found.

(IMPFD-3) Import Field Translate does not
exist in ImportTranslate table:                         No rows found.

(IMPXL-1) Import Translate Field does not
exist in ImportField table:                             No rows found.

(RECLANG-1) Base Language Records found in
the PSRECDEFNLANG table:                                No rows found.

(RECLANG-2) Foreign Language Records found
in PSRECDEFNLANG table without related Base
Records from PSRECDEFN:                                  No rows found.

(FLDLANG-1) Base Language Fields found in
the PSDBFIELDLANG table:                                No rows found.

(FLDLANG-2) Foreign Language Fields found in
the PSDBFIELDLANG table without related Base
Fields from PSDBFIELD:                                   No rows found.

(XLTLANG-1) Foreign Language Translate
Fields found in the XLATTABLE table without
related Base Language Translate Fields:                  No rows found.

(PNLLANG-1) Foreign Language Panels found in
the PSPNLDEFN table without related Base
Lanaguage Panels:                                              No rows found.

(ECINMPFL-1) Inbound work records not found
in the PSRECDEFN table:                                        No rows found.

(ECINMPFL-2) Inbound work record EC Map ID
not found in the PS_ECMAPDEFN table:                           No rows found.

(ECINMPFD-1) Inbound work record fields not
found with valid EC Map ID and EC File Row
ID combination  from the PS_ECINMAPFILE
table:                                                         No rows found.

(ECINMPFD-2) Inbound work record fields from
PS_ECINMAPFLD not found in PSRECFIELD:                         No rows found.

(ECINMPFD-3) Inbound work record field type
does not match field type definitions in
PSDBFIELD. *** This Audit is informational
only. ***                                                      No rows found.

(ECINMPRC-1) Target inbound records not
found in the PSRECDEFN table:                                  No rows found.

(ECINMPRC-2) Target inbound EC Map ID not
found the PS_ECMAPDEFN table:                                  No rows found.

(ECINMPRF-1) EC Map ID/EC File Row ID
combination not found in PS_ECINMAPREC for
the target inbound record field in
PS_ECINMAPRECFLD:                                              No rows found.

(ECINMPRF-2) A Field for a Record in
PS_ECINMAPRECFLD was not found in
PSRECFIELD:                                                    No rows found.

(ECINMPRF-3) A field type for a field in
PS_ECINMAPRECFLD did not match the field
type for the same field in PSDBFIELD. ***
This Audit is informational only. ***                         No rows found.

(ECINMPRF-4) A related record in
PS_ECINMAPRECFLD was not found in PSRECDEFN:                   No rows found.

(ECINMPRF-5) An EC Related Record in
PS_ECINMAPRECFLD does not have a valid EC
Related Row ID from PS_ECINMAPREC:                    No rows found.

(ECINMPRF-6) A related field in
PS_ECINMAPRECFLD was not found in
PSRECFIELD:                                           No rows found.

(ECOTMPRC-1) Target outbound records not
found in the PSRECDEFN table:                         No rows found.

(ECOTMPRC-2) Outbound work record EC Map ID
was not found in the PS_ECMAPDEFN table:              No rows found.

(ECOTMPRC-3) Parent records from the
outbound work record not found in the
PSRECDEFN table:                                      No rows found.

(ECOTMPRC-4) File records from the outbound
work record not found in the PSRECDEFN
table:                                                No rows found.

(ECOTMPFD-1) Outbound work record fields not
found with valid EC Map ID and EC File Row
ID combination from the PS_ECOUTMAPREC
table:                                                No rows found.

(ECOTMPFD-2) Outbound work record fields
from PS_ECOUTMAPFLD not found in PSRECFIELD:          No rows found.

(ECOTMPFD-3) Outbound work record field type
does not match field type definitions in
PSDBFIELD:                                            No rows found.

(SYSCLRLIST-1) Entries in PSACTIVITYDEL and
PSACTIVITYDEFN are not mutually exclusive:            No rows found.

(SYSCLRLIST-2) Entries in PSAEAPPLDEL and
PSAEAPPLDEFN are not mutually exclusive:              No rows found.

(SYSCLRLIST-3) Entries in PSBUSCOMPDEL and
PSBUSCOMPDEFN are not mutually exclusive:             No rows found.

(SYSCLRLIST-4) Entries in PSBUSPROCDEL and
PSBUSPROCDEFN are not mutually exclusive:             No rows found.

(SYSCLRLIST-5) Entries in PSCOLORDEL and
PSCOLORDEFN are not mutually exclusive:                 No rows found.

(SYSCLRLIST-6) Entries in PSFMTDEL and
PSFMTDEFN are not mutually exclusive:                   No rows found.

(SYSCLRLIST-7) Entries in PSHOLIDAYDEL and
PSHOLIDAYDEFN are not mutually exclusive:               No rows found.

(SYSCLRLIST-8) Entries in PSHOMEPAGEDEL and
PSHOMEPAGEDEFN are not mutually exclusive:              No rows found.

(SYSCLRLIST-9) Entries in PSIMPDEL and
PSIMPDEFN are not mutually exclusive:                   No rows found.

(SYSCLRLIST-10) Entries in PSMENUDEL and
PSMENUDEFN are not mutually exclusive:                  No rows found.

(SYSCLRLIST-11) Entries in PSPCMPROGDEL and
PSPCMPROG are not mutually exclusive:                   No rows found.

(SYSCLRLIST-12) Entries in PSPNLDEL and
PSPNLDEFN are not mutually exclusive:                   No rows found.

(SYSCLRLIST-13) Entries in PSPNLGRPDEL and
PSPNLGRPDEFN are not mutually exclusive:                No rows found.

(SYSCLRLIST-14) Entries in PSPRCSRUNCDEL and
PSPRCSRUNCNTL are not mutually exclusive:               No rows found.

(SYSCLRLIST-15) Entries in PSPROJECTDEL and
PSPROJECTDEFN are not mutually exclusive:               No rows found.

(SYSCLRLIST-16) Entries in PSQRYDEL and
PSQRYDEFN are not mutually exclusive:                   No rows found.

(SYSCLRLIST-17) Entries in PSRECDEL and
PSRECDEFN are not mutually exclusive:                   No rows found.

(SYSCLRLIST-18) Entries in PSRECURDEL and
PSRECURDEFN are not mutually exclusive:                 No rows found.

(SYSCLRLIST-19) Entries in PSSTYLEDEL and
PSSTYLEDEFN are not mutually exclusive:                 No rows found.

(SYSCLRLIST-20) Entries in PSTOOLBARDEL and
PSTOOLBARDEFN are not mutually exclusive:               No rows found.

(SYSCLRLIST-21) Entries in PSTREEBRADEL and
PSTREEBRANCH are not mutually exclusive:                No rows found.

(SYSCLRLIST-22) Entries in PSTREEDEL and
PSTREEDEFN are not mutually exclusive:                 No rows found.

(SYSCLRLIST-23) Entries in PSTREESTRDEL and
PSTREESTRCT are not mutually exclusive:                No rows found.

(SYSCLRLIST-24) Entries in XLATTABLEDEL and
XLATTABLE are not mutually exclusive:                  No rows found.

# *The ParseName Function for Microsoft Excel*

## FEATURING

▶ **EXAMPLE OUTPUT**

▶ **VBA CODE**

▶ **PARAMETERS**

▶ **REGISTRATION IN EXCEL**

developed a Microsoft Excel function called ParseName that parses the PeopleSoft name field into its various parts. ParseName is a good example of the power that is available through both the Query and nVision links with Excel. My company found this to be such a useful function that we made it available to all the Human Resources users. They can now extract any part of the name they need while doing an ad hoc query from PeopleSoft. I created this function to allow the users to create their own ad hoc mail merges using Microsoft Excel and Microsoft Word. ParseName has saved our technical staff untold hours in programming support time.

# Example Output from the *ParseName* Function

Figure C.1 contains examples of the ParseName function being used on the People-Soft name field. In this figure, the formula that you enter is shown in column B. The results are shown in column C. Let's look at how the function works.

**FIGURE C.1**   ParseName **example**

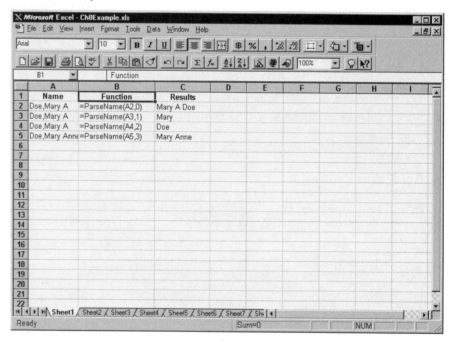

**TIP**   My company found that most mail merge requests requiring employee data can be completed by the end users with data from the PS_EMPLOYEES reporting table.

# VBA Code for the *ParseName* Function

The following code is the VBA code used to create this function. Following the code is a brief description that explains how to create this code as a Microsoft Excel function. For more information, see the Excel online Help.

```
Public Function ParseName(namein As String, rettype As Integer) As String
  Namein = namein + " "
  Scomma = Application.Search(",", namein, 1)
  Sblank = Application.Search(" ", namein, Scomma)
  Nblank = Application.Search(" ", namein, 1)
  Slength = Len(namein)
  If rettype = 1 Then
    If Application.IsErr(Sblank) Then
      ParseName = Mid(namein, Scomma + 1, Slength - Scomma)
    Else
      ParseName = Mid(namein, Scomma + 1, Sblank - Scomma)
    End If
  ElseIf rettype = 0 Then
ParseName = Application.Trim(Mid(namein, Scomma + 1, Slength -
        Scomma)) & " " & Mid(namein, 1, Scomma - 1) /* this is one line */
  ElseIf rettype = 2 Then
    If Nblank < Scomma Then
      ParseName = Mid(namein, 1, Nblank)
    Else
      ParseName = Mid(namein, 1, Scomma - 1)
    End If
  ElseIf rettype = 3 Then
      ParseName = Mid(namein, Scomma + 1, Slength - Scomma)
  End If
End Function
```

**N O T E**  The first line of the code (in **boldface**) is used to append a space to the name being read in. This is done to prevent an error if an employee has no middle name or initial.

**W A R N I N G**  This code is relatively simple, but I do not guarantee that there are no bugs in it.

# Parameters for the *ParseName* Function

When you execute this function, you pass two parameters: the name field and the desired return type. The valid return types are 0–3, as shown in Table C.1.

**TABLE C.1**    Valid Return Types for the ParseName Function

| Return Type | What It Means |
| --- | --- |
| 0 | The full name in correct order |
| 1 | The first name |
| 2 | The last name |
| 3 | Preferred name (Mary Ann instead of Mary) |

**N O T E**    Return type 3 also assumes that the preferred name field you are using is in PeopleSoft format of last name, first name.

# Registering the *ParseName* Function in Excel

Let's look at how you create and register the ParseName function as a Microsoft Excel function.

**N O T E**    I originally created this function using Microsoft Office 95.

1. When you have the macro window open in Excel, select Tools **>** Make Add-In to create the add-in file (*.xla) for Microsoft Office 95. If you are using the Microsoft Office 97 VBA editor, select File **>** Save and select the Microsoft Excel add-in type.

2. Save this file in the Excel\library directory for your Microsoft Office 97 system. If you are using Office 95, this file is automatically stored in the Excel\library directory of the system on which you are creating the function.

3. Register this function by selecting Tools > Add-Ins in Excel. The dialog box shown in Figure C.2 appears. Check the box next to the name of your function, in this case "Custom." This function is now available for use with the Excel Function Wizard.

> **NOTE**  Functions created using Office 95 still work in Office 97.

**FIGURE C.2**    Microsoft Excel Tools Add-In menu

Once we defined the ParseName function, we created an extra step in our network login procedure that copied this function file to the add-in function library for each user group that needed the function. We also provided e-mail instructions on how to activate the add-in in Excel.

We used a generic filename, CUSTOM.XLA, for the add-in file. This allowed us to add other custom functions as needed, since a single add-in file can contain multiple functions. A new version of the file can now be installed and the users do not have to re-register the function in their library.

# INDEX

**Note to the Reader:** Throughout this index **boldfaced** page numbers indicate primary discussions of a topic. *Italicized* page numbers indicate illustrations.

# X

# Y

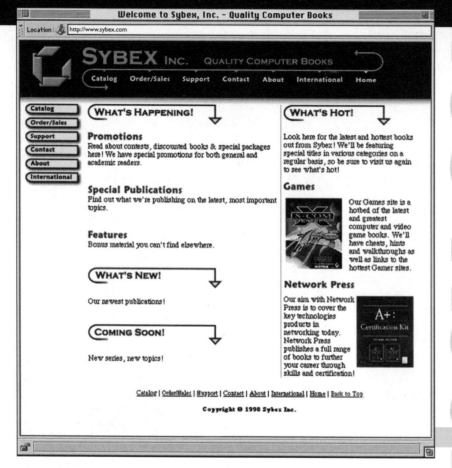